OF THE

LEWIS AND KINDRED FAMILIES

EDITED BY

JOHN MERIWETHER McALLISTER
Atlanta, Georgia
AND
LURA BOULTON TANDY
Columbia, Missouri

PRINTED BY
E. W. STEPHENS PUBLISHING COMPANY
Columbia, Missouri
1906

Reprinted by Higginson Book Company
Derby Square

Dedication

EXPLANATION.

The full-size figures preceding a name indicate the number of the generation; the small figures indicate the number in the family. This plan could not be followed out uniformly for lack of data, but its value will be apparent to those interested in family history.

INTRODUCTION.

In the preparation of this work the authors have had the assistance of so many friends who take a general interest in genealogy that they could not undertake in the space allotted to them to mention the names of a tithe of them. Conspicuous among those, however, to whom their sincere thanks are due, are Mr. Thomas M. Green, of Danville, Kentucky, the late Henry Howell Lewis, of Baltimore, Dr. Edmond J. Lee of Philadelphia, Dr. James A. Dibrell, of Little Rock, Arkansas, Mr. Robert S. Hatcher, Lafayette, Indiana, the late Mrs. Mary Starling Payne, of Hopkinsville, Kentucky, and Mrs. Sarah T. L. Anderson of Ivy Depot, Virginia, also her brother R. L. Scott of Texas.

In making up the genealogies of the different families whose names appear in this volume, completeness has been the main object in view. It has not, of course, been possible to entirely accomplish this object, but enough has been given to enable any one interested to supply the missing links and thus connect the different parts which may become apparent in any broken chain. At the outset it was the design of the authors to prepare a history exclusively for their children, but as usual in such cases the work has far outgrown the original design. While it is true that no name has been included in this volume, the bearers of which are not related in some degree of consanguinity to the children of the authors, it has been found necessary to include even the very remote, in order to even approximate the completeness which was desired in the general scope of the work. While it may be charged that in this the writers were actuated by selfish motives, it may also be replied that it was a selfishness prompted not by pecuniary gain, but a pardonable pride, in which every descendant of every name contained in the book is entitled to a full share.

This is strictly a work of genealogy, and is in no sense intended to trench on the field properly belonging to the biographer. Where sketches of individuals appear, the author's aim has been to connect the person alluded to with contemporaneous history. In a few instances more extended notices have been given of individuals whose lives have been intimately associated with the upbuilding of the country and whose deeds have contributed to her greatness.

It is not to be supposed that in the preparation of a family history embracing many names, extending through several hundred years and covering from seven to eleven generations, the writers claim to set forth an unbroken line of heroes, statesmen, saints and sages, superior to any families that have existed in this or any other country. On the contrary, all that is claimed for this volume is that some of those whom it mentions have left their impress upon the times in which they lived. Others, disregarding tradition, and failing to avail themselves of ancestral advantages, have illustrated the irrevocable law of cause and effect and passed out of view.

Every source has been exhausted to obtain all available information. Libraries have been ransacked, records have been overhauled; deeds, marriage certificates, church registers and tombstones, grown gray with centuries of age, all have been brought into requisition.

It may be proper to add that this has been a labor of love,

both for the work itself and for those who will be benefited by it. Having spent years of labor and much money, and having traveled hundreds of miles in search of information, we bequeath our work, incomplete as it is, to posterity with a hope that some other lover of genealogy may take it up where we have left off, remedy our errors and complete what we have left undone.

The American people have neglected nothing so much as family history, and it is only after one hundred years of national existence that we have waked up to a realisation of a failure to retain our identity. With the close of the Revolution which resulted in our independence, this great boon having been obtained at the cost of every conceivable sacrifice, we were naturally carried away with the idea of freedom. The victory to our arms had not been achieved by any one class, nor had questions of ancestral precedence played any part in the struggle. All classes and conditions in whose veins coursed patriotic blood had stood shoulder to shoulder against a common foe, and these old heroes, seeking no distinction the one over the other, allowed their family histories to be swallowed up for the time in the national glory. This feeling, very natural and proper under the circumstances which gave rise to it, would not, however, have predominated had not other causes arisen which conspired to cast odium upon American heraldry. A very considerable Tory element remained in the country after the war was over, while there were others who did not rise to the standard of the Tories, having taken no part in the politics of the country or exposed themselves to the dangers and hardships of war. Still another and lower class, who had neither ancestral nor individual standing, had prospered and become prominent under the liberal opportunities afforded by the new government. These three classes made up a large proportion of the population and had no sentiments in common with the patriot element, and by the time the second generation had come upon the stage of action, the term "first families" had become one of reproach instead of distinction, and any attempt to trace an ancestry or erect a family tree was held up to derision and laughed to scorn.

The fact that one family chooses, for reasons satisfactory to itself, not to write its history, or that another family has no history to write, is no reason why family history should not be written. Families make up nations and a history is as important to one as the other. A nation of families who have no histories is without material for a national history. It is not national history that makes great names. But names who have performed great deeds and thus established historic families make a nation great and give it a history. The names which go to make up this history are so closely interwoven with the history of the country that it is impossible to trace their genealogy without interspersing many historical events of national interest.

Several of the families date back to a very early period in English history, and some were quite well established in France before coming to England, but only such reference will be made to these families prior to their coming to America as will be necessary to trace their line of descent.

The Rev. Mr. Hayden, in his "Virginia Genealogies," argues in his article on descent that the most prominent Virginia families are not able to trace their descent beyond the fifteenth century, and asserts that neither George Washington nor General Robert E. Lee knew anything, save by tradition, of the immediate line of their English descent.

LEWIS AND KINDRED FAMILIES.

It is known that the name of Lee was interwoven with the history of England since the days of William the Conqueror, 1066, although Dr. Edmond J. Lee, in his "Lee of Virginia," ignoring current and authentic history and recognising nothing but the public records, does not bring the name down from that period. It is well known that the first Richard Lee of American history brought his lineage with him when he came to America. That many lost sight of the lineage in the lapse of generations is not denied, but the history was preserved nevertheless.

While there are very few families who can trace their descent with equal certainty from so remote a period as that of Lee, yet there are others who have no trouble in tracing their lineage much further back than that of the fifteenth century. The Bruce family of Virginia, and other American names descending from and connected with them, trace their Scotch descent from the eleventh century, and the same may be said of some of the families of this volume.

Trusting to the charity of indulgent friends and the magnanimity of the reading public, this volume is given to the numerous descendants of the names of which it treats, with a full knowledge of its imperfections but in the confident belief that the original information, heretofore unpublished, will compensate to a large extent for its shortcomings.

THE AUTHORS.

LEWIS FAMILIES.

This is one of the oldest names in English history and one of the most numerous and distinguished in American history. It is claimed by many reputable genealogists that the name was originally spelled "Louis," and was known in France as early as the eighth century, when that country was an integral part of the Roman Empire. Louis I, born 778, came to the throne upon the death of his father, Charlemagne, in the year 814, and his son, Louis, upon the dismemberment of the empire, A. D. 817, became king of Bavaria and other German provinces. These facts show that the surname was well known at this early period of European history, and a ta later period genealogy proves that it became one of the most numerous and distinguished of family names in France and England. It is a favorite past time with many genealogists to attempt to prove that all of the Lewis name in America descended from one common stock of Huguenot refugees who fled from France on the revocation of the "Edict of Nantes" in 1685, that three brothers fled to England, and that from these the American supply was furnished; but the records show that in many of the counties of England there were any number of the name to be found several centuries before this event, and, indeed, there were numbers of them in Virginia previous to this time.

There is ample proof, however, that Louis of France and Lewis of England are identical. It is equally true that many of the former name fled from France to England upon the revocation of the "Edict of Nantes." It is also well known that the Huguenot refugees who spelled the name "Louis" in France, adopted the English spelling as soon as they crossed the channel; and as the name was known in France centuries before it appeared in England, it is an accepted proposition that the family name, regardless of its spelling, was originally French.

LEWIS AND KINDRED FAMILIES.

It is not claimed that the Lewis families of America, or any one of them, are of royal descent. The fact that Charlemagne named his son Louis, and that several centuries afterwards some of the name crossed to England and called themselves Lewis, does not prove that they were descended directly or collaterally from Charlemagne, nor does the fact that an exuberant author with a vivid imagination runs through twenty generations and about six hundred years of English history from Alfred the Great to Robert Reade without a single specific record reference or historical citation, prove that the descendants of Robert Reade were of royal descent; but these and kindred incidents do show that wherever found, whether on the banks of the Tiber or Seine, the Thames, the Shannon or the James, they were the peers of royalty and the leaders of men, and the sequel shows that when they were transferred to a free soil and were permitted to breathe a free atmosphere, they became the foremost champions of human liberty. Mr. Hayden copies from the pen of Mr. John Lewis of Llangollen, Spottsylvania county, Virginia, the early history of the Lewis family. Of the three brothers, heads of the respective Lewis lines in Virginia, he brings Zachary to Virginia as a pioneer of the family in 1692, and adds that his brother, from whom the nephews of Washington descended, having favorable accounts from him, came to Virginia also, and settled on the Rappahannock, when in fact General Robert Lewis from whom Washington's nephews descended, came to Virginia in 1635 more than forty years before Zachary came, and indeed, before Zachary was born. In the attempt of Mr. William Terrell Lewis to account for the early history of the Lewis family, Mr. Lewis is more extravagant than most genealogists. He provides us with four brothers, but disposes of one of them by sending him to Portugal, thus leaving three as founders of the Virginia family. On the ninth page of his book, quoting from "Washington and his Generals," by Lippincott, he says: "Andrew Lewis, son of a gentleman who came to Virginia from Ireland, whither a Huguenot ancestor had fled from

13

France upon the revocation of the Edict of Nantes, settled in Augusta county, Virginia," etc.; when in fact General Robert Lewis, one of the alleged brothers of this Huguenot ancestor, who he says fled at the same time, was in Virginia fifty years prior to the event referred to.

The name of Louis in continental Europe and Lewis in England is too old and too numerous to be traced to a common origin. The name doubtless had a common origin, but it would be folly to undertake to trace it. Indeed, the name Lewis is too numerous in America, too widely diffused and traceable to too many different sources to admit of the "three-brothers" theory.

It is not known how many distinct branches of the Lewis family there are in America. For several centuries previous to the settlement of this country, the name of Lewis was as numerous by comparison in Wales as that of Smith in America to-day, and in every portion of the country are to be found distinct branches that run back to a period so remote as to render reliable trace impossible. Francis Lewis, one of the signers of the Declaration of Independence, was from New York, while Ellis Lewis, an eminent jurist, was of Pennsylvania. Every portion of New England has its representative Lewis families, all of them of Welsh origin, but traceable to different sources. These pages, however, will be confined to the Lewis families of Virginia, which embrace five distinct branches, between whom there is no traceable relation. These branches may be considered under their respective heads, as follows; General Robert Lewis, of Wales, who settled in Gloucester county, Virginia, in 1635; John Lewis, also of Wales, who settled in Henrico county, Virginia, in 1660; John Lewis, also of Wales, who settled in Hanover county in 1675; Zachary Lewis, also of Wales, who settled in Middlesex county, Virginia, 1692; and John Lewis from Donegal county, Ireland, who settled in Augusta county, 1732.

LEWIS AND KINDRED FAMILIES.

GENERAL ROBERT LEWIS.

General Robert Lewis, the first of the name in America known to history or genealogy was a native of Brecon, Wales. Together with his wife, Elizabeth, he sailed from Gravesend, England, April, 1635. So much has been asserted and denied concerning this ancestor that the very mention of his name invites criticism. It may be that too much has been claimed for him, and that these claims have given rise to adverse criticisms. However this may be, whatever the claims may have been that have aroused the swarm of critics into action, certain it is that they have denied every claim that has ever been made, and do not hesitate even to deny his existence. In the "William and Mary Quarterly" for January and April, 1901, it was boldly assumed that no such person had ever existed, and that General Robert Lewis was simply a "traditional myth."

The history of General Robert Lewis, however, was not allowed to become extinct in consequence of the destruction of the records, but was preserved by Captain Henry Howell Lewis, Thomas Warring Lewis, and others with the assistance of data furnished by their immediate ancestors; so what we have of this ancestor of the Lewis family is not tradition, but a revival and perpetuation of the records.

The controversy between Mr. Tyler, Mr. Stanard and J. M. McAllister upon the early history of Gen. Robert Lewis will be found published in full in the second volume of the "Historical Collections of the Joseph Habersham Chapter, Daughters American Revolution," on file in the Carnegie Library, Atlanta, Georgia.

According to Mr. Henry Howell Lewis of Baltimore, who devoted years of his life to the pursuit of his family history both in England and in America, General Lewis, with his wife, Elizabeth, sailed from Gravesend, England, and settled in Gloucester county, Virginia. The maiden name of his wife is not known and his descendants have been unable to trace it in England. We refer to him in these pages as General Robert Lewis upon the authority of Bishop Meade and others who speak of him as being favorably known to English history and having held a commission in the British army, and his standing at home may be inferred from the fact that, according to the same authority, he brought with him a grant from the crown of 33,333 1-3 acres of land which was located in that portion of York county which is now included in the county of Gloucester. According to Mr. Thomas M. Green of Danville, Kentucky, who is most eminent authority on all genealogical subjects, General Lewis died about 1645, and previous to 1650 his widow married Major Longley or Langley. Mr. Henry Howell Lewis further states that Robert Lewis had two sons, William Lewis, and John Lewis; that William Lewis died without issue, and that John Lewis married Isabella Warner, and built Warner Hall on the Severn river, which enters into Mob Jack bay, near the mouth of the York. "Their tombs are there. I have seen them. It is to be supposed that their father and mother lie there also, as the cemetery is large and has many tombs and slabs. These are facts from the tombs and church records. What more can we desire."

It is evident that Mr. Lewis, in speaking of the numerous tombs and slabs at Warner Hall, refers to those that have become defaced and illegible from age, and doubtless the tombs of Robert Lewis and his wife are among those. It is a noteworthy fact that he says that, "these facts are taken from the tombs and church records." He asserts that John Lewis, who married Isabella Warner, was buried at Warner Hall, that he saw the tomb and that he was the son of Robert Lewis, the emigrant. "What more can be desired." No reputable authority has been known to question the authenticity of Mr. Lewis' statements. Mr. Tyler and Mr. Stanard in their controversy with Mr. McAllister, insisted that what Mr. Lewis said was tradition. Mr. Lewis, however, emphatically asserts that his statements were facts taken from the tombs and church record. Both high character and the thoroughness of his research have given currency to any utterance that he might make on the subject.

It is claimed that Robert Lewis was the son of Sir Edward Lewis of a noble line of ancestry, and Mr. Henry Howell Lewis

16

is quoted as authority; but this is not considered authentic, though it may be true. Mr. Lewis never at any time intimated to the authors that he had succeeded in establishing the English line of General Lewis from the records, although generally accepted tradition goes far to establish this theory.

In addition to the statement of Mr. Henry Howell Lewis in regard to the identity of John Lewis, who married Isabella Warner, we have the authority of Mr. Thomas M. Green of Danville, Kentucky, who furnishes the most unquestioned record proof, and leaves no room to doubt that this John Lewis was the son of Robert the emigrant. Mr. Green cites Henning's Statutes at Large, 1769 and at other times, with reference to entailed estates. These statutes show that entailed estates in New Kent and Hanover counties, settled upon William Lewis by his father, reverted to the descendants of John Lewis who married Isabella Warner, William Lewis having died without issue. These statutes further prove that General Robert Lewis had two sons, only one of whom left issue, William Lewis as is shown above having died without issue, and his estates having reverted to the descendants of his only brother; and John Lewis the survivor, having married Isabella Warner built Warner Hall.

2   THE FIRST JOHN LEWIS.

This member of the Lewis family was the second son of General Robert Lewis of Brecon, Wales, born about 1640. He married Isabella Warner and built Warner Hall on the Severn river in Gloucester county, Virginia. Mr. William Terrell Lewis, author of "Genealogies of Lewis family," gets the Warner Hall line very much confused. Mr. Lewis himself is a descendant of John Lewis of Hanover who came to Virginia about 1675. Three-fourths of his book is devoted to genealogies of this line, on which he is undoubted authority, but on other lines he has been doubtless misled by unfounded traditions. These genealogies make William Lewis the father of Charles Lewis, of the Byrd, who married Mary Howell, and hence the ancestor of a

numerous line of descendants; while Hennings's Statutes at
Large show conclusively that William Lewis, the son of Robert
the Welshman, died without issue.

The John Lewis we now have under consideration was the
sole survivor of his family, so far as we have any account. He
married Isabella Warner, daughter of Captain Augustine Warner of the British army, and sister of Speaker Augustine Warner. It has been claimed by some genealogists that this John
Lewis was born in England and that he married there, but all of
the circumstances and data go to prove that he was born several
years after his father came to America, and that his wife's parents were in Virginia long before he was married, and, indeed,
before either he or his wife were born. The exact date of the
arrival in Virginia of Captain Augustine Warner of the British
army is not known. The first that is definitely known of him
in the colony, is the registry of his son Augustine when he entered the "Merchant's Tailors School" in London, in which he
stated that he was born in Virginia in 1642. The first appearance of Captain Augustine Warner on the Virginia records is
the entry of a tract of 2,500 acres of land, in connection with
his wife Mary, about the branches of old Cheese Cake Town,
south side of the Piankitank river, October 26, 1652, and his
name first appears as burgess from York in the same year.

From the fact that Augustine Warner, Sr., and his wife,
and Speaker Augustine Warner, were buried at Warner Hall,
and their tombs were marked 1662, 1674, 1681, respectively,
and that of General Robert Lewis cannot be located, it has been
insisted by the school of chronic objectors that the Warner Hall
property belonged to the Warner and not to the Lewis family.
Several facts stand forth prominently, however, which preclude
the possibility of any such contention being successfully made.
General Robert Lewis died about 1645 while Speaker Augustine
Warner did not die until 1681. Mr. Henry Howell Lewis tells
us that there are numerous slabs that could not be deciphered
on account of age and that doubtless the tomb of Robert Lewis
was among them. He tells us further that Robert Lewis settled on the Severn and that John Lewis built Warner Hall on

the same river. Thus we have the location of the estate of Robert Lewis settled, and we find that Warner Hall was built upon this property. The first record evidence that we have of the presence of Augustine Warner, Sr., in Virginia is the entry of the tract of land above referred to at Cheese Cake Town, south side of Piankitank river, October 26, 1652. Thus we have record evidence of the Warner homestead fifteen or twenty miles northwest of Warner Hall. In confirmation of this fact, the epitaph of Elizabeth Warner Lewis states that she was born at Cheese Cake, the name of the Warner homestead. November 24, 1672. So that, taking it for granted that Elizabeth Warner was born at home, there can be no question as to the homestead of the two families. There is nothing remarkable about the elder Warners being buried in the Lewis burying ground when it is considered that their oldest daughter had married John Lewis about 1660. Another fact which goes to prove that this was not a Warner burying ground is that none of the younger Warners were buried there.

Mrs. Stubbs of New Orleans, author of "Early Settlers of Alabama," in an article published in the Joseph Habersham column of the Atlanta Constitution, June, 1902, asserted that the Warner Hall property was patented by the first Augustine Warner, and undertook by a series of arguments to prove her position. It is clear that Mrs. Stubbs was conscientious in her claims, but her premises being erroneous, all that followed was simply a comedy of errors. She claimed that Augustine Warner resided within the bounds of Abingdon Parish and that he gave a communion service to that church; and as Warner Hall was in Abingdon Parish she claimed that fact settled the location of his residence. Bishop Meade, however, asserts that Augustine Warner lived in Pettsworth's Parish and gave the communion service to that church, and this parish takes in the Cheese Cake and Piankitank territory. Mrs. Stubbs endeavors to reconcile the birth of Elizabeth Warner Lewis at Cheese Cake by saying that Speaker Augustine Warner resided for a time long enough for Elizabeth to be born, on lands given to Speaker

19

Augustine Warner's wife by her father, George Reade, but these lands were not in Abingdon or Pettsworth parish, but as shown by Henning's Statutes, were in the Parish of Ware, and according to the records none of the Warners ever resided in that Parish.

READE AND WARNER.

As these names become a part of the Lewis history at this point, they will be noticed briefly before going farther on the main line. Mr. Thomas M. Green says: "Among others of the younger sons of the English nobility who sought to improve their fortunes in the Colony of Virginia, was George Reade, whose sole importance to history consisted in the fact that he was one of the first ancestors of General Washington who ventured across the Atlantic, and it was from him that the first and greatest of Americans derived his given name."

George Reade came to Virginia about 1637. He was secretary of the colony 1637, acting governor 1638-9, member of House of Burgesses from James City 1649, and for York 1656, member of King's Council from 1657 until his death 1671. (Henning's Statutes at Large, Vol. I, pp. 358, 414, 421, 429, 432, 499, 505.) He married Elisabeth, daughter of Colonel Nicholas Martian (pronounced Marchen) and had four sons and one daughter. This Nicholas Martian was evidently a Frenchman, as his name would indicate, and from the further fact that the records of North Hampton county show that he obtained denization papers in England before coming to Virginia which would not have been the case if he had been an Englishman. He was born 1591, and came to Virginia about 1620. He was justice of York county from 1632 to 1657, member of the House of Burgesses from time to time, as shown by Henning's Statutes, Vol. 1, pp. 129, 154, 179, 203. His will, dated March, 1656, and proved April 24, 1657, is on record in York county, and divides his estate between his three daughters, Elisabeth, wife of Colonel George Reade, Mary, wife of Colonel

20

Sarbrook, and Sarah, wife of Captain William Fuller, at one time governor of Maryland. As appears from the will of Nicholas Martian, he left no son, and so far as is known the name has become extinct or fallen into obscurity.

George Reade, who married Elizabeth Martian, as has been seen, had four sons and one daughter. His will was admitted to probate 1671. His sons, Robert, Francis, Benjamin and Thomas, were the respective heads of numerous families of the name, and from the Reades, either directly or through the Warners, have descended the numerous Roots family, Thomas Reade Roots being a combination of names which has become stereotyped in many households.

Before dismissing George Reade, it is proper that we should refer briefly to his English history, as he was first taken up after reaching Virginia. As a matter of fact, all of the names in which this volume will deal have European histories. They are strictly historic families, but they came to America to make history and left their past history behind them. George Reade is no exception to the rule, but such were his associations that his English history followed him. This is true of many other names.

The first clue to the English history of George Reade was the fact, shown by several letters in the first volume of the English Calendar of Colonial Papers, that he had a brother, Robert Reade, who was private secretary to Sir Francis Winderbank, secretary of state during the reign of Charles I, from which it was ascertained that George Reade was a descendant of the Reades of Faccombe, in the county of South Hampton.

Andrew Reade of Faccombe, was born about 1550. His will was dated October 16, 1619, with a codicil dated November 15, 1621, and was proven October 24, 1623. He married Miss ———— Cook, of New Kent, and had five sons and four daughters, Henry, Robert, George, John and Andrew, being the sons. The eldest son married Anne, daughter of Sir Thomas Windebank, and died April 4, 1647. The second son, Robert, who lived at Linkenholdt, married three times. His third wife was

Mildred, daughter of Sir Thomas Windebank, of Haines' Hill, Parish of Hurst, Berkshire, who was clerk of the signet of Elizabeth and James. It does not appear whether or not the wives of Henry and Robert were sisters, or whether there were two Thomas Windebanks, contemporaneous with each other, but it is certain that Robert's wife was a sister of Sir Thomas Windebank.

Robert Reade and Mildred Windebank had five sons, Andrew, William, Thomas, Robert (who was secretary to his uncle, Sir Francis Windebank), and George, the subject of this sketch, who came to Virginia in 1637. George Reade is mentioned several times in volume I, Calendar Colonial State Papers. He was a friend and adherent of Governor Harvey and Secretary Kemp, and during their absence in England was secretary and acting governor of the colony at different times.

Augustine Warner, Sr., is referred to in the "William and Mary Quarterly" as "Colonel," and by Mr. Green and others as "Captain" Augustine Warner. It is more than probable that he was a captain in the British army and colonel in the Colonial service. The Quarterly says that he came to Virginia as early as 1628, but I find no record of his presence there previous to 1642, and none between that time and 1652.

Augustine Warner, Sr., and his wife, Mary, had only three children so far as is known, though Mrs. Stubbs tells us of a fourth, a daughter who married Major Cant. I have found no record or even reference to this marriage from any other source. Augustine Warner, Jr., who married Mildred Reade, Isabella, who married the first John Lewis, and Sarah, who married Lawrence Townley and was the ancestress of General Robert E. Lee, are all for whom the records vouch. Mr. Green says: "It was the fashion as well as the necessity with the wealthier Virginians to send their oldest sons to England to be educated, and thither went the younger Augustine Warner, who in 1657 was entered on the books of the Merchants Tailors School in London as Augustine, eldest son of Augustine Warner, gentleman, born in Virginia, October 20, 1642. Matriculating at

Cambridge and returning to Virginia, he was elected to the House of Burgesses from Gloucester as early as 1666, whence he passed to the Royal Council, under Sir William Berkley. In 1676 he was speaker of the Burgess of the Assembly which succeeded the one which had been in existence since 1666, and which Berkley dissolved in consequence of Bacon's rebellion. It was at the Bar of the Assembly of Burgess, presided over by this Augustine Warner, that Bacon knelt and sued for pardon.

Speaker Augustine Warner married Mildred, only daughter of George Reade and his wife, Elisabeth Martian. Mr. Green says: "They left sons who handed down the name, but we have no well-authenticated history of any of the name, or their lines of descent." It may be said that so far as the records show, all of Speaker Augustine Warner's sons died without issue. Speaker Warner had three daughters, Mildred, Elisabeth and Mary, who married, respectively, Lawrence Washington, John Lewis, and John Smith of Purton, Gloucester county. It was necessary to designate who John Smith was, otherwise, it would never have been known who Mary Warner married.

Nothing further is known of the history of the first John Lewis than has already been given, except that he was the sole heir of Robert and the founder of that line of the Lewis family in America. Councilor John Lewis, who married his first cousin Elizabeth Warner, was his only child so far as is known.

Thus we have brought the two lines of descent from General Robert Lewis of Wales on the one side, and from Nicholas Martian and George Reade, through Augustine Warner, on the other, and find the union consummated in the marriage of Councilor John Lewis to Elizabeth Warner.

3. THE SECOND JOHN LEWIS.

3 Councilor John Lewis was the grandson of General Robert Lewis the Welshman, born in 1669, and died 1725. He married his first cousin, Elisabeth Warner, granddaughter of George Reade and great-granddaughter of Nicholas Martian. On the tombstone of Elisabeth Warner Lewis it is stated that she was the loving mother of fourteen children. It is not known

how many of these reached maturity or left issue. We have only the history of three sons, John Lewis, born 1692, Charles Lewis, born 1696, and Robert Lewis, born 1704. The names of five daughters have been preserved through the records of Abingdon Parish, and Henning's Statutes, but there is no data in regard to any of them except Isabella who married Dr. Thomas Clayton July 14, 1720. They had one child, Juliana.

ROBERT LEWIS OF BELVOIR.

4 Robert Lewis, the youngest son of John Lewis and Elizabeth Warner, taken up at this time for the sake of convenience, was born 1704, at Warner Hall, the old ancestral home in Gloucester county, Virginia. He married Jane Meriwether, daughter of Nicholas Meriwether and Elizabeth Crawford, 1725.

For three successive generations and for nearly one hundred years, the Lewis family have in every essential sense of the term been among the "Lords of Gloucester." Unbroken tradition, supported by the highest standard of record proof, goes to sustain this assertion. The founder of the family having brought with him a grant from the Crown to immense tracts of land, and having been possessed of large estates before leaving Wales, had no difficulty in establishing in his new home the foundation of an immense fortune, baronial indeed in its extent and value. Up to the time when the fourth generation found it expedient, like bees from an over-crowded hive, to withdraw from Gloucester, Warner Hall had been to the Lewises and Warners what Windsor Castle had been to British royalty. It must not be inferred, however, that this was the breaking up of the Lewis family. It was the opposite. Warner Hall stood and a John Lewis still continued to occupy it; and it was as much as ever the scene of gaiety and of hospitality, while the Lewises, Warners and Washingtons continued to meet there and hold high carnival. But the family had grown too large and their operations too extensive to be confined within the limits of a single county, and so we find them establishing themselves in other localities and laying the foundations of other estates.

One of Mr. Jefferson's biographers says that his father, Peter Jefferson, was one of the earliest settlers of Albemarle county, being the third or fourth to settle in Shadwell district; but Bishop Meade, in his "Old Churches and Families," finds Peter Jefferson's name on the vestry book of St. James Northam Parish, Goochland county, in 1744, while he finds the name of Robert Lewis on the vestry book of Fredericksville Parish, Albemarle county, in 1742. So that there can be no doubt but that Robert Lewis was one of the pioneers of Albemarle. What the earlier members of this family had been to Gloucester, Robert Lewis was to Albemarle, and as an evidence of his estates it may be mentioned that in his will he devises to his children 21,660 acres of land. He married a second time, in his old age, the widow of his old friend, Thomas Meriwether, whose maiden name was Elizabeth Thornton. He died 1765.

To Robert Lewis and Jane Meriwether were born eleven children all of whom lived to be grown and married. Their names are as follows:

5 ¹John Lewis, born about 1726, married Catherine Fauntleroy.
5 ⁶Nicholas Lewis, born 1728, married Mary, daughter of Dr. Thomas Walker and Mildred Thornton, of Castle Hill, Albemarle county, Virginia. She was born July 24, 1742.
5 ³Charles Lewis, born 1730, married his cousin Mary, daughter of Charles Lewis of Buck Eye land and his wife Mary Randolph.
5 ⁴William Lewis, born about 1735; married his cousin Lucy, daughter of Thomas Meriwether and Elizabeth Thornton.
5 ⁵Robert Lewis, born about 1738; married his cousin Frances, daughter of Charles Lewis of the Byrd.
5 ⁶Jane married first Thomas Meriwether, second John Lewis of the Byrd.
5 ⁷Ann married John Lewis, "the honest lawyer," son of Zachary Lewis, of Spottsylvania county, Virginia.

5 ⁸Mildred married Major John Lewis of Goochland, son of
Joseph Lewis, and great-grandson of John Lewis of
Henrico.

5 ⁹Sarah married Dr. Waller Lewis of Spottsylvania, son of
Zachary and Mary Waller.

5 ¹⁰Elizabeth married Rev. Robert Barrett of Richmond, Virginia.

5 ¹¹Mary married first Samuel Cobbs of Louisa, and second
Waddy Thomson.

JOHN LEWIS.

5 John Lewis, oldest son of Robert Lewis of Belvoir, and
Jane Meriwether, born about 1726; married Catherine Fauntleroy, daughter of Col. Wm. Fauntleroy of Richmond, Virginia.
His last appearance on the records of Albemarle was as executor
of his father's will, 1766, and the execution of a deed, with his
wife Catherine, a few years afterwards, when he is described
as "John Lewis of Halifax," after which other genealogists
seem to have lost sight of him. The best evidence, however,
locates him on Dan river about five miles east of Danville, in
Halifax county, Virginia. It has been only by the most persistent search and constant perseverance that any of his descendants have been located and identified. Four children, two
sons and two daughters, have however been successfully located:
John, Francis, Apphia and Sallie.

6 John Lewis, oldest son of John Lewis and Catherine
Fauntleroy, born August 31, 1753; married Elizabeth Kennon,
daughter of Wm. Kennon and Elizabeth Lewis and granddaughter of Charles Lewis of "The Byrd," born November 13, 1754.
They were married February 8, 1776. Issue as follows:

7 ¹John Lewis, oldest son of John Lewis and Elizabeth Kennon,
born December 28, 1776.

7 ²Wm. Lewis, born December 7, 1778.

7 ³Elizabeth Lewis, born December 28, 1780, married a man
named Sturgis and died at birth of first child. This child
was named Elizabeth Sturgis and married Richard Hines.

7 ⁴Augustine Lewis, born November 3, 1784.

7 [5]Jane Lewis, daughter of John Lewis and Elizabeth Kennon, born October, 1786, married Capt. Wm. Kennon, her first cousin, and had issue:

8 [1]Woodson Kennon married Hester Witherspoon, of Green county, Alabama.

8 [2]Mary Kennon married Wm. Jones of Alabama.

8 [3]Apphia Kennon married Martin Lea.

7 [6]Catherine Lewis married Major Wm. Dowsing and left issue:

8 [1]Elizabeth Dowsing married a Simms.

8 [2]William Dowsing.

8 [3]James Dowsing married a Lonby.

8 [4]Mary Dowsing married Chives of Mississippi.

8 [5]Martha married Hamton of Mississippi.

8 [6]Caroline married Dr. Alexander.

8 [7]Fielding Dowsing and several others. Names unknown.

7 [7]Fielding Lewis, son of John Lewis and Elizabeth Kennon, born July 3, 1788, died September 15, 1875; married Elizabeth A. Berryman, February 2, 1827, and had issue as follows:

8 [1]Americus Washington Lewis, son of Fielding Lewis and Elizabeth Berryman, born November 2, 1827.

8 [2]John Fielding Lewis, born January 10, 1831.

3 [3]Thomas Jefferson Lewis, born November 12, 1833.

8 [4]Catherine Lewis, born May 22, 1838.

8 [5]Mary Jane Lewis, born May 15, 1842.

7 [8]Charles Lewis, son of John Lewis and Elizabeth Kennon, born April 24, 1790.

8 [1]Catherine Lewis, born January 20, 1792, died young.

7 [9]Ulysses Lewis, son of John Lewis and Elizabeth Kennon, born February 7, 1799, married in 1824 Miss Ambercomby. Ulysses Lewis was first mayor of Columbus, Georgia, and afterwards judge of the county court of Russell county, Alabama. He left issue:

8 [1]John A. Lewis, born 1825, married Miss Spivy.

8 [2]Thomas J. Lewis, born March, 1827, married Miss Eiland; was killed at Fredericksburg, December 12, 1862.

8 [3]Elizabeth Lewis, born 1829, married Judge Porter Ingraham.

8 [4]Claudia A. Lewis, born 1831, married Benjamin R. Palmer. They removed to Texas where they both died.

8 [5]Sarah E. Lewis, born 1833; married Lyman P. Cowdry.

8 [6]Martha J. Lewis died in infancy.

8 [7]Martha G. Lewis, born 1837; married Dr. James Freeney.

8 [8]Jane H. Lewis, born 1840; married first Lyman P. Cowdry, husband of her deceased sister Sarah, and married second Lafayette Murdock.

8 [9]Joseph H. Lewis, born December 3, 1847; married Miss Decker of Alabama.

8 [10]Ulysses Lewis, Jr., son of Ulysses Lewis and Miss Ambercromby, born February 27, 1845; married Miss Frances Stewart, daughter of John D. Stewart of Columbus, Georgia. Mr. Lewis is a lawyer who, for legal ability, ranks with the first members of the profession. He is not startling or sensational, nor is he versed in the tricks and short cuts of the "Shyster," but his ability is recognized by all who know him, and his integrity is unquestioned. Were it not for the fear of shocking the nerves of the public, we would class him with John Lewis of Spottsylvania, of a past generation, and say that he was entitled to the appellation of "the honest lawyer."

Following are the names of the children of Ulysses Lewis and Miss Stewart:

9 [1]Eugene.

9 [2]John.

9 [3]Emma, died in infancy.

9 [4]Elizabeth.

9 [5]Thomas.

9 [6]Frank.

9 [7]Cephalie.

9 [8]Henry.

9 [9]Joseph.

Miss Elizabeth Lewis, oldest daughter of Mr. Ulysses Lewis, is deeply pious, as is also her father, and strongly imbued with the missionary spirit. She is now at Nyack, New York, training for the work.

7 [10]Fauntleroy Lewis, youngest son of John Lewis and Elizabeth Kennon, born February 7, 1796; married Miss Lucy Garland and had issue as follows:

8 [1]Edward Garland Lewis; married first Elizabeth Brown, and second Laura Bynum.

8 [2]Eliza Lewis, married Phillip Bathea.

8 [3]Margaret Lewis (twin); married Youngblood.

8 [4]Lucy Lewis (twin); married Newton Carr.

8 [5]Fannie Lewis; married first Thomas Richmond, second Fayette Grooms.

8 [6]Fauntleroy Lewis; married Martha Renfroe.

8 [7]Celestine Lewis married James Oliver; both died; no issue.

8 [8]Mildred Lewis married Everett Arnold.

8 Edward Garland Lewis and Elizabeth Brown had two children:

9 [1]William Lewis.

9 [2]John Lewis.

And by Laura Bynum he had four daughters:

9 [3]Jane Lewis.

9 [4]Kittie Lewis.

9 [5]Eva Lewis.

9 [6]Agnes Lewis.

8 Eliza Lewis and Phillip Bathea had six children:

9 [1]Mary Bathea married Dan Green.

9 [2]Anne Bathea married Dolly Deveraux.

9 [3]Elizabeth Bathea married Joseph Bowyer.

9 [4]Kittie Bathea married Silas Shell.

9 [5]Axcie Bathea married Wm. Renfroe.

9 [6]Linden Bathea married Fannie Beavens.

9 Mary Bathea and Dan Green have four sons:

10 [1] Phillip Green.
10 [2] Samuel Green
10 [3] Charles Green.
10 [4] Daniel Green.

8 Margaret Lewis (daughter of Fauntleroy Lewis and Lucy Garland) and her husband George Youngblood had two children:

9 [1] James Youngblood.
9 [2] Julia Youngblood.

8 Fannie Lewis, daughter of Fauntleroy Lewis and Lucy Garland; married first Thomas Richmond and second Fayette Grooms.

9 By first marriage one son, Thomas Richmond.
9 By second marriage two sons, John Grooms, Robert Grooms.

8 Fauntleroy Lewis, Jr., son of Fauntleroy Lewis and Lucy Garland; married Martha Renfroe and had issue:

9 Elisa Lewis married William Rateree and has son and daughter.
9 Bettie Lewis married John Hodo and had three children:
　　10 Walter, Robert and Albert Hodo.

9 James Youngblood, son of Margaret Lewis and Geo. Youngblood and grandson of Fauntleroy Lewis and Lucy Garland; married Mary Brookins and has a family of eight or nine children.
　　Julia Youngblood married Wm. Arnold and has three children.
8 Mildred Lewis, daughter of Fauntleroy Lewis and Lucy Garland; married Everett Arnold, had one daughter, Virginia Arnold.

8 Lucy Lewis, daughter of Fauntleroy Lewis and Lucy Garland, and twin sister of Margaret who married Youngblood; married Newton Carr. They had one child, Sarah Elizabeth.

9 Sarah Elizabeth Carr married William Renfroe; issue, two children:
   10 ¹Carlton Eugene Renfroe.
   10 ²James Renfroe.

7 ¹¹Elizabeth Lewis, youngest daughter of John Lewis and Elizabeth Kennon, born about 1800, and so named because of the early death of her oldest sister Elizabeth; married about 1818, in Milledgeville, Georgia, Colonel Wm. Stone, of Savannah, Georgia. They had one daughter:

8 Mary Stone married James Sorley, a banker of Galveston. They had one son:
   9 James Stone Sorley, captain in United States Army, stationed in the Philippines.

6 Sallie Lewis, daughter of John Lewis and Catherine Fauntleroy, born May 29, 1761; married August 10, 1780, Phillip Taylor, born March 25, 1759, son of Phillip and Mary (Anderson) Taylor of Chatham county, North Carolina. Issue:

7 ¹Iphegenia Taylor, born August 21, 1781.
7 ²Apphia Taylor, born March 10, 1783.
7 ³Phillip Taylor born October 7, 1784.
7 ⁴John Taylor, born October 7, 1786.
7 ⁵Polly Walker Taylor, born April 10, 1788, married Charles Judson Williams, son of John and Philadelphia Williams, son of John A. Williams of Asheville, North Carolina.
7 ⁶James Taylor, born July 30, 1791. Infant son died 1793.

6 Francis Lewis, son of John Lewis of Belvoir and his wife Catherine Fauntleroy, born about 1755 married and left sons and daughters, indeed, a long line of descendants. Francis Lewis settled in Georgia, and many of his descendants removed

to Alabama, one of whom, Dixon H. Lewis was in the United States Senate from that State, his history belongs to the country, and would require more space than a work of this character would admit. He was a man of ability, rare personality, and striking figure, he bordered very nearly upon the domain of giants, his weight approximate 500 pounds, and as the stage coach was, at that time, the only public means of travel, he always paid double fare.

7 Mary Lewis, daughter of Francis Lewis, and grand-daughter of John Lewis and Catherine Fauntleroy, married a gentleman by the name of Glenn and left issue:

9 Mary Glenn, granddaughter of Mary Lewis Glenn and great-granddaughter of Francis Lewis, great-great-granddaughter of John Lewis and Catherine Fauntleroy, married Judge Brickel, Chief Justice of the Supreme Court of Alabama, one of the most distinguished Jurists of his day, whose opinions are accepted as authority throughout the United States.

6 Apphia Fauntleroy Lewis daughter of John Lewis and Catherine Fauntleroy, married David Allen and had issue.

7 Mary Meriwether Allen married John Ross, issue three, girls: Sarah, Lizzie, and Kate, who married respectively, Ross, Turpin and Patton.

8 Sarah Allen Ross married Thomas B. Doe and had issue. Six girls one boy.

9 Sallie Allen Doe, second daughter of Sallie Allen Ross and Thomas B. Doe, married Joseph L. Lyack and had issue, 3 girls and one boy; Mayme Doe Lyack, Sallie A. Lyack, Sue Lyach, Thomas Doe Lyack, the last three unmarried.

10 Mayme Doe Lyack married Thomas G. Moore and has issue: Adalaide Moore, Mary Weeks Moore, Sarah Moore, born respectively, 1897, 1898, 1900.

9 Mary Virginia Doe third daughter of Thomas B. Doe and Sarah Allen, and great-great-granddaughter of John Lewis and Catherine Fauntleroy, married John Thomas Keene and had issue: Sallie Ross Keene, Nannie F. Keene, W. Witcher Keene, the two last unmarried.

10 Sallie Ross Keene married George A. Watson, and had issue: John Thomas Watson, Ross Watson, Sallie R. Watson, aged respectively 12, 18, 22.

9 Mattie Weeks Doe, daughter of Thomas B. Doe and Sarah Allen Ross, and great-great-granddaughter of John Lewis and Catherine Fauntleroy, married Samuel M. Embry and had issue: Sallie Doe Embry, and Mary Allen Embry, both unmarried at last accounts.

9 Kate Patton Doe, fourth daughter of Thomas B. Doe and Sarah Allen Ross married Samuel R. Street, Newbern, North Carolina, issue two boys, living: Samuel Street aged 20, and Thomas Doe Street, aged 13.

9 Sue Rickie Doe, fifth daughter of Thomas B. Doe and Sarah Allen Ross, married John R. Hutchings and had issue, as follows: Lucy Allen Hutchings, and Sue Hutchings, unmarried.

9 Thomas B. Doe, Jr., only son of Thomas B. Doe and Sarah Allen Ross, married Dora Williamson; issue, 3 boys and 3 girls: Thomas B., Jennie Dora, Weldon, Willie, Sarah.

8 Catherine Apphia Ross, or Kate, as used elsewhere, married William S. Patton; issue, 4 boys. John R. Patton married Hellen Flournoy; issue one son.

10 William F. Patton, unmarried.

9 William F. Patton, second son of W. S. Patton and Catherine Ross, married Sallie Fuller; issue two boys: Fearn Patton and Albert Patton, both unmarried.

9 James Dodridge Patton, third son of W. S. Patton and Catherine Ross, married Nannie Leary; issue, 1 boy and 1 girl. Nannie Leary Patton, James D. Patton, both unmarried.

9 Julian Allen Patton, fourth son of W. S. Patton and Catherine Ross, married Hennie C. Crew. Issue three children: Henry C. Patton, Kate Patton, Blanch Patton, all unmarried.

8 Elizabeth Ross, daughter of Mary Meriwether Allen and John Ross and granddaughter of Apphia Lewis, married John Turpin. Issue, Willie Turpin, 4 years old.

7 Lewis Buckner Allen, son of Apphia Fauntleroy Lewis and David Allen and grandson of John Lewis and Catherine

Fauntleroy, married Mary Catherine Jones; issue, Elizabeth Crawley Allen; three sons and three daughters.

8 Elizabeth Crawley Allen married Clinton Heeley; issue, Mary Cornelia Heeley and 4 sons.

9 Mary Cornelia Heeley married John Murray Hood; issue, Mary Chalmers Hood and 7 sons and one other daughter.

5 NICHOLAS LEWIS.

Second son of Robert of Belvoir, although a man of about 45 years of age at the time the Revolution broke out, was nevertheless in the full vigor of life. Mr. Jefferson, in his notes on "Virginia," vol. VIII, p. 481, says of Nicholas Lewis: "He commanded a regiment of militia in a successful expedition of 1776, against the Cherokee Indians, who, seduced by the agents of the British Government to take up the hatchet against us, had committed great havoc on our southern frontier, by murdering and scalping helpless women and children according to their cruel and cowardly principles of warfare. The chastisement they then received closed the history of their war, prepared them for receiving the elements of civilisation, which, zealously inculcated by the present Government of the United States, have rendered them an industrious peaceable and happy people. This member of the Lewis family, whose bravery was so usefully proved on this occasion, was endeared to all who knew him, by his inflexible probity, courteous disposition, benevolent heart and engaging modesty of manner. He was the umpire of all the private differences of his county, selected always by both parties. He was also the guardian of Meriwether Lewis."

The foregoing by Mr. Jefferson, is only a side reference, so to speak, in his biographical notice of Meriwether Lewis. The Revolutionary services of Nicholas Lewis would be sufficient in itself to fill a volume. He married Mary, daughter of Dr. Thomas Walker and Mildred Thornton of Castle Hill, Albemarle county, Virginia. She was born July 24, 1742, and had nine children. Following are some of the marriages of these children:

Nicholas Meriwether married Mildred Hornsby; Thomas Walker married Betsy Meriwether; Jane married Mr. Dickerson; Mildred married David Wood; Mary married Isaac Miller; Elizabeth married William Meriwether of Clover Field; Peggy married Charles S. Thomas. The descendants of these names have scattered to different parts of the country, many of whom no doubt having lost all trace of their ancestry. It is to be hoped that interest may be aroused and the attention of the younger generations bearing these names may be called to the subject.

Following is the issue more in detail:

6 [1]Thomas Walker Lewis, son of Nicholas Lewis and Mary Walker, born 1765, died June 1807; married 1788, Elizabeth Meriwether.

6 [2]Nicholas Meriwether Lewis second son of Nicholas Lewis and Mary Walker; born August 18, 1767; Died September 22, 1818, married his cousin Mildred Hornsby, daughter of Joseph Hornsby of Williamsburg, Virginia, and his wife Mildred Walker. They emigrated to Kentucky, near Louisville.

6 [3]Elizabeth Lewis, daughter of Nicholas Lewis and Mary Walker, born 1769, married February 28, 1788, William Douglas, or William Meriwether.

6 [4]Margaret Lewis, daughter of Nicholas Lewis and Mary Walker, born 1785, married Charles Lewis Thomas.

6 [5]Mary Lewis, daughter of Nicholas Lewis and Mary Walker; married Isaac Miller of Kentucky.

6 Nicholas Meriwether Lewis, son of Nicholas Lewis and Mary Walker; married Mildred Hornsby and had issue as follows:

7 [1]Joseph Lewis died young.

7 [2]Annah Hornsby Lewis, married Hancock Taylor, son of Col. Richard Taylor, brother of Zachary Taylor, President of the United States. They resided on a handsome estate five miles from Louisville, named Springfield. They had issue as follows. There were ten children, but only two living:

8 [1]Robert Hornsby Taylor, now of Florida.

8 [2]Mary Louise Taylor, born May 20, 1824; married Archibald McGill Robinson of Louisville, Ky., born in Winchester, August 23, 1821; he is a great-grandson of Alexander Robinson who settled in Baltimore, Maryland, about 1780.

8 Mary Louise Taylor and her husband, Archibald McGill Robinson, had issue as follows:

9 [1]Richard Goldsborough Robinson married Laura Picket Thomas.

9 [2]Lewis Magill Robinson.

9 [3]John Hancock Robinson married Frances L. Scruggs.

9 [4]Annah Walker Robinson married October 5, 1870, James Henry Watson of Mississippi. She is now a resident of Memphis, Tennessee. Author of "A Royal Lineage" etc.

9 [5]Elizabeth Lee Robinson.

9 [6]Robert Tyler Robinson.

9 [7]William Bryce Robinson married Elizabeth Boyd Rainy.

9 [8]Arthur Edwards Robinson.

9 [9]Zachary Taylor Robinson married Susan Luckett.

9 [10]Alexander Meade Robinson, married Lillian Hammond.

9 [11]Henry Wood Robinson.

The children of Mrs. Annah Robinson Watson, Author of a "Royal Lineage," and other genealogical works which have attracted wide attention are:

10 [1]Archibald R. Watson.

10 [2]James Henry Watson.

10 [3]Katherine Davis Watson.

10 [4]Elizabeth Lee Watson.

James Henry Watson, son of Mrs. Annah Robinson as above married June 12, 1900, Miss Katherine Julia Black.

6 Thomas Walker Lewis, son of Nicholas Lewis and Mary Walker; married Elizabeth Meriwether and had issue:

7 [1]Jane Warner Lewis, married Walker Meriwether.

7 [2]Margaret Douglas Lewis, married James Clark.

Jane Warner Lewis and Walker G. Meriwether had:

8 [3]Alice B. Meriwether married Henry V. P. Block of Pike county, Mo.

Alice V. Meriwether and Henry V. P. Block are said to have ten children, but I have the names of only eight, as follows:

9 [1]George M. Block, a lawyer of St. Louis, Mo., married Hellen L. Sylvester.

9 [2]Robert C. Block, married Annie Scott.

9 [3]Harry L. Block, married Nannie B. Livermore.

9 [4]Sarah C. Block, unmarried.

9 [5]Mary M. Block, unmarried.

9 [6]Helen L. Block, unmarried.

9 [7]Alice V. Block, married Fred A. Hamilton.

9 [8]Walker M. Block, married Annie Lynott.

George M. Block and Hellen Sylvester had:

10 [1]Hellen S. Block.

Harry L. Block and Nannie Livermore have 2 children:

[1]Mary B. Block.

[2]Ann M. Block.

Alice V. Block and Fred Hamilton have a daughter:

[1]Alice B. Hamilton.

Walker M. Block and Annie Lynott have a son:

[1]Henry V. P. Block.

7 Margaret Douglas Lewis, daughter of Thomas Walker Lewis and Elisabeth Meriwether, granddaughter of Nicholas Lewis, and great-granddaughter of Robert Lewis of Belvoir married James Clark and had issue:

[1] Ellen Judith Clark, married Andrew Cochrane.

Andrew Cochrane and Ellen Judith Clark had: Margaret Douglas Cochrane, married Frank E. Block.

Frank E. Block and Margaret Douglas Cochrane had:

[1]Francis Cochrane Block, married Elizabeth Ormo.
[2]Ellen Douglas Block, married Augustus Hugh Bancker.
[3]Edward Bates Block, M. D.
[4]Lucretia Parker Block.
[5]Isabel Margaret Block, married Brooks Sanderson Morgan.
[6]Hamilton Block.

Francis Cochrane Block and Elizabeth Ormo had:

[1]Margaret Douglas Block.

Miss Ormo is a daughter of Dr. Frank Ormo of Atlanta. They trace their lineage back to Somerled, Wayne, Arguyle and first Lord of the Isles. They were also maternally descended from a sister of "The Bruce," who married a Highland Chief of the "Clan McAllister."

Isabel Margaret Block married Brooks Sanderson Morgan as seen above and had one daughter:

[1]Margaret Douglas Morgan.

Mr. Frank E. Block is from St. Louis, Missouri, having commenced business in Atlanta more than 30 years ago. He has been universally successful, and to day he does a manfacturing business second to none in the South. He belongs to what we are fond of calling "The Old School."

5 CHARLES LEWIS.

This member of the Lewis family, the third son of Robert of Belvoir, was also an active participant in the American Revolution, having taken a leading part in the events which led up to it. Mr. Jefferson in his "Notes on Virginia," vol. VII, p. 481 says of him; "He was one of the earlier patriots who stepped forward at the commencement of the Revolution, and commanded one of the regiments first raised in Virginia, and placed on continental establishment. Happily situated at home with a wife and young family, and a fortune placing him at ease, he left all to aid in the liberation of his country from foreign usurpation, then first unmasking their ultimate end and aim. His good sense, bravery, integrity, enterprise and remarkable bodily prowess marked him an officer of great promise, but he unfortunately died early in the Revolution." As remarked in regard to Colonel Nicholas Lewis, the foregoing are only side notes of Mr. Jefferson. The military record of Charles Lewis would be too extensive for the scope of this work. He married his cousin, Mary, daughter of Charles Lewis, of Buckeyeland, and his wife Mary Randolph. His will probated May, 1777, is on record in the Clerk's office of Albemarle county, Virginia, and is as follows:

"I, Charles Lewis of the county of Albemarle and Parish of St. Ann do constitute this my last will and testament in manner and form following, viz.:

"1. It is my will and desire that all my just debts be paid, and to enable my executors the better to do so, it is my will and desire that they should sell all my land on Ivy Creek.

"2. I lend my beloved wife, Mary Lewis, during her natural life, five hundred acres of land, including the houses and plantation, also, the fourth part of my negroes, and all my household furniture, and the fourth part of all my stock of all kinds.

"3. I give and bequeath the residue of my negroes and other personal estate, to be equally divided among my children, to them and their heirs forever, and in the case of the death of either of my children, their part of the estate to be equally divided among the survivors.

"4. I give and bequeath to my sons Howell, and Charles Warner and their heirs forever, my tract of land in the North Garden, to be equally divided between them in quantity and quality.

"5. I do hereby appoint, my beloved wife, Mary Lewis, executrix, Colonel Charles Lewis of Buckeyeland, Charles L. Lewis, Bennett Henderson, Charles Hudson and my brother, Nicholas Lewis, executors of this my last will and testament.

"Given under my hand and seal, this eleventh day of June, 1776.

"CHARLES LEWIS,   Seal.

"Signed, sealed and delivered in presence of John Thomas, Bennett Henderson, Charles L. Lewis.

"Codicil providing for unborn child added September 7, 1776.

"Admitted to record at a court held for Albemarle, May, 1777.

"JOHN NICHOLAS, Clk."

From the foregoing will it will be seen that Charles Lewis died previous to May, 1777, less than a year after the breaking out of the American Revolution. It will also be seen that he had only two sons, Howell and Charles Warner. It may be that he had daughters but if so they were included in the term "all my children."

We have no authentic account of his descendants further than this as seen by the foregoing will, only two names are mentioned, Howell and Charles Warner.

Having obtained the lineage of one of the descendants of Howell Lewis, son of Col. Charles Lewis, too late to give a more extended account, we will give what we have that others may add more. We are indebted to Mrs. Julia Lewis Shay, wife of A. K. Shay of Seattle, Washington, for this line. She says: "My great-grandfather was Col. Charles Lewis, son of Col. Robert Lewis and Jane Meriwether of Albemarle county, Virginia. My grandfather was Howell Lewis who married Mary Carr. My father was James Howell Lewis who married Sarah Ann Stanford and were the parents of twelve children; six sons and six daughters. One daughter died infant. Mrs. Julia Lewis Shay was one of these daughters and she has seven sons and one daughter. One son is married and has two children a son and daughter. Her daughter is married and has a little girl three months old. Mrs. Shay is a D. A. R., member of the Lady Sterling Chapter of Seattle, Washington."

WILLIAM LEWIS.

5 William Lewis was the fourth son of Robert Lewis of Belvoir, and was also an officer in the Revolutionary army, and

bore a conspicuous part in that struggle. He married Lucy Meriwether, sixth daughter of Thomas Meriwether and Elizabeth Thornton, and made his home at Locust Hill, seven miles west of Charlottesville. Locust Hill was a part of the vast estate owned by his father, on Ivy Creek, and was bequeathed to him, as will be seen by reference to his father's will. It is a noteworthy fact that, notwithstanding the vast increase in the value of lands and the radical changes in the methods of life, this property has never passed out of the hands of the family. Governor Gilmer in referring to this branch of the Meriwether family, says of the gentlemen: "Mr. Anderson who married the daughter of Colonel William Lewis was remarkable for nothing specially except the faculty for squandering his wife's estate," but it must be remembered that Governor Gilmer was not only a paralytic, but also a dispeptic and a misanthrope. About half a mile from Ivy Station on the Chesapeake and Ohio railroad is the residence of Mr. C. Harper Anderson, great-grandson of Captain William Lewis, and on its walls hangs the oil painting of his great-grandmother, Lucy Meriwether Lewis, known to her descendants, as "Aunt Marks." That part of the land belonging to the estate upon which the former home of William Lewis stood, has passed into other hands, but Mr. Anderson still owns several hundred acres of this historic patrimony, and a new residence stands not far distant from Locust Hill.

William Lewis and Lucy Meriwether had only three children, two sons and one daughter; Meriwether, Reuben and Jane. Meriwether never married. Reuben married his cousin, Mildred Dabney, daughter of Samuel Dabney, and "pretty Jane" Meriwether. They left no children. Jane Lewis married Edmond Anderson, also a first cousin. Mr. Harper Anderson, mentioned above is a descendant of this marriage, and notwithstanding the caustic remarks of Governor Gilmer in regard to Edmond Anderson, it is nevertheless true that Mr. Harper Anderson is still the owner by regular line of descent, of valuable property which has come down to him through a succession of five generations.

MERIWETHER LEWIS.

6. Meriwether Lewis was the oldest son of Captain William Lewis and Lucy Meriwether, and was born at Locust Hill, seven miles west of the town of Charlottesville, August 18, 1774. The station on the Chesapeake and the Ohio railroad which runs within half a mile of the old homestead of the Lewis family, is known as Ivy Station. Fifteen minutes' ride over a smooth road, full in sight of the Blue Ridge mountain, brings you within a short walk of Locust Hill, the birthplace of Meriwether Lewis, a place remarkable alike for its historic surroundings, and its long continuance in the same family; longer, perhaps than any other homestead in America, unless, some of the older entailed estates may prove exceptions. Locust Hill, however, was not an entailed estate. Purchased by Robert Lewis of Belvior, about 1730, it has descended from father to son for five successive generations, and more than a hundred and seventy years, with no entail or other legal provision to save it from the sheriff's hammer; and it therefore stands as a monument to the patriotism, paternal love and frugality of its successive owners.

Although Locust Hill was the birthplace of Meriwether Lewis, and although he entered the United States army from that place, there is an event in his life that historians, biographers and genealogists seem alike to have overlooked, or never to have known. His father died when he was a small boy, and his mother afterwards married Colonel William Marks, also a Revolutionary patriot, and in a sort of exodus, so to speak, of the Meriwethers,' Mrs. Marks, together with her second husband, and her Lewis children, removed to Georgia. Governor Gilmer, in his "Georgians" mentions this fact, but so incidentally that the reader is not impressed with it. Georgia, like Kentucky, was at that time (1785-1790) the far West, where the Indian roamed at will over her hills and through her valleys.

Mr. Jefferson, no doubt drawing upon his imagination, tells us of the early childhood of Meriwether Lewis, of his hunting the "raccoon and the opossum," in the darkness of the night

MERIWETHER LEWIS.

among the spurs of the Blue Ridge, and in this way accounts for his habits of hardihood in after life.

Mr. Jefferson was doubtless ignorant of the removal of Mrs. Marks and her Lewis children to Georgia, and wholly ignorant of the early life of Meriwether Lewis, who had spent all of his coon-hunting days in Georgia, where Indians were the only game that the white man could afford to hunt, or at school, where coons were not to be found. It is more than probable that Meriwether Lewis was never on a coon hunt in his life. It is true that he was inured to hardships and accustomed to danger in his boyhood, and that this had much to do with shaping his character in after life; but it is to the Indian, and not to the coon and opossum, that we must look for the explanation of this fact.

After the death of Colonel Marks, "Aunt Marks" returned to Locust Hill, Albemarle county, Virginia, and shortly after her return Meriwether Lewis entered the United States army. He volunteered in 1794, with the troops called out to suppress the whiskey rebellion, and in 1795 entered the regular army. He was promoted to the rank of Captain in 1800, and in 1801, when Mr. Jefferson was inaugurated president, he became his private secretary, and in 1803, upon the recommendation of the President was appointed to take command of the exploring expedition, which has become a part of our country's history as the expedition of "Lewis and Clark." The scope of this work will not admit of historical or biographical reference, except of the briefest character, and therefore this notice of Meriwether Lewis will be closed with a quotation from instructions which accompanies his appointment, and which will show the purport and scope of the undertaking, together with extracts from letters going to show the confidence reposed in him by the Government:

MR. JEFFERSON'S LETTER OF INSTRUCTIONS.

"Meriwether Lewis, Esq., Captain of 1st Regiment of Infantry of the United States of America.

"Your situation as secretary of the President of the United States has made you acquainted with the object of my confidential message of January 18, 1803, to the Legislature. You have seen the act they passed, which, though expressed in general terms, was meant to sanction those objects, and you are appointed to carry them into execution.

"Your mission has been communicated to the ministers here from France, Spain and Great Britain, and through them to their respective governments, and such assurance given as to its object as we trust will satisfy them. The country of Louisiana having been ceded by Spain to France, the passport you have from the minister of France, the representative of the present sovereign of that country, will be a protection, with all its subjects, and that from the minister of England will entitle you to the friendly aid of any traders of that allegiance with whom you may happen to meet. The object of your mission is to explore the Missouri river and such principal streams of it or any other river as may offer the most direct and practicable water communication across the continent.

"As it is impossible to foresee in what manner you will be received by the people with whom you may come in contact, Indians, traders and others, whether with hospitality, or hostility, so is it impossible to prescribe the exact degree of perseverance with which you are to pursue your journey. We value too much the lives of citizens to offer them to probable destruction. Your numbers will be sufficient to secure you against the unauthorised opposition of individuals or small parties, but if a superior force authorised or not authorised by a nation, should be arrayed against your further passage, and inflexibly determine to arrest it, you must decline its further pursuit and return. In the loss of yourselves we should lose all the information you will have acquired. By returning safely with that, you may enable us to renew the essay with better calculated means. To your own discretion, therefore, must be left the degree of danger you may risk, and the point at which you should decline, only saying we wish you to err on the side of your safety, and to bring us back your party

44

safe, even if it be with less information.

"On your arrival on the Pacific coast, endeavor to learn if there be any port frequented by the sea vessels of any nation, and to send two of your trusted people back by sea, in such way as shall appear practicable, with a copy of your notes; and should you be of the opinion that the return of your party by the way they went will be imminently dangerous, then ship the whole and return by sea by the way either of Cape Horn or the Cape of Good Hope, as you shall be able. As you will be without money, clothes or provisions, you must endeavor to use the credit of the United States to obtain them, for which purpose open letters of credit will be furnished you, authorising you to draw on the Executive of the United States or any of its officers in any part of the world, on which drafts can be disposed of, and to apply with our recommendations to the consuls, agents, merchants or citizens of any nation with which we have intercourse, assuring them in our name that any aids they may furnish you shall be honorably repaid and on demand. Our consuls, Thomas Hughes at Batavia in Java, William Buchanan in the isles of France, and John Elmsly at the Cape of Good Hope, will be able to supply your necessities by drafts on us.

"Should you find it safe to return by the way you go, after sending two of your party around by sea, or with your whole party, if no conveyance by sea can be found, do so, making such observation on your return as will serve to supply, correct or confirm those made on your outward journey.

"On re-entering the United States and reaching a place of safety, discharge any of your attendants who may desire and deserve it, procuring for them immediate payment of all arrears of pay and clothing which may have been incurred since their departure, and assure them that they shall be recommended to the liberality of the Legislature for the grant of a soldier's portion of land each, as proposed in my message to Congress; and repair yourself, with your papers, to the seat of government.

"To provide, in the accident of your death, against anarchy, dispersion and consequent danger to your party and total failure of the enterprise, you are hereby authorised by any instrument signed and written in your own hand, to name the person among them who shall succeed to the command on your decease, and by a like instrument to change the nomination from time to time as further experiences of the characters accompanying you shall point out superior fitness; and all the powers and authorities given to yourself are in the event of your death transferred and vested in the successor so named, with further powers to him and his successor in like manner to name each his successor who, on the death of his predecessor shall be vested with all the powers and authorities given to himself. Given under my hand in the city of Washington this 20th day of June, 1803."

Meriwether Lewis died October 11, 1809. After the completion of his expedition, the success of which secured to the United States by right of discovery all of that territory now embraced in the States of Oregon and Washington and some of the other Rocky Mountain States, he was appointed governor of Louisiana, now Missouri the capitol site of which at the time was in St. Louis. While en route to Washington on official business, unattended save by a single companion, who doubtless proved to be his assassin, he was murdered while passing through what is now the State of Tennessee, near where the town of Franklin is at present situated. Although it was believed at the time that he had committed suicide, and was so reported by Mr. Jefferson as a historical fact, the theory is not only not plausible but contradictory in its every bearing. Governor Gilmer, who perhaps knew more of Meriwether Lewis than any man of the time, being a near relative, and about the same age, who was many years in public life, having been twice governor of Georgia and having served several terms in Congress, did not believe the suicide theory, but emphatically contradicted it and gave the best of reasons to disprove it; while Mr. Jefferson's own account of the circumstances, when analysed, furnishes its own refutation. No one could suspect Mr. Jefferson of doing intentional injustice to the memory of Meriwether Lewis, but that his credulity was

46

imposed upon is proven by his own statements.

Paul Hayne's account of the expedition of Lewis and Clark is the most comprehensive of any that has been published, and shows the vast scope of the undertaking, together with its difficulties and dangers, as well as the great benefits resulting to the country therefrom. Mr. James Parton has also published a very interesting, and at the same time correct, account of this expedition.

Of one fact we are assured, that he made a noble record while living and died true to his country, true to his duty as a man, and true to the trusts reposed in him. Capt. Lewis died at the age of 35 years, and was buried in the center of Lewis county, Tennessee. In a dense oak forest, remote from human habitation, stands a simple granite monument, erected by the State of Tennessee over the grave of Meriwether Lewis; upon which is cut the eulogy, written of him by President Jefferson: "His courage was undaunted, his firmness and perseverance yielded to nothing but impossibilities. A rigid disciplinarian, yet tender as a father of those committed to his charge; honest, disinterested, liberal, with a sound understanding and a scrupulous fidelity to truth." It also bears this Latin epitaph, "*Immaturus obi; sed to felicior annos vive meos, bone republica vive tuos.*" His own family motto: "*Omne solumforti patria est,*" might have been more appropriate.

August 12, 1905, will be the Centennial anniversary of the arrival of Captain Lewis in the Oregon country, and the Loyal Lewis Legion, a fraternal, genealogical and historical society, composed of those by the name of Lewis and their kin, will hold a Congress in Portland, Oregon, under the auspices of the Lewis and Clark Exposition. One entire day has been set aside and designated as Lewis Day (as was also September 23, 1904 at the Louisiana Purchase Exposition), in honor of the intrepid explorer Meriwether Lewis. The Tennessee Lewis Society, through Hon. E. C. Lewis of Nashville, will decorate the tomb of Meriwether Lewis with flags and flowers while Lewis' Congress will meet in Portland, Oregon, to honor his life, character and services, to pay royal homage to his memory, to sing his praises and record their estimate of his worth. He was a history maker. He achieved honor for honor's sake, by which he is now remembered one hundred years afterwards. May the Lewises of today emulate all that was good, just and generous; emulate the sturdy character, the strenuous life of our honored hero, and win honor in *this day and generation by which they* may be *remembered* and *honored* one hundred years hence.

Reuben Gold Thwaites has edited a very authentic account of the expedition from the original journals of the Lewis and Clark Expedition.

6 *Reuben Lewis*, born February 14, 1777. Second son of William Lewis and Lucy Meriwether, went west with his brother, Governor Meriwether Lewis in 1807. Was Indian agent among the Maudans and Cherokees, returned to Ivy, Virginia, 1820 where he married December 18, 1822, his cousin, Mildred Dabney. They left no children. She was born September 5, 1790, and died October 5, 1851.

6 Jane Lewis, only daughter of William Lewis and Lucy Meriwether, born March 31, 1770, died March 15, 1845. Married Edmund Anderson, and had nine children, Meriwether L., Edmond, Jane, Anne, Sarah, Lucy Elisabeth Thornton, David, William L.

6   EDMUND ANDERSON AND JANE LEWIS.

7 [1]Dr. Meriwether Anderson, oldest son of Jane Lewis and Edmund Anderson, married Miss Lucy Harper, and left children only three of whom we have been able to trace: Meriwether Lewis, killed in the Confederate army, Charles Harper and Mary Miller.

8   Charles Harper Anderson, only surviving son of Dr. Meriwether Anderson and Lucy Harper, married Miss Scott, who was a descendant of Zachary Lewis and also of Robert Lewis of Belvior. He resides seven miles west of Charlottesville, Virginia, on the Chesapeake and Ohio railroad at Ivy Depot. Mr. An-

derson is a successful merchant at that place, and owns a subdivision of the old Lewis estate, known as Locust Hill. They have an interesting family of four sons and three daughters.

8. Mary Miller Anderson, daughter of Dr. Meriwether Anderson, and Lucy Harper, married B. R. A. Scott, a prominent lawyer of Galveston, Texas. This Mr. Scott is a brother of Mrs. Anderson mentioned above and hence, is also a descendant of Zachary Lewis and Robert of Belvior. The descendants of Jane Lewis and Edmund Anderson given more fully in detail below:

7 [1]Elizabeth Thornton Anderson, daughter of Jane Lewis and Edmund Anderson, born May 14, 1786, died young.

7 [2]Jane Lewis Anderson, daughter of Jane Lewis and Edmund Anderson, born July 15, 1789, married Benjamin Wood; residence near Ivy Depot, Virginia.

7 [3]William L. Anderson, born December 4, 1792, married Mary Webb and died in West Virginia.

7 [4]Lucy M. Anderson, born July 30, 1795, died October 19, 1854; married Ballard Buckner.

7 [5]Anne E. Anderson, born October 20, 1800, died June, 1845; married Thomas Fielding Lewis, son of Howell and Mary (Carr) Lewis, son of Charles and Mary Lewis, son of Robert and Jane M. Lewis.

7 [6]David Anderson, born 1803; married in the West, Mary Buckner of Natches, Mississippi.

7 [7]Meriwether Lewis Anderson, born Albermarle county, Virginia, June 23; 1805; married Lucy Sidney Harper; born 1811, died December 4, 1885. Residence Locust Hill.

7 [8]Sarah Thornton Anderson, born June 22, 1807; married December 8, 1823, Gabriel Smithes Harper; died in Prince Edward county, Virginia.

7 [9]Mary Herndon Anderson, born October 4, 1809, died young.

8 [1]Marion Wood, daughter of Jane Lewis Anderson and Benjamin Wood; married William G. Rogers, a direct relative of George Rogers Clark and William Clark, through their mother, Ann Rogers.

49

8 ²Martha Wood, daughter of Jane Lewis Anderson and Benjamin Wood; married Daniel Perkins.

8 ³Alice Wood, daughter of Jane Lewis Anderson and Benjamin Wood; married Charles Price.

8 ⁴Lucy Wood, daughter of Jane Lewis Anderson and Benjamin Wood; married William Barrett.

The children of William L. Anderson and Mary Webb are:

8 ¹Reuben M. Anderson died 1888.

8 ²Mary J. Anderson, born December 1824, died September 1846; married July 29, 1845, Robert H. Mosby.

8 ³Robert Meriwether Anderson, born October 19, 1826 died November 9, 1880 in Essex county, Virginia; married 1864 Harriet S. Lewis.

8 ⁴Tempte Anne Anderson, born January 30, 1828; married Kosciusco Hopkins.

8 ⁵Lucy M. Anderson, born March 4, 1829; married W. F. Green.

8 ⁶Sarah H. Anderson married ——— Hedges.

8 ⁷Laura Anderson, born 1834; married William Landis.

8 ⁸Richard Webb Anderson, born 1836, died October 22, 1867.

8 ⁹Henning Fisher Anderson, born February 19, 1840, died October 18, 1869; married Laura McCoy of Texas.

The issue of Ballard Buckner and Lucy M. Anderson are:

8 ¹Mary Jane Buckner married, first, David Anderson; second, ——Cunningham, and third, McCrocklie.

8 ²Edmund A. Buckner, born December 27, 1815; married Mary Graf.

8 ³Maria Buckner, born January 1, 1818; married William Davidson.

8 ⁴Alice Buckner, born February 24, 1820; married Joseph Thornton.

8 ⁵Robert Buckner, born July 12, 1824, died 1864; married Willie Abbott.

8 ⁶Caroline Buckner, daughter of Lucy M. Anderson and Ballard Buckner, born October 21, 1827; married her cousin Archie Anderson.

Children of Anne E. Anderson and Thomas Fielding Lewis:

8 ¹Charles Wm. Lewis, M. D., son of Anne E. Anderson and Thomas Fielding Lewis, born January, 1820.

8 ²Matilda Lewis, born September 3, 1822; married Henry Wood, January 4, 1847.

8 ³John Marks Lewis, born November 17, 1826; married Margaret Tapp.

8 ¹Jane Lewis Anderson, daughter of Meriwether Lewis Anderson and Lucy Sidney Harper; died in infancy.

6 ²Meriwether Lewis Anderson, born August 24, 1845; killed in war between the States near Fishers Hill, October 8, 1864. Age 19.

8 ³Charles Harper Anderson, son of Meriwether Lewis Anderson and Lucy Sidney Harper, born June 28, 1848; married February 15, 1872. Sarah Travers Scott, great great granddaughter of Robert Lewis of Belvoir through his daughter Mary by her second marriage with Waddy Thompson. Mr. Charles Harper Anderson is the nearest living relative of Meriwether Lewis the Explorer.

8 ⁴Mary Miller Anderson, daughter of Meriwether Lewis Anderson, born September 5, 1851; married September 27, 1877, B. R. A. Scott for some years a prominent lawyer of Galveston, Texas, but since the Galveston flood he has resided and practiced law in San Antonio, Texas.

8 ¹Mary J. Harper, daughter of Sarah Thornton Anderson and Gabriel Smither Harper, born 1824, died 1846; married William Woods.

8 ²Wilmuth Harper, born 1826, died 1842.

8 ³Annie Harper, born 1828, died 1846.

8 ⁴Sarah Harper, born 1831, died 1853; married Dr. James Terry.

8 ⁵Alice Harper, born 1835, died 1860; married Joel Watkins Daniels. Also children of Gabriel Harper.

8 ⁶Robert Harper, born 1840, died 1874; unmarried.

8 ⁷Charles Harper, born 1847, son of Sarah Thornton Anderson and Gabriel Harper; married Alice Gates 1875, died 1877.

8 Matilda Lewis, daughter of Annie E. Anderson and Thomas
Fielding Lewis; married David Henry Wood and had issue
as follows:

9 [1] Margaret Lewis Wood, born October 1842; married
Frances Lobban.

9 [2] Henry Grattan Wood, born June 6, 1846; married Miss
Hudspeth.

9 [3] Paulus Powell Wood, born August 10, 1854; married
Miss Ware.

9 [4] Annie J. M. Wood, born January 10, 1855; married as
her second husband, James Terrell Lewis, son of Howell and Sarah (Stanford) Lewis, who was son of Howell and grandson of Charles, Residence, Ivy, Virginia.

8 John Marks Lewis, son of Annie E. Anderson and Thomas
Fielding Lewis; married Margaret Tapp. Issue:

9 [1] Thomas Fielding Lewis; married Josephine Johnson and
resides in Dallas, Texas.

9 [2] Walter Tapp Lewis married Nellie ——— residence, Ft.
Worth, Texas.

9 [3] John M. Lewis married Sallie Lewis, grand-daughter of
Howell and Sarah (Stanford) Lewis married in Richmond, Virginia; residence in Norfolk, Virginia.

9 [4] William H. Lewis married Annie Strayor; residence
Charlottesville, Virginia.

9 [5] Matilda Lewis married Winslow Garth of Albemarle,
Virginia.

9 [6] Howell C. Lewis married Bessie Smith; residence Charlottesville, Virginia.

10 ———Woods, daughter of Wm. Woods, Jr., and fifth in line
of descent from Wm. Lewis, through his daughter Jane
Lewis and her husband Edmund Anderson; married Wm.
Scott.

10 Elizabeth Terry, Sarah Terry, Delia Terry and Giles Terry,
children of Nathaniel Terry and Elizabeth Terry and Elisa-

beth Sydnor, and fifth in line of descent from Wm. Lewis and Lucy Meriwether through their daughter, Jane Lewis and Edmund Anderson.

10 Nathan B. Topping, Harriet P. Topping and Ruth Topping, children of Sarah E. Daniels and Nathan B. Topping and fifth in line of descent from Wm. Lewis and Lucy Meriwether.

10 Mary Harper Cobb, daughter of Martha M. Harper and Wm. S. Cobb and fifth in line of descent from Wm. Lewis and Lucy Meriwether.

9 Robert Meriwether Anderson, Philip Lewis Anderson, H. Temple Anderson, Henning Webb Anderson, and W. M. Anderson, children of Robert Meriwether Anderson and his wife, Harriet S. Lewis.

9 Lucy Anderson Hopkins, Mary M. Hopkins, children of Temple Anderson and her husband Kosciusco Hopkins.

9 Mary Buckner and three sons died. Edmund Buckner, Meriwether Lewis Buckner, now living in Louisville, Kentucky. All children of Edmund A. Buckner and great-grandchildren of Edmund Anderson.

9 Mary Davidson, daughter of Maria Buckner and William Davidson; married Nathan Ragland.

9 Edmund Davidson, son of Maria Buckner and William Davidson; married Miss Ware.

9 Lulie Thornton, daughter of Alice Buckner and Joseph Thornton; married Hardin Magruder.

9 Willie Abbott Buckner, daughter of Robert Buckner and Willie Abbott; married James Osbourne.

9 Robert Anderson, Judge William, who was in the Interior Department with Hoke Smith during Cleveland's administration. Alice Anderson who married Graves, Sallie Anderson, and Archie Anderson, who died young, were all children of Caroline Buckner and Archie Anderson.

10 Jennie Ragland, Alice Ragland and Edward Ragland, all daughters of Mary Davidson and Nathan Ragland.

10 Maria Davidson, Harry Davidson, Edward Davidson, Frank

Davidson, Cora Davidson, Flora Davidson and George Davidson, all children of Edmund Davidson and Miss Ware.

10 Bessie Magruder, Willie Magruder, Thornton Magruder, all children of Lulie Thornton and Hardin Magruder and grandchildren of Alice Buckner and Joseph Thornton.

10 Robert B. Osborne, son of Willie Abbott Buckner and James Osborne; resides in Louisville, Kentucky.

5. ROBERT LEWIS.

Youngest son of Robert Lewis of Belvoir, was not twenty-one years old when his father's will was written in 1757, hence it follows that he was born subsequent to 1736. He married his cousin, Mary Frances Lewis, daughter of "Charles Lewis of the Byrd," and settled in Granville county, North Carolina. He appears upon the records of that state quite prominently, and was a member of the Constitutional Convention which met just previous to the breaking out of the Revolution. He died comparatively young, leaving several children as follows: James is one of the executors of his will, as shown by settlement of guardian; Howell Lewis 1791; Jane and Nicholas as shown by guardian Thomas Hynes; Charles, and is shown in book three, page 86, division of slaves among the children; Frances who married Dr. John Payne; Charles and Nicholas. Thus we have, Jane, Charles, Nicholas, James and Frances Payne, and from other sources we have John and Richard. Mrs. General Gordon, the first wife of Chief Justice Bleckly of the Supreme Court of Georgia, and Judge Haralson of the Supreme Court of Alabama, descended from this line.

Miss Latimer, daughter of James Latimer of Charles county, Maryland, married, first, a gentleman named Posey who died and left her a widow and in her widowhood she determined to cast her lot in Georgia, which was then the "far. west" and passing through North Carolina, traveling herself, with proper protection in her carriage, while her slaves and manager traveled with the wagons and the stock. She met Dr. John Lewis, son of

Robert Lewis. They married, settled in Warren county, Georgia, and were the ancestors of Mrs. Frank Graham of Augusta, Georgia, Judge Hal Lewis, Supreme Court, and many others in Georgia.

5 JANE LEWIS.

Jane Lewis, oldest daughter of Robert of Belvoir, born about 1728; married first, Thomas Meriwether, who was a grandson of old Nicholas Meriwether and Elizabeth Crawford and son of their son Nicholas, and second, John Lewis her first cousin, who was a son of "Charles Lewis of the Byrd." Of the descendants of the first marriage very little is known. The descendants of the second marriage will be taken up under the head of John Lewis. Following are the children of Jane Lewis and Thomas Meriwether. William born 1751. Robert born 1752. Thomas born 1754. Jane, Elizabeth, Nicholas, Mary, who married Richard P. White, and Richard.

6 · William Meriwether, son of the above named Thomas Meriwether, married and had issue as follows: Thomas, born 1781; Jane born 1783; Frances born 1785; Matilda born 1790; William born 1792; Robert born 1795; Lucinda born 1800.

7 William Meriwether, grandson of Thomas Meriwether and Jane Lewis, married and had issue as follows: Robert born 1828; Mary Ann born 1830; Eveline born 1832; William A. born 1834; Susan B. born 1837; Moody B. born 1839; Thomas born 1843, and C. V. (Mrs. Furlow) born 1846.

8 Mrs. C. V. (Meriwether) Furlough, great granddaughter of Thomas Meriwether and Jane Lewis married Chas. T. Furlough, July, 1864; assistant treasurer of the State of Georgia through a succession of administrations. They have issue as follows:

9 [1] Floyd C. Furlough married Miss Johnson, whose father was prominent in Georgia history. [2] Felder, [3] Meriwether, [4] Chas. T., Jr., [5] Eugene (daughter), [6] Hal.

5 MARY LEWIS.

5 Mary Lewis, born about 1735; married first, Samuel Cobbs; second, Waddy Thomson. Issue by first marriage: Robert Cobbs; Jane Cobbs, Judith Cobbs.

6 Robert Cobbs, only son of Samuel Cobbs and Mary Lewis, was born 1754 and married Ann G. Poindexter, daughter of John Poindexter, of Louisa county, Virginia; he died in Campbell county, Virginia in 1829. Robert Cobbs was a unique character whose highest estimate of life was a straightforward and unswerving integrity. He christened his home "Plain Dealings" and was known as "Robin Cobbs of Plain Dealing," he was an officer in the Revolutionary army and left a record of which any descendant could well afford to be proud. Robert Cobbs and Ann G. Poindexter left a family of nine children, six sons and three daughters, who together with their descendants will be taken up under the head of the "Cobbs Family."

6 Jane Cobbs, daughter of Mary Lewis and Samuel Cobbs, married a gentleman by the name of Waddy, had one child whom she named Samuel Cobbs, and died. This child was raised by his grandmother but all trace of him has been lost.

6 Judith Cobbs, youngest child of Samuel Cobbs and Mary Lewis, died in girlhood. Issue by second marriage.

6 Ann Thomson married first John Slaughter, second Phillip Grafton; Mary Thomson married James Poindexter; Susannah Thomson married Jesse Davenport; Judith Thomson married William J. Poindexter; Mildred Thomson, born September 22, 1775, died October 9, 1829; married December 9, 1801, as his second wife, Dr. James McClure Scott, born February 17, 1760, died April 14, 1822.

A daughter of Judith Thomson Poindexter married a man named Mills; went west and left descendants, scattered from Iowa to Texas.

7 Mary Ann Lewis Scott, born October 28, 1808; married as her second husband, Lewis A. Boggs, February 15, 1827; died August 27, 1840. She was a daughter of Mildred Thomson.

7 John Thomson Scott, born February 26, 1810; married Huldah Lewis, January 5, 1832; died in Savanah, Georgia, October 19, 1832. She was a daughter of Dr. Richmond Lewis·

and Elisabeth Travers (Daniel) Lewis.

7 James McClure Scott, Jr., born August 17, 1811; married at "Prospect Hill," Spottsylvania county, Virginia, December 13, 1832, Sarah Travers Lewis, born November 7, 1813, died July, 1890. She was a sister of Huldah Lewis, of Zachary Lewis line.

8 Eliza Hart Boggs, daughter of Mary Ann Lewis Scott and Lewis A. Boggs, born March 3, 1839; died September 28, 1879; married May 1, 1861, Valentine M. Johnson.

8 John Thomson Scott born January 7, 1834; died January 15, 1869; married May 18, 1865, Grace McMorris, Houston, Texas; he was a son of James McClure Scott, Jr., and Sarah Travers Lewis.

8 Elizabeth Lewis Scott, born December 31, 1835; married September 4, 1851, Dr. John Minor, born Albemarle county, Virginia, April 7, 1822.

8 Alfred Lewis Scott, C. S. A., born February 12, 1838; married July 22, 1862, Fanny Herbert Taylor, of Alabama.

8 Mary Ann Scott, born October 6, 1839; died October 13, 1860.

8 Dr. Jas. M. Scott, Jr., born July 13, 1841; married February 24, 1875, Sarah L. Dickinson.

8 John Zachary H. Scott born March 14, 1843; married December 18, 1872, Lucy Prentis Doswell, second Claudia Keenan. Mr. Scott was a prominent lawyer of Galveston, Texas. He died in 1904.

8 Richmond L. Scott, born September 21, 1845; died March 30, 1847.

8 Sarah Travers Lewis Scott, born March 31, 1847; married Charles Harper Anderson, February 15, 1872. Mr. Anderson is a merchant at Ivy Depot, and resides at "Locus Hill." They had issue as follows:

9 [1]Dr. Meriwether Lewis Anderson, oldest son of Charles Harper Anderson and his wife Sarah Travers Lewis Scott, born November 13, 1872; married September 23, 1903, Annie Tatum, residence Richmond, Virginia.

9 [2]Sarah T. S. Anderson, born February 1, 1874.

9 [3]Charles Harper Anderson, Jr., born December 3, 1875; married April 23, 1902, Caroline Gwynn of Galveston, Texas.

9 [4]Alfred Scott Anderson, born February 14, 1878; married May 18, 1903, Katherine Morris of Georgia.

9 [5]Jane Lewis Anderson, born 1881; died 1882.

9 [6]Son born and died February 18, 1883.

9 [7]Lucy Butler Anderson, born August 15, 1885.

9 [8]Alden Scott Anderson, born February 24, 1888.

8 R. Lewis Scott, born September 17, 1848; married Abbie Agnes Boyle of Texas, postoffice Clifton, Texas.

8 Lucian Minor Scott, born December 11, 1849; died March 2, 1854.

8 Bradford R. A. Scott, born June 23, 1851; married September 27, 1877, Mary M. Anderson. Mr. Scott is a lawyer and resides in San Antonio, Texas.

8 Ann E. Scott, born December 25, 1852.

8 Mildred Scott, born April 1, 1855; married J. R. Thurman.

8 Frances G. Scott, born July 18, 1857.

8 Wm. W. Scott, youngest son of James McClure Scott, Jr., and Sarah Travers Lewis, born October 19, 1861.

9 James Scott and John Travers Scott, children of John Thomson Scott, both died young.

9 Lucian Minor, son of Elizabeth Lewis Scott and Dr. John Minor, born October 12, 1852; married February 14, 1877, Elizabeth Webb.

9 James L. Minor, born October 14, 1854.

9 Lucy L. Minor, born February 5, 1857; died August 28, 1857.

9 Catherine G. Minor, born August 25, 1858.

9 Mary Love Minor, born March 15, 1862.

9 John Baily Minor, born April 25, 1866; died September 1, 1883.

9 Margaret, Eleanor, Virginia, Elizabeth Minor, daughters of Dr. John Minor and Elizabeth Lewis Scott, born May 12,

1874, all children of Dr. John Minor.

9 Alfred L. Scott, Augusta Daniel Scott, Edmund Perry Scott, Catherine T. Scott, Frances G. Scott, James Scott, Dunklin B. Scott, Sarah T. Scott, Richmond L. Scott and Nathan Scott, are all children of Alfred Lewis Scott and Fannie Herbert Taylor, and reside at San Antonio, Texas.

9 McClure Scott, born November 13, 1876; Cassandra D. Scott, born June 25, 1879; Ann Brooks Scott, born July 29, 1885; were children of Dr. James M. Scott and his wife Sarah Dickinson.

9 Helen Sarah Scott, daughter of John Zachary Scott and Lucy Prentis, born February 22, 1874.

9 Lewis Raymond Scott, Lucy Estelle Scott, born January 12, 1878, James McClure Scott, born April 2, 1879, Richard Doswell Scott, born February 17, 1881, Mary Travers Scott, born February 19, 1883, Caroline Prentis Scott born August 15, 1884, Elizabeth Scott, born September 17, 1885, are also children of John Zachary Scott and Miss Prentis.

9 Zachary Scott, Pauline Scott, Lewis Scott and Abbie Scott, children of R. Lewis Scott and his wife, Agnes Boyle, reside in Clifton, Texas.

Bradford R. A. Scott, of San Antonio, Texas. Issue as follows: Lucy Scott, Mary Scott, Thomas Scott, Sarah Scott, Alden Scott, Harper A. Scott.

5 MILDRED LEWIS.

Mildred Lewis fourth daughter of Robert of Belvoir, married Major John Lewis. He was thus described in her father's will, and numerous records, both of Albemarle and Goochland, locate him in Goochland county. The early genealogists insisted on marrying Mildred to John Lewis, son of Zachary, and some of the later writers are unwilling to admit that she married John Lewis, the son of Joseph, but about this there can be no doubt.

John Lewis, husband of Mildred, whose will is on record in Goochland, 1796, was great-grandson of John Lewis, of Henrico, who came to Virginia about 1660 from Wales.

The will of Major John Lewis mentions four married

daughters, Ann Mosely, Elizabeth Halsy, Mary Atkison and Sarah Mann, and two sons, John and Joseph. John Lewis Robard of St. Joseph, Missouri, and Judge Joseph Lewis, of Kentucky, are descended from this line.

5 ANN LEWIS.

5 Ann Lewis, daughter of Robert Lewis, of Belvoir; married John Lewis, son of Zachary, who was known as "the honest lawyer of Spottsylvania;" he was born October 18, 1729, died September 12, 1780. For years the genealogists, having married Mildred to this John Lewis, were unable to place Ann, but the will of Samuel Cobbs and other record proofs have settled all doubt about the matter, and both Mildred and Ann are provided with a husband without any conflict of authority.

The will of this John Lewis, on record in Spottsylvania county, Virginia, names three sons, John Zachary Lewis, ·Robert Lewis `and ·Nicholas Lewis. The fact that he mentions no daughters does not necessarily preclude the idea that he had daughters, and at most it is only a negative inference that he had no daughters, as at that time daughters were never mentioned in the distribution of estates, except when some special provisions were made. The parentage of Mary Lewis, who married David Wood Meriwether in 1784, has been a matter of dispute among genealogists for years, not a few of whom have claimed that she was not a daughter of. Ann Lewis and "the honest lawyer." We have controverted this claim, but have yielded our opposition, for first her undisputed association with this family of Lewis, second, the general and unbroken tradition through successive generations, third, the utter failure of ourselves, or any one else, after years of search, to locate her anywhere else; hence we do not hesitate to include the descendants of ·Mary Lewis and David Wood Meriwether under this head. In addition to these circumstantial proofs we have recently found in the published records of Spottsylvania where the children of this John Lewis give a deed of release which is signed by the sons of John Lewis and David Meriwether, on the part of his wife Mary.

6 ¹Nicholas Lewis, son of Ann Lewis and her husband John .

Lewis, an attorney of Spottsylvania, went west and all trace of him has been lost.

6 ²Robert Lewis, another son of John and Ann Lewis, has also been lost sight of.

6 ³John Zachary Lewis, son of Ann Lewis and her husband John Lewis of Spottsylvania, is the only one of whom we have any record account, and his will dated March 7, 1784, and probated at Spottsylvania court house September 7, 1784, is all that we know of him. He names in his will his wife Elisabeth and three children, Augustine, Ann and Betsy; makes Augustine Woolfolk guardian of these three children, and appoints Col. Joseph Brock, "guardian of my children I may have by his daughter."

6 ⁴Mary Lewis, daughter of Ann Lewis and her husband John Lewis of Spottsylvania; married David Wood Meriwether, son of Wm. and Martha (Wood) Meriwether. He was born 1756 and died 1795; Mary Lewis died 1801.

7 ¹Ann Meriwether, daughter of David Wood Meriwether and Mary Lewis, born July 7, 1785; married January 8, 1806, John Burruss, born December 14, 1774, in Virginia.

7 ²Martha Meriwether, daughter of David Wood Meriwether and Mary Lewis; married Robert Pollard, died April 2, 1856, at Shipman, Illinois.

7 ³Jane Meriwether, daughter of David Wood Meriwether and Mary Lewis; married John P. Tunstall; reside in Illinois.

7 ⁴Henry Wood Meriwether, born February 3, 1790, son of David Wood Meriwether and Mary Lewis; married first, March 10, 1811, Jane Meriwether, his cousin, daughter of Wm. and Sarah (Oldham) Meriwether. He married second Dorothea Lewis Hill, October 22, 1829.

7 ⁵Mary Meriwether, daughter of David Wood Meriwether and Mary Lewis; married September 28, 1813, Dr. Samuel Meriwether.

7 [6]Sarah Lewis Meriwether, daughter of David Wood Meriwether and Mary Lewis, born September 9, 1794, died 1851; married first January 2, 1814, David Farnsley, and second September 3, 1832, Ebenezer Williams died, 1854.

8 [1]John Henry Burruss born March 16, 1808, in Jefferson county, Kentucky; moved to Greene county, Illinois, 1836, died December, 1882; married Martha J. Ballenger, May, 1840.

8 [2]Mary Meriwether Burruss, born June 11, 1810; died March 10, 1818.

8 [3]David Nelson Burruss, born June 25, 1813; married November, 1839, Frances Burruss Henly; died August, 1853. Issue, Mary A. Burruss; married W. B. Robinson; Frances Burruss married R. G. Robinson, resides near Carrollton, Illinois.

8 [4]Barbara Terrill Burruss, born December 10, 1816; married April, 1839, George Winston, died November 27, 1853. Issue, Judith and Lucy K. Winston.

8 [5]George Lewis Burruss, born February 15, 1820; married April 22, 1846, Maria J. Wood; she was born December 21, 1825. Issue:

9 [1]John Campbell Burruss, born September 16, 1847; married November 30, 1871, Mary K. Beaty.

9 [2]Henry David Burruss, born November 20, 1850; married November 20, 1879, Kittie A. Beaty. Issue, a daughter.

9 [3]George Wood Burruss, born August 1, 1853; died November 12, 1856.

9 [4]Alfred Leslie Burruss, born September 1, 1856; married December 24, 1877, Minnie Pollock. Issue, two sons; married second Ida Schoen.

9 [5]Nancy Lewis Burruss, born March 22, 1860; married Howard B. Nelson. No issue.

9 [6]Edward Wood Burruss, born June 14, 1864.

9 [7]Maria Frances Burruss, born October 20, 1870.

Children of John Henry Burruss, son of John Burruss and Ann Lewis Meriwether, who married Martha J. Ballenger, May, 1840:

9 [1] John Burruss, born in Greene county, Illinois, April 20, 1841, when his parents emigrated from Illinois to San Antonio, Texas, in 1849; he went with them and remained there until 1867 when he came to Missouri. Resides 22 Ripley street, Columbia, Missouri. He married November 22, 1870, Sadie Turpin of Kentucky.

9 [2] Henry Burruss, born January, 1843; married Annie M. Rhodes.

9 [3] Joe Frank Burruss, born September, 1844; married Flora J. Parsons.

9 [4] George L. Burruss died single in 1882.

9 [5] David N. Burruss, born December, 1854; married Edna Sanfley. Issue, a son David Nelson Burruss twelve years of age.

9 [6] Lucy Burruss, born August, 1859; married John D. Fristoe. Issue, a son about seventeen years old, John D. Fristoe, Jr.

9 [7] Mary Burruss born March 16, 1864; married H. M. Harvey, now deceased. Issue, H. M. Harvey.

Children of John Burruss and Sadie Turpin:

10 [1] Martha Burruss, born March 3, 1872, at Miami, Missouri; married April 29, 1896, Robert Martin Rea, of Carrollton, Missouri. Issue, Ruth Rea, born November 25, 1901.

10 [2] Frank M. Burruss, born October 6, 1875; married August 23, 1899, Minnie Casebolt, of Missouri.

10 [3] William B. Burruss, born May 17, 1878; married February 24, 1904, Ida Louise Lapsley, of Kentucky. Issue, William Lapsley Burruss, born March 7, 1905.

10 [4] Marion Burruss, born April 1, 1882.

10 [5] John Lewis Burruss, born April 3, 1886.

Children of Henry Burruss and Annie M. Rhodes: Henry R. Burruss, George L. Burruss, Mrs. Margaret Squires (widow), James H. Burruss, Dollie Burruss and David N. Burruss.

Children of Joe Frank Burruss and Flora J. Parsons: John P. Burruss, Joe Frank Burruss, Mary Weir Burruss, Sewall Burruss, Lucy Burruss, Emma Burruss, Camilla Burruss, George L. Burruss, Flora Burruss and Merrill Burruss.

8 [1]Letitia Meriwether, [2]Mildred Meriwether, [3]Nicholas Hunter Meriwether, [4]Wm. A. Meriwether, [5]David Samuel Meriwether. Marion Wood Meriwether born in Todd county, Kentucky, December 25, 1821; married in Jeffersonville, Indiana, December 24, 1840, James Weir Gilson, born in Westmoreland county, Pennsylvania, January 6, 1810. He died August 30, 1864; she died August 30, 1873. They are buried in Brighton, Illinois, cemetery; all children of Henry Wood Meriwether and grandchildren of David Wood Meriwether and Mary Lewis, great-grandchildren of John Lewis and Ann Lewis.

8 Waller Lewis Meriwether and two daughters made up the family of Dr. Samuel Meriwether and his wife Mary.

8 Mary Rebecca Farnsley, born December 26, 1814; married John Loyd, M. D.

8 James Marten Farnsley, born May 9, 1817.

8 David Henry Farnsley, born September 24, 1819; died young.

8 Wm. Joshua Farnsley, born September 24, 1820; died young.

8 Martha E. Farnsley, born August 10, 1825; married George Williams.

8 Leah Ann Williams, daughter of Sarah Lewis Meriwether, second marriage, and Ebenezer Williams, and granddaughter of David Wood Meriwether and Mary Lewis, born May 26, 1834; died December 30, 1876; married November 16, 1852, Charles Pawson Atmore.

8 Sarah E. Williams, daughter of Sarah Lewis Meriwether and Ebenezer Williams, and granddaughter of David Wood Meriwether and Mary Lewis, born November .17, 1837; died November 25, 1867; married Samuel Taylor Suit.

9 [1]Jane Elizabeth Gilson, born December 9, 1841, graduated from Monticello Seminary; died at Brighton, Illinois, February .23, 1867.

9 [2]Mary Frances Gilson, born November 24, 1845; married October 22, 1867, M. S. Brown, of Brighton, Illinois.

9 [3]Sarah Gilson born March 9, 1847; died July 16, 1848.

9 [4]Martha (Meriwether Lewis) Gilson, born at Brighton, Illinois, May 24, 1849; received into Presbyterian church in 1864; educated at Monticello Seminary, Godfrey, Illinois; married Hugh Henry Herdman, born in New York, March 25, 1841; married December 14, 1871; now a grain merchant of Morrisonville, Illinois. Mrs. Herdman is a member of the Springfield, Illinois, chapter of the Daughters of the American Revolution and of the Loyal Lewis Legion, and lover of family history.

9 [5]Edward Payson Gilson, born July 19, 1851, educated at Carlinsville and Chicago, Illinois. Resides at Brighton, Illinois, unmarried.

9 [6]George Herbert Gilson, M. D., born September 15, 1853; in 1883 was married to Mary Preston who died in 1888. He was educated at Blackburn College and St. Louis Medical College; having completed his medical course in 1876. He practiced his profession in Illinois nearly thirty years; a member of American Medical Association; honorary member of Macoupin county, Illinois, Medical Society; a resident of Raymond, Illinois, where he died November 17, 1905.

9 [7]David Henry Gilson born November 30, 1854, died September 7, 1857, at Brighton, Illinois.

The above seven were children of James W. Gilson and Marion Wood Meriwether.

9 [1]Wm. E. Atmore, born November 28, 1854.

9 [2]Charles P. Atmore, born December 5, 1856.

9 [3]Mary Lloyd Atmore, born December 8, 1858.

9 [4]Annie Atmore, born December 8, 1859; married December 8, 1880, Paul Caine, born July 11, 1859, son of John Strange Caine and Amanda Matilda Pepper, of Louisville, Kentucky. Their children are:

10 [1]Sydney Atmore Caine, born June 26, 1883.

10 [2]Idelle Meriwether Caine, born August 3, 1884.

Children of H. H. Herdman and Martha M. L. Gilson, of Morrisonville, Illinois:

10 [1] Marion Gilson Herdman, born June 1, 1873, baptized
August 3, 1884; graduated from Monticello Semi-
nary, June 7, 1892; died at Crawfordsville, Indiana,
October 12, 1895; buried at Morrisonville, Illinois.

10 [2] Hugh Henry Herdman, Jr., born November 11, 1875,
baptized August 3, 1884; graduate of Morrisonville
High School, 1892; A. B. Wabash College, 1896; M.
A. degree, Columbia University, New York City, September, 1899; appointed to chair in English in Portland Academy, Portland, Oregon, where he is still
teaching; chairman executive committee Lewis Day,
August 12, 1905, at Lewis and Clark Exposition; member Presbyterian church, Crawfordsville, Indiana.

10 [3] Jessie Weir Herdman, born March 2, 1881, died November 10, 1881.

10 [4] Albert Meriwether Herdman, born September 15,
1883; attended Holbrook Military Academy and Wabash College, 1903, 1904, 1905; manager Athletic
Track Team.

10 [5] Ellis Francis Herdman, born March 18, 1886, at Morrisonville, Illinois; died June 10, 1887.

5 SARAH LEWIS.

5 Sarah Lewis, about whom we have been able to learn so
little, was the daughter of Robert of Belvoir; married Dr. Waller Lewis, born September 11, 1739, died in Spottsylvania
county, Virginia, last of January, 1808; son of Zachary and
brother of John Lewis, "the honest lawyer," who married her
sister Ann. They had issue as follows:

6 [1] Waller Lewis, Jr., married Sarah ———, removed to Kentucky, and died May 8, 1818, postoffice, Russellville, Kentucky.

6 [2] Charles Lewis from whom Lewis Store, Spottsylvania, is
named, married Susan Waller, probably a daughter of Wm.
Waller, of Waller's Tavern; removed to Lynchburg, Virginia, and died February 2, 1822.

6 [3]Ann Lewis, born August 21, 1769, married Samuel Hill of Spottsylvania county, Virginia, who was a brother to John Hill who married Mary Waller Lewis, daughter of Colonel Zachary and Ann (Terrell) Lewis. Mary Waller Lewis was a sister of Reverend Addison Murdock Lewis, grandfather to Dr. M. D. Lewis, now of Columbia, Missouri. Samuel Hill and wife removed to Kentucky, postoffice, Russelville, Kentucky.

6 [4]Elisabeth Lewis, daughter of Dr. Waller Lewis and his wife Sarah Lewis, born 1772, married 1791 in Spottsylvania county, Virginia, John Woolfolk, born September 9, 1760, son of John Woolfolk, Sr., who was a son of Joseph Woolfolk. John Woolfolk, Sr., born November 6, 1727, died January 13, 1816, married about 1750, Elisabeth Wigglesworth, daughter of John and Mary Wigglesworth, born March 23, 1732. John Woolfolk, Jr., emigrated to Christian county, Kentucky, in 1811, where his wife died and he moved to Boone county, Missouri, in 1835, where he died October 11, 1843, and was buried near Deer Park on the farm of his son Waller Lewis Woolfolk, now owned by his grandson, Robert Henry Woolfolk.

6 [5]Lucy Lewis, daughter of Dr. Waller and Sarah Lewis, married John Wigglesworth of Spottsylvania county, Virginia.

6 [6]Dorothea, daughter of Dr. Waller and Sarah Lewis, married Dr. Harris Coleman of Nelson county, Virgina.

6 [7]Sallie or Dolly Lewis; no record.

7 [1]William Lewis, son of Waller Lewis Jr., resided in Hopkinsville, Kentucky.

7 [1]Robert Hill, son of Ann Lewis and Samuel Hill, and grandson of Waller and Sarah Lewis, born at Russelville, Kentucky.

7 [2]Dorothea Lewis Hill, daughter of Samuel Hill and Ann Lewis, as above, married Henry Wood Meriwether, son of David Wood Meriwether and Mary Lewis.

7 [1]Ann Waller Woolfolk, daughter of Elisabeth Lewis and John Woolfolk, and granddaughter of Waller and Sarah

Lewis, born in Spottsylvania county, Virginia, October, 1792, married in Kentucky in 1821, Judge Benjamin Young of Callaway county, Missouri.

7 [3]Waller Lewis Woolfolk, son of Elizabeth Lewis and John Woolfolk, as above, born in Spottsylvania county, Virginia, March 19, 1794; removed with his parents to Christian county, Kentucky, in 1811; married December 12, 1816, his cousin, Maria Susannah Woolfolk daughter of Elijah and Phoebe Woolfolk. Maria was born in Scott county, Kentucky, February 10, 1796. They moved to Boone county, Missouri, in 1834, where she died April 25, 1857, and he died October 22, 1874.

7 [3]Elizabeth Woolfolk, daughter of Elizabeth Lewis and John Woolfolk, and granddaughter of Waller and Sarah Lewis, born December 2, 1797, in Spottsylvania county, Virginia, married in Christian county, Kentucky, October 16, 1823, Thomas Beasley, Rev. Wm. Tandy performing the ceremony. She came with her husband to his home in Boone county, Missouri, where she died September 30, 1852. Thomas Beasley was born in Spottsylvania county, Virginia, fourteen miles south of Fredericksburg on March 16, 1793, and died at his residence eight miles south of Columbia, Missouri, July 11, 1879. His father was from England and married in Spottsylvania county, Virginia, a Miss Carleton daughter of Ambrose Carleton and sister to Catherine Carleton who married Richard Estes. It is stated in the obituary of Mr. Beasley that his father and his wife's father were soldiers in the Revolutionary War. He enlisted as a private in the War of 1812, in the United States Army serving with the first regiment of Virginia Volunteers, Colonel Stapleton Crutchfield, Brigadier-General Madison, brother of the President, commanding Brigade. Mr. Beasley drew a pension for several years before his death for services in the War of 1812. He united with the Bonne Femme Baptist church July 6, 1823, and was a deacon for more than forty years.

7 [4]Sarah Woolfolk, daughter of John Woolfolk and Elizabeth Lewis, and granddaughter of Waller and Sarah Lewis, born in Spottsylvania county, Virginia, moved with her parents to Christian county, Kentucky, in 1811; married Joseph Holaday, born in Fayette county, Kentucky, 1791; fourth child of Stephen Holaday and Ann (Hickman) Holaday. She was a daughter of James and Hannah (Lewis) Hickman of Culpepper county, Virginia.

7 [5]Dr. John Woolfolk, son of Elizabeth Lewis and John Woolfolk, and grandson of Waller and Sarah Lewis, born in Virginia, moved to Kentucky and from there to St. Louis, Missouri, where he died, unmarried, in 1834.

7 [6]Mary Woolfolk, daughter of Elizabeth Lewis and John Woolfolk, and granddaughter of Waller and Sarah Lewis, born in Spottsylvania county, Virginia; married in Kentucky, Washington Mansfield, and lived and died in Kentucky.

7 [7]Charles Woolfolk, son of Elizabeth Lewis and John Woolfolk, and grandson of Waller and Sarah Lewis, born 1804, in Virginia; moved to Kentucky and married Polly Ann Payne, and moved to Missouri. Aunt Polly Ann in now living with her daughter in Henry county, Missouri, being over ninety years of age.

7 [8]Alice Woolfolk, daughter of Elizabeth Lewis and John Woolfolk, and granddaughter of Waller and Sarah Lewis, born in Spottsylvania county, Virginia, August 15, 1806; married at Pembroke, Kentucky, December 7, 1826, Wm. Henry Tandy, born September 24, 1806, son of Mills and Amelia (Graves) Tandy, son of Henry Tandy and Ann Mills, son of Roger and Sarah (Quarles) Tandy from Orange county, Virginia. Wm. H. Tandy moved from Kentucky to Adams county, Illinois, in 1833, where he died July 29, 1864, and his wife died February 8, 1878.

7 [1]Lucy Wigglesworth, daughter of Lucy Lewis and John Wigglesworth, and granddaughter of Waller and Sarah Lewis, married Warren Wigglesworth of Spottsylvania county, Virginia.

69

7 [2]Dorothea Wigglesworth married Peter Dudley of Spottsylvania county, Virginia. They lived before the "war between the states" near Twyman's Store; they afterwards
moved to Texas and died there.

7 [3]Sarah Wigglesworth, daughter of John Wigglesworth and
Lucy Lewis, married Henry Duerson. They left only one
child, a daughter—Sarah Wigglesworth, who married a
Baptiste by name. It is not known whether or not he belonged to the Baptist church, nor is it known whether or not
the left any children. Mrs. Baptiste's postoffice is Dulce,
Albemarle county, Virginia.

7 [4]Elizabeth Wigglesworth, daughter of John and Lucy Wigglesworth, married H. B. White, who, Mrs. Baptiste says,
left quite a number of children, all of whom reside in Georgia.

8 [1]Ann Eliza Young, daughter of Ann Waller Woolfolk and
Judge Benjamin Young and great-granddaughter of Wal-
ler and Sarah Lewis, born October 5, 1822, married Wm.
M. George, May, 1841. She now lives in Dallas, Texas.

8 [2]Martha Virginia Young, daughter of Ann Waller Woolfolk
and Judge Benjamin Young and granddaughter of Waller
and Sarah Lewis, born 1829, married Alfred Moore of Fulton, Missouri, about 1850. He was killed in war and she
married second Fountain Letcher, residence Fresno, California.

8 [1]Claudius Marcellas Woolfolk, son of Waller Lewis Woolfolk, and his wife, Maria Susannah Woolfolk and great-
grandson of Waller and Sarah Lewis, born in Scott county,
Kentucky, September 16, 1817, married Adeline Heflin.

8 [2]John Edwin Woolfolk, son of Waller Lewis Woolfolk and his
wife Mariah Susannah Woolfolk, and great-grandson of
Waller and Sarah Lewis, born November 27, 1819, married
Bettie Wright.

8 [3]Elizabeth Emiline Woolfolk, daughter of Waller Lewis Woolfolk and his wife Mariah Susannah Woolfolk, and great-
granddaughter of Waller Lewis and Sarah Lewis, born

March 19, 1821 in Kentucky, married October 18, 1844, Michael Fisher, Sr., born August 17, 1811 near Moorefield, West Virginia; now living with his daughter, Mrs. Laura Williams in Boone county; his wife died September 24, 1852.

8 ⁴Waller Lewis Woolfolk, Jr., son of Waller Lewis Woolfolk and his wife Mariah Susannah Woolfolk, and great-grandson of Waller and Sarah Lewis, born December 7, 1824.

8 ⁵Charles Elijah Woolfolk, born May 19, 1827, married Susan Abel, also son of Waller Lewis Woolfolk and his wife Susannah.

8 ⁶Robert Henry Woolfolk, son of Waller Lewis Woolfolk and his wife Mariah Susannah Woolfolk, and great-grandson of Waller and Sarah Lewis, married Elizabeth Slaughter, daughter of John Hampton Slaughter and Sarah Reid of Kentucky. Resides near Deer Park, Missouri.

8 ⁷Phoebe Ann Woolfolk, daughter of Waller Lewis Woolfolk and his wife, Mariah Susannah Woolfolk, and great-granddaughter of Waller and Sarah Lewis, married Michael Fisher as his second wife (his first wife being her sister Emiline), January 4, 1853. They lived in Boone county near Bonne Femme. She died 1899.

8 ⁸Mariah Lewis Woolfolk, daughter of Waller Lewis Woolfolk and his wife Mariah Susannah Woolfolk, married Joseph Flemming.

8 ¹Elizabeth Lewis Beasley, daughter of Elizabeth Woolfolk and her husband, Thomas Beasley, and great-granddaughter of Waller and Sarah Lewis, born near Rockbridge, Boone county, Missouri, August 20, 1824; married 1846 Stephen Watkins, son of John Watkins of Kentucky. He was a lawyer and Circuit Judge of Sullivan county, Missouri. She died in Columbia, Missouri, June 24, 1905.

8 ²William Wallace Beasley, son of Elizabeth Woolfolk and her husband Thomas Beasley, and great-grandson of Waller and Sarah Lewis, born October 17, 1826, married, first his cousin Ellen Woolfolk, daughter of Charles, and second, Emma

Johnston, daughter of J. T. M. Johnston. Mr. Beasley was Surveyor of Boone county for several years. Residence Willow Springs, Missouri.

8 ³John Woolfolk Beasley, son of Elizabeth Woolfolk and her husband, Thomas Beasley, and great-grandson of Waller and Sarah Lewis, born October 19, 1828, married December 20, 1855, Sallie Lynes, daughter of Madison Lynes. He died May 24 1862.

8 ⁴Mary Catherine Beasley, daughter of Elizabeth Woolfolk and her husband Thomas Beasley, and great-granddaughter of Waller and Sarah Lewis, born in Boone county, Missouri, July 19, 1831; married her cousin Adrain Tandy, at the home of her parents near Rockbridge, Boone county, Missouri; married by Rev. Dr. David Doyle, June 5, 1851; died at her home in Columbia, October 28, 1901. She was a noble, faithful christian woman for more than fifty years, and in generations to come, wherever her memory is known, posterity will rise up and call her blessed.

8 ⁵Reuben Gant Beasley, son of Elizabeth Woolfolk and her husband, Thomas Beasley, and great-grandson of Waller and Sarah Lewis, died young.

8 ⁶Robert Thomas Beasley, son of Elizabeth Woolfolk and her husband Thomas Beasley, and great-grandson of Waller and Sarah Lewis, born July 18, 1834, married in Henry county, Missouri, December 4, 1866, Olivia Perry, daughter of Wm. Perry. They both now live on their farm adjoining his father's in Boone county, Missouri.

8 ⁷Henry Lewis Beasley, son of Elizabeth Woolfolk and her husband Thomas Beasley, and great-grandson of Waller and Sarah Lewis, born in Boone county, Missouri, September 11, 1836, married first in Illinois, Mary Scott, and married second Anna Emmitt, daughter of Judge Emmitt of Ohio. He died in Kansas City, Missouri, March 18, 1906.

8 ⁸Richard Estes Beasley, son of Elizabeth Woolfolk and her husband Thomas Beasley, and great-grandson of Waller and

Sarah Lewis, born November 29, 1838, married Alice Mc-
Conathy, daughter of James McConathy and Miss Todd of
Boone county, Missouri, who was the father of Sallie Mc-
Conathy who married Dr. A. W. McAlester of Columbia.
They are now living at Seymour, Missouri.

8 Stephen Holladay; James Holladay, born in Kentucky, married McLane; Wm. Holladay; Betsy Holladay, married C.
Ferguson; John Holladay; Sally Holladay, married John
McCalla; Benjamin Holladay, married A. E. Brown in Kentucky, 1855; David Holladay, died young; Lewis Holladay,
married ——— Brown, sister of his brother's wife; Marie
Holladay, married McPike, resides in Pike county, Missouri
children of Sarah Woolfolk and Joseph Holladay.

8 Ann Mansfield, born in Kentucky, and Erskin Mansfield, children of Mary Woolfolk and her husband, Washington Man-
field, and great-grandchildren of Waller and Sarah Lewis.

8 [1] Angeline Woolfolk, daughter of Charles Woolfolk and Polly
Ann Payne.

8 [2] Ellen Woolfolk, married her cousin, W. W. Beasley.

8 [3] Wm. Woolfolk.

8 [4] Elizabeth Woolfolk, married first Julius Wall, married second, ——— Bass.

8 [5] John Lewis Woolfolk, born November 4, 1850, married November 20, 1878, Alice V. Dawson of St. Louis county. Now
a wealthy and influential citizen of Kansas City, Missouri.

8 [6] Narcissa Woolfolk.

8 [7] Charles Woolfolk.

8 [8] Sallie Woolfolk, daughter of Charles Woolfolk and Polly Ann
Payne, married in the Spring of 1865, James Mason Avery,
born in Henry county, Missouri, June 7, 1838, died at Clinton, Missouri, November 23, 1903. When the first Baptist
Church of Clinton was organized September 16, 1866, he
was received into its membership, was elected one of its first
deacons, and filled the office of deacon, trustee and Sunday
School teacher during his entire Church life.

The foregoing eight are children of Charles Woolfolk and
Polly Ann Payne.

8 [1]Catherine Virginia Tandy, daughter of Alice Woolfolk and
her husband William Henry Tandy, and great-granddaughter of Waller and Sarah Lewis, born in Kentucky, October
31, 1827, married in Adams county, Illinois December 26,
1847, John Franklin Richards born in Virginia, died in Illinois, 1902.

8 [2]Adrain Tandy, son of Alice Woolfolk and her husband, William Henry Tandy, and great-grandson of Waller and Sarah Lewis, born in Kentucky May 19, 1831, married his
cousin, Mary Catherine Beasley. He died August 14, 1878
at his residence near Rockbridge, Boone county, Missouri,
and was buried at Bethel Cemetery. His parents removed
from Kentucky to Adams county, Illinois, where he was
reared to manhood. He came to Boone county, Missouri, in
1850, where he married June 5, 1851. He was a successful
teacher, farmer and inventor, a faithful member of the
Bonne Femme Baptist church for twenty years. His con-
tributions to the columns of the Central Baptist, were able
deductions of the doctrinal truths to which he adhered.

8 [3]Herbert Lewis Tandy, son of Alice Woolfolk and her husband, William Henry Tandy, and great-grandson of Waller and Sarah Lewis, born in Kentucky, August 1, 1833;
married December 12, 1854, in Adams county, Illinois, Cerilla Lewis, daughter of Giles Lewis and Sophronia Daniels. He is also a faithful worker in his Master's Cause.
He and his wife are both living near Adams postoffice,
beloved and respected by all who know them. He is a farmer and fruit grower.

8 [4]John Mills Tandy, born in Illinois, September 16, 1835, died
May 16, 1839.

8 [5]Amelia Ann Tandy daughter of Alice Woolfolk and her husband, William Henry Tandy, and great-granddaughter of
Waller and Sarah Lewis, born in Illinois, January 7, 1838,
died July 10, 1839.

8 [6]Mary Alice Tandy, born in Illinois, April 10, 1841; married
July 17, 1861, in Adams county, Illinois, William A. Wal-

LEWIS AND KINDRED FAMILIES.

lace, born in Ohio died in Denver, Colorado.

8 [7]William Henry Tandy son of Alice Woolfolk and her husband Wm. Henry Tandy, and great-grandson of Waller and Sarah Lewis, born in Illinois, August 10, 1843; enlisted in the 99th Illinois Volunteers, Col. John Wood's regiment, and was killed at Memphis, Tennessee.

8 [8]Louisa Emily Tandy, born in Illinois, January 17, 1846; married October 4, 1868, William Conants died January 9, 1881.

8 [9]Mark Tandy, son of Alice Woolfolk and her husband William Henry Tandy, and great-grandson of Waller and Sarah Lewis, born in Adams county, Illinois, April 18, 1848; married November 1, 1869, Laura Tibbets. She is the great-great-great-granddaughter of Joseph and Ann (Enos) Case of Hartford, Connecticut. They are now living in Dallas City, Illinois, where he is a prominent hardware merchant.

8 A daughter of Lucy Wigglesworth and her husband, Warren, is said to have married W. G. Miller of Richmond, Virginia.

8 Sarah Dudley, daughter of Dorothea Wigglesworth and Peter Dudley, and great-granddaughter of Waller and Sarah Lewis through their daughter Lucy, married Charles K. Battaile, originally from Caroline county, Virginia.

9 Rev. Benj. Y. George, son of Ann Eliza Young and her husband Wm. M. George, and great-great-grandson of Waller and Sarah Lewis through their daughter, Elizabeth, born near Fulton, Callaway county, Missouri, June 3, 1843; married in Columbia, Missouri, January 27, 1869; Adaline Gilman, born in Washington District of Columbia, January 22, 1851. Now located at Elmwood, Illinois.

9 [1]Scott Woolfolk, married Minerva Owens.

9 [2]Lucien Woolfolk, married Ellen Rouse.

9 [3]William Walter Woolfolk; married Alice Elkins, sister to N. B. Elkins of Columbia, Missouri.

9 [4]Warren Woolfolk, married Price Paxton—all four of whom are children of Claudius Marcellus Woolfolk and his wife Adaline Heflin, and great-great-grandchildren of Waller

75

and Sarah Lewis.

9 [1]Annie Maria Fisher, daughter of Elizabeth Emiline Woolfolk and her husband Michael Fisher, and great-great-granddaughter of Waller and Sarah Lewis, married W. U. Billingsly and reside in Boone county, Missouri.

9 [2]Susannah Fisher, daughter of Elizabeth Emiline Woolfolk, and her husband, Michael Fisher, and great-great-granddaughter of Waller and Sarah Lewis; married in Boone county, Missouri, W. T. Cunningham of Virginia, residence Columbia, Missouri.

9 [2]Sallie Fisher, descent as above, married Paul Hume of Callaway county, Missouri.

9 [1]Lewis Thompson Woolfolk, son of Charles Elijah Woolfolk and his wife Susan Abel, and great-great-grandson of Waller and Sarah Lewis, married Lola Matheny; residence, Atchison, Kansas; issue, two children.

9 [1]Louise Woolfolk, daughter of Robert Henry Woolfolk and his wife Elizabeth Slaughter, and great-great-granddaughter of Waller and Sarah Lewis, unmarried; residence with her parents, Deer Park, Missouri.

9 [2]Paul E. Woolfolk, same descent as above, born February, 1866, in Boone county, Missouri; married Flora Emmett, daughter of David Emmett; residence in Evansville, Indiana.

9 [1]Mark Woolfolk, son of Robert Henry Woolfolk and his wife, Elizabeth Slaughter, and great-great-grandson of Waller and Sarah Lewis, born and died 1868.

9 [2]Mary and [3]Elizabeth Woolfolk, twins, born June 1874; Mary died 1876; Elizabeth married her cousin Waller Joseph Fleming and resides in Jefferson City, Missouri. He died January, 1905. She married second, D. D. Henry of Jefferson City, Missouri.

9 [4]Esther Woolfolk, born January, 1876, died young. The descent of last three is the same as Mark, above.

9 Wm. Fisher, dead; Charles Fisher, dead; Michael Fisher married ——— Baker; Clarence Fisher married Mattie Allen;

Mary Fisher married Dr. J. O. Grubbs. She died 1899. Laura Fisher married Benjamin Williams, son of Isom Williams of Boone county, Missouri.—These six above are all children of Michael Fisher and his wife, Phoebe Ann Woolfolk, and great-great-grandchildren of Waller and Sarah Lewis.

9 [1]Stella Fleming, daughter of Joseph Fleming and Maria Woolfolk, and great-great-granddaughter of Waller and Sarah Lewis, married Wettlesby.

9 [2]Waller Joseph Fleming, descent same as above, married Elizabeth Woolfolk.

9 [1]Mary E. Watkins, daughter of Stephen Watkins and his wife Elizabeth Beasley, and great-great-granddaughter of Waller and Sarah Lewis, married May 24, 1883, Marshall Hults, who died 1891. Mrs. Hults resides in Columbia, Missouri.

9 [2]John Thomas Watkins married January 24, 1884, Fannie G. Lane. He is a farmer near Browning, Linn county, Missouri.

9 [3]Robert Watkins, born and reared in Boone county, Missouri; now living near Temple, Oklahoma, unmarried.

9 [4]Mattie Watkins, born in Boone county, married March 3, 1886, John L. Dodd, a farmer of Boone county, Missouri.

9 [5]Edward Lewis Watkins, married March 4, 1887, Gertrude Armstrong and resides near Gallup, New Mexico.

9 [1]Alice Beasley, daughter of Wm. Wallace Beasley and his wife Ellen Woolfolk, and great-great-granddaughter of Waller and Sarah Lewis; married Thomas Ragland.

9 [2]Mary Beasley married Jacob Johnston, brother to her father's second wife.

9 [3]Edgar Beasley resides in Howell county, Missouri.

9 [4]Hattie Beasley, daughter of Wm. W. Beasley and Emma Johnston, born September 26, 1873, in Boone county, Missouri, married September 14, 1904, Nathaniel Dodd.

9 [5]Minerva Beasley born January 6, 1875, married December 22, 1897, W. D. Hart of Hartsburg, Missouri.

9 [6]Archibald Beasley, born March 17, 1876.

9 [7]Noah Beasley, no record.

9 [8]Frederick Beasley, unmarried; residence, Willow Springs, Missouri.

9 [1]Thomas L. Beasley, son of John Woolfolk Beasley and his wife Sally Lynes, and great-great-grandson of Waller and Sarah Lewis, born in Boone county, Missouri, April 28, 1858; residence Boone county, Missouri, unmarried.

9 [2]James D. Beasley descent same as that of Thomas, born February 8, 1860, died March 16, 1906.

9 [3]Sarah E. Beasley (Betty), descent same as above, born April 16, 1862, unmarried.

9 [1]William Tandy, son of Adrian Tandy and his wife Mary Catherine Beasley, and great-great-grandson of Waller and Sarah Lewis, born June 23, 1852, died March 7, 1868.

9 [2]Charles Tandy, born March 22, 1854, died in Illinois, March 16, 1876.

9 [3]Ann Elizabeth Tandy born in Boone county, Missouri, March 31, 1855, married October 17, 1878 at the home of her parents near Rockbridge, Boone county, Wm. S. Johnston, son of Jacob and Pauline (Payne) Johnston, son of Captain Wm. and Rebecca (Spears) Johnston, son of Robert Johnston and Peggy McClannahan Mr. W. S. Johnston is now proprietor of the Athens, Columbia, Missouri. Mrs. Johnston is a woman of striking personality and fine intelligence, deeply interested in family history.

9 [4]Ephraim Tandy, born April 8, 1857; died September 30, 1879.

9 [5]Robert Thomas Tandy, son of Adrain Tandy and his wife Mary Catherine Beasley, and great-great-grandson of Waller and Sarah Lewis, born April 6, 1859, near Rockbridge, Boone county, Missouri; married March 4, 1885, Lura May Boulton, born Feb. 11, 1858, daughter of John Rice and Margaretta (Estes) Boulton of Boone county, Missouri. R. T. Tandy resides 705 Tandy avenue, Columbia, Missouri; is now a live stock dealer and owner of fine stock; formerly

farmer and merchant.

9 [6]Henry Herbert Tandy, born June 21, 1861, married November 29, 1899, Grace T. Jackson of Horton, Kansas, born in Hancock county, Illinois, July 5, 1874, daughter of J. H. and Sarah Jackson now of Lawrence, Kansas. H. H. Tandy is one of Columbia's substantial and representative citizens. Owns large property interests in Columbia and Boone county. He also conducts a large lime, cement and plaster business and has recently established a lumber yard at Hallsville, Boone county, Missouri.

9 [7]Richard Tandy, born April 15, 1865; unmarried.

9 [8]John Lewis Tandy, born July 8, 1868; unmarried, and is proprietor of a furniture store in Horton, Kansas, but resides in Kansas City, where he manufactures and sells the National Display Cabinet, and Sanitary Folding Bed, of which he is the inventor.

9 [9]Felix Adrain Tandy, born September 10, 1870, married November 8, 1893, Eva Dodd, born December 23, 1871; he lives at his father's old homestead, which he owns; he is also a member of Tandy Brothers Lumber Co.

9 [10]Mary Alice Tandy, born April 25, 1874; unmarried and re-sides with her sister, Mrs. W. S. Johnston, at "The Athens," Columbia, Missouri, a lady of decisive opinions and sterling worth.

9 [11]Mark Tandy, born January 7, 1876, married May 12, 1897, Cora Christian, born near Ashland, Missouri. He is a farmer and lumber dealer.
All the eleven of the foregoing of the Tandy name are of the same descent as that given to William and Robert Thomas Tandy.

9 [1]Infant son of Robert Thomas Beasley and his wife, Olivia Perry, died in infancy.

9 [2]Mary Ella Beasley, daughter of Robert Thomas Beasley and his wife Olivia Perry, and great-great-granddaughter of Waller and Sarah Lewis, born November 17, 1868; unmarried.

9 [3]Arthur Perry Beasley, born August 25, 1870; married Hattie Bartlow of Horton, Kansas; residence, Horton, Kansas.

9 [4]John Beasley, born March 7, 1874; married Cora Pearman; resides in Boone county, Missouri.

9 [5]Bessie Beasley, twin, born February 19, 1877; dead.

9 [6]Anna Beasley, twin, born February 19, 1877, is now a saleslady for A. Fredendall, Columbia, Mo.

9 [7]Robert Beasley, died young.

All of the above name of Beasley are children of Robert Thomas and Olivia Perry Beasley, and great-great-grandchildren of Waller and Sarah Lewis.

9 [1]Everett Beasley, son of Richard Estes Beasley and his wife Alice McConathy, and great-great-grandson of Waller and Sarah Lewis, married Olive Lowe Wood of Winona, Missouri. He is now a merchant in Winona.

9 [2]Lillian Beasley married William Mants; residence, West Plains, Missouri.

9 [3]Mabel Claire Beasley, married J. H. Livingston.

9 [4]Lewis Beasley.

9 Julius Wall and Eugene Wall, children of Elizabeth Woolfolk by her first marriage with Julius Wall. Eugene Wall resides in Windsor, Missouri. They are great-great-grandchildren of Waller and Sarah Lewis.

9 Sallie Bass and Kate Bass, children of Elizabeth Woolfolk by her second marriage with Bass. They married Hayden and Carmichael, respectively. The latter resides in Henry county, Missouri. They are great-great-grandchildren of Waller and Sarah Lewis.

9 Mary Woolfolk, daughter of John L. and Alice V. Woolfolk, born January 12, 1880; married November 20, 1902, Beverly C. Platt of Kansas City, Missouri.

9 [1]Ella C. Avery, daughter of Sallie Woolfolk and her husband Mason Avery, and great-great-granddaughter of Waller and Sarah Lewis, married Robert Edgar Lewis, now judge of District court, Colorado Springs, Colorado, who is descended from Charles Lewis and Mary Howell.

9 [2]Charles Avery, residence, Clinton, Missouri.

9 [3]Belle Avery, married William Livingston, residence, Windsor, Missouri.

9 [4]Frank Avery, residence, Memphis, Tennessee.

All of whom are children of Mason Avery and his wife Sallie Woolfolk, and great-great-grandchildren of Waller and Sarah Lewis.

9 [1]Effie Richards married Dr. Cranston, Indian Territory.

9 [2]Amelia Richards married Dr. Durant of Topeka, Kansas.

9 [3]Ellodie Richards married Mr. Reade, residence, Galesburg, Illinois.

9 [4]Dr. Walter Richards married Mary Willis, residence, Quincy, Illinois.

All children of Catherine Virginia Tandy and her husband, John Franklin Richards and great-great-grandchildren of Waller and Sarah Lewis.

9 [1]Annetta Tandy married Robert Beckett of Adams county, Illinois, residence, Deerfield, Kansas.

9 [2]Ellen Tandy married Rev. Charles H. Hands, late of Connecticut now pastor of Forest Grove Church, St. Louis, Missouri.

9 [3]Cerilla Tandy married E. B. Harkness and lives in Lakin, Kansas.

9 [4]Sophronia Tandy married R. V. Elliott, residence, University Place, Nebraska.

9 [5]Elmer Tandy married Mary Sexton, residence the old Tandy Homestead, Adams county, Illinois. She died January, 1905, leaving several children.

9 [6]Louise Tandy married Frank Bradshaw, residence, Philipsburg, Montana.

9 [7]Amelia Tandy, unmarried; on account of her health now resides in Denver, Colorado.

9 [8]William H. Tandy married Myra Nipher, postoffice Dunn, Tennessee.

9 [9]Mamie Tandy resides with parents in Adams county, Illinois, unmarried.

All children of Herbert Lewis Tandy and his wife Cerilla Lewis and great-great-grandchildren of Waller and Sarah Lewis.

9 William Wallace died young; Elodie Wallace; Mattie Wallace, dead; Frank Wallace; Florence Wallace—children of Mary Alice Tandy and her husband Wm. A. Wallace and great-great-grandchildren of Waller and Sarah Lewis, residence, Denver, Colorado.

9 Hay Battaile; Fitzhugh Battaile; Edwin Battaile; Eleanor Battaile; Madison Battaile; Rosalie Battaile; Francis Battaile; Charles Battaile—All children of Sarah Dudley and her husband Charles K. Battaile, originally from Caroline county, Virginia, and great-great-grandchildren of Waller Lewis and his wife Sarah Lewis.

10 [1]Margaret G. George, born in Columbia, Missouri, November 25, 1869, married, April, 1895, W. T. Davidson of Lewiston, Illinois; died November 23, 1897.

10 [2]Robert Dunbar George born in Columbia, January 12, 1873, married 1896, Bessie Bailey of Lewistown, Illinois.

10 [3]Anne Everett George, born in Columbia, July 12, 1878, now teaching in Illinois.

Above three are children of Benjamin Y. George and his wife, Adeline Gilman, grandchildren of Wm. M. George and Annie Eliza Young, great-grandchildren of Judge Benjamin Young and Ann Waller Woolfolk, and great-great-great-grandchildren of Waller and Sarah Lewis.

10 Lillian Billingsly, great-great-great-granddaughter of Waller and Sarah Lewis through their daughter Elizabeth and John Woolfolk, Waller Lewis Woolfolk, Pheobe Ann Woolfolk and Michael Fisher, and Ann Maria Fisher and W. U. Billingsly; died aged 2 years and 8 months.

10 Kenneth Cunningham, same descent as Lillian Billingsly, born 1880, unmarried, residence, Jefferson City, Missouri.

10 [1]Mary Louise Woolfolk, born January 16, 1898.

10 [2]Lewis Emmett Woolfolk, born May, 1901.

10 [3]Joseph Waller Woolfolk, born April 19, 1904.

These three are great-great-great-grandchildren of Waller and Sarah Lewis, through their daughter Elizabeth, who married John Woolfolk, Waller Lewis Woolfolk, Robert Henry Woolfolk and Paul E. Woolfolk.

10 [1]Clarence Grubbs, Boone county, Missouri.

10 [2]Raymond Grubbs, Indian Territory.

10 [3]John O. Grubbs, Indian Territory.

These three are great-great-great-grandchildren of Waller and Sarah Lewis, through their daughter, Elizabeth, who married John Woolfolk, Waller Lewis Woolfolk, Phoebe Ann Woolfolk and Michael Fisher, and Mary Fisher who married Dr. Grubbs.

10 [1]Commodore P. Hults, born June 2, 1884, unmarried, residence, Temple, Oklahoma.

10 [2]Elizabeth Lewis Hults born in Boone county, September 13, 1885, now student in Missouri State University, Columbia, Missouri.

10 [3]Mary Hults, born April 29, 1887, now Columbia High School student.

10 [4]M. J. Hults, born January 13, 1891.

These four are children of Mary E. Watkins and Marshall J. Hults, grandchildren of Elizabeth Lewis Beasley, great-grandchildren of Elizabeth Woolfolk, great-great grandchildren of Elizabeth Lewis and John Woolfolk, and great-great-great-grandchildren of Waller and Sarah Lewis.

10 Willie Watkins and Keith Watkins, children of John Thomas Watkins, Stephen Watkins, Elizabeth Woolfolk, Elizabeth Lewis, Waller and Sarah Lewis.

10 Stella Lewis Dodd, Lena Dodd, Mattie Gertrude Dodd, Mary Elizabeth Dodd—children of John Dodd, Stephen Watkins, Elizabeth Woolfolk, Elizabeth Lewis, Waller and Sarah Lewis.

10 John Armstrong Watkins, born 1888; Lewis Hunt Watkins, born 1894—children of Edward Lewis Watkins, Stephen Watkins, Elizabeth Woolfolk, Elizabeth Lewis, Waller and Sarah Lewis.

10 Claude Ragland and Mary Ellen Ragland, children of Thomas Ragland, Wm. Wallace Beasley, Elizabeth Woolfolk, Elizabeth Lewis, Waller and Sarah Lewis.

10 Edgar Johnston, born 1882, son of Jacob Johnston, Wm. Wallace Beasley, Elizabeth Woolfolk, Elizabeth Lewis, Waller and Sarah Lewis.

10 Hallie Beasley, Wm. Henry Beasley, Earl Beasley—children of Edgar Beasley, Wm. Wallace Beasley, Elizabeth Woolfolk, Elizabeth Lewis, Waller and Sarah Lewis.

10 Douglas Hart, born January 1899, Wallace Hart, born March 24, 1902, Catherine Hart, born December 31, 1904 —children of W. D. Hart, Wm. Wallace Beasley, Elizabeth Woolfolk, Elizabeth Lewis, Waller and Sarah Lewis.

10 [1]Leila Bryant Johnston, born in Boone county, Missouri, September 6, 1879; married Wm. Martin of Doniphan, Missouri.

10 [2]Mary Pauline Johnston, born September 30, 1881; residence Athens Hotel, Columbia, Missouri.

10 [3]Margaret Bass Johnston, born February 25, 1885.

10 [4]Lucile Keller Johnston, born September 1, 1887.

10 [5]William Spears Johnston, born December 12, 1892.

These five are children of Wm. S. Johnston, Mary Catherine Beasley, Elizabeth Woolfolk, Elizabeth Lewis, Waller and Sarah Lewis.

10 [1]Herbert Leroy Tandy, born May 9, 1886, died January 6, 1898; buried at Bethel, Boone county, Missouri.

10 [2]Frances Lewis Tandy, born in Boone county, October 17, 1887; now a student in Columbia High School.

10 [3]Ruth Estes Tandy, born in Columbia, February 5, 1891.

10 [4]Mary Elizabeth Tandy, born December 18, 1892.

10 [5]Excell Boulton Tandy, born February 1, 1895.

10 [6]Margaretta Tandy, born December 6, 1896.

10 [7]Mabel Estelle Tandy, born December 8, 1898.

10 [8]William Berkeley Tandy, born March 6, 1902, died August 5, 1903, in Columbia, Missouri.

These eight are children of R. T. Tandy, Adrian Tandy, Elizabeth Woolfolk, Elizabeth Lewis, Waller and Sarah Lewis.

84

10 [1]Sarah Catherine Tandy, born May 17, 1903; Grace Truman Tandy, born December 7, 1905 in Columbia, Missouri; children of Henry Herbert Tandy, Adrian Tandy, Elisabeth Woolfolk, Elisabeth Lewis, Waller and Sarah Lewis.

10 [1]Wm. Henry Tandy, born April 26, 1899.

10 [2]Mary Mildred Tandy, born September 10, 1902.

10 [3]Gladys, born February 24, 1905.

These three are children of Felix Adrian Tandy, Adrian Tandy, Elisabeth Woolfolk, Elisabeth Lewis, Waller and Sarah Lewis.

10 Alma Tandy, born in Boone county, July 16, 1898; James Keith Tandy, born June 9, 1902—children of Mark Tandy, Adrian Tandy, Elisabeth Woolfolk, Elisabeth Lewis, Waller and Sarah Lewis.

10 Robert Beasley, born October 10, 1903, son of Arthur Perry Beasley, Robert Thomas Beasley, Elisabeth Woolfolk, Elisabeth Lewis, Waller and Sarah Lewis.

10 Lucile Beasley, born April 11, 1898, daughter of John Beasley, Robert Thomas Beasley, Elisabeth Woolfolk, Elisabeth Lewis, Waller and Sarah Lewis.

10 Everett Beasley, Jr., and Margaret Alice Beasley—children of Everett Beasley, Richard Estes Beasley, Elisabeth Woolfolk, Elisabeth Lewis, Waller and Sarah Lewis.

10 Herbert Mantz, Allene Mantz, Maria Mantz, Dorothea Mantz —children of William Mantz, Richard Estes Beasley, Elisabeth Woolfolk, Elisabeth Lewis, Waller and Sarah Lewis.

10 Harold Livingston, Mildred Livingston, Vivion Livingston, Mabel Eunice Livingston, Harry Morris Livingston, Lewis Max Livingston—children of J. H. Livingston, Richard Estes Beasley, Elisabeth Woolfolk, Elisabeth Lewis, Waller and Sarah Lewis.

10 Mason A. Lewis, and a daughter whose name is unknown—children of Robert Edgar Lewis, Sallie Woolfolk, Charles Woolfolk, Elisabeth Lewis, Waller and Sarah Lewis.

11 Randolph Gilliam, son of Marion Mildred Perkins, by first marriage with Richard Gilliam.

11 Daniel Moncrek, Joseph Moncrek, John Moncrek, Rhett Moncrek, Mason Moncrek—children of Marion Mildred Perkins by second marriage with Moncrek, Joseph Perkins, Daniel Perkins, Jane Lewis Anderson, Jane Lewis and Edmund Anderson, William Lewis and Lucy Meriwether.

11 Wm. G. Davidson, son of W. T. Davidson, Benjamin Y. George, Wm. M. George, Ann Waller Woolfolk, Elisabeth Lewis, and Waller and Sarah Lewis.

11 Margaret Elisabeth George, born October 16, 1901, daughter of Robert Dunbar George, Benjamin Y. George, Wm. M. George, Ann Waller Woolfolk, Elisabeth Lewis, Waller and Sarah Lewis.

11 Beasley Ragland, son of Claude Ragland, Thomas Ragland, Wm. Wallace Beasley, Elisabeth Woolfolk, Elisabeth Lewis, Waller and Sarah Lewis.

11 Christopher Harold Martin, son of Lelia and Wm. Martin, Ann Elizabeth Tandy, Adrian Tandy, Elizabeth Woolfolk, Elisabeth Lewis, Waller and Sarah Lewis.

5 ELIZABETH LEWIS.

5 Elisabeth Lewis, daughter of Robert of Belvoir; married Rev. Robert Barret of Richmond, Virgina, rector of St. Matens Parish. She is mentioned in the will of her father as "Eliza Barret, deceased," and as that will was written in 1757, it follows that she died young, as Robert Lewis did not marry until 1725; and Elisabeth was not one of the older children. There is no other record of her history, nor is it known how many children she left. The history of only one is known and that is very meager, though the descent from him has been preserved.

6 [1]Capt. Wm. Barret, born January 2, 1756, died February 16, 1815; was so far as is known, the only child of Elisabeth Lewis Barret; married 1784, Dorothea Winston, removed to Kentucky, 1799, and settled on his farm, "Rockcastle."

7 [1]Ann Barret, born Louisa county, Virginia, May, 1786; married June, 1802, Genl. James Allen, died in Kentucky, 1842.

General Allen served in Hopkins Division, Kentucky army in 1812.

7 [2]James Winston Barret, born Virginia, 1788; married Maria Allen in Kentucky, about 1812. He emigrated to Illinois in 1835; died about 1872.

7 [3]Mary Lee Barret; married Wm. Barret of Cumberland county, Kentucky, lived on a cotton and sugar plantation in Louisiana; owned a grant of land near Waco, Texas, died in St. Louis, January 1867.

7 [4]Wm. Derricoat Barret born in Virginia, 1790; married Eliza Allen, sister of his brother James' wife, died December 24, 1844.

7 [5]Dr. and Professor Richard Farril Barret, born in Green county, Kentucky, 1804, died April 16, 1860; married Maria Lewis Buckner, daughter of Judge Richard Aylett and Elisabeth Lewis Buckner, November 5, 1832, at her home "Clifford," Green county, Kentucky.

The above five are children of Wm. Barret, Elizabeth Lewis.

8 Rev. Richard H. Allen; residence, Philadephia, Pennsylvania; John R. Allen, married 1840, Elisabeth Robards Buckner—children of Gen. James Allen and Ann Barret, Wm. Barret, Elisabeth Lewis.

8 [1]Wm. Barret, born 1815, Green county, Kentucky, now of Virginia City, Illinois.

8 [2]Jas. A. Barret, colonel 10th Illinois Dragoons during Civil War.

8 [3]Richard F. Barret, Mexican War Veteran.

8 [4]Dr. Edward Barret, died Troy, Missouri, 1850.

8 [5]Dr. Joseph Addison Barret; married Ellen Moore, daughter of John S. Moore, St. Louis.

The above are children of Dr. Richard Farrell Barret.

8 [1]Eliza Barret, married first, —— Johnson, married second, Pascal Enos, of Springfield, Illinois.

8 [2]Mary Barret, no record.

8 ³Jane M. Barret married Charles Ridgley.

The above three are children of Jas. Winston Barret, Wm. Barret, Elizabeth Lewis.

8 ¹Robert T. Barret, born 1823, Green county, Kentucky, died in Texas, 1861.

8 ²John R. Barret, born 1825, Green county, Kentucky, married 1846, Elisa Simpson of Winchester, Kentucky.

8 ³Dedie Nichols Barret, Louisville, Kentucky.

8 ⁴Mary Barret, married Mathew Kenedy.

8 ⁵Overton Winston Barret, born 1834; Major First Missouri Battery Artillery, C. S. A., died in Boston, Massachusetts.

8 ⁶Laura Barret, now of Washington, District of Columbia.

The above six are children of Wm. Derricoat Barret, Wm. Barret, Elizabeth Lewis.

8 ¹Richard Aylett Barret, born at Cliffland, Kentucky, June 21, 1833; married February 21, 1862, Mary Finney, daughter of Wm. and Jane Finney; retired capitalist, now of 1335 Washington avenue, St. Louis.

8 ²Arthur Buckner Barret, born Sangamon, county, Illinois, August 21, 1835, died April 16, 1875; married June 5, 1859, Anna Farrar Sweringen who is now living with her son 4520 West Pine boulevard, St. Louis, Missouri. He was President Agricultural and Mechanical Association 1866 to 1874. Mayor of St. Louis, 1875.

8 ³Dr. Wm. Lee Barret, born March 5, 1837; married Nannie Lemoine.

8 ⁴Julia Allen Barret, born November 5, 1839; married January, 1865, Charles Alexander, Surgeon United States Army; resides in Washington, District of Columbia.

8 ⁵Winston L. Barret, resides in New York City.

8 ⁶John A. Barret, born March 5, 1843; resides in Bloomfield, Stoddard county, Missouri.

The last six names are the children of Dr. Richard Farril

Barret, Captain Wm. Barret, Elizabeth Lewis.

9 Wm. Barret Ridgley, Washington, District of Columbia; a daughter, name unknown, 15 South Sixth street, Springfield, Illinois—children of Chas. Ridgley and Jane Barret, James Winston Barret, Capt. Wm. Barret, Elizabeth Lewis.

9 ——Kenedy, daughter, residence in New York City; —— Kenedy, daughter married ——Denny, residence, New York City—children of Mathew Kenedy and Mary Barret, Mary Lee Barret, Capt. Wm. Barret, Elizabeth Lewis.

9 James Barret married Miss Melton, St. Louis, Missouri; Arthur Buckner Barret, 4520 W. Pine boulevard, St. Louis; Mattie Barret, born April 5, 1860; married John M. Frost —children of Arthur Buckner Barret, Dr. Richard Barret, Capt. Wm. Barret, Elizabeth Lewis.

9 Mary Barret, Maria Barret, Arthur Buckner Barret, died at Ashville, North Carolina, August 1886, Dr. Wm. Barret, died at Ashville, North Carolina—children of Dr. Wm. Lee Barret, Dr. Richard Farrel Barret, Capt. Wm. Barret, Elizabeth Lewis.

9 Richard Barret and two daughters, children of John A. Barret, Dr. Richard Farrel Barret, Capt. Wm. Barret, Elizabeth Lewis.

· 9 [1] Bettie Allen married Judge B. M. Great, Memphis, Tennessee; Buckner Allen; John Allen, Lexington, Kentucky— children of John R. Allen and Elizabeth Robards Buckner.

4   CHARLES LEWIS OF "THE BYRD."

Charles Lewis was the second son of Councilor John Lewis and his wife Elizabeth Warner, born October 13, 1696, died 1779. His will is on record in Goochland county, Virginia. He married May 28, 1717, Mary Howell, daughter of John Howell, gentleman. Col. Charles settled the Byrd plantation in 1733, and it is from the name of this estate that he has always been designated, "Charles of the Byrd," by way of distinction from others of the same name. His children, as shown by his will, are as follows:

5 [1] John Lewis, born October 8, 1720, married his first cousin, Jane Lewis. She was at the time of this marriage the widow of Thomas Meriwether.

5 [2] Charles Lewis, born May 14, 1722, died May 14, 1782; married Mary, daughter of Isham Randolph, of Dungeness.

5 [3] Elizabeth Lewis, born April 23, 1724, married May 3, 1744, Wm. Kennon of Chesterfield county, Virginia.

5 [4] James Lewis, born October 6, 1726, died May 1, 1764, said to have married Isabella or Elizabeth Taylor.

5 [5] Mary Lewis born April 26, 1729, died January 12, 1733.

5 [6] Howell Lewis, born September 13, 1731, died 1814; his will was admitted to probate in Granville county, North Carolina, February 1814. He married a daughter of Henry Willis, the founder of Fredericksburg, Virginia, a lady variously named by the genealogists, Elizabeth, Mildred, Mary and Isabella, of which more will be said hereafter. He settled in Granville county, North Carolina.

5 [7] Ann Lewis, born March 2, 1733, married Edmund Taylor.

5 [8] Mary Lewis, born September 25, 1736, died April 26, 1740.

5 [9] Robert Lewis, born May 29, 1739, married February 26, 1760, Jane Woodson, daughter of Tucker Woodson.

5 [10] Frances Lewis, born August 1, 1744; married September 3, 1760, Robert Lewis of Louisa county, Virginia, son of Robert of Belvoir. He also removed to Granville county, North Carolina, where his will is on record.

LEWIS AND KINDRED FAMILIES.

JOHN LEWIS.

5 John Lewis oldest son of "Charles of Byrd" and his wife Mary Howell, was born about 1720, or perhaps earlier, as his parents were married 1717. Of the early history of this John Lewis we have no definite account, and it is not until 1769, or when he was at least 49 years old, that he appears distinctively on the records. At this period of the Lewis family, there were so many by the name of John that it was difficult to distinguish one from the other, when their names appeared in a general way. John Lewis married his cousin Jane Meriwether, daughter of Col. Robert Lewis of Belvoir, and widow of Thomas Meriwether. It is very probable, indeed, almost certain that this John was married twice, though neither the records nor tradition sustain this conclusion, but the circumstances point very strongly in that direction. The first husband of Jane Lewis was living in 1765 when John Lewis was 45 years old, and very few men of that period lived to this age without marrying.

Mr. Alexander Brown, author of the "Cabels and their Kin," insists that this was the Major John Lewis referred to in the will of Robert of Belvoir, and that he was the husband of Mildred at the time the will was written, and that he married Jane Lewis, the widow of Thomas Meriwether after the death of Mildred; but this is mere conjecture for which there is no authority, and besides, there can be no doubt that the husband of Mildred was the son of Joseph Lewis.

The most authentic account we have of this John Lewis is based upon generally accepted traditions, against which there is no proof, and is sustained by such conclusive circumstances that it is accepted as history. That he married Jane Lewis of Belvoir, daughter of Col. Robert Lewis, and widow of Thomas Meriwether, there can be no doubt.

As will be seen from the will of this John Lewis, written 1791, he left six children, three sons and three daughters. The sons were all twenty-one years old when the will was written, as they were all appointed Executors, and the daughters were all married. The names of the children were, John, Charles, Robert, Jane Read, Mary Williams, and Elizabeth Hopkins, all married. We have the partial record of Mary Williams and Jane Read, also of Charles and Robert Lewis.

6 Mary Lewis, daughter of John Lewis and Jane Meriwether married Wm. Williams and had issue as follows:

7 William Robert Lewis, Warner Lewis, Howell Lewis, Fielding Lewis, Charles Lewis, Coleman, Mildred Lewis, or, as corrected by Coleman Williams: Robert, Howell, William Lilburn, Warner, Fielding, Charles, Coleman, and Mildred.

7 Wm. Lilburn Williams married and had issue, Mary, who married Albert Wheatley.

7 Fielding Lewis Williams married Frances Pemberton Boyd, sister of Lucy Porter and Harriet Bullock, and had issue: Wm. Boyd Williams; Mary Frances Williams, died June, 1886; Mildred Lewis Williams; Fielding Lewis Williams;

7 Coleman Williams, son of William Williams and Mary Lewis and grandson of John Lewis and Jane Meriwether, married, first, Mary B. Wheatley, married second, Sarah M. Floyd Jones, and had issue, as follows: Robert F., died unmarried; Mary Mildred, died unmarried; Howell L., died unmarried; Leonidas P.; Harriet E.

7 Mildred Williams married Dr. James Wheatley, issue, James and Elvira, both deceased.

8 Mary, daughter of Wm. Williams married Albert Wheatley, had issue, two boys and four daughters and many grandchildren.

8 Harriet E. Williams, daughter of Coleman Williams and his wife Mary Wheatley married James S. Brownson, had 7 children, all young, being in the 9th generation.

8 Fielding Lewis Williams, son of Fielding Lewis Williams and Frances Boyd, grandson of Mary Lewis and William Williams, and great-grandson of John Lewis and Jane Meriwether, married Abby Louisa Miller, daughter of Augustus N. Miller and his wife, Harriet J. Waldron; residence Bristol, Rhode Island. They had issue as follows: Fielding

Lewis Williams; Mildred Lewis Williams married Dr. W. Fred Williams; no children.

8 Mary M., daughter of Coleman Williams, married John Gandy and had issue, one daughter, Mary M. Gandy and Wm. B. Gandy. These children are also in the ninth generation.

8 James H. Wheatley married Ella B. Bowen—one son now living, James Bowen Wheatley.

8 Leonidas P. Williams, son of Coleman Williams, grandson of Wm. Williams and Mary Lewis, and great-grandson of John Lewis and Jane Meriwether, married Mary Roberts; issue: two children, Fannie R., and Leonidas P., Jr.

The foregoing is made up from notes taken from time to time, and while they are fragmentary, as to arrangement, they are positively reliable and give more information of the descent of Mary Lewis and William Williams than I have been able to obtain from all other sources. They bring down several of the descendants of this couple to the ninth generation, and furnish data from which the descendants of that line will be enabled to make up a complete genealogy.

Mrs. A. Louise Williams, wife of Mr. Fielding Lewis Williams of Bristol, Rhode Island, is responsible for the foregoing data.

Mr. Fielding Lewis Walker of Danville, Virginia, has kindly furnished us with the descent of Jane Lewis, daughter of John Lewis and Jane Meriwether, and her husband Jonathan Read, which may be relied on as correct.

6 Jane Lewis, daughter of John Lewis and Jane Meriwether, married Jonathan Reade, and had issue as follows: Margaret, married a Harrison; Thomas, married Miss Panel; Eliza, married Hobson and had two children, Howell and George; Mary, no record; Howell, married Eliza T. Boyd; Charles Lewis, born 1795, died December 20, 1869.

7 Howell Reade, son of Jane Lewis and grandson of John Lewis and Jane Meriwether, married Eliza T. Boyd and had issue as follows: Frances married ——— McLin and had a daughter who married Tom Walker; and James married

Helen Read; John married Isabella Boyd and had children: Lizzie, John, Fanny and Bobby.

8 Charles Fox Reade married Harriet Cotter. Children: Mary; Emma married Charles Taylor; Charles; Howell; Eliza; Hattie; Alexander, never married; Harriet married James Haywood. Children: Bettie, John, James, Mary, William; Elizabeth married first, Isham Boyce, second, John Haywood and had one child, Eliza Boyce; Howell died in childhood; Alfred married first, Miss Partee, second, Miss Conner, no issue; Mary Jane married Robert Haywood.

7 Thomas Reade, son of Jane Lewis and Jonathan Reade, and grandson of John Lewis and Jane Meriwether, married Miss Pannel; issue, Margaret, married a Mr. Reade; Jane; Ann; John; Virginia; Clement; Mary; Drusilla; Thomas.

7 Charles Lewis Reade, son of Jane Lewis and Jonathan Reade, and grandson of John Lewis and Jane Meriwether, married Jane Boyd and had issue:

8 ¹Jane Eliza Reade married James Beverly Daniel.

8 ²Wm. Boyd Reade married Ann Eliza Boyd.

8 ³Jonathan Reade married Ann Barbee.

8 ⁴Charles Lewis Reade, Jr., married first, Sarah Estes, married second, Mary Taylor; children: Sarah; Lewis married Baskerville; Charles married Pepper.

8 ⁵Edmund Reade, died in infancy.

8 ⁶Howell Reade, died in infancy.

8 ⁷Lucy Frances, born April 29, 1830, married Rev. R. E. Sherril.

8 ⁸Mildred Reade married Wm. Bullock Tyler. Children: Rosa Tyler, married Bonde; Charles married Emma Read.

8 ⁹Harry Read, died in infancy.

7 Charles Lewis Read by second marriage with Elizabeth Daniel had issue:

8 ¹⁰Isaac Henry Reade married first, Lizzie Green, second, Martha Green, third, Alice Green.

8 [11]Nannie, died young, never married.

8 [12]Priscilla Margaret married John Y. Barbee.

8 [13]Sarah Elizabeth married William Bond.

8 [14]Louisa Hellen married James McLin.

8 Jane Eliza Reade, daughter of Charles Lewis Reade, granddaughter of Jonathan Reade, who married Jane Lewis, great-granddaughter of John Lewis and Jane Meriwether, married James Daniel, and had issue:

9 [1]Nancy Venable Daniel married Nathaniel Venable Watkins.

9 [2]Martha Elizabeth Daniel married David Flournoy Morton. Children: Jane Morton, David, James, Daniel, and Martha Morton.

9 [3]Charles Reade Daniel, died young.

9 [4]Mildred Daniel married Richard Edward Booth. Children: Lucy, Daniel and Samuel.

9 [5]Nathaniel Daniel married a Wilson; Lucy Frances, no record.

8 Wm. Boyd Reade, son of Charles Lewis Read, grandson of Jane Lewis and Jonathan Read and great-grandson of John Lewis and Jane Meriwether, married Ann Eliza Boyd and had issue:

9 [1]Lucy Frances married Wm. Scott; one child, William Scott.

9 [2]Jesse married India Peyton.

9 [3]Anna married Peoples.

9 [4]Ella, no record.

8 Lucy Frances Reade, daughter of Charles Lewis Read, born April 29, 1830, granddaughter of Jane Lewis and Jonathan Read, and great-granddaughter of John Lewis and Jane Meriwether, married Rev. R. E. Sherril and had issue as follows:

9 [1]Charles Reade Sherril, born November 5, 1857.

9 [2]Richard Ellis Sherril, born March 17, 1861, married Kittie H. Taylor.

9 [3]Lizzie Frances Sherril, born April 24, 1863, died July 25, 1863.

9 [4]Eugenia Laura Sherril, born January 27, 1865, married
Alfred H. Smith.

9 [5]Wm. Enos Sherril, born August 29, 1868.

9 Richard Ellis Sherril and Kitty H. Taylor, as above, married
March 21, 1889 and had one son, Lewis Joseph Taylor, born
April 18, 1892.

9 Eugenia Laura Sherril, born January 27, 1865, daughter of
Lucy Francis Reade, granddaughter of Charles Lewis
Reade, great-granddaughter of Jane Reade and great-great-
granddaughter of John Lewis and Jane Meriwether, married Alfred H. Smith, and had issue:

10 [1]Mamie Reade Smith, born September 15, 1884.

10 [2]Howard Lee Smith, born May 1, 1886.

10 [3]Ines and [4]Sherril Smith, no record.

9 Frances Reade, daughter of Howell Read, granddaughter of
Charles Lewis Reade, great-granddaughter of Jane Lewis
and great-great-granddaughter of John Lewis and Jane
Meriwether, married Robert McLinn. Issue: Betty, married
Tom Walker; and James, married Louise Hellen Reade.

10 Louise Hellen Reade and James McLinn had issue as fol-
lows: Fannie married W. B. Johnson, January 24, 1895;
Alfred married Miss Claiborn; James died young; Nannie
Morton; Bessie; Charles Lewis; Robert Spencer; Hellen;
Chester; Fred and Margie. No record of the last names.

8 Priscilla Margaret Reade, daughter of Charles Lewis Reade,
granddaughter of Jane Lewis, and great-granddaughter of
John Lewis and Jane Meriwether, married John Y. Barbee
and had issue: Allen married Miss Herbert; Bessie Reade
married Moriarity; Reade Barbee, Taylor Barbee, Susie
Barbee, Pannel Barbee, Isaac Barbee, Nelson Barbee. No
record of the last six names.

8 Isaac Henry Reade; son of Charles Lewis Reade, grandson of
Jane Lewis, and great-grandson of John Lewis and Jane
Meriwether, married three times, most probably three sis-
ters, as they were all of the same name, Lissie, Martha and
Alice Green. Issue: Lillie Reade married Elias King, one

child, Bessie King; Lewis Reade died young; Edward married Cora Fields; Sarah Ann married John King; Isaac, James, Lizzie, Maggie and Alice, no record.

8 Sarah Elizabeth Reade, daughter of Charles Lewis Reade, granddaughter of Jane Lewis, great-granddaughter of John Lewis and Jane Meriwether, married Wm. Bond and had issue: Margaret Bond, Pugh Bond, Henry Lewis Bond, Lucy Bond, Priscilla Bond, Sarah and Julian.

9 Children of Nancy Venable Daniel and Nathaniel Watkins: Mildred Henry; Lucy Morton; Richard Henry.

10 Children of Mildred Henry Watkins and John Robert Morton: John, Richard, James, Reade, Nannie, Henry, Lucy, Lewis Warner.

9 Mildred Reade Daniel, daughter of Jane Eliza Reade, and James Beverly Daniel, granddaughter of Chas. Lewis Reade, and great-granddaughter of Jonathan Reade and Jane Lewis, married Richard Edward Booth and had issue: Lucy Daniel Booth, Samuel Patrick Booth.

9 James Nathaniel Daniel, married Ellen Scott Wilson and had seven children: William Goodridge, Jane Reade, Margaret Ringold, Norvel Watkins, James Venable, Ellen Wilson, Edward Abbott.

10 Lucy Morton Watkins married John Flood Morton and had one child, Mildred Watkins Morton.

10 Richard Henry Watkins married Josephene Crits and had one child: Richard Henry Crits.

10 Samuel Patrick Booth married Alma Smith Brooks and has one child: Willie Lee Booth.

6 Charles Lewis, son of John Lewis and Jane Meriwether, and grandson of Charles Lewis of the Byrd married Miss Garthrey Glover. They had issue:

7 [1] Nicholas Meriwether Lewis married Miss Lucy Bullock, no issue.

7 [2] Lucy Meriwether Lewis married Dr. Ajax Walker. Issue: Nicholas Lewis Walker married Emily F. Hunt; Henry Ajax Walker married Mary McCotter Owens; Fielding

Lewis Walker married Penelope Campbell Wilson.

8 Fielding Lewis Walker and Miss Wilson had: Henry Ajax Walker, married Miss Ida Thames of Mobile; Maitland Walker; Mary Wilson Walker; Agnes Campbell Walker; Annie Louise Walker; Lewis Meriwether Walker; Charles Baylor Walker; Lucy Meriwether Lewis Walker married Lovie Pierce Morgan; Penelope Wilson Walker married Wm. Humphreys Jones; Fielding Lewis Walker, Jr., married Mary Dowd.

9 Henry Ajax Walker and Ida Thames had: Mary Ellis Walker; Ida Thames Walker; Henry Ajax Walker.

9 Lucy Meriwether Walker and Lovie Pierce Morgan had: Penelope Campbell Morgan, Fielding Lewis Morgan.

8 Henry Ajax Walker and Mary McCotter Owens, had: John Owens Walker.

8 Nicholas Lewis Walker, son of Lucy Meriwether Lewis and Ajax Walker, grandson of Charles Lewis and Miss Glover, and great-grandson of John Lewis and Jane Meriwether, married Jean Resbrow of Aurora, Missouri, and had issue as follows:

9 [1]Lewis Walker married Sue Sumerville Cunningham. No issue.

9 [2]Robert Lewis Walker married Cornelia Wilson.

9 [3]Lucy Lewis Walker, not married.

9 [4]Leonard Hunt Walker married Lockie White, of Hendersonville, Kentucky.

9 [5]William Hunt Walker, married Kate Dibrell.

9 [6]Nicholas Walker, marriage unknown.

9 Robert Lewis Walker and Cornelia Wilson had one daughter, Margaret Walker.

9 William Hunt Walker, son of Nicholas Lewis Walker and his wife, Kate Dibrell, had issue as follows: Alphonso Dibrell Walker, Nicholas Lewis Walker, Kate Dibrell Walker, Emily Frances Walker, Elizabeth Walker.

6 Robert Lewis, son of John Lewis and Jane Meriwether, and grandson of "Charles of Byrd," married Ann Ragland and

left issue:

7 [1]Warner Meriwether Lewis, married first Elisabeth Hinton.

7 [2]Ann Susan Lewis, married Captain Wm. Irvine.

7 Warner Meriwether Lewis and Elisabeth Hinton had one son, John Willis Lewis, who married three times, first Annie Hinton.

8 John Willis Lewis and his first wife Annie Hinton had:

9 [1]Elisabeth Lewis, married Nathaniel M. Richmond.

9 [2]Annie Hinton Lewis, who never married.

9 Elisabeth Lewis and her husband Nathaniel M. Richmond, had issue as follows: Annie Hinton Richmond, Nathaniel Macon Richmond, Lucy Mayfield Richmond, John Willis Richmond, Charles Hunton Richmond, Sue Lewis Richmond, Elisabeth Richmond, David Hunton Richmond.

9 John Willis Lewis married second Elizabeth Baskerville and had:

10 [1]Susan B. Lewis, married Hiram Ford.

10 [2]Warner Meriwether Lewis, not married.

10 [3]Wm. Baskerville Lewis, married Maggie Watkins.

10 [4]Lucy Lewis, married Hammet Gregory, no issue.

10 [5]Mary B. Lewis.

10 [6]Kate Watkins Lewis.

9 John Willis Lewis married third Elisabeth Walker and had: Sallie Brown Lewis.

7 Warner Meriwether Lewis married second Phoebe Sewell and had: Ellen Lewis, married Caleb Haygood Richmond. They had: Meriwether Lewis Richmond; Ellen Ramseur Richmond; Caleb Haygood Richmond; George Gilbert Richmond married Mary Kirkland; Annie Zell Richmond married George L. Cunningham; Mary Dodson Richmond.

10 Susan B. Lewis married Hiram Ford. They had two children: Elisabeth B. Ford, Meriwether Lewis Ford.

10 Wm. Baskerville Lewis married Maggie Watkins and had four children: Claudia Lewis, Warner Meriwether Lewis, Charles Watkins Lewis, William B. Lewis.

9 George Gilbert Richmond and Mary Kirkland had one child:
Caleb Haygood Richmond.

9 Annie Zell Richmond and Geo. L. Cunningham had one child:
John Wilson Cunningham.

·7 Ann Susan Lewis, daughter of Robert Lewis and Anna Ragland, and granddaughter of John Lewis and Jane Meriwether, married, 1819, Captain Wm. Irvine of Bedford
county, Virginia. Issue:

8 [1]Wm. Meriwether Irvine, married, 1857, Virginia A.
Jeffries.

8 [2]Elizabeth Juliet Irvine, married, 1853, Dr. Thos. W.
White.

8 [3]John Lewis Irvine, married, 1856, Elizabeth C. Hoge.

8 Wm. Meriwether Irvine and Virginia Jeffries had one child:
Annie Irvine, married John S. Early, no issue.

8 Elizabeth Juliet Irvine and her husband Thos. W. White
had:·

9 [1]Beverly White, not married.

9 [2]Sallie Howard White.

9 [3]Isadore White.

9 [4]John Irvine White, married Mary T. Barksdale.

9 [5]Fannie Lewis White, married George P. Ball.

9 [6]Thomas Warner White, married Emma J. Farmer.

9 [7]Wm. Irvine White, married Annie A. Rives.

9 John Irvine White and Mary Barksdale had issue: Beverly
Barksdale White, Juliet Irvine White, Elizabeth High·
tower White, Thos. Winston White, Claiborne Barksdale
White, Ann Early White.

9 Fannie Irvine White and Geo. Ball had issue as follows: Julia
Irvine Ball, Geo. Wallace Ball, Wm. Irvine Ball, Thomas
Warner Ball, Claiborne White Ball.

9 Wm. Irvine White and Annie A. Rives had one daughter,
Emma A. White.

8 John Lewis Irvine married Elizabeth C. Hoge. They had
issue: Mary Whitlock Irvine, married Chas. W. Heuser
of Wythville, Virginia; Annie Lewis Irvine; Whitlock

Hoge Irvine; Moses Hoge Irvine; John Lewis Irvine; Thos. Hoge Irvine.

9 Mary Whitlock Irvine and Charles W. Heuser had: Bettie Hoge Heuser, Claire Heuser, Augustine Heuser, Willie Irvine Heuser.

5 CHARLES LEWIS.

5 Charles Lewis, of Buckeye Land, second son of "Charles of Byrd," born May 14, 1722, died May 14, 1782; married Mary, daughter of Isham Randolph of Dungeness. There is very little known of his descendants, as many of them went west at a very early day, and all of them have evidently scattered. His wife, Mary Randolph, was a sister of President Jefferson's mother, and his oldest son married a sister of Mr. Jefferson, Lucy Jefferson, who was his first cousin. As shown by his will on record in Albemarle county, Virginia, he had five children: Charles Lilburn Lewis, Isham Lewis, Ann Jefferson Lewis, Mary Lewis, and Mildred Lewis. He also mentions a grandson, Howell Lewis.

6 Charles Lilburn Lewis married Lucy Jefferson and emigrated to Kentucky. They left descendants.

6 Mary Lewis married Colonel Charles Lewis, her cousin, and son of Colonel Robert of Belvoir. The other daughters married Bennet Henderson and Charles Hudson, whom he names in his will as two of his executors, and as his sons-in-law.

7 Howell Lewis, whom Charles Lewis mentions as his grandson, is evidently the son of Colonel Charles, who had previously died, and his daughter Mary.

7 Randolph Lewis, son of Charles Lilburn Lewis and Lucy Jefferson, married his cousin Mary, daughter of Robert Lewis of "the Byrd" and his wife Jane Woodson. Issue: Lilburn Lewis, Tucker Woodson Lewis and Randolph Lewis, went west; Howell Lewis married a sister of Hancock Lee of Richmond, Virginia; Warner Lewis died young, unmarried; Mary Lewis married Charles Palmer of Richmond, Virginia; Susan Harrison Lewis married Douthat of Botetourt

101

county, Virginia; Lucy Jefferson Lewis, no record.

8 Children of Mary J. Lewis, who married Charles Palmer of
Richmond, Virginia, grandchildren of Randolph Lewis, and
great-grandchildren of Charles Lilburn Lewis and Lucy
Jefferson: William Palmer, M. D., surgeon C. S. army, ed-
ited calendar Virginia State Papers, unmarried; Charles
Palmer, Randolph L. Palmer, Richard Palmer, Catherine
C. Palmer.

5 ELIZABETH LEWIS.

5 Elizabeth Lewis, oldest daughter and third child of Charles
Lewis and Mary Howell, born April 23, 1724, married May
3, 1744, William Kennon of Chesterfield county, Virginia,
son of Wm. Kennon and Ann Eppes, grandson of Richard
Kennon and Elizabeth Washam. Their son John Kennon
married in 1779 Elizabeth Woodson, daughter of John
Woodson and Elizabeth Hughes. Their daughter Elizabeth
Kennon married in 1809, D. L. White, son of David L.
White and Mary Lyne.

8 Pleasant Woodson White, son of D. L. and Mary (Lyne)
White, married in 1848, Emily Gibson, daughter of Edward
R. and Jeanette (Tilton) Gibson. Emily White died in
1902. Woodson Tilton White, their son, born July 26,
1849, now a resident of Waco, Texas.

6 Howell Lewis was the fourth son of "Charles of the Byrd,"
born 1731 in Goochland county, Virginia. He married a daughter of Captain Henry Willis, of Fredericksburg, Virginia. The
name of the wife of Howell Lewis has been a matter of dispute
among genealogists for years. It was known among many of
her descendants that in household circles she was known as
Mary; and her grandson, John Adison Cobb, who grew up in
his grandfather's household, was raised and educated by him,
and who was necessarily familiar with his grandmother's name,
handed it down to posterity as "Mary," and named one of his
daughters "Mary Willis" in perpetuation of her memory, but the
records of Spottsylvania having disclosed the fact that Henry
Willis had a daughter Mary, who married Hancock Lee, in 1816,
put the genealogists to guessing, and they turned their attention

to finding another name for the wife of Howell Lewis. Byrd Willis, grandson of Henry Willis, had left it on record that the wife of Howell Lewis, who was his aunt, was named "Elisabeth." Mr. Thos. M. Green of Danville, Kentucky, and Miss Minor, author of "Meriwether Genealogy," insisted that her name was Mildred, and Miss Hinton of North Carolina who had found a newspaper clipping in her grandfather's Bible, which referred to her demise under the name of Isabella, furnished Mrs. Watson, author of a "Royal Lineage," with that name, and Mrs. Watson, having given it to the secretary of Virginia Historical Society, it was claimed by that authority that Isabella, to the exclusion of all others, was the name of Howell Lewis' wife. There can be no doubt that in the numerous marriages of Henry Willis, he gave this daughter the name of Mary Isabella, notwithstanding the fact that his first born, who married Hancock Lee, was named Mary, nor will this appear at all strange or unusual, when it is considered that the wife of Hancock Lee was the child of his first wife, and the wife of Howell Lewis the child of his third wife and about twenty years apart.

In a deed from Howell Lewis to John Johnson, book H, page 283, Granville county, North Carolina, the wife of Howell Lewis is referred to as Isabella. In 1769, two years after the date of the foregoing deed, Howell Lewis and Mary are subscribing witnesses to a deed to land sold to John Cobbs, who was about to marry their daughter Mildred. So that it is seen that she appears on the records both as Isabella and Mary, and that she is also known to indisputable tradition under both names, and therefore no other conclusion can be reached than that she was named Mary Isabella, and this is accepted by the author as a solution. They had issue as follows:

6 ¹Charles Lewis.
6 ²Willis Lewis.
6 ³Isabella Lewis married Jeffries.
6 ⁴Ann Lewis married Morton.
6 ⁵Frances Lewis married Bugg.
6 ⁶Jane Lewis married David Hinton, Wake county, North

Carolina, where they still reside with their great-grand-daughter, Mary Hilliard Hinton, at "the Oaks."

6 [7]Mildred Lewis married John Cobbs, born in Goochland; lived in Louisa county, Virginia, afterwards in Albemarle; removed to Granville county, North Carolina, and lastly established himself in Georgia.

6 [8]Mary Lewis married a Kennon.

6 [9]Elizabeth Lewis married William Ridley, Granville county, North Carolina.

6 [10]Howell Lewis, born April 2, 1759, married in 1780 Betsy Coleman, daughter of Robert Coleman of Goochland county, Virginia.

Of the descendants of the children of Howell Lewis very little is known. There are many of his name in Granville county, North Carolina, but their line of descent could not be ascertained.

7 Elizabeth Ridley, daughter of Howell Lewis, left issue: Dr. Robert Ridley of Atlanta, Georgia, whose first wife was a daughter of the "great Ben Hill," is one of her descendants.

6 Willis Lewis appears on the rolls of the North Carolina State troops with the rank of captain, in the Revolutionary Army; beyond this nothing is known of him or his descendants.

6 Mildred Lewis has long been recognized as the oldest child of Howell Lewis, though this is disputed by some genealogists. She was married September 6, 1769, when her father was only thirty-seven years old, and it is hardly possible in the nature of things, that there could have been any older children. Mildred Lewis, was married to John Cobbs September 6, 1769, in Granville county, North Carolina. The records show that John Cobbs purchased land in Granville that year, of Wm. Moore, and in 1784, or fifteen years after his marriage, we find him described on the tax books of Goochland county, Virginia, as John Cobbs, of Georgia.

The sons of John Cobbs, as well as those of Thomas Cobbs, left off the "s" and spelled the name "Cobb," which accounts for the Cobb family of Georgia and Alabama. This change was made previous to 1800, as Howell Cobb entered the army under appointment from General Washington under the name of Cobb. A curious and interesting coincidence, in connection with it, is presented in the will of Howell Lewis, written in 1812 and probated in 1814, in which he makes bequests to the children of "my deceased daughter, Mildred Cobbs;" and the sons of John Cobbs and Mildred Lewis, who had changed their name to Cobb, became beneficiaries under that will under the name of Cobbs. Of course their identity was unmistakable, but the name of Cobbs, even in this line, is established up to a time that takes in General Howell Cobb of Georgia, who was born previous to the settlement of the estate of Howell Lewis. Issue of John and Mildred Lewis Cobbs as follows:

7 [1]Howell Cobbs, born 1771, married Martha Jacquiline Roots.

7 [2]John Addison Cobbs, born 1773, married Sarah Robinson Roots.

7 [3]Mildred Lewis Cobbs.

7 [4]Mary Willis Cobbs.

7 [5]Susanna Cobbs.

7 [6]Henry Willis Cobbs.

7 Howell Cobbs was the oldest of the children of John Cobbs and Mildred Lewis. He was appointed, during General Washington's administration, an officer in the United States Army, but after his marriage he resigned and settled on his plantation in Georgia. He represented his district in Congress from 1807 to 1812, at which time he resigned his seat in Congress to re-enter the army. He served as captain during the War of 1812, after which he again resigned his commission. He left no issue.

7 John Addison Cobbs, second son of John Cobbs and Mildred Lewis, is very little known to history, but the prestige of his family and all of his surroundings point unmistakably

to the fact that he was a man of mark in his day. He left issue as follows:

8 [1] Howell Cobb, born 1815, married Miss Lamar of Georgia.

8 [2] Thomas R. R. Cobb, married Miss Lumpkin, daughter of Chief Justice Lumpkin of the Supreme Court of Georgia.

8 [3] Mary Willis Cobb married first —— Erwin, and second Dr. J. M. Johnson.

8 [4] Mildred Lewis Cobb married Colonel Lucien Glenn.

8 [5] Sarah Martha Cobb married Major John C. Whitner.

8 Howell Cobb, son of John Addison Cobb and Sarah Robinson Roots, belongs to history. He was born at "Cherry Hill," Georgia, in 1815. He entered Congress in 1843, was re-elected successively until 1851, when he was elected governor of Georgia. He was made speaker of the House in 1849, and in 1857 Mr. Buchanan appointed him secretary of the treasury, from which position he resigned to share the fortunes of the Southern Confederacy. He left issue as follows: Judge Howell Cobb of the Athens Circuit; Judge Andrew Cobb of the Supreme Court of Georgia; John B. Cobb of Americus, Georgia, and others, a daughter who married Tinsley Rucker.

10 Thomas R. R. Cobb, son of Judge Howell Cobb, who married Miss Barker of Atlanta, was a brilliant young lawyer, who easily took the lead in his profession, but consumption claimed him as a victim. He died before he was thirty.

9 John B. Cobb married first Mary Lamar, and married second Alice Cutler. They left issue, one of whom, a daughter, married Wm. B. Lowe, Jr., of Atlanta.

8 Thos. R. R. Cobb also belongs to history. He was never in political life. He was strictly a lawyer and wedded to his profession. When the war between the states broke out, however, he went to the front and followed the fortunes of war, as brigadier-general, and was killed at the battle of Fredericksburg, December 12, 1862. He left several daugh-

ters, no sons. They married respectively, Harry Jackson, son of General Henry R. Jackson, an Athens gentleman by the name of Hull, and Hoke Smith, who was secretary of the interior in Cleveland's second administration.

10 Dr. Marion Hull, a distinguished physician of Atlanta, is a grandson of General Thomas R. R. Cobb.

8 Mildred Lewis Cobb, daughter of John Addison Cobb, who married Colonel Lucien Glenn, died in 1900, at an advanced age. Colonel Glenn was a distinguished lawyer. They left issue:

9 Sallie Glenn, who married a Mr. McBride, had two sons, Glenn and William, and three daughters. The older, Sallie, married Geo. W. Adair; the two younger not married.

9 Howell Glenn, son of Colonel Lucien Glenn, was a lawyer by profession, and at one time was city recorder. He went to New York City and died.

9 Colonel John Thomas Glenn, a distinguished lawyer of Atlanta, who has held many positions of trust and honor, is a son of Lucien and Mildred (Cobb) Glenn. He died very suddenly while yet in the prime of life, about 1900. He had been mayor of the city and solicitor general of the judicial circuit. He married Miss Garrard of Columbus, Georgia. They left issue, one son and two daughters. The family reside for the present in the city of New York, where their daughter, Miss Isa, has for some time been a leader in society. I see from a letter from her that she signs herself "Isa Urquhart Glenn, president general of the Order of the Crown," etc., from which it seems that she is at the head of that branch of "Colonial Dames" who claim "Royal Descent," certainly the most exclusive, if not the most worthy or meritorious, of any of the historical societies.

8 Mary Willis Cobb, daughter of John Addison Cobb, married first ——— Erwin, and second Dr. J. M. Johnson. Issue by first marriage: Howell Cobb Erwin, an attorney of At-

lanta, and Miss Lucy Erwin, who married Mr. Welborn
Hill of Atlanta, and by the second marriage, James Johnson, who had an appointment under Cleveland's second administration in some of the Indian agencies and remained
in the west; and Sarah Cobb or Sallie, as she was always
called, who, as a girl, was one of the brightest of an ex-
ceedingly bright family. She married first Dr. Hagan of
Richmond, Virginia, by whom she had two children, Hugh
Hagan and Willis Cobb Hagan; and she married second a
lawyer of Roanoke, Virginia, by the name of Cocke, a
member of a distinguished Virginia family of that name,
and a descendant of General Phillip St. George Cocke.

8 Sarah Martha Cobb, daughter of John Addison Cobb, and
granddaughter of John Cobbs and Mildred Lewis, married
Major John C. Whitner, of a South Carolina family, but
who have long resided in Atlanta, where Major Whitner
and his sons have long conducted a successful fire insurance business. They are both living at an advanced age,
and have issue as follows: John A. Whitner, Thomas Cobb
Whitner, Charles F. Whitner, Elisa S. Whitner—unmarried, Sarah Whitner, Mary A. Whitner, Mattie Mildred
Whitner.

9 John A. Whitner married Lidie Farrow of Atlanta. They
have eight children: John A. Whitner, Jr., Henry F.
Whitner, Caspar S. Whitner, John C. Whitner, Lidie F.
Whitner, Cornelia S. Whitner, Martha Cobb Whitner, Joseph Whitner.

9 Thomas Cobb Whitner married Miss Emily L. Tichenor, of
Atlanta, and have two children: Thomas C. Whitner, Jr.,
James T. Whitner.

9 Charles F. Whitner married Miss Margaret Badger, who is
a member of the distinguished Badger family of North
Carolina. Her immediate family, however, reside in Atlanta. They have two children: Charles F. Whitner, Jr.,
John S. Whitner. Mr. Charles Whitner is the genealogist
of his family and is very much interested in Lewis history.

9 Sarah R. Whitner married Warren Howard and had two children: Martha Cobb Howard, Whitner Howard.

9 Mary A. Whitner married B. C. Milner and had four children: Charles W. Milner, B. C. Milner, Jean S. Milner, John Cobb Milner.

9 Martha Mildred Whitner married Willis J. Milner and had six children: Willis J. Milner, Jr., B. C. Milner, Spann Whitner Milner, Mildred Milner, and two children died in infancy.

5 ROBERT LEWIS.

5 Robert Lewis, youngest son of "Charles of Byrd," born May 29, 1739, married February 26, 1760, Jane Woodson, daughter of Tucker Woodson. Appointed Colonel of Goochland county militia in 1779, died January 10, 1803; he had issue as follows: Howell Lewis, born November 18, 1760; Charles Lewis, born June 25, 1765; Robert Lewis, born March 26, 1763; James Lewis, born June 6, 1768; John Woodson Lewis, born May 21, 1770; Sarah Lewis, born June 8, 1772; Mary Howell Lewis, born December 25, 1774; Elizabeth Lewis, born August 14, 1779; Warner Lewis, born May 2, 1777, died October 6, 1820; married June 11, 1798, Sarah Pleasant Woodson; daughter, name unknown, born July 24, 1784. Fielding Lewis, born October 20, 1782.

6 Warner Lewis, son of Robert Lewis above, born May 2, 1777, married June 11, 1798, Sarah Pleasants Woodson; emigrated to St. Louis county, Missouri; issue: Robert Lewis, born May 9, 1799; Charles Lewis, born February 4, 1801; Samuel Lewis, born February 23, 1803, married Miss Bates of Iowa; Warner Lewis, born November 28, 1804, settled in Dubuque; Sarah P. Lewis, born August 8, 1806; Robert Lewis, born March 8, 1808, died July 8, 1875, married December 21, 1829, Lucy Bacon of St. Louis, born September 3, 1814; moved to Cass county, Missouri, in 1855, where he lived until the civil war; his family moved to Henry county, Missouri, in 1862, where she died August 13, 1903; James Howell Lewis, born November 18, 1809; Jane

Lewis, born November 20, 1811, married first Ferguson, married second Colonel Wm. Talbot of Loutre Island, Missouri; John Lewis, born July 4, 1818; Ann Lewis, born May 11, 1818; Elisabeth Lewis, born July 1, 1814, married Captain Robert Freeland; Wm. Price Lewis, born June 4, 1816; John Pleasants Woodson Lewis, born August 27, 1819.

7 Robert Lewis, son of Warner Lewis, and grandson of Robert Lewis and Jane Woodson, born March 8, 1808, married December 21, 1829, Lucy B. Bacon, of St. Louis, Missouri, and had issue:

   8 [1]Elvira Ferguson Lewis, married first James Orr, February 8, 1852, married second Jeptha D. Elliston, November 5, 1863.

   8 [2]Warner Lewis, Colonel C. S. A., commanded regiment in the Transmississippi department, married first Sarah M. Griffith of Cass county, Missouri, married second Mary (Morrison) Glenn, resides in Montgomery county, Missouri.

   8 [3]Ann Lewis died young.

   8 [4]James Lewis died young.

   8 [5]Anne E. Freeland Lewis married Dr. John H. Britts, Clinton, Missouri, November 1, 1865.

   8 [6]Garland Bacon Lewis, soldier C. S. A., killed at siege of Vicksburg.

   8 [7]Sarah L. Lewis married Dr. T. T. Thornton, of Hartwell, Missouri.

   8 [8]Lucy B. Lewis married Robert W. Covington of Garland, Missouri.

   8 [9]Robert Lewis died young.

   8 [10]Louisa Lewis married Wm. Covington.

   8 [11]Samuel Woodson Lewis married Sterling Price Covington.

8 Warner Lewis, Colonel C. S. A., great-grandson of Robert Lewis and Jane Woodson, January 5, 1834, married first Sarah M. Griffith, June 21, 1855; married second, June 27, 1882, Mary (Morrison) Glenn, had issue as follows:

LEWIS AND KINDRED FAMILIES.

9 [1]Robert Edgar Lewis, born April 3, 1857, married Ella
C. Avery of Clinton, Missouri, daughter of James and
Sallie (Woolfolk) Avery of Henry county, Missouri.
He is now judge at Colorado Springs, Colorado.

8 [1]Samuel Woodson Lewis, great-great-grandson of Robert
Lewis and Jane Woodson, married Sterling Price Covington. Issue: Annie and Kate Lewis. No record.

8 Elvira Ferguson Lewis, daughter of Robt. Lewis and his wife
Lucy Bacon, Warner, Robert and Jane Woodson, "Charles
of Byrd," married Jeptha D. Elliston and had one son,
James Lee Elliston.

9 Robert Edgar Lewis, son of Warner Lewis and Mary Glenn,
Robt. Lewis and Lucy Bacon, Warner Lewis and Sarah
Pleasants, Robt. and Jane Woodson, married Sallie Woolfolk Avery. Issue: Mason A. Lewis, and daughter, name
unknown.

9 Annie Lewis and Kate Lewis, daughters of Samuel Woodson
Lewis and Sterling Price; descent same as Robert Edgar
Lewis.

JOHN LEWIS OF WARNER HALL.

4 John Lewis of Warner Hall, the third of the name in
regular succession, was the oldest son of Councilor John Lewis
and Elizabeth Warner, born 1692, baptized same year; married Frances Fielding, and as the oldest son inherited Warner
Hall and the historic Bell farm, both entailed estates. There
is no record evidence in regard to this John Lewis, except
church registries and such inferential proof as has been gathered from the records of other members of the Lewis family.
He remained in Gloucester, the records of which county having
been almost totally destroyed, not even his will could be obtained.
It is known from church records that he married Frances Fielding and that they left five children:

5 [1]Warner, the oldest, born 1720.

5 [2]A second child, next to the oldest, whose name could not be

111

made out because of the frayed condition of the page.

5 [3]Fielding Lewis, born 1725.

5 [4]Charles, born about 1727.

5 [5]John, born about 1729, who has been completely lost sight of.

5 Warner Lewis married the widow of Wm. Gooch, who was Eleanor Bowles before she was married, daughter of James Bowles of Maryland; her first husband was a son of Sir William Gooch, governor of Virginia. They had issue as follows:

> 6 [1]Warner Lewis married first Mary Chiswell, married second Mary Fleming, said to have been a descendant of Pocahontas.
>
> 6 [2]Fielding Lewis of Weyanoke, married Agnes, daughter of William Harwood.
>
> 6 [3]James Lewis married Miss Thornton.
>
> 6 [4]John Lewis, no record.
>
> 6 [5]Addison Lewis married Susan Fleming, sister to Mary.
>
> 6 [6]Thomas Lewis married Nancy Harwood, sister to Agnes.
>
> 6 [7]Rebecca Lewis married Dr. Robert Innis.

6 Warner Lewis, son of Warner, and grandson of John Lewis and Frances Fielding, married first Mary Chiswell, married second Mary Fleming, issue as follows:

> 7 [1]Warner Lewis married Courtney Norton, daughter of J. H. and Ann Norton.
>
> 7 [2]John Lewis married Ann C. Griffin.
>
> 7 [3]Elizabeth Lewis, never married.
>
> 7 [4]Eleanor Lewis married first John Fox, married second Augustus Oliver.
>
> 7 [5]Caroline Lewis married Charles Barnett or Barrett.
>
> 7 [6]Julia Lewis married Thos. Throckmorton of Williamsburg, Virginia.
>
> 7 [7]John Lewis married his cousin, Eleanor Lewis.
>
> 7 [8]Phillip Warner Lewis, never married.

6 Fielding Lewis of Weyanoke, son of Warner, and grandson of John Lewis and Frances Fielding, married Agnes Harwood. Issue:

7 [1]Nancy Lewis.

7 [2]Fanny F. Lewis married Archibald Taylor.

7 [3]Margaret Lewis, born 1792, at Wyanoke, Charles City
county, Virginia, died at Oakhill, Fauquier county,
February 2, 1829; married October 19, 1809, Thos.
Marshall, son of Chief Justice Marshall, born in Richmond, Virginia, July 21, 1784, died in Baltimore, June
29, 1835.

7 [4]Eleanor W. Lewis, married Robert Douthat.

6 James Lewis, son of Warner, and grandson of John and
Frances Fielding, married Miss Thornton and had issue:
Elleanor Lewis and Sally Lewis who married Dr. Griffin.

6 Addison Lewis, son of Warner, and grandson of John Lewis
and Frances Fielding, married Susan Fleming and had
issue: Susan Lewis, born 1782, died November 12, 1865,
married William Byrd, son of Colonel Wm. Byrd.

7 Warner Lewis, son of Warner Lewis, grandson of John and
Frances Fielding Lewis, married Courtney Norton and had
issue:

8 [1]Mary C. Lewis, married John Peyton, son of Sir John
Peyton.

8 [2]Elizabeth Lewis, married Mathew Brook, M. D.

7 Eleanor Lewis married first John Fox, married second ———
Oliver. Issue:

8 [1]John W. Fox married Mary F. Ball, died in Gloucester
county, Virginia.

8 [2]Eliza Lewis Fox married Dr. Geo. D. Baylor, New
Market, Caroline county, Virginia.

8 [3]Warner Lewis Oliver.

8 [4]Margaret P. Oliver.

8 [5]Mary A. Oliver married John Fox Whiting.

7 Fanny F. Lewis, daughter of Fielding Lewis of Wyanoke,
Warner, John Lewis and Frances Fielding, married Archibald Taylor. Issue:

8 [1]Colonel F. L. Taylor married E. L. Fauntleroy.

8 [2]Dr. Archibald Taylor married Martha Fauntleroy.

8 [3]Robert Taylor.

8 [4]Thomas Taylor.

7 Margaret Lewis, born 1792, at Weyanoke, daughter of Fielding Lewis of Weyanoke, Warner, John and Frances Fielding, married October 19, 1809, Thomas Marshall and had issue:

8 [1] John Marshall, born 1811, died 1854, married 1837, Annie E. Blackwell.

8 [2] Agnes H. Marshall married General Alexander Taliferro.

8 [3] Mary Marshall married William B. Archer.

8 [4] Fielding L. Marshall married first Rebecca F. Coke, second Mary V. Thomas.

8 [5] Annie L. Marshall married James F. Jones.

8 [6] Margaret L. Marshall married John Thomas Smith.

8 [7] Colonel Thomas Marshall married Maria Barton.

7 Eleanor W. Lewis, daughter of Fielding Lewis of Wyanoke, Warner, John and Frances Fielding, married Robert Douthat. Issue:

8 [1] Robert Douthat married Mary A. Marshall.

8 [2] Jane Douthat married Dr. Wm. A. Selden.

8 [3] Agnes Douthat married Robert Lewis McGuire.

8 [4] Fielding L. Douthat married Mary Willis Marshall.

7 Sallie Lewis, daughter of James Lewis and Miss Thornton, Warner, John and Frances Fielding, married Dr. Griffin. Issue: James Griffin, Cyrus Griffin, Louisa Griffin married Dr. Wright.

7 Susan Lewis, daughter of Addison Lewis, Warner, John and Frances Fielding, married William Byrd, son of Colonel William Byrd. Issue as follows:

8 [1] Addison Byrd married Sue Coke.

8 [2] Mary W. Byrd married Richard C. Coke.

8 [3] Jane O. Byrd married G. W. McCandish.

8 [4] Samuel P. Byrd married first Catherine C. Corbin, married second Mary L. Brooke.

8 Mary C. Lewis, daughter of Warner Lewis and Courtney Norton, Warner, Warner, John and Frances Fielding, married John Peyton. Issue: Rebecca C. Peyton, married

Edward C. Marshall, son of Chief Justice Marshall, died in Fauquier county, Virginia, February 8, 1882.

8 Elizabeth Lewis, daughter of Warner, Warner, Warner, John and Frances Fielding, married Mathew Brooke, M. D. Issue:

9 [1] Elizabeth Brooke, born October, 1813, married May 16, 1834, H. M. Marshall.

9 [2] Courtney W. Brooke married Robert Selden.

9 [3] Mary L. Brooke married Dr. S. P. Byrd.

9 [4] John L. Brooke married Maria Louisa Ashby, born 1828, died 1882.

8 John Marshall, son of Margaret Lewis of Weyanoke, and Thomas Marshall, Fielding Lewis of Weyanoke, Warner, John and Frances Fielding, married Annie E. Blackwell. Issue:

9 [1] Anna G. Marshall married Richard Byrd.

9 [2] Fanny L. Marshall, born 1847, died 1860.

9 [3] John Marshall, born 1852.

9 [4] William C. Marshall married S. R. Taylor.

8 Agnes Marshall, daughter of Margaret Lewis, Fielding of Wyanoke, Warner, John and Frances Fielding, married General Alexander G. Taliaferro. Issue:

9 [1] Mary J. Taliaferro married Dr. Charles W. Chancelor.

9 [2] Leah S. Taliaferro.

9 [3] Agnes M. Taliaferro married R. W. Maupin.

9 [4] Margaret L. Taliaferro married 1870, Chapman Maupin.

9 [5] Eleanor W. Taliaferro married 1871, George Nelson.

9 [6] William A. Taliaferro married Charlotte Franklin.

8 Mary Marshall, daughter of Margaret Lewis, Fielding of Weyenoke, Warner, John and Frances Fielding, married Wm. B. Archer and had issue as follows: Wm. S. Archer and Lizzie Archer.

8 Fielding L. Marshall, son of Margaret Lewis, Fielding of Weyenoke, Warner, John and Frances Fielding, married first Rebecca Coke, married second Mary Thomas. Issue:

9 [1]Margaret L. Marshall married C. B. Hite.

9 [2]Richard Marshall married Catherine Willson.

9 [3]Mary W. Marshall married J. R. Yates.

9 [4]Susan L. Marshall married B. E. Armistead.

9 [5]Fielding L. Marshall married Caroline B. Gwatkin.

9 [6]Rebecca married C. R. Nash.

9 [7]Agnes H. Marshall married W. P. Helm.

9 [8]Thomas Marshall married Maud G. Barhydt.

8 Annie L. Marshall, daughter of Margaret Lewis, Fielding of Weyenoke, Warner, John and Frances Fielding, married James F. Jones. Issue:

9 [1]Cary R. Jones married Charles S. Marshall.

9 [2]Thomas M. Jones married Bessie W. Payne.

9 [3]Fannie B. Jones married Hugh McIllhany.

9 [4]William S. Jones married Kate U. Smoot.

9 [5]James S. Jones married Jane S. McGuire.

9 [6]Fielding L. Jones married Nellie C. Stanly.

9 [7]Agnes H. Jones married Dr. W. W. Butler.

8 Colonel Thomas Marshall, son of Margaret Lewis, Fielding of Weyanoke, Warner, John and Frances Fielding, married Maria Barton. Issue:

9 [1]David B. Marshall married Miss Roberts.

9 [2]Margaret L. Marshall married A. A. Duer.

9 [3]Thomas Marshall.

9 [4]Fanny J. Marshall married Rev. C. J. Holt.

9 [5]Fielding L. Marshall married Sue L. Waller.

8 Robert Douthat, son of Eleanor Lewis and Robert Douthat, Fielding Lewis of Weyanoke, Warner, John and Frances Fielding, married Mary A. Marshall. Issue:

9 [1]Lizzie Douthat, born 1842, died 1880, Eleanor, born 1844.

9 [2]Agnes A. Douthat married Colonel R. M. Stribling.

9 [3]Jacq. M. Douthat married Caroline Harrison.

9 [4]Mary Douthat, no record.

8 Louisa Griffin, daughter of Sallie Lewis and Dr. Griffin, James Lewis, Warner, John and Frances Fielding, mar-

LEWIS AND KINDRED FAMILIES.

ried Dr. Wright and had one daughter, "Sallie," who married Captain Ball.

(Warner Lewis line has not been traced any farther than the ninth generation.)

FIELDING LEWIS.

5 Fielding Lewis, second son of John Lewis and Frances Fielding, born 1725, married first, 1746, Catherine, daughter of John Washington and Catherine Whiting and first cousin of General George Washington, and married second, 1750, Bettie Washington, only sister of General George Washington. He was not in field service during the Revolutionary War, being over the military age, but was engaged during the struggle in manufacturing arms for the patriot army. His home was "Kenmore," Fredericksburg, Virginia.

6 John Lewis, born June 22, 1747, was the only surviving child of Kate Washington and Fielding Lewis. The other two children died in infancy. The first wife of John Lewis was Lucy Thornton, daughter of Col. John Thornton and a granddaughter of his grand-aunt, Mildred (Washington) Gregory. By the first marriage of John Lewis with Lucy Thornton, he had only one child. Mildred, at whose birth the mother died.

7 Mildred Lewis, daughter of John Lewis and Lucy Thornton, married Col. Wm. Minor and left three children: Warner Minor, Lucy Minor, and Elizabeth Minor.

8 Warner Minor, son of Col. Wm. Minor and Mildred Lewis, married Maria Timberlake and had three children: Lewis Minor, Virginia Minor, and Mary Minor.

9 Virginia Minor, daughter of Warner and Maria Timberlake Minor was an advocate of Woman's Rights. She married her cousin, Dabney Minor, and died without issue.

9 Lewis Minor married and left children in Texas.

10 Mary Minor, daughter of Warner and Maria Timberlake Minor, married a Mr. Swan of Georgia.

8 Lucy Minor, second child and oldest daughter of Col. Wm.

117

Minor and Mildred Lewis, married James Byars and had four children: William, James, Elizabeth Minor and Warner.

9 James Byars, son of James Byars and Lucy Minor married Mary Vincent, and their son James Vincent Byars is a successful journalist, was for some time on the editorial staff of the New York World.

8 Elizabeth, youngest daughter of Col. William Minor and Mildred Lewis, married Col. Wm. Campbell and left children. The second wife of John Lewis was Elizabeth Thornton, daughter of Col. Thomas Thornton, and double first cousin of his first wife. She left no children.

The third wife of John Lewis was Elisabeth Jones, daughter of Gabriel Jones, one of the most distinguished lawyers of Virginia, and known as the "Valley Lawyer." By this marriage he had three sons; Warner, Fielding, and Gabriel, the two first died young.

7 Gabriel Lewis, born September 16, 1775, son of John Lewis and Elizabeth Jones, married, November 24, 1807, Mary Bibb and had four children: John Lewis, Fielding Lewis, Mary Lewis, and Elizabeth Lewis. John married Mary Martin and left children; Fielding and Mary left no issue; Elisabeth, born November 11, 1813, married September 29, 1831, Col. Samuel McDowell Starling and left several children, but only one left issue.

9 Mary Starling, daughter of Col. Samuel McDowell Starling, married W. R. Payne, and after her marriage was known as "Mrs. Mary Starling Payne," and was emphatically one of the most thorough genealogists of her time. She died very suddenly about 1896. She left no issue.

9 ———— Starling, son of Col. Samuel McDowell Starling, married Nannie Killebrew and left five children: Nannie, Lizzie, Kate, Lewis, and Ellis, all unmarried except Kate. Kate Starling married Mr. Harvie Brithell and has one little boy, Harvey Brithell, Jr.

The fourth wife of John Lewis was Mary Ann Armistead, nee Foutaine, widow of Boyles Armistead, and his fifth wife was Mildred Carter, daughter of Landon Carter, and widow of

Robert Mercer, who was a son of General Hugh Mercer. Her mother was granddaughter of Mrs. Roger Gregory, and also of Col. Henry Willis. John Lewis died November 23, 1825.

5 Col. Fielding Lewis, by his second marriage with Bettie Washington, daughter of Augustine Washington and only own sister of General George Washington, had issue as follows: Fielding Lewis, Jr., born February 14, 1751; Augustine, born January 22, 1752; Warner, born June 24, 1755; George W. Lewis, born March 14, 1757; Mary, died in infancy; Charles, born October 3, 1760; Samuel, born May 14, 1763; Bettie, born February 23, 1765; Lawrence Lewis, born April 4, 1767; Robert, born June 25, 1769; Howell, born December 12, 1771.

6 Fielding Lewis, Jr., married Ann Alexander of Fairfax county, Virginia, where he died July 5, 1803. They had issue:

    7 [1]Charles Lewis, born in Fairfax county, Virginia, November 15, 1775; was appointed lieutenant in the army by his granduncle, General Washington; also served in the War of 1812; married Ann Davison, died August 9, 1829.

    7 [2]John Augustine Lewis, married Rebecca Ann Latimer.

    7 [3]George Lewis.

    7 [4]Catherine Lewis married Henry Chew Dade.

    7 [5]A daughter said to have married Spotswood.

6 Capt. George Lewis, son of Fielding Lewis and Bettie Washington, married Kate Dangerfield and had issue: Dangerfield Lewis, Samuel Lewis, Mary Lewis married Byrd Willis.

6 Bettie Lewis, daughter of Col. Fielding Lewis and Bettie Washington, married Charles Carter of Culpepper county, Virginia, and had issue:

    7 [1]Maria Carter married Prof. George Tucker.

    7 [2]Sarah Carter married Sir John Peyton.

    7 [3]Eleanor Carter married Henry Brown.

    7 [4]Farley Carter married Eliza A. Conn of Kentucky.

7 ⁵Otway Ann Carter married Dr. Owens of Lynchburg, Virginia.

7 ⁶Fielding Carter married Miss Smith of Arkansas.

7 ⁷George Washington Carter married Mary Wormley.

6 Lawrence Lewis, said to have been the favorite nephew of General Washington, because he was more intimately associated with him, born April 4, 1767, was aid to General Morgan 1794, married February 22, 1799, Eleanor Park Custis, granddaughter of Mrs. Martha (Dandridge) Custis, who afterwards became Mrs. Martha Washington. Lawrence Lewis and Eleanor Park Custis had issue:

7 ¹Eleanor Parke Lewis, born December 1, 1799; married Col. E. G. Butler.

7 ²Angela Lewis, born 1801; married Charles M. Conrad of New Orleans.

7 ³Lorenso Lewis, born November, 1803, died August, 1847; married 1826, Esther Maria Coxe, daughter of John R. Coxe of Philadelphia.

6 Robert Lewis, son of Fielding Lewis and Bettie Washington, at one time private secretary for his uncle General Washing, born January 25, 1769, married Judith Brown, daughter of Wm. Barnett Brown and Judith Carter, had issue:

7 ¹Bettie Lewis married George W. Bassett of Hanover county, Virginia.

7 ²Judith Lewis married Rev. John McGuire.

6 Howell Lewis, born December 12, 1771, married Ellen Hackney Pollard of Culpepper county, Virginia, moved to Kanawha, West Virginia, where he died December 26, 1822. They had issue: Bettie Washington Lewis; Robert Pollard Lewis; George Richard Lewis; Ellen Joel Lewis; Frances Fielding Lewis; Virginia Lewis; Howell Lewis married Emily G. Burch and moved to Henry county, Missouri, about 1836, where he died April 11, 1883, at Lewis station, named for him; Mary Ball Lewis; John Edward Lewis; Lawrence Lewis; Henry Dangerfield Lewis.

7 Dangerfield Lewis, son of Capt. George Lewis, Fielding, John and Frances Fielding, married unknown, has issue: Lucy Lewis, married Michael Wallace, son of Gustavus Brown Wallace and Frances Lurty.

7 Samuel Lewis, son of Capt. George Lewis, Fielding, John and Frances Fielding, married unknown and had issue: Alloway Lewis married John Putnam; Henry Howell Lewis, late of Baltimore; Mary Lewis of Morgansfield, Kentucky, married John Casey; George Lewis; Thomas Lewis; John Lewis.

7 Mary Lewis, daughter of Capt. George Lewis, Fielding, John and Frances Fielding, married Byrd Willis and had issue: Fannie Willis, born 1805; died 1867. Lived in Florida. married Achille Murat, son of Caroline Bonaparte and received a pension from the Emperor Napoleon III.

7 Maria Carter, daughter of Bettie Lewis, Fielding, John and Frances Fielding, married Prof. George Tucker and had issue: George Tucker; Lelia Tucker; Maria Tucker married George Rives; Elisa Tucker married Gesner Harrison of the University of Virginia.

7 Farley Carter, son of Bettie Lewis, Fielding, John and Frances Fielding, married Eliza A. Conn of Kentucky and had issue:

8 [1]Eleanor C. Carter married William C. Child.

8 [2]Rose C. Carter married Edward Baughman.

8 [3]Mary Carter married Dr. A. L. Robinson.

8 [4]William Farley Carter, marriage not known, banker, Clinton, Missouri.

8 [5]Phillip B. Carter.

8 [6]Charles Carter.

7 George Washington Carter, son of Bettie Lewis, Fielding, Lewis, John and Frances Fielding, married Mary Wormley and had issue:

8 [1]Maria E. Carter married Stephen Cobb.

8 [2]Eleanor Carter.

8 [3]Rosalind Carter married M. A. Jenkins of Mississippi.

121

8 ⁴Sophia F. Carter married W. D. Postlewaite, of Louisiana.

8 ⁵Georgianna Carter married E. L. Bower of Louisiana.

8 ⁶Anna B. Carter married Judge E. J. McGhee of Mississippi.

8 ⁷Harriet Carter, no record.

8 ⁸Virginia Carter married Judge D. O. Merwin of New Orleans.

7 Judith Lewis, daughter of Robert Lewis and Judith Brown, Fielding, John and Frances Fielding, married and had issue as follows: Bettie Burnett McGuire, born April 23, 1827, died April 29, 1856, married July 29, 1851, Rev. Charles E. Ambler, born Fauquier county, Virginia, June 6, 1827, died June 21, 1876.

7 Lorensa Lewis, son of Lawrence Lewis, Fielding, John and Frances Fielding, married Esther Maria Cox. Issue: Capt. Edmund Park Custis Lewis, born Clark county, Virginia, February 7, 1837, died Audley, Virginia, September, 1866; married March 23, 1859, Lucy Belmain Ware, born 1839. He married second, Mary Picton (Stevens) Garnett, widow of Hon. Muscoe Garnett. Capt. Lewis moved to Hoboken, New Jersey and was appointed by President Cleveland, April 2, 1885, resident minister to Portugal.

7 Bettie Lewis, daughter of Robert Lewis and Judith Brown, Fielding, John and Frances Fielding, married George W. Bassett; issue.

8 ¹Bettie Bassett married Ronald Mills.

8 ²George W. Bassett.

8 ³Virginia Bassett married J. H. Claibourne.

8 ⁴Ella Bassett married Col. Lewis Washington.

8 ⁵Fanny Bassett married C. T. Mitchell.

8 ⁶Mary Bassett married Benjamin Harrison Bassett.

8 ⁷Annetta Bassett married Julian Ingle.

8 ⁸Robert Bassett married Sallie Jeffries.

8 ⁹Wm. Bassett.

7 Judith Lewis, daughter of Robert Lewis and Judith Brown,

Fielding, John and Frances Fielding, married Rev. John McGuire. Issue:

8 [1]Rev. E. C. McGuire, married, first, Murphy, married second, Miss Fitzhugh.

8 [2]Dr. Robert McGuire married Agnes Douthat.

8 [3]Wm. McGuire married Miss Alexander.

8 [4]Marianna McGuire married H. A. Claibourne.

7 Howell Lewis, son of Howell, Fielding, John and Frances Fielding, married Emily Burch, and left issue:

8 [1]George Lewis.

8 [2]Augustus Dana Lewis.

8 [3]Mary Ellen Lewis married Dr. R. H. Hogan.

8 [4]Fielding Lewis married Mary Rains.

8 [5]Columbia Lewis.

8 [6]Virginia Lewis.

8 [7]Bettie Fitzhugh Lewis married ———— Finks.

8 [8]Wm. Henry Lewis married Bettie Dean.

8 [9]Emma Lewis.

7. Catherine (Kitty) Lewis, daughter of Fielding Lewis, Jr., Fielding, John, and Frances Fielding, married Henry Chew Dade, and had issue as follows:

8 [1]Elisabeth married James L. Dabney and moved to Texas.

8 [2]Henry Chew, also moved to Texas.

8 [3]Robert Fielding, died.

8 [4]Francis Huger married Miss Gray of Louisiana and moved to Marshall, Texas.

8 [5]Lucinda Frances married Judge H. W. Foote of Macon, Mississippi, where she died. They left issue, seven children:

9 [1]Ann married Dr. Early C. Clements of Mississippi.

9 [2]Catherine Lewis married T. T. Patty of Mississippi.

9 [3]William H. Foote married and resides in Louisville, Kentucky.

9 [4]Henry Dade Foote married Susan C. Walker, of Columbus, Mississippi.

9 [5]Thomas Dade Foote married Ann Allen of Virginia, now of Mississippi.

9 [6]Huger Lee Foote married Kate Shelby and resides in Mississippi.

9 [7]Emmie Foote, daughter of Lucinda Frances Dade, Catherine Lewis, Fielding Lewis, Jr., and Fielding and Bettie Washington, John and Frances Fielding, married Mr. H. M. Patty, formerly of Mississippi, but more recently of Texas, where he practiced his profession successfully for a number of years, but on account of the health of his family, he located in Atlanta. He is a gentleman of the highest standing and a lawyer of recognized ability. They have only one child, a daughter, just entered into womanhood.

7 Charles Lewis, son of Fielding Lewis, Jr., Fielding, John and Frances Fielding, married Ann Davidson and had issue, one son, George Washington Lewis of Louisville, who married and had issue, John C. Lewis, dry goods merchant of Louisville, and is reputed to be wealthy. He is vice-president general of Sons of the American Revolution.

7 Dr. John Augustine Lewis, born in Virginia in 1778, son of Fielding Lewis, Jr., and Ann Alexander, married Rebecca Ann Latimer of Virginia. He was an eminent surgeon and a man of great culture and ability. Issue: Mary Mildred Lewis married Hon. Beader Proctor of Virginia; Elizabeth Ann Lewis; Fielding, Addison, Alexander, William Robert Lewis.

10 Children of Hon. Beader Proctor and Mary M. Lewis are: Ann Rebecca Proctor, married Hon. Lawrence Battle, a capitalist of Georgia; Virginia Elizabeth Proctor; Nancy Alexander Proctor, Emily Mildred (called Matilda); George Washington Proctor and others.

11 Children of Ann R. Proctor and Hon. Lawrence Battle: [1]Claude Pierce Battle, deceased; [2]Marye Lulu Battle deceased; [3]Minnie Adelaide Battle, the family genealogist of Sharon, Georgia, who married James Frederick Allen, a distinguished and wealthy banker and financier of Warren-

ton, Georgia, president of Georgia and South Carolina banks, president of Georgia Cotton Mills, vice-president of Georgia Bankers Association; [4]Maude Lillian Battle, married Charles R. Smith of Georgia, and have a daughter Agnes Lillian Smith of Washington, Georgia; [5]Hon. Beader Lawrence Battle a capitalist and manufacturer of Georgia, now residing in Atlanta, Georgia, married Marie Stella Allen and have two children, Beader Lawrence Battle, Jr., now of Atlanta, Georgia, and Jacob Lawrence Battle; [6]James Hartwell Battle a banker of Georgia, married Bessie Cason, and have a daughter, Louise Battle of Warrenton, Georgia.

8 Lucy Lewis, daughter of Dangerfield Lewis, Capt. George Lewis, Fielding and Bettie Washington, John and Frances Fielding, married Michael Wallace and had issue:

    9 [1]Gustavas Brown Wallace, born "Marmion," K. G. county, Virginia.

    9 [2]Mary Boyd Wallace married first, Taylor, married second Taliaferro.

8 Maria Tucker, daughter of Maria Carter, Bettie Lewis, Fielding Lewis, John and Frances Fielding, married George Rives. Issue: Tucker Rives, Rosalie Rives, Edward Rives, Alexander Rives.

8 Elisa Tucker, daughter of Maria Carter, Bettie Lewis, Fielding Lewis, John and Frances Fielding, married Gesner Harrison and had issue as follows:

    9 [1]Maria Harrison married Rev. John A. Broaddus.

    9 [2]Mary Harrison married Professor Frank Smith.

    9 [3]George Harrison married Lelia Belle Edwards.

    9 [4]Peachy Harrison.

    9 [5]Robert Harrison.

    9 [6]Rosalie Harrison married Professor Wm. M. Thornton.

8 Wm. Farley Carter, son of Farley Carter, Bettie Lewis, Fielding Lewis, John and Frances Fielding, married unknown and left issue: Wm. F. Carter, Mary Carter, Nannie Carter. Resides at Clinton, Missouri.

8 Maria Carter, daughter of George Washington Carter, Bettie

Lewis, Fielding Lewis, John and Frances Fielding, married Stephen Cobb and had issue: Ellen Cobb, Wm. Farley Cobb, Mary Cobb, Henry Cobb.

8 Rosalind Carter, daughter of G. W. Carter, Bettie Lewis, Fielding Lewis, John and Frances Fielding, married M. A. Jenkins and had issue: George Jenkins, Mary Jenkins, Sarah Jenkins, Frank Jenkins, Rosalie Jenkins, Augustus Jenkins.

8 Sophia F. Carter, daughter of G. W. Carter, Bettie Lewis, Fielding Lewis, John and Frances Fielding, married W. D. Postlewaite and left issue: Ann Postlewaite, Mary Postlewaite, Amelia Postlewaite, Wm. Postlewaite, Fannie Postlewaite, Helen Postlewaite, Georgiana Postlewaite.

8 Georgiana Carter, daughter of G. W. Carter, Bettie Lewis, Fielding Lewis, John and Francis Fielding, married E. L. Bower and had issue: Mary Bower, Stella Bower, Lewis Bower.

8 Annie B. Carter, daughter of G. W. Carter, Bettie Lewis, Fielding Lewis, John and Frances Fielding, married Judge E. J. McGehee, and had issue: Mary McGehee, Edmund McGehee, Mervin McGehee.

8 Capt Edward Park Custis Lewis, son of Lorenzo Lewis, Lawrence, Fielding, John and Frances Fielding, married Lucy Ware and had issue as follows:

9 [1] Eleanor Angella Lewis, born July 27, 1859, died February 18, 1860.

9 [2] Lawrence Fielding Lewis.

9 [3] Lucy Ware Lewis.

9 [4] John Glassel Ware Lewis.

9 [5] Edward Park Custis Lewis, born Aug. 1864, died about 1866.

9 [6] Edward Augustus Lewis, by second marriage with widow Garnett.

9 [7] Julia Stevens Lewis, by second marriage with widow Garnett.

9 [8] Esther Maria Lewis, by second marriage with widow Garnett.

9 *Eleanor Park Custis Lewis, by second marriage with
widow Garnett.

8 Virginia Carter, daughter of G. W. Carter, Bettie Lewis,
Fielding, John and Frances Fielding, married Judge D. O.
Merwin and had issue: George W. Merwin, Samuel Merwin,
Fielding Merwin, Julia Merwin.

8 Bettie Bassett, daughter of Bettie Lewis and George W. Bassett, Robert Lewis, Fielding, John and Frances Fielding,
married Ronald Mills. Issue: Virginia Mills, W. L. H.
Washington Mills.

8 Fanny Bassett, daughter of Bettie Lewis and George W. Bassett, Robert Lewis, Fielding, John and Frances Fielding,
married C. T. Mitchell. Issue: Fanny Mitchell, Virginia
Mitchell, Laura Mitchell, Bassett Mitchell, Lucy Mitchell.

8 Mary Bassett, daughter of Bettie Lewis, Robert Fielding,
John and Frances Fielding, married Benjamin Harrison
Bassett. Issue: Eleanor Bassett, Lewis Bassett, Lucy
Bassett, Hope Bassett, Benjamin Bassett.

8 Dr. Robert McGuire, son of Judith Lewis and Rev. John Mc-
Guire, Robert, Fielding, John and Frances Fielding, married Agnes Douthat and had issue: Jane S. McGuire married James F. Jones.

8 Fielding, son of Howell Lewis and Emerly Burch, Howell,
Fielding, John and Frances Fielding, married Mary Rains,
and had issue: Lawrence Howell Lewis.

8 Bettie Fitzhugh Lewis, descent same as Fielding above, married ——— Finks, issue, Leland Finks, now of Calhoun,
Missouri.

8 Wm. Henry Lewis, descent same as Fielding and Bettie, married Nellie Dean and had issue as follows: Emmett Lewis,
died aged 8; Olla Lewis, and Howell Lewis.

9 Maria Harrison, daughter of Gesner Harrison and Eliza
Tucker, Maria Carter, Bettie Lewis, Fielding, John and
Frances Fielding, married Rev. John A. Broadus, a distinguished Baptist minister of Virginia, who for many years
was president of the Baptist Theological seminary, located

first at Greenville, South Carolina, and afterwards at Louisville, Kentucky. Dr. Broadus was presiding officer of that institution up to the time of his death.

10 Anna Broadus, daughter of Rev. John A. Broadus and Maria Harrison and granddaughter of Dr. Gesner Harrison, so long chairman of the faculty of the University of Virginia, married Rev. Wyckliffe Yancey Abraham, a Baptist minister of Virginia. She died about 1895; he died 1903. They left two children: John Abraham, who is married and in business in St. Louis, Missouri, and Annie Lou, about 12 years old, who lives with her stepmother in Richmond. Mr. Abraham, several years after the death of Anna Broadus, married Miss Christian of Buckingham county, Virginia, a a most worthy and estimable lady, and it proved a fortunate marriage. She is indeed a mother to his orphan daughter. His death was very sudden and indeed tragic. He had been in attendance on a Baptist Convention in Staunton, Virginia, and had returned to Richmond and boarded a street car for his home, when he was struck down with heart failure and was taken off the car in a dying condition and carried home a corpse.

10 Mary Harrison, daughter of Gesner Harrison and Elisa Tucker, Maria Carter, Bettie Lewis, Fielding, John and Frances Fielding, married Prof. Frank Smith, and had issue: Elisa Smith, Lelia Smith, Harrison Smith, Eleanor Smith, Tucker Smith.

COL. CHARLES LEWIS OF CEDAR CREEK.

5 Charles was the youngest son of John Lewis and Frances Fielding, born, according to the register of Abington Parish, in Caroline county, Virginia, 1729. He was brother of Warner and Fielding Lewis and Nephew of "Charles of Byrd," and Robert of Bellvoir. He married Lucy Taliaferro, daughter of John Taliaferro and Mary Catlett of Snow Creek near Fredericksburg. They had three children: Dr. John Taliaferro Lewis,

Charles Augustine Lewis, and Mary Warner Lewis.

6 Dr. John Taliaferro Lewis, oldest son of "Charles of Cedar Creek," was a graduate of Edinburgh College, Scotland. He settled at "Mulberry Green," in Culpepper county, Virginia, where he practiced his profession, successfully and profitably but died in the prime of life. He married first, Hannah Green of Essex county, Virginia, and married second, Susannah Warring, also of Essex. Dr. John Taliaferro Lewis, by his marriage with Hannah Green had only one son, no daughter; Augustine Lightfoot Lewis, who married his cousin, Mary Warner Lewis, daughter of Charles Augustine Lewis of Caroline county, Virginia. By second marriage with Susannah Warring, he had several children. We have only the record, however, of four:

7 ¹Lucy, oldest child of Dr. John Taliaferro Lewis, by his second marriage, was born September 5, 1783. She married Col. John Thom of Culpepper county, Virginia. They left several children, one of whom, Lucy Lewis Thom married Col. William Taylor of Louisiana, a cousin of President Zachary Taylor.

7 ²John Lewis, second child of Dr. John Taliaferro Lewis and Susannah Warring, was born July 18, 1785. He married his cousin, Frances Tasker, daughter of Spencer Ball, Esq., and his wife Bettie Landon, daughter of Robert Carter. John and Frances Tasker Lewis left three sons: John Taliaferro Lewis, Robert Motrum Lewis, and Frank Warring Lewis, all of whom reside in Prince William County, Virginia. They also left a daughter who married Dr. Bowen.

7 ³Warner Lewis third child of Dr. Taliaferro and Susannah (Warring) Lewis, was born December 13, 1786 and resided at Lewis Level, Essex county, Virginia. He was of the "Old County Court," was high sheriff of Essex, and vestryman of South Farnham Parish, in 1820. In 1810 he married his cousin, Susannah Latane, daughter of Wm. Latane, Esq., of Langle, Essex county, Virginia. This Wm. Latane was grandson of the Rev. Lewis Latane, a French Huguenot who fled from France upon the revocation of the Edict of

Nantes in 1685, first to England, then emigrated to Virginia and took charge of South Farnham Parish in 1700.

8 Thomas Warring Lewis, son of Warner and Susannah (Latane) Lewis, was born August 15, 1815. He married August 11, 1842, Ann Ursula, only daughter of Henry Warring Latane of Essex county, Virginia. On the second of June, 1892, Mr. Thomas Warring Lewis, in a letter to Mr. A. St. M. Cliflin of Chicago, gave the lineage of his ancestor, "Charles Lewis of Cedar Creek," which we have copied in these pages, and concluded by saying: "I have seven sons and five daughters who are sources of joy to me in my old age." There is no record, however, of his children or their descendants.

6 Mary Warner Lewis, only daughter of "Col. Charles Lewis of Cedar Creek," married Phillip Lightfoot of "Sandy Point," on James River. They resided at Cedar Creek. He lived but a short time and left only one son, Phillip Lightfoot, Caroline county, Virginia.

7 Phillip Lightfoot, son of Phillip Lightfoot and Mary Warner Lewis and grandson of "Charles of Cedar Creek," married Sally, daughter of William Bomard, Esq., of Mansfield, near Fredericksburg, Virginia.

6 Mary Warner Lewis married second Dr. John Bankhead of Caroline county, Virginia, who was a graduate of Edinburgh, and a nephew of President Monroe. They had two sons: Charles Lewis Bankhead and Dr. Wm. Bankhead.

7 Charles Lewis Bankhead married Cary Randolph, granddaughter of Mr. Jefferson. They left many descendants who moved to Missouri years ago.

7 Dr. Wm. Bankhead married Dorothea Minor, daughter of Garrett Minor of Fredericksburg, Virginia. They have many descendants in Virginia.

6 Charles Augustine Lewis, second son of "Charles of Cedar Creek," was educated at William and Mary. He was a member of the "Old County Court" of Caroline, and in the language of Mr. Thomas Warring Lewis, was the peer of

any of his associates. He married Catherine Battaile of Caroline county, Virginia and left six children as follows:

7 [1]Mary Warner, named for her aunt, married her cousin, Charles Augustine Lightfoot Lewis, and lived at Maringo, Spottsylvania county, Virginia.

7 [2]Charles Augustine Lewis was a graduate of the University of Virginia, married Elizabeth Goodwin of Blenheim, Caroline county, Virginia and left an only child, Elizabeth Meriwether, who married Professor R. Massie of Virginia. He commanded a cavalry company from Caroline in the War of 1812, and saw hard service at Camp Holly, near Norfolk, Virginia.

7 [3]Arthur Lewis, a captain in the United States army, died without issue.

7 [4]Lawrence Battaile Lewis married and removed to Missouri years ago.

7 [5]Bettie Battaile Lewis died single.

7 [6]Rebecca Lewis married her cousin, John Taliferro Lewis of Prince William, and died in Mississippi.

FIRST ZACHARY LEWIS.

This head of the Lewis name in Virginia was not the first that came, but when he did come he came to stay. It may be said of him, as of many other emigrants to Virginia at that period, that he most emphatically "had his hat in his hand" and was prepared for the mission upon which he came. It was about 1692 that Zachary Lewis landed on the "Old Virginia Shore." The first record evidence of his presence in Virginia was a land grant for 500 acres of land in King and Queen county in 1694. His birth is believed to have been about 1650. The name of his wife is unknown, nor is it known whether he married in England, or after he came to Virginia. That he had a number of children there is abundant proof, but little is known of their history beyond that of the second Zachary. It is known that he had a son John who married Sarah Iverson, but little is known definitely of the descendants of this marriage. The records show many families in which the name of Zachary has been perpetuated, and there is no lack of evidence that the first Zachary Lewis left many representatives. On the records of Albemarle county, Virginia, may be found the will of "John Lewis Planter," about whom other genealogists know nothing. He is contemporaneous with six or eight others of the same name, whose identity is known, yet his line of descent has never been traced. The name of Zachary, however, is perpetuated with his descendants and we have unhesitatingly placed him in the Zachary Lewis line. There are doubtless many of the descendants of John Lewis and Sarah Iverson who have been entirely lost sight of.

This name is recognized as a distinct head of one of the branches of the Lewis family, in Virginia.

Whatever may have been said of the identity of the Lewis name, whether in France, or subsequently in England, it is nevertheless true, in spite of the intermarriages between the different lines after coming to Virginia, the distinctness between the repective lines continue to be marked.

The head of this family, as has been seen, first appears on the Virginia records during the last quarter of the seventeenth century, and on the land books the first grant of land to Zachary Lewis is for 500 acres of land in King and Queen county, in 1694, he was probably born about 1650, and believed to have come to Virginia in 1692. He first settled in Middlesex county, in the vicinity of Dragon Swamp, where he laid the foundation of his future fortunes and like other pioneers of this historic family, proceeded to establish his own line, which, having borne his name for more than 200 years, will always be known as the Zachary Lewis line; indeed, it is more than probable that this distinction was observed in England previous to their establishment in Virginia.

It has been said, and is borne out by the facts, that Irish John Lewis of Augusta, in his sons and grandsons, furnished more warriors, officers of rank and distinction, for their country's defence, than any other name and it may be said with equal truth that Zachary and other heads of the Lewis families in eastern Virginia, while furnishing their full quota of soldiers and officers to the army, at the same time led in the professions, and were not behind in the ranks of statecraft; and in this they are still conspicuous.

It is not known, and perhaps will never be ascertained, how many children the first Zachary Lewis had. The Rev. Mr. Hayden mentions only two: Zachary, born 1702, and John, date of birth not given; but it is nevertheless true that there were cotemporaneous with these sons, other Lewises, in whose families is perpetuated the name of Zachary, and as Mrs. Mary Starling Payne used to say: "Nothing less than the most unbounded filial devotion could ever induce anyone to give his son such a name." Owen Lewis, the birth and baptism of whose children appear on the church registry, and who was himself born 1690, was cotemporaneous with the other known sons of the first Zachary Lewis, and his descendants are brought down with the name of Zachary perpetuated in the succeeding generation.

The Rev. Mr. Hayden in his "Virginia Genealogies" devotes a chapter to "The Lewis family," and with the exception of some merely incidental remarks, confines himself entirely to the Zachary Lewis line; but he only gives a limited account of this line, and hence in justice to this branch of the Lewis family, I shall seek to give, as far as possible, a more complete genealogy. In doing this, however, it will be necessary for me to reproduce much that Mr. Hayden has already given, but with some additions and corrections. In dealing with this branch of the family, I shall present them under three general heads:

First Zachary Lewis, emigrant, born about 1650, who came to Virginia 1692. Name of wife unknown.

Second Zachary Lewis, born in Virginia 1702, married Mary Waller 1725.

Third John Lewis, born about 1704, married Sarah Iverson.

SECOND ZACHARY LEWIS.

Born 1702, married Mary Waller, January 3, 1725; and died 1765. His will is probated February, 1765. Mary Waller was born 1699, baptized by the Rev. John Munroe, October 17th of that year, and died March 23, 1781. She was the daughter of Col. John Waller and his wife Dorothy King. The best established traditions, as well as the court records for generations previous to this, go to show that the Lewises of this line were a wealthy family, and this number was no exception to the rule. As a result of a large and lucrative law practice, Mr. Lewis amassed a fortune and left his children wealthy. As an attorney he was a recognized leader, being retained in the most important cases and receiving the largest fees. In his will he names four sons: John, Zachary, Waller and Benjamin; daughters, Mary Meriwether, Betsy Littlepage, Lucy Ford, and Dorothea Smith, and makes his four sons executors; but from the church registers and other records we find the name of Ann Lewis, born November 30, 1726, died August 8, 1784, married Chancellor George Wythe who was one of the most distinguished lawyers and jurists of his age. They were married about 1746.

Chancellor Wythe was born in the county of Elizabeth City in 1726 and died June 8, 1806. He studied law with Mr. Dewey of Prince George county and came to the bar at Williamsburg after 1756. In 1758 he was burgess, at which time Thomas Jefferson came under his instruction, and they were ever afterwards warm friends. In 1764 Mr. Wythe was a member of the Commission of the House which presented resolutions of Remonstrance to the House of Commons. In 1774 he joined the Continental forces against Lord Dunmore. In 1776 he was elected to the Continental Congress and was one of the signers of the Declaration of Independence.

In 1778 Chancellor Wythe was appointed one of the three judges of the High Court of Chancery, and when that court was reorganized in 1788 he was made sole Chancellor, which position he continued to hold the remainder of his life.

An incident in the life of Chancelor Wythe which has never been published is worthy of notice here, as it gives an insight. not only to his own character, but to his fine judgment of the character of others. It was related to the writer by Robert L. Cobbs, an intimate friend and relative of General White, who was surgeon on his staff through the war of 1812, and afterwards read law in his office. As was the custom with Virginia planters at that time, Mr. White, a wealthy Virginia planter, and special friend of Chancelor Wythe, had delivered his entire crop of tobacco to Richmond, and commissioned his son William to attend to the sale for him. The sale having been made, and the money collected, young White fell into the hand of sharpers and was swindled out of the last dollar. Mortified and chagrined at the turn of affairs, he determined never to return home until he could carry with him the full amount of his father's losses. He sought Chancelor Wythe, laid his plans before him, detailing in the meantime his misfortune, requested the loan of enough money to carry him to Nashville, then a frontier town in Tennessee. Having been furnished with the needed amount he set out, a youth of seventeen, on his journey to the "Far West." For several years Mr. White knew nothing of his son except such information as was given him by Chancelor Wythe, and even then he knew nothing of his whereabouts, was only assured that he was determined to reinstate himself in his father's confidence. Confident of the integrity of young White, Chancelor Wythe gave the father such assurances that his confidence in his son was unshaken and he was content to await results. In an incredibly short time the amount with interest, which had been advanced by Chancelor Wythe was returned, and all of Mr. White's losses made good by his son. This youth turned out to be General William White who had command of one of the divisions of General Jackson's army during the war of 1812, and commanded the left wing at New Orleans on the 8th of January, 1815. He had become a distinguished lawyer before the war, and after the close of the war he resigned his commission in the army and resumed the practice in Nashville, Tennessee.

Chancellor Wythe did not live to see White in the zenith of his fame, as he died in 1806, while White, at that time, had just entered upon his brightest career, but he lived to see him prove himself a man, in the redemption of the most sacred pledges of his early life.

Chancelor Wythe married a second time, Elizabeth Taliferro of Williamsburg, but we have no account of any children by either marriage. He removed to Richmond in 1789 where he spent the remainder of his life.

3 MARY LEWIS.

3 Mary Lewis, second daughter of Zachary Lewis and Mary Waller, was born January 30, 1728, married Frank Meriwether, son of Col. David Meriwether and his wife Ann Holmes. born 1717. They removed to South Carolina, and had issue: Zachary Lewis, Nicholas Lewis, and Mary Lewis.

LEWIS AND KINDRED FAMILIES.

3. JOHN LEWIS.

The third child, in order of age, of Zachary Lewis and Mary Waller, was born October 18, 1729, baptised by the Rev. Rodham Kenner, November 23, 1729, died September 12, 1780. Will dated May 31, 1766. Codicil added 1776. Admitted to record October 19, 1780. He married Ann Lewis, daughter of Robert Lewis of Belvoir and his wife Jane Meriwether, and reference to his descendants will be found under the head of Robert Lewis of Belvoir. The Rev. Mr. Hayden says that John Lewis married, first, Sarah Iverson, but this is altogether improbable. John Lewis, son of the first Zachary, and uncle of this John, married Sarah Iverson, and this fact no doubt confused Mr. Hayden's authorities. All of the circumstances preclude the idea of a previous marriage. Equally erroneous is Mr. Hayden's assertion that John Lewis married Mildred Lewis, as the records and a letter preserved by his descendants positively prove that he married Ann Lewis, a sister of Mildred.

Mr. Lewis had only three sons, John Zachary, Robert and Nicholas. Charles Lewis who married Susan R. Waller and died in Lynchburg, Virginia, 1822, was not a son of this John Lewis. Nicholas Lewis, his son, married Ann Meriwether. Their children were: Eliza, James, Hunter, Susan and Laura Lewis.

While Mr. Lewis does not mention any daughters, the records show, as explained on another page, that he had two daughters: Mary, who married David Wood Meriwether, and Jane who married Zachary Meriwether. (See Records of Spottsylvania.)

3. COLONEL ZACHARY LEWIS.

The second son of Zachary Lewis and Mary Waller was born May 6, 1731, died July 31, 1803. Will dated February 20,

1803, and probated in Spottsylvania county. Married May 8, 1771, Ann Overton Terrell of Louisa county, Virginia, daughter of Richmond Terrell. The records show that Col. Lewis was made captain of the Spottsylvania foot company February, 1758, and was also an officer in the Revolutionary army. He left children as follows:

4 ¹Ann Overton Lewis, born April 23, 1772, married July 28, 1795, James McClure Scott.

4 ²Richmond, born March 14, 1774, died July 31, 1831; married first, October 28, 1802, Elizabeth Travers Daniel, second, September 3, 1830, Margaret B. Richardson.

4 ³Cadwalader Lewis, born November 25, 1776, died February 4, 1796.

4 ⁴Mary Waller Lewis, born April 10, 1779; married John Hill, 1797.

4 ⁵Huldah Fountain Lewis, born February 4, 1781, died October 25, 1863; married September 23, 1802, Waller Holladay.

4 ⁶John Lewis, born February 25, 1784, died August 27, 1858; married November 21, 1808, Jean Wood Daniel.

4 ⁷Elisa Lewis, born May 27, 1786, died September 4, 1816; married Walter Raleigh Daniel.

4 ⁸William Lewis, born August 20, 1788, died same day.

4 ⁹Addison Murdock Lewis, born September 26, 1789, died August 27, 1857; married first, December, 1810, Sarah Billingsby, second, March 2, 1821, Sarah Ann Minor.

3. WALLER LEWIS.

The third son of Zachary Lewis and Mary Waller appears on the records of Spottsylvania county as one of the executors of his brother John's will, and his will is on record in the same county. Mr. Hayden gives his birth September 11, 1739. It is more than probable that this is a traditional approximation, as Waller Lewis was married previous to September 1, 1757, at which time the will of Robert of Belvoir was written, which would have made him, at that time not quite eighteen, and it is not known how long previous to this time he had been married; from which it follows almost necessarily that Waller Lewis was born at least two or three years previous to the date given by Mr. Hayden. Not until very recently has it been possible to break through the crust, so to speak, which has hidden the history and family of Waller Lewis from posterity; and even now it has not been possible to obtain anything like a complete record.

Waller Lewis, M. D., married Sarah, daughter of Robert Lewis, previous to September 1, 1757. They had seven children, as will be seen by reference to the family line of Robert Lewis of Belvoir, under the head of his daughter, Sarah, who married Waller Lewis, but only the line of one of their children has been wholly rescued from oblivion, that of Elizabeth, born 1772, who married John Woolfolk in 1791 and removed to Kentucky 1811; and this has been done by the untiring zeal and persistent energy of the wife of one of her descendants.

3. BENJAMIN LEWIS.

The youngest son of Zachary Lewis and Mary Waller was born in King and Queen county, Virginia, June 16, 1744. He married Martha Bickerton, of Hanover county, Virginia, but the date of his marriage is unknown. He left five children:

4 ¹Benjamin Lewis, M. D., died unmarried.
4 ²John Lewis, married Matilda Nelson.
4 ³Patsy Bickerton Lewis, married Snellson Smith and left several children, one of whom (Dorothea) married Edmund Swift and left issue, Martha, who married William Cook and also left children.
4 ⁴Alice Lewis married a Mr. Jewett.

4 [3]Elisabeth Lewis married George Greenhaw, and left several children, one of whom (Samuel), married Mary Johnston, whose daughter married Rev. Frances Marsh Baker, rector of Grace Church, Richmond, Virginia.

4. RICHMOND LEWIS, M. D.

The oldest son of Col. Zachary Lewis and his wife Ann Overton Terrell, was born March 14, 1774, in Spottsylvania county, Virginia, died July 31, 1831; married Elizabeth Travers Daniel, daughter of Travers and Frances Monners Daniel. He married second, Margaret B. Richardson. He first located at Urbana, Middlesex county, Virginia, and in 1800 at Fredericksburg. He was surgeon, United States army during the war of 1812.

4. ANN OVERTON LEWIS.

Oldest daughter of Col. Zachary Lewis and his wife, Ann Overton Terrell, was born in Spottsylvania county, Virginia, April 23, 1772, baptised by Rev. Robert Barret, June 7, 1772; married July 28, 1795, James McClure Scott, M. D.

Dr. Scott was from Pennsylvania and, as informed by one of his grandsons, was the only one of his family who ever came South. There is no account of any children by this marriage, and the records show that Ann Overton Lewis died shortly after marriage.

Dr. Scott married a second time, Mildred Thomson, daughter of Waddy Thomson and his wife Mary Lewis Cobbs, daughter of Col. Robert Lewis of Belvoir, Albemarle county, Virginia, and had two sons: John Thomson Scott and James McClure Scott, both of whom married back into the Zachary Lewis family, daughters of Dr. Richmond Lewis, and nieces of their father's first wife.

The marriages in this family go to show somewhat the extent to which the different branches of the Lewis name have merged. Two sons of Zachary Lewis, Waller and John "The honest lawyer," married daughters of Robert Lewis of Belvoir, while another daughter of Robert, Mildred Lewis, married a great-grandson of John Lewis of Henrico, and these are only a few of the many instances of similar intermarriages between the different branches of this name.

John Lewis of Llangollen was no exception to his family, but was simply another variety of genius. A ripe scholar and a man of letters, and although Mr. Hayden says that he failed to find his name among the Alumni of any of the colleges that he examined, that is no proof that he was not an alumnus of some one that he did not examine. Certain it is that as a scholar his rank was equal to the standard of the best universities. A lawyer by profession, but all of his tastes turned to literature and he employed his time principally as an educator.

3. ELIZABETH (BETTIE) LEWIS.

Daughter of Zachary Lewis and Mary Waller, born October 9, 1732, married first, 1760, Col. James Littlepage, of Hanover county, and second, March 5, 1774, Major Lewis Holaday of Spottsylvania county, Virginia. By her first marriage with Col. Littlepage she had two children:

4 [1]General Lewis Littlepage, born December 9, 1762, died July 19, 1802; he never married.

4 [2]Mary Littlepage, born 1764, married Robert Shelbe Coleman. By her second marriage with Major Holaday she had two children.

4 [3]Ann Holaday, born April 18, 1775; died January 26, 1846, married Hugh Corrans Boggs.

4 [4]Waller Holaday, born August 17, 1776, died August 27, 1863, married September 23, 1803, Huldah Fountain Lewis.

4 GENERAL LEWIS LITTLEPAGE.

Lewis Littlepage is known to history with this title, which was doubtless conferred by one or more of the European Countries, as he was in the service of France, Spain and Poland. His was strictly a European career. His history reads like a romance and belongs not only to the country, but to the civilised world, and, for lack of space, will not be reproduced here; only brief references will be made to it:

At the age of 17, delicate, precocious, and of an unnatural mental development, Lewis Littlepage, by permission of his guardian, left America, on what was at first intended as a European tour, but he entered at once actively into European politics, and as above stated, was at different times in the service of France, Spain and Poland, and did not permanently return to America until a short time before his death. Lewis Littlepage died July 19, 1802, in Fredericksburg, Virginia, and was buried by the Masonic Fraternity with the following inscription on his tomb: "Here lies the body of Lewis Littlepage, who was born in the county of Hanover, in the State of Virginia, December 19, 1762, and departed this life July 19, 1802, aged 39 years and 7 months. Honored for many years with the esteem and confidence of the unfortunate Stanislaus Augustus, King of Poland. He held under that monarch until he lost his throne, the most distinguished offices among which was that of Ambassador to Russia. He was by him created the Knight of St. Stanislaus, chamberlain and confidential secretary in his cabinet, and acted as his special envoy in the most important negotiations. Of talents, military as well as civil, he served with credit, as an officer of high rank, in different armies. In private life he was charitable, generous and just, and in the various public offices which he filled, he acted with uniform magnanimity, fidelity and honor."

4 Mary Waller Lewis, daughter of Zachary Lewis and Ann Overton Terrell, granddaughter of Zachary and Mary Waller and great-granddaughter of the first Zachary Lewis, born in Spottsylvania county, Virginia, April 10, 1779, baptised by the Rev. Robt. Barret, May 23, 1779; married May, 1797, John Hill of Hillsboro, Virginia, and had issue as follows: Ann Overton Hill, married John Overton Harris; John Minor Hill, married Harriet Lowry Hill; Huldah

Lewis Hill; Mary Ann Hill; Robert Zachary Hill; Martha B. Hill; Edward H. Hill; Mary Clark Hill; Sarah Frances Addison Hill.

4 John Lewis of Llangollen, son of Zachary, Zachary, Zachary, born in Spottsylvania county, Virginia, February 25, 1784, baptized by Rev. Wm. Douglas, May 14, 1784, died in Franklin county, Kentucky, August 15, 1858; married November 21, 1808, Jean Wood Daniel, born at Frankfort, Kentucky, 1786, died same place January 3, 1853, aged 67. They had issue as follows:

5 [1]Frances Ann Lewis, born March 3, 1810, married May 31, 1836, William Mitchell.

5 [2]Cadwalader, born November 5, 1811, died April 22, 1882, married February 13, 1830, Elizabeth Henry Patterson.

5 [3]Elizabeth Travers Lewis, born July 10, 1813; and died October 15, 1836.

5 [4]George Wythe Lewis, born February 9, 1815, died July 19, 1845, married Mary Jane Todd.

5 [5]Mary Overton Lewis, born November 7, 1816.

5 [6]John Moncure Lewis, born May 11, 1820, died March 21, 1845.

4 Rev. Adison Murdock Lewis, son of Col. Zachary Lewis and his wife Ann Overton Terrell, and grandson of Zachary Lewis and Mary Waller, born at "Bel Air," Spottsylvania county, Virginia, September 26, 1789, died at Huntsville, Missouri, August 27, 1857; married first, December 10, 1810, Sarah Billingsly, and married second, March 20, 1821, Sarah Ann Minor. By his first marriage with Sarah Billingsly he had three children:

5 [1]Virginia Ann, born May 30, 1813, died February 1867, married December, 1838, James D. Brown, Franklin county, Kentucky.

5 [2]John Lewellen, born February 23, 1815, married April, 1809, Mary Eliza Woolfolk.

5 [3]Joseph Addison, born October 18, 1818, died in Glasgow,

143

Missouri, December, 1876; married September, 1848, Mary Elizabeth McCoy.

6 Virginia Ann Lewis and James D. Brown had one child: Sarah Addison Brown married Colley Taylor, Franklin county.

5 John Lewellen Lewis and Eliza Woolfolk had:

6 [1] Thomas Addison.

6 [2] Isabel married Oscar Stephens.

6 [3] Malcolm Duane married first, Julia McKinney, second, Amanda Prather.

6 [4] Charles Orville, M. D.

6 [5] Ann Maria married Walter Scott.

5 Joseph Addison Lewis and Mary Elizabeth McCoy had: Ellery Channing; Nannie married Dr. Berry; Josephine; Adison Thomas; Elizabeth.

5 Malcolm Duane Lewis, M. D., is now located in Columbia, where he is practicing his profession; he married Julia McKinney and had:

6 [1] Mildred Lewis educated at Missouri State University.

6 [2] Carl Lewis, a druggist in connection with his uncle Phillip Prather of Columbia, Missouri.

6 [3] Pierre Lewis, Columbia, Missouri.

4 Rev. Addison Murdock Lewis by his marriage with Sarah Ann Minor had nine children and with the three by a previous marriage, he had a family of twelve children:

5 [4] Thomas Minor Lewis, born January 19, 1822, married July 17, 1844, Louisiana Cleveland Hughes.

5 [5] Richmond Zachary Lewis, born August 12, 1823, died December 20, 1844.

5 [6] Jane Elizabeth Taylor Lewis, born March 14 ,1825, unmarried.

5 [7] Waldo Lewis, M. D., born May 6, 1827, died September 6, 1864; married December 26, 1855, Sophia Miller Shafer, died 1872.

5 [8] Ann Terrell Lewis, born June 30, 1829, died October 17, 1883,

5 [9] John Henry Lewis, born September 30, 1831, residence

144

St. Louis; is in the lumber business; married January, 1855, Mary Susan Hix.

5 [10]Sarah Billingsly Lewis, born in Kentucky, June 23, 1834, married December 1850, Theodore Washington Dunica of St. Louis, died 1874.

5 [11]Lucy May Lewis, born in Kentucky, May 5, 1836; married December, 1859, Gordon Cloyd McGarvock.

5 [12]Huldah Fontain Lewis, born in Kentucky, November 11, 1838, died October 12, 1872; married September 1, 1861, D. Alexander J. Bibb.

5 Thomas Minor Lewis and his wife Louisianna Cleveland Hughes had ten children as follows: Florence Howell Lewis married W. B. Brown; Alice Minor Lewis married Joseph Drake; Overton Earnest; Caroline Virginia married Robert W. Hughes; Kate Richmond; Thomas Minor Lewis, Jr.; John Hughes; Frances May; Robert Roy Earnest.

5 Dr. Waldo Lewis and his wife Sophia Miller Shafer had no issue, so far as known.

5 John Henry Lewis and Mary Susan Hix left five children, as follows: Mary, born February, 1857; Leonora, born December, 1859; Frank, born January, 1863; Nannie Lay, born August, 1871; Robert Hunter, born December, 1875.

5 Sarah Billingsly Lewis and her husband, Theodore Washington Dunica, had three children:

6 [1]Sarah B., born 1857, married December, 1882, Henry D. Stewart.

6 [2]Eudora, born October, 1859, married September, 1881, Phillip Winchester.

6 [3]Mills Hapwood.

5 Lucy May Lewis and her husband, Gordon Cloyd McGarvock, had six children:

6 [1]John Lewis McGarvock, born 1861.

6 [2]Sally Ann McGarvock, born February, 1863.

6 [3]Mary, born 1866.

6 [4]Louisa, born 1869.

6 [5]Hugh, born 1871.

6 [6]Robert, born 1876.

145

6 Overton Lewis, son of Thomas Minor Lewis and grandson of
Rev. Murdock Lewis, marriage not known, had: Hugh
Lewis and Max Lewis.

6 Sarah B. Donica, daughter of Sarah Billingsly Lewis and her
husband, Theodore Washington Doica, and granddaughter
of Rev. Murdock Lewis, married Harry J. Stewart and had
one child: Harry Stewart.

As has been said of John Lewis of Llangollen, Rev. Addison
Murdock Lewis was no exception to his family, but his genius
was of an exceptional kind. While his uncle John Lewis of Spottsylvania was gifted with the rare faculty of combining great
legal ability with stern and rigid honesty, and his brother, John
of Llangollen, excelled in scholarship and literature, and his cousin Lewis Littlepage filled with distinction the most difficult positions in European politics, the Rev. Murdock Lewis threw the
weight of all of his great gifts, and bent all of his energies, to
the building up of the Master's cause, during a period of nearly
half a century. He was a Baptist minister, and in the years
between 1810 and 1820, he traveled through Kentucky, Indiana,
Illinois and Missouri, preaching and organizing churches. In
1828 he removed to Kentucky and took charge of a church and
a school for girls at Georgetown. In 1833 he settled on a farm
in Franklin county, taking charge of Buck Run Baptist church.
In 1839 he removed his family to Howard county, Missouri. In
1855 he resided in Glasgow. He died in Huntsville, Randolph
county, Missouri, August 27, 1857, having been forty-eight years
in the ministry.

3 LUCY LEWIS.

3 Lucy Lewis, daughter of Zachary Lewis second and Mary
Waller, born December 5, 1735, married a Mr. Ford of
Amelia county, Virginia. They left several children and
as a Waller Ford was visiting Mr. Holladay of Virginia
who was from Kentucky, it is probable they moved to Kentucky after marriage.

LEWIS AND KINDRED FAMILIES.

3 DOROTHY LEWIS.

3 Dorothy Lewis, daughter of Zachary Lewis second and Mary Waller, born September 3, 1737, married Charles Smith, an Englishman. They had three sons: one of them, Snelson Smith, married his cousin Martha B. Lewis, a daughter of Benjamin Lewis; Christopher Smith (called Kid Smith) died unmarried; Charles, or Nat, Smith.

PLANTER JOHN LEWIS.

In will book 4, pages 42 to 45, Albemarle county, Virginia, will be found a will, written July, 1786, codicil 1792, and June, 1794, probated January 6, 1800, beginning with the significant language: "I, John Lewis, Planter, etc." In Albemarle and adjoining counties at that time there were forty or fifty of that name, and the most of them were planters. There were very few people of any means in Virginia at that time who were not planters, but there were many by the name of John Lewis who were also doctors and lawyers and some few were preachers; and one of the name was known as "the honest lawyer," but this old ancestor chose to designate himself in a way that could not be misunderstood, as no one had ever selected this designation.

This member of the Lewis family seems to have effectually escaped the attention of the genealogists, and even the most intelligent and best posted of his descendants seem to have known nothing of him from a genealogical standpoint. As a genealogist I claim him by right of discovery, never having seen any reference to him by any other genealogist, or found any trace to him in any family records. I found him on the records of Albemarle county and run down the descendants of his daughter, Sarah Cobbs, and his son, Owen Lewis, to the present generation, before these descendants knew, or had any idea of what line of the Lewis family they had descended from.

There is no record trace of the father of Planter John Lewis, but all of the circumstances point very clearly to the conclusion that he belonged to the Zachary Lewis line, and that he was a son of the first Zachary Lewis, and brother of the second Zachary who married Mary Waller. The Reverend Mr. Hayden gives the names of only two of the sons of the first Zachary: Zachary, born 1702, and John, birth not given; but there is no doubt that there were others, and perhaps younger sons.

LEWIS AND KINDRED FAMILIES.

Owen Lewis appears on the church register of the Theological Seminary, Fairfax county, Virginia, cotemporaneously with the second Zachary, and as the name comes down in the same line with that of Zachary, he was no doubt an older brother, the birth of his oldest child being given March 19, 1714, and Planter John Lewis has a son Owen, and Zachary is perpetuated in his family.

The will of Planter John Lewis names two sons Owen and John; and six daughters, all married: Elisabeth Davis, Ann Tindell, Sarah Cobbs, Mary Nevill, Susan Wingfield, and Lucy Davenport. The names of the six married daughters of Planter John Lewis have gone to make up some of the most prominent families of Virginia, many of whom have played a conspicuous part in the stirring events of the past century.

4 Sarah, who married Edmund Cobbs, was the ancestress of Bishop Nicholas Hamner Cobbs of the Diocese of Alabama, and others of the same family, distinguished in other professions, will be mentioned more prominently under the head of the Cobbs family.

Of John Lewis, son of "Planter John," nothing is known further than what has been obtained from the records of Albemarle county. From these records we find that he was born 1749 and died 1804. His will was admitted to probate February 6, 1804. Owen Lewis and Zachary Lewis, brother and nephew, and John Staples are named as executors, and provision is made for wife and three children: Sally Ming, a married daughter; Elisabeth Anderson Lewis; and John Waddy Lewis.

4 Owen Lewis, second son of "Planter John" Lewis, is the only member of that family, numerous as it is, whose descendants I have been able to trace, except Sarah Cobbs, whose line will be taken up under the head of the Cobbs family, as before stated, and traced more fully. Deed book 6, page 204, Albemarle county, Virginia, shows Owen Lewis to have been born 1752; and will book 4, page 281, shows that he died 1812. He married Miss Sallie Perkins about 1775. In the settlement of the estate July 6, 1812, the children of Owen Lewis are named

as follows: William, John, Harding, Howell, Nicholas, and Zachary, and Mr. Zachary Lewis of Nelson county, Virginia, furnishes me with the name of an additional son, Robert, and a daughter, Sally.

5 William Lewis, oldest son of Owen Lewis, born between 1775 and 1780, married about 1800, Miss Elizabeth Lee Patterson, daughter of David Patterson and his wife Judith Dibrell of Buckingham county, Virginia, by which marriage he had three daughters: Judith Dibrell, Sarah, and Elizabeth Lee; and by a second marriage, with Mrs. Glover, he had three other daughters: Susan, who married a Mr. Hooker; Mary, who married a Harris; and Caryann, who married a Mr. Christian. He had no sons by either marriage. The three first named daughters of William Lewis and Miss Patterson, Judith, Sarah, and Elizabeth, married, respectively, Edward H. Mosely of Buckingham, a Mr. Morris, and Mr. Thomas of Nelson county, Virginia; of the descendants of the two latter nothing is definitely known.

6 Judith Dibrell Lewis, daughter of William Lewis and Elizabeth Lee Patterson, married Edward H. Mosely of Buckingham county, Virginia, about 1825. The issue of this marriage was three daughters and no sons. Their daughters were: Mary Elizabeth, Sarah Ann Lewis, and Virginia Edward.

7 Mary Elizabeth Moseley, daughter of Edward Moseley and his wife Judith Dibrell Lewis, born 1826, married Reverend Thomas N. Johnson, one of the most distinguished Baptist ministers in Virginia, who for more than half a century, was in the forefront of his profession and filled some of the most important stations within the bounds of the state. They had five children: Sarah Louisa, Thomas Edward, Ella, Lafayette Dibrell, and Mary Lewis.

8 Sarah Louisa Johnson, daughter of Rev. Thomas N. Johnson and Mary Elizabeth Mosely, married Rev. William Shipman of Nelson county, Virginia, a gentleman of fine family and high standing, both as a man and a minister, having filled some of the most important stations in the State, having been stationed at one time at Richmond.

9 Rev. Thomas Johnson Shipman, oldest son of Rev. William Shipman and Sarah Louisa Johnson, is yet quite a young man, only recently married. He has been called to appointments in Virginia and Kentucky, and has also served a charge in Savannah, Georgia. He is a young man of rare ability and promise, and is in demand with Baptist congregations.

7 Sarah Ann Lewis Mosely, daughter of Edward Mosely and Judith Dibrell Lewis, married first, Dr. Lafayette Dibrell, oldest son of Mr. Charles Lee Dibrell, then of Richmond, but afterwards of Lynchburg, Virginia. Doctor Dibrell was a young man of rare attainments and deep piety. He had graduated with distinction in his chosen profession, and gave promise of a brilliant success, but consumption had fastened itself upon him and claimed him as its victim. He lived only eight months after his marriage. He died in Lynchburg, Virginia, February 1847, aged 24 years. He left no issue. After the death of Doctor Dibrell his widow married Mr. John Abraham of Buckingham county, Virginia, but moved soon thereafter to Rockbridge county, near the Rockbridge Alum Springs. Mr. Abraham was a man of high character and sterling qualities, and of him it may be said that the world, so far as he come in contact with it, was the better by his having lived in it. One son was the issue of this marriage, Wyckliffe Yancy Abraham, born about 1850.

About 1880, Sarah Ann Mosely was left a widow a second time and in the long interval, has followed her son, for the most part, in his various homes as Baptist minister, and now still lives at the advanced age of 77 years, in Richmond, Virginia.

8 Rev. Wyckliffe Yancy Abraham married Miss Anna Broadus, daughter of Rev. John A. Broadus, formerly of Virginia, but for a long time, and up to his death, president of the Southern Baptist Theological Seminary, located first at Greenville, South Carolina, but subsequently removed to Louisville, Kentucky. Two children blessed this union: John Abraham; now married and doing business in St. Louis, Missouri, and Annie Louise who is about 12 years old and at school in Richmond, Vir-

151

ginia. Mrs. Abraham died about 1895; and the Rev. Mr. Abraham died 1903.

7 Virginia Edward Mosely, youngest daughter of Edward Mosely and Judith Lewis, married Mr. John Armstrong of Rockbridge county, Virginia. Issue: William Mosely Armstrong, Alexander Lewis Armstrong, Percy Stanly Armstrong, Lelia Jordon Armstrong, Sallie Ann Armstrong. Mrs. Armstrong when a young lady possessed rare beauty and was very much admired and very much courted. I remember seeing her at home, Goshen, Virginia, soon after she was married, when she was indeed a picture for a painter; having been left a widow she removed to Staunton, Virginia, about 1885; where she spent the remainder of her days. She died soon thereafter.

Susan Lewis, daughter of William Lewis by his second marriage with Miss Glover, married a gentleman by the name of Hocker of Buckingham county, Virginia, and her son is one of the Superior Court Judges of Florida.

Judge Hocker married a Miss Venable of Virginia, and his oldest son, Wm. Hocker, Jr., graduated in the law class of 1894 at the University of Virginia.

A daughter of Mrs. Susan (Lewis) Hocker married Howell Venable of Virginia. He also removed to Florida.

5 Zachary Lewis, son of Owen Lewis, and grandson of Planter John Lewis of Albemarle, was born about 1780. His name first appears on the record of Albemarle February 6, 1804, as one of the Executors of the will of his uncle John Lewis. The perpetuation of the name Zachary in this family is sufficient proof of the line to which they belong and if this was not sufficient proof of itself, the perpetuation of the name in other branches would be sufficient corroboration. Mary, daughter of Planter John Lewis, who married a Neville, named her oldest son "Zachary Lewis Neville." The fact that Planter John did not perpetuate the name is doubtless owing to his having only two sons. The older named after himself, and the other, Owen, no doubt, after his father; but as we have seen, the name was very promptly revived and has been very faithfully perpetuated by his descendants.

Zachary Lewis, the subject of this sketch, married Sallie Patterson of Buckingham county, Virginia, and sister of Elizabeth Lee Patterson who married William Lewis an older brother. These sisters were granddaughters of the first Anthony Dibrell and Elizabeth Lee, and will be more fully noticed under the head of the Dibrell family.

5 Zachary Lewis and his wife Sallie Patterson had six children as follows: Agnes Lewis, Sarah Lewis, John Lewis, David Lewis, Leannah Lewis Zachary Lewis. Nothing is known of any except John and Zachary, and very little is known of them, although there are many of the name and kin that can not be traced, but it is to be hoped that information contained in these sketches will enable others to trace their lines.

6 Zachary R. Lewis, fourth in line from Planter John Lewis, is the youngest child of Zachary Lewis and Sallie Patterson. In a letter to me about twelve years ago (1893) he said: "My mother died when I was a baby and I am now 76 years old." No doubt he has been gathered to his father's ere this. On account of his advanced age he has ceased to write. This letter was an answer to my inquiries in regard to his branch of the family, and gave more information than I have been able to obtain from all other sources. I have also had very interesting and valuable letters from his youngest daughter, Miss Mary Lewis, who has been especially kind in answering my letters. The latest that I had from her was a "Richmond State" containing an account of her marriage to Mr. W. D. Patterson, no doubt a relative. Mr. Patterson is a member of one of the leading law firms of Scottsville, Virginia.

6 Mr. Lewis married Miss Mary Garth of Albemarle, one of the wealthiest families of that county. Issue: Howell Lewis, William Lewis, Zachary Lewis, John , Sallie, Mary and Henry Lewis. Their postoffice address is Howardsville, Nelson county, Virginia.

6 John Owen Lewis, son of Zachary Lewis and Sallie Patterson, and hence brother of the last named Zachary, married twice and left ten children. This much we learned in a general

way from his brother, but we have not been able to obtain any thing definite, either in regard to his marriages or his descendants. It is to be hoped, however, that this reference will meet the eye of some of them, and serve the purpose, at least, of directing their attention to their ancient and honorable as well as distinguished ancestry.

JOHN LEWIS OF HENRICO.

This is another distinct head of the Lewis families in Virginia, and is so distinctively designated. Every circumstance by which he was surrounded goes to show that he had no connection, or even intimate association with any of the name who came to Virginia in the seventeenth century, or with Irish John Lewis who came later. This John Lewis first appears on the records of Henrico in 1660 and, as subsequent events show, was quite a young man at that time; therefore he could not have been a brother of Robert of Gloucester who was more than forty years older, nor could he have been a son, as Robert's son, John, his marriage and descendants, are fully accounted for; So is John the brother of Zachary and John, of Hanover, while Irish John is too remote to be taken into consideration.

Whatever may be said of the identity of the different branches of the Lewis family, or of their relationship, one thing is certain: so far as their American history is concerned, there is no means of tracing this identity or of establishing the relationship. Nearly one hundred years intervened between the arrival of General Robert Lewis and Irish John, while the arrivals of the other occurred at such intervals, as to preclude the idea of identity of interest or concert of action on the part of any of them.

It is a generally conceded fact, or at least, proposition, that all of them sprung from the same stock, but this doubtless had its foundation in a generally accepted tradition, but while tradition is valuable to the extent that it gives rise to inquiry and investigation; with no confirmation of this tradition, we shall continue, as we have started out, to treat them separately.

However distinct these respective families or their respective heads may have been when they first set out on their American

155

GENEALOGIES OF THE

life, or how long they may have remained so after settling down
in their new homes, it is nevertheless true that, in the lapse of
time, the intermarriages between the respective branches have
been so numerous as to largely merge them into each other.

John Lewis of Henrico seems to have been entirely lost sight
of not only by other genealogists, but by his own descendants.
Like "Planter" John Lewis of Albemarle, I claim "John of Henrico" by right of discovery, for I virtually dug him out from
among a mass of Henrico records where he had been lost to his
own posterity for more than one hundred years. When in 1892,
I was in search of Lewis history among the Virginia records,
I very naturally, when in Richmond, repaired first to the rooms
of the Secretary of the Virginia Historical Society. Doctor
Brock, who was then secretary, and who had just spent years in
reviving Virginia genealogies, and to some extent, made a specialty of the Lewis family, although his office was within six or
eight squares of the Henrico Court House, where the clerk's office containing the records, was open to his inspection, did not
know of the existence of this John Lewis. The records show,
and the character and standing of his descents confirm, that
John Lewis of Henrico was no obscure man in his day and generation. He died, however, at the age of forty-five in the prime
of his usefulness. He is described on the records as being from
Wales, and was therefore a direct emigrant.

The records of Henrico shows that the estate of John Lewis
was finally wound up in 1689 and that his widow married a second time, hence, it follows that he died about 1686. They also
show that he died intestate; that he left two children—son and
daughter—William and Sarah; that Sarah was a minor at the
time of her father's death and that her brother William qualified
as her guardian in 1689; that the widow of John Lewis married
a second time, Samuel Trottman in 1688, which no doubt accounts for William Lewis qualifying as his sister's guardian in
1689. Nothing further is known of the widow of this John Lewis, or of his minor daughter Sarah, as they appear no more on
the records.

156

LEWIS AND KINDRED FAMILIES.

2 William Lewis, only son of John Lewis of Henrico, was born 1660, as shown by a deposition made by him in 1679 in which he describes himself as nineteen years old and as shown by his nuncupative will, made December 24, 1706, and proven May 1, 1707, upon the evidence of George Payne and Elizabeth Johnson. He died December 25, 1706.

"NUNCUPATIVE WILL OF WILLIAM LEWIS.

"At a court held at Varna for ye County of Henrico. The first day of May, 1707. Present Her Majesty's Justices:

"That upon ye 24th day of December in Ye year of our Lord 1706, Wm. Lewis did, lying very sick, but of perfect mind and memory, declare the manner and form of will in disposing of his worldly estate vis.: He allotted to his eldest son, John Lewis, the plantation whereon he lived, one hundred acres of land purchased of Wm. Porter, Jr., one hundred acres of land upon the north side of Whiteoak Swamp. He allotted to his two sons, William and Joseph Lewis, two hundred acres of land upon a place known by the name of the 'Runs,' with a parcel of land lying upon the 'Whiteoak swamp' and 'Deep Run' to be divided between them, but withall, would wish that his son John should have the privilege of carrying and keeping a stock of hogs and cattle, and of getting timber for his own use, upon the said William and Joseph's land lying upon the Whiteoak 'Swamp and Deep Run.'

"He disposed of all the residue of his estate to his wife, adding concerning his children, that they were her children as well as his, and for that reason doubted not but that she would do as well for them as he would do if in her place; therefore he would give nothing from her, but leave all to her disposal. The words or the same in effect, were declared and publicly spoken by the deceased the day and year abovewritten in the presence of George Payne and Elizabeth Johnson who are ready to evidence and testify the same if required, in behalf of the deceased's wife.

157

"Henrico county May first Anno: 1707: Presented to the County Court by Elizabeth Lewis relict of the deceased William Lewis, and proved by George Payne and Elizabeth Johnson, who upon oath declared that the words (or the same in effect) in the above said will or writing, expressed, were declared and publicly spoken by the said William Lewis in their presence and hearing the day before his death, and that he was at the same time of perfect mind and memory, to the best of their judgments, wherefore, on the motion of the said Elizabeth Lewis, it is ordered that the same be entered on record.

"Teste. "JAMES COCKE,
"Clerk of Court."

Of the many "Quaint and Curious Volumes of Forgotten Lore," through which I have had to search in quest of genealogical information, this is the only specimen of its kind that has fallen under my observation. Nuncupative wills were recognised by the English law for hundreds of years, and as a matter of learning in the pursuit of the law, we have been familiar with them through a lifetime of literary pursuit, but this is the only one that I have even found on record.

This will shows that Wm. Lewis left three sons, John, William and Joseph, but while he may have left daughters to be provided for out of property left to his wife, no daughters are mentioned.

3 John Lewis, oldest son of Wm. Lewis, appears on the records of Goochland, but there is no record evidence that he married in that county. He disappears, however, from the records of Goochland and reappears at different times on the records of Loudon, Berkeley and the border counties of Maryland. His identity is unmistakable and the best evidence is that he married a daughter of Jacob Woodson of Goochland. He had a son Jacob and this Jacob Lewis had a son who was an officer in the Revolutionary army from Berkeley county, Virginia, or it is more than probable that Jacob himself was an officer in the army.

LEWIS AND KINDRED FAMILIES.

3 William Lewis, the second son of Wm. Lewis and grandson of John of Henrico, had his residence in that county, while
John and Joseph are shown to be residents of Goochland. It
is not known whether the last two removed to Goochland, or were
simply cut off from Henrico by the formation of Goochland, that
county having been cut off from Henrico; most probable the latter. Nothing further is known of him than that he was the second son of William, Sr., and is found on the records of Henrico
in the transfer of titles to lands. It is not known that he ever
married, or if he did he left no descendants that are known.

3 Joseph Lewis, youngest son of William Lewis Sr. and
grandson of John of Henrico, and his descendants have firmly
planted him in the minds of posterity and in the history of the
country. The will of Joseph Lewis, of record in Goochland
county Virginia, 1783, shows that he had seven children. Three
sons and four daughters as follows: John Lewis, William Lewis, Joseph Lewis, Elisabeth RoBards, Sarah Bedford, and Ann
Mosely; and grandchildren named Cocke—Susan Cocke and
James Cocke. It will be seen that all of his daughters had married and one had doubtless died. Of all of these children no definite trace of any of the descendants can be found, except one
or two of John and Elisabeth RoBards.

4 John Lewis of Goochland, great-grandson of John Lewis
of Henrico, and son of the above Joseph Lewis, born about 1735,
married about 1755, Mildred Lewis, daughter of Robert Lewis
of Belvoir, Albemarle county, Virginia, and is the Major John
Lewis, mentioned in the will of Robert Lewis as "the husband
of my daughter Mildred."

So completely had John Lewis of Henrico been lost to the
Virginia genealogists that, notwithstanding, one of his great-
granddaughters had married a member of the distinguished
Cocke family and another a RoBards, two of the wealthiest and
most influential families of Virginia all previous genealogists
have utterly failed to locate Major John Lewis, who married
Mildred of Belvoir. They persisted in claiming that he was a
son of Zachary Lewis and Mary Waller, but when it was proven

that this John had married Ann Lewis, another daughter of Robert of Belvoir, they turned us loose being compelled to give up the claim, and if they did not accept our solution, they at least withdrew their objections.

It was not because John of Henrico was not a man who was fully the peer of his fellows, nor because his descendants did not measure up to the full standard of their surroundings, but because the Gloucester family owing to a combination of circumstances, and an overpowering concentration of conditions, simply overshadowed all of the other Lewises. It is true there was no such thing as keeping them down, but whenever a Lewis did anything to attract attention of the public, or distinguished himself in any way in the departments of life, no one made any attempt to locate him, or stopped to ask any questions about him, but without making any inquiries, assigned him at once to the ranks of the Warner Hall family.

Whether Robert Lewis of Gloucester was an officer in the English army, with the rank of general, or not or whether he had a grant from the Crown for 33,333 1-3 acres of land such was his reputation, and such was the wealth, influence and success of his immediate, and many of his more remote descendants, in all of the departments of life, they, and the public generally were prepared to accept his reputation at face value; and when his grandson and Lawrence Washington had married the daughter of the speaker of the House of Burgeses and member of the Royal Council, and John Lewis had himself become a member of the Royal Council, the early history of Robert Lewis of Brecon, Wales, was readily accepted; and when his descendants become identified with Washington and Jefferson, and the leading men of the country generally, and indeed had become leaders themselves, all of the Lewises, if not swallowed up were, at least overshadowed by the Warner Hall family. It is true that many of the name in Virginia, who were in no way related to that family, or to each other, were equally distinguished in civil and military affairs, but the public did not stop to draw the distinction, and so the Virginia Lewises, were all bunched together under one general head.

Major John Lewis, son of Joseph Lewis of Goochland, was the great-grandson of John of Henrico, as shown by the records of that county and of Goochland. Robert Lewis of Belvoir mentions Major John Lewis in his will as "husband of my daughter Mildred," and I find him on the records of Albemarle with his wife Mildred, described as John Lewis of Goochland. The will of this John Lewis is of record in the county of Goochland, 1796. His wife had evidently died previously, as no wife is mentioned. He mentions three sons: John, William, and Joseph. William, however, had previously died. His daughters had all married previous to the making of the will and are as follows: Ann Mosely, Elizabeth Halsy, Mary Atkisson, and Sarah Mann.

We have no definite account of the descendants of Major John Lewis and Mildred of Belvoir. Enough, however, is known to establish the fact that, for the most part, they emigrated to Kentucky. Mr. Thomas M. Green is authority for the assertion that Joseph, their youngest son, removed to Kentucky and was the ancestor of Judge Joseph Lewis of the Supreme Court of that State. Mr. John Lewis RoBards of Hannibal, Missouri, confirms this statement.

Elizabeth Lewis, daughter of Joseph Lewis of Goochland and sister of John who married Mildred Lewis of Belvoir, married a RoBards as shown by her father's will.

Mr. John Lewis RoBards of Hannibal, Missouri, with whom I have corresponded, has given me much valuable information. From him I learn that Elizabeth Lewis, who was his great-grandmother, was married September 6, 1781, and that her husband, his great-grandfather, was William RoBards, Jr., and that the later generation of their family had chosen to employ a capital B in the second syllable of their name in order to preclude the possibility of its being confounded with "Roberts," which he considered commonplace, to say the least. From him I also learn that Captain George RoBards of the Revolutionary army was a son of Elizabeth Lewis RoBards, and was his grandfather. He also says that his grandmother was Elizabeth Barbour Sampson, daughter of Anne Sampson, so that it appears that Captain George RoBards of the Revolutionary army, married Elizabeth Barbour Sampson, and that all through this remarkable family, the most conclusive proof of the highest family alliances are to be found.

EXITUS ACTA PROBAT

George Washington

READE, WARNER, WASHINGTON.

The three names which head this page are taken up at this point in connection with the Lewis family of Warner Hall because of their intimate association with that family, and a short review of them is important to a better understanding of these associations.

The first clue to the English ancestry of George Reade was the fact, shown by several letters in the first volume, English Calendar Colonial State papers, that he had a brother, Robert Reade, who was private secretary to Sir Francis Windebank, secretary of State during the reign of Charles the first; from which it was ascertained that George Reade was a descendant of the Reades of Facombe in the county of Southampton.

Andrew Reade of Facombe married Miss ——— Cook and had five sons; Henry, Robert, George, John, and Andrew, and four daughters, names not given.

Robert Reade, the second son of Andrew Reade and Miss Cook who lived at Lenkenholdt, married three times. His third wife was Mildred, daughter of Sir Thomas Windebank, of "Haines Hill," Parish of Hurst, Berkshire, who was clerk of the signet of Elizabeth and James.

George Reade, as is seen, was a grandson of Andrew Reade and Miss Cook and son of Robert Reade and Mildred Windebank. The will of Andrew Reade, grandfather of George Reade, bears date October 2, 1619, with a codicil November 15, 1621, and was proved October 24, 1623.

Robert Reade and Mildred Windeband had five sons: Andrew, William, Dr. Thomas, Robert who was secretary to his uncle, Sir Francis Windebank, and George who came to Virginia in 1637. Robert Reade's will was dated September 23, 1626.

George came to Virginia in 1637, and is mentioned several times in vol. 1, Calendar of Colonial State papers. He was a

friend and adherent of Governor Harvey and secretary Kemp.
Mr. Thomas M. Green of Danville, Kentucky, one of the best informed genealogists in the country, says of George Reade:
"Among others of the younger sons of the English nobility who
sought to improve their fortunes in the Colony of Virginia, was
George Reade whose sole importance to history consisted in the
fact that he was probably the first ancestor of General Washington who ventured to cross the Atlantic, and that it was from him
that the first and greatest of Americans derived his given name.
This George Reade was brother to Robert Reade who was private
secretary to Sir Francis Windebank, secretary of State to the
first Charles of England. The fact appears from letters written to him by Edward Norgate, dated from the king's army at
Berwick, May 29, 1639, and published in the 'Life and Times
of Charles the first,' and from several letters to him in Sarns-
burg's Calendar of State papers, 1654-1660.

The exact year of Reade's departure from England is not
known, but letters written by him in 1637 state that he was still
at the governor's house, and that he had received many favors
from him, from which it is clear that he had been in America
some time previous to that. The governor referred to was John
Harvey, and while Harvey's secretary (Richard Kemp) was absent in England, Reade was secretary of the Colony. And Harvey, either having been called to England or finding it to his
interest to go without being called, went to England before
Kemp's return; and, hence, during this interregnum, so to speak,
Reade was acting governor of the colony and whether appointed
by the Crown or not, he was recognised for the time. The histories of the times, loosely thrown together make no mention of
Reade, but the data is amply sustained by the records and borne
out by Hennings Statutes at large. George Reade was member
of The House of Burgesses from James City county, 1649, and
for York 1656, and member of King's Council from 1657 to
1671, or until his death. (Hennings Statutes at Large, vol. 1,
pp. 358, 414, 421, 429, 432. He married Elizabeth Martian
(pronounced Marchen), daughter of Captain Nicholas Martian,

and had five children, four sons and one daughter: Robert Reade, Benjamin Reade, Francis Reade, Thomas Reade married Lucy Gwynn, Mildred Reade married Speaker Augustine Warner. George Reade, as has been seen, died in 1671 and his will was admitted to record at Yorktown in November of the same year.

Thomas Reade, youngest son of George Reade, married Lucy Gwynn, granddaughter of Col. Hugh Gwynn, left a large family of children, only six, however of whom are known to history: Col. Clement Reade, born January 1707; Thomas Reade, born 1697 died 1739; John Reade, born at Munster, in King and Queen; Lucy Reade, born 1701, married John Dixon; Mildred Reade, married Major Phillip Roots; Mary Reade married Mordica Throckmorton.

Colonel Clement Reade, or Read was born in Virginia, January 1, 1707. Was left an orphan before he was twelve years of age. John Robinson of King and Queen county, known as "President" Robinson, was his guardian and superintended his education, which was completed at William and Mary College, Williamsburg, Virginia. He was given a legal education and qualified as an attorney in Brunswick, Goochland and Albemarle counties. On May 5, 1746, he was appointed clerk of Lunenberg county. The county had just been formed and he was the first clerk, which office he held until his death, seventeen years later. He was a member of the House of Burgesses from 1748 to 1758. He married Mary Hill, daughter of Wm. Hill and granddaughter of Governor Edmund Jennings, and they had eight children; five sons and three daughters. His eldest son Clement, Jr., was born in 1736. He married 1757, Mary Nash, eldest daughter of Judge John Nash, who was chairman of the Safety Committee.

Clement Read, Jr., and his wife, Mary Nash, had five children—Clement, who was a lieutenant in the Revolutionary Army, died in Richmond, Virginia, at the age of 21 years; Mary, who married Robert Bedford, moved west and died in 1803. John Nash who served under General Green at Guilford

Court House, Cowpens, etc, married three times—his first wife, Elizabeth Julia Spencer, first cousin to President Jefferson, eldest daughter of Sion and Mary Spencer. By this marriage he had twelve children, nine of whom died early in life. His son, Sion Spencer, married 1819, Hardenia Spencer and had eight children, four of whom died without issue. His daughter Laura married Harrison Barksdale of Yazoo City, Mississippi, and had a large family. His son, John Thomas, married Laurena Caroline Rankin, daughter of David Rankin of Jasper, Tennessee, and had five children: Laura, who married Samuel McCall and had one son, Alpheus Wright; Mary, who married W. W. Frater and had four children—Mary, Caroline, Hannah and Elizabeth; Hallie, married Rev. H. H. Sneed and had John, Nellie, Samuel, Carrie, Harrison, William and Robert; Samuel Robertson of Chattanooga, Tennessee, married Lizzie H. Sims and had four children—Mary Hill, Elizabeth Nash, Margaret and Sims: Carrie Rankin, married Letcher Pickens and had John and Henry.

Harriet, daughter of Sion Spencer Read, married Samuel Pennybaker and had several children.

Dr. Cronin Read, son of Sion Spencer Read, married Ada Sally and had John and Eulerah. Is now living in Arkansas.

Dr. Thomas Hill Read, son of Sion and Mary Read, married a Miss Allen of Decatur, Illinois, and had two sons and five daughters.

Elizabeth Julia, daughter of Sion and Mary Read, married David E. Allen and left one daughter, Laura, now living in Chicago.

John Nash Read, by his second marriage (Elizabeth Fisher Nash), had two children, one of whom died early and the other, James Allen, married a Miss Lannon and had nine children.

John Nash Read married, for his third wife, Mary Barksdale and had ten children the greater number of whom died early in life. One son, Nathaniel Barksdale, married Margaret Jane Bryan and had a son, Edwin Randolph, now living in Texas, who married and had a large family.

LEWIS AND KINDRED FAMILIES.

Col. Clement Read's second son, Thomas, married Elisabeth Nash, and they had a daughter, Peggy, who died about the year 1815, unmarried. A third son, Isaac, married Sarah Embrey. This son, Isaac Read, built a home in Charlotte county, Virginia, and called it "Greenfield." He was a colonel in the Revolutionary War. They had three children, Clement, Priscilla and Isaac. Clement was a minister, married a Miss Edmunds and they had eleven children; Priscilla married Captain Charles Scott and had eight children; Isaac, the youngest son, married Anna Mayo Venable and had nine children.

Edmund, the fourth son of Col. Clement Read, was a major in the Revolutionary War and married, first, a Miss Lewis, and second, a Miss Cabel. He died without issue.

Jonathan, the fifth son of Col. Clement Read, married Miss Jane Lewis daughter of John Lewis and Jane Meriwether Lewis of Warner Hall and left a large family in Virginia.

Margaret, the eldest daughter of Col. Clement Read, married Judge Paul Carrington and left a large family. Mary, second daughter, married Thomas Nash; Annie, third daughter, married, first a Mr. Jamieson, and second, Richard Elliott.

It is claimed however by the best genealogical authority, including Dr. Lyon G. Tyler, editor of William and Mary Quarterly, that Col. Clement Reade, first Clerk of Lunenburg county, Virginia, born 1707 was a son of this Thomas Reade. Mr Thomas M. Green says of the three other sons of George Reade, of whom less is known than of Thomas, that they were of local prominence, and their descendants numerous and noteworthy. He says that Benjamin owned the land on which the Assembly in 1601, ordered the town of York to be built, and that his sons were conspicuous in church matters in Gloucester county.

Scotch Tom Nelson, the first of that name so celebrated and so highly honored in Virginia, married a lady of this family and name. But it is with the daughter of George Reade, Mildred by name, who married Augustine Warner, that this sketch has to do, that is to say, with her descendants more especially.

Augustine Warner of Gloucester county, who married Mildred Reade, was a son of Captain Augustine Warner of the English army, whose name first appears on the Virginia records, in connection with that of Mary, his wife, as entering a tract of 2,500 acres of land about the branches of old Chesscaketown, South side of Pianketank river, October 26, 1652. They had however, lived in Virginia some years previous to that time, as the young Augustine Warner was born in Virginia 1642. It was a fashion as well as a necessity with the wealthier Virginians to send their oldest sons to England to be educated, and thither went the younger Augustine Warner, who, in 1657, was entered on the books of the Merchant Tailors School, London, as Augustine, eldest son of Augustine Warner, gentlemen, born in Virginia, October 20, 1642. Matriculating at Cambridge and returning to Virginia, he was elected to the House of Burgesses from Gloucester as early as 1666, whence he passed to the Royal Council under Sir Wm. Berkley in 1676. He was Speaker of the House of Burgesses, of the assembly which had succeeded the one that had been in existence from 1666 to 1676 which Berkley was forced, by Bacon's Rebellion, to dissolve, and to issue writs for a new election. It was at the bar of the assembly presided over by this Augustine Warner that Bacon knelt, confessing himself "guilty of unlawful and mutinous practices, and promised, if pardoned, to demean himself dutifully, faithfully and peaceably." The military title of Augustine Warner, was, "Colonel Commanding the Militia of Gloucester," but he is better known in history as "Speaker Augustine Warner," from the fact that he was so long speaker of the House of Burgesses.

Col (or Speaker) Augustine Warner and Mildred Reade had three sons and three daughters. None of the sons ever married. The daughters, Mildred, Mary and Elisabeth, married respectively Lawrence Washington, John Smith "of Purton," and Councilor John Lewis, who was the son of John Lewis and Isabella Warner and the grandson of General Robert Lewis of Brecon, Wales. These were the immediate ancestors of the Lewis family of Warner Hall, and their three sons, John of Warner Hall, Charles of the Byrd, and Robert of Belvoir, were the respective heads of that numerous family which now numbers many hundreds and are scattered over many States. The descendants of Elizabeth Warner Lewis, or at least many of them, will be found in this book under the three respective heads mentioned above.

Mildred, oldest daughter of Speaker Augustine Warner, as seen above, married Lawrence Washington and hence was the ancestor of General George Washington and others of that distinguished family.

Later than George Reade and Captain Warner there came to Virginia two brothers, John and Lawrence Washington. They were sturdy Royalists, men of education, fair estates, and excellent social connections in England. This was about 1657. At the date of the emigration they were men of middle age and both widowers, Lawrence, having a daughter who had married in England. By his will, February 26, 1675, and proved January 10, 1677, Lawrence Washington bequeathed his whole estate in England to his daughter, Mary, she being the child of the first wife that he had buried there, while to his American wife, and to John and Ann, his children by her, he left all the handsome property he had accumulated in Virginia.

Henceforth, all that can be traced to this Lawrence Washington directly, disappears from history. Yet General Washington, in his letter to Sir Isaac Heard, states that his descendants were numerous.

From this Lawrence Washington came Bailey Washington, whose son was the gallant cavalry officer of the Revolution, Col. Wm. Washington and probably Robert and Lawrence of Chatanck Stafford, whom the General mentions in his will, without claiming them as relatives, as "friends of his juvenile days," and also many other Washingtons in Virginia and elsewhere, who assert their relationship to the General without being able to trace it.

Far more conspicuous, however, in every respect was the other brother, John Washington, for whom the Parish in Westmoreland, in which he lived, was named. His military talents entitled him to the command of all the forces of the "Northern Neck." His successful campaign against the Indians in Maryland and elsewhere, culminated in the murder of the Chiefs of the Saranacs, after they had surrendered and led to reprisals for which Bacon marched against the hostile Indians, contrary to Berkley's command, and thus inaugurated Bacon's rebellion. As Burgess and Magistrate for the county, standing high in the confidence of Berkley in the suppression of this rebellion, in which he took an active part, Col. John Washington became prominent in all public affairs, and amid the universal complaint, "the happy land of Westmoreland" alone reported to the king's commissioners, that it had no grievances to be redressed.

In Virginia Col. Washington did not fail to add largely to the patrimony he had left in England. A widower, he took unto himself a second wife in the person of Ann Pope, the daughter of a wealthy planter, and sister of Thomas Pope, from whom the celebrated John Pope, territorial Governor of Arkansas, and his namesake nephew, who lost the second battle of Manassas, descended. By this marriage he gained the handsome property on which they lived, between Brydges and Pope's Creek, near the Potomac. They had three children, Lawrence, John and Ann, among whom, by his will, proved on the 6th of January, 1677. his property in England as well as in Virginia, was divided, the homestead on Bridges falling to the portion of Lawrence.

The second son, John married and had many children, but the maiden name of his wife is unknown. Among the children was Mildred, who married a gentleman named Brown, and after his death became the wife of Col. Henry Willis, the founder of Fredericksburg. This is the Mildred Washington concerning whom Mr. M. D. Conway is in so much doubt as to her identity and relationship to the other Washington. Mr. Thomas M. Green from whom the main facts of this sketch has been obtained says this Mildred Washington was the Mother of Mary Willis who married Captain Hancock Lee, and also of the wife of Howell Lewis, but as "Old Henry Willis" had three wives (as good authority as Mr. Green undoubtedly is), it would be difficult to settle, with any degree of certainty the maternity of two children whose births were twenty years apart. The wife of Hancock Lee was born 1716 and the wife of Howell Lewis about 1736, and in that interval Col. Willis no doubt married once or twice. He had three wives in rapid succession.

Lawrence Washington, son of John Washington and Ann Pope as has been seen, married Mildred Warner, the oldest daughter of Speaker Augustine Warner and Mildred Reade. He was born at King, England, baptised, June 23, 1635. As he was cotemporaneous with Councilor John Lewis, who married a younger sister of Mildred, the approximate date of Lawrence Washington's marriage may be safely placed at 1660. Not much is to be learned from the records concerning this Lawrence Washington. That he was a Burgess, a magistrate by a sort of hereditary right, a "Colonel" and a prominent man in Episcopal vestries, is nearly all that is known.

In the more peaceful times that followed Bacon's rebellion less opportunity was afforded Lawrence Washington for improving himself upon his generation, than fell to the lot of his father, "The sturdy Col. John." Inheriting the larger share of the paternal estate in England and Virginia, dispensing a liberal hospitality, albeit, a trifle pompous, after the manner of educated and wealthy Virginia planters of the day, a devout believer in the Apostolic succession and a sturdy Royalist, not failing to add to his acres and increase his stores: This is about all that one can learn or imagine of Lawrence Washington. He died 1697 and was interred in the family vault near the Potomac. His widow married a second time, George Gale, but nothing is known of her second marriage after it occurred; the records are silent.

Lawrence and Mildred (Warner) Washington had three children: John, Mildred, and Augustine.

John Washington, oldest son of Lawrence Washington and Mildred Warner, and the third in this line of the name in Virginia, married Catherine Whiting, a wealthy heiress of Gloucester county, Virginia, and his daughter Catherine was the first wife of Fielding Lewis of Fredricksburg; and the descendants of this marriage, and other children of John Washington, have intermarried with the Nelsons, Fairfaxes, Throckmortons, and others of the "Northern Neck."

Augustine Washington, second son of Lawrence Washington and Mildred Warner was born 1694 and died 1743, at the age of 49. He married first Jane Butler, of Westmoreland, and second, Mary Ball, "Belle of Lancaster." In both marriages he exhibited the family characteristic of seeking good alliances. Prudent, industrious, energetic, and conservative, punctual, discreet and decided, he was a man of mark in the colony. A burgess, a magistrate, a zealous churchman, fond of company, and maintaining the state that belonged to his degree; in his social relation, aristocratic in a quaint way, and yet Augustine Washington was a lover of liberty. His second wife, Mary Ball, was the granddaughter of Col. Wm. Ball, whose rank entitled him to armorial bearings. This Col. Wm. Ball settled at the mouth of Corotoman river in 1650, and died in 1669, leaving two sons, Wm. and Joseph; the latter being the father of Mary, before named, the wife of Augustine Washington.

According to Mr. Paxton, Augustine Washington had four children by his first marriage with Jane Butler, but he does not give their names. By his second marriage with Mary Ball he had several children, General George Washington and other sons, but only one daughter, Bettie, who became the second wife of Fielding Lewis.

It is not the purpose of this sketch to give a history of the Washington family, for that would be foreign to the scope of this work. Nor is it intended to give their genealogy, as that would involve more space than is allotted to us. Their history belongs to the country, and their genealogy would require a separate work.

It is only because of the association of the name with the Lewis family and others connected with them that the Washington name has been brought in.

Bettie Washington, as has been seen, was the second wife of Col. Fielding Lewis of Fredricksburg, his first wife having been

Catherine, daughter of Col. John Washington, and first cousin of Bettie; and it may be added that Col. Lewis was second cousin to both of his wives.

General George Washington, son of Augustine Washington and Mary Ball, is too well known to history to have any thing more than a passing notice here. He married the widow Custis, nee Martha Dandridge, one of whose sisters was the wife of Col· Burwell Bassett, and was the ancestress of Delia Claiborne, the beautiful and accomplished young wife of Simon Bolivar Buckner of Kentucky, one of the leading generals of the Confederate army, who has redeemed his promise to her that she should reside in the governor's mansion at Frankfort.

Mildred Washington, daughter of Lawrence Washington and Mildred Warner, and hence an aunt of General Washington, was born about 1696. The Rev. Phillip Slaughter, author of St. Marks Parish, is authority for the statement that the first husband of this Mildred Washington was a Lewis, one of the Warner Hall family, but General Washington does not mention this marriage in any of his letters to Sir Isaac Heard; and yet it is a fact that the name of Lewis obtains among her descendants, even with those who did not afterwards marry into that family. This fact would go far to confirm that statement.

Whether as the first or second husband, Mildred became the wife of Roger Gregory, one of the wealthiest land owners in the colony, by whom she had three daughters: Frances, Mildred and Elizabeth. These three daughters married three brothers, Col. Francis Thornton, Col. John Thornton and Reuben Thornton, all of Spottsylvania county and sons of Francis Thornton, an English emigrant.

Col. Francis Thornton, who married Frances Gregory, was the proprietor of "Fall Hill" near Fredricksburg where seven generations of the same name have lived in succession. Their daughter Mildred married Charles Washington, half-brother of the General. Col. Francis Thornton and Frances Gregory had several sons among whom were Col. William Thornton of Montpelier, and Col. John Thornton of the Revolution. The latter married Jane Washington, daughter of Augustine Washington, who was the eldest half-brother of the General.

Col. John Thornton, who married Mildred Gregory, had four daughters, Mildred, Mary, Elisabeth and Lucy.

Mildred Thornton became the second wife of Samuel Washington, brother of the General, and was the mother of Thornton Washington, from whom the Washingtons of Newport, Kentucky, are descended.

Mary Thornton married General Woodford of the Revolution and was the ancestor of the countless Woodfords and Buckners of central Kentucky.

Elisabeth Thornton married John Taliaferro of Dessington.

Lucy, daughter of Col. John Thornton was one of the five wives of John Lewis, son of Fielding Lewis and Catherine Washington.

About 1733, Mildred Washington, daughter of Lawrence and Mildred (Warner) Washington, who had been previously married twice, first to a Lewis, and second to Roger Gregory, became the third wife of Col. Henry Willis of Fredricksburg. Col. Willis had himself been previously married twice, one of his wives having also been Mildred Washington, daughter of John Washington and first cousin of this Mildred. Their residence was on the heights near Fredricksburg, now known historically as "Mayrees Heights."

At this point arises a very decided delemma as to the maternity of one of Col. Henry Willis' children, the wife of Howell Lewis. As has been seen, Col. Henry Willis was married three times. His first wife was Mildred, daughter of John Washington, his third was Mildred daughter of Lawrence Washington, who, as has been seen, had been twice married before. Mildred, daughter of John Washington, having been the first wife of Col. Henry Willis, she could not have been the mother of Howell Lewis' wife, as she was necessarily born within a short time of the third marriage, as her husband Howell Lewis was born in 1732. It is therefore impossible, in the absence of positive record proof to tell whether, Mary or Isabella Willis who married Howell Lewis, was the daughter of the second or third wife of Henry

Willis, as the death of the second wife, the birth of this daughter, and the third marriage, were so close together that nothing short of record proof could settle the question. It is more than probable that Howell Lewis' wife was the daughter of Henry Willis' third wife, as it is fair to conclude that she was younger than her husband, and hence born about 1734, which would make her descendants of the Washington line; but when it is remembered that she had a daughter married 1769, only 35 years after the date we give for her birth, there is rather a narrow margin left for the events which occurred.

Col. Lewis Willis, oldest child of Col. Henry Willis by his third wife, Mildred Washington, whose birth Mr. Green puts at 1734, married Mary, daughter of Col. John Champe, whose sister Jane was the wife of Samuel Washington—brother of the General.

Byrd Willis, son of Lewis Willis, married Mary Lewis, daughter of George Lewis and granddaughter of Fielding Lewis, and Bettie Washington.

Fannie Willis, daughter of Byrd Willis and Mary Lewis, became the wife of Achille Murat, son of Caroline Bonaparte, and Napoleon's great marshal of that name.

Col. Henry Willis and his third wife, Mildred Washington, had also a daughter, Ann, who married Duff Green. Their youngest son, William, was a soldier at fifteen with the army at Valley Forge. After the war he removed to Kentucky, married the daughter of Markham Marshall, and was the father of General Duff Green who was the editor of the old Washington Telegraph in the days of General Jackson.

Willis Green, oldest son of Duff Green and Ann Willis, emigrated to Kentucky in 1779, to pursue the vocation of surveyor, traveling the old wilderness road by Cumberland Gap marked out by Daniel Boone. In 1783, he married the oldest daughter of John Reed and resided several years in the fort built by his wife's father. When Kentucky was divided into three counties he was clerk of Lincoln, which county he represented in a number of conventions held for the purpose of separating from Virginia.

Lewis Warner Green, the eloquent divine, president of Hampden Sidney College, and afterwards of Center College, Kentucky, was the youngest son of Willis Green and Miss Reed. His oldest daughter was the accomplished wife of Mr. Scott of Bloomington, Illinois, and his youngest daughter was the wife of A. E. Stevenson, Vice-President of the United States during Cleveland's second administration.

Ann Willis Green followed her sons to Kentucky, lived with them for a time in Reeds Fort, and died in 1820 at Moreland, then the home of her grandson, Judge John Green. Her tombstone still stands in the old burying ground in Reeds Fort, near Danville, Kentucky.

By the intermarriage of the granddaughters of Mildred Washington by her marriage with Roger Gregory, and those of Henry Willis with the brothers of the General, and of the grandsons and great-grandsons, with his nieces and grand-nieces, the larger portion of the descendants of her brother Augustine are also her descendants.

Col. Fielding Lewis was nearly related, by a common descent from Col. George Reade and Speaker Augustine Warner, with both of his wives, Catherine and Bettie Washington, being related in the same degree to both of them—second cousin. His son Lawrence Lewis married Eleanor Custis, granddaughter of Mrs. Martha Washington. The daughter of Lawrence Lewis and Eleanor Custis married Col. E. G. W. Butler, and their son, Col. Lawrence Butler, of St. Louis unites in his person the blood of the Warners, Lewises, Washingtons, Custises and Dandridges. Not less distinguished is that of the race whose name he bears. So many of the name were officers in the war of 1812, that a British officer, who accidentally trod upon the foot of one of them at a military ball in New Orleans, apologized saying: "The Butlers are so numerous I cannot miss them."

It has been definitely ascertained that the first wife of Henry Willis was Mildred Washington, daughter of Col. John

Washington, who was the widow Brown at the time of her marriage to Col. Willis. "From whom Mr. Thomas M. Green informs us he descended." This last sentence in quotations, however, seems to be erroneous, as the name of Green is interwoven with the descendants of the third marriage. Mr. Green has, however, furnished unmistakable data in regard to the second wife of Col. Henry Willis. It transpires in recently discovered records that Mildred Willis, wife of Col. Henry Willis, and Mary Lewis, wife of "Charles Lewis of the Byrd," were residuary legatees in the will of John Howell; from which it would seem to follow necessarily that the second wife of Henry Willis was a daughter of John Howell, as it is a well known fact that the wife of Charles Lewis was Mary Howell, and hence it follows that the second wife of Henry Willis was Mildred Howell and not Mildred Washington.

JOHN LEWIS OF DONEGAL.

Although others of this name had preceded "Irish John" nearly one hundred years and were identified with the settlement and growth of the country and distinguished in colonial history, yet he was pre-eminently fitted for the niche which he filled in the development of frontier life and in shaping the destiny of a new country. Plunging, as it were, from the start into the midst of a dense and unexplored forest, where the foot of the white man had rarely ever trod and through which a savage foe roamed at will, it matters not how long he had been preceded by others of this or any other name in other sections of the state, he was emphatically the pioneer of Augusta county, which at that time embraced the greater part of Northwest Virginia.

Whatever may be said about the identity of the different branches of the Lewis family at some anterior date, there is a striking contrast in the surroundings of the Warner Hall family and the subject of our sketch, at the time the respective heads came to America. General Robert Lewis was an officer in the English army, and to say nothing of his English holdings, he brought with him a grant from the crown for 33,333 1-3 acres of land, while John Lewis of Donegal was clearly not a landholder, but in consequence of having to slay his Irish landlord, was compelled to flee the country. Notwithstanding this contrast, true to the traditions of the name, he proved himself equal to his surroundings in his new home, too far removed from royalty to be any longer the victim of tyranny.

John Lewis and his wife, Margaret Lynn, and six children, came to Virginia, 1732 and settled in Augusta county where the town of Staunton now stands, of which he was the founder.

JOHN LEWIS OF AUGUSTA COUNTY.

Irish John Lewis, as he was best known was one of the first and most distinguished pioneers of the valley of Virginia. He

was one of the first settlers of Augusta county and indeed founder of the town of Staunton. A marble slab in the cemetery at
that place, beneath which rests his remains, tells of his parentage
and birthplace, as well as the date of his death and his age. The
inscription reads:

> "John Lewis was the son of Andrew
> Lewis and Mary Calahan. Born in Donegal
> county, Ireland, 1678. Died in Augusta
> county, Virginia, February 1, 1762, in the
> 84th year of his age."

He married Margaret Lynn, who, tradition says, was the
daughter of a Scotch Laird, and to this marriage was born seven
children, all of whom, except one, was born in Ireland:

Samuel Lewis, son of John Lewis and Margaret Lynn was
born in Ireland, 1716.

Thomas, born in Ireland, 1718, married Jane Strother.

General Andrew Lewis, born in Ireland, 1720, married
Elizabeth Givens.

Col. Wm. Lewis, born in Ireland, 1724, married Ann Montgomery.

Margaret, born in 1726, died unmarried.

Ann, born in Ireland, 1728, died unmarried.

Col. Charles Lewis, born in Virginia, 1736, married Sarah
Murray.

It is not known, as matter of record, that there was any
connection between Irish John Lewis and the other Virginia families of that name, but the members always claimed relationship,
and Robert Lewis of Belvoir mentions large business transactions with Mr. John Lewis of Augusta, in his will.

After the departure of John Lewis from Ireland, on account
of having slain his Irish landlord, he is said to have sojourned
for a few years in Portugal before coming to America, coming
first to Pennsylvania, where he remained but a short time, and
in 1732 he came to Virginia. An unbroken forest lay out be-

fore our frontiersman, predatory bands of Indians roamed the woods without hindrance, and the shrieks of a savage foe, as from time to time they rang out upon the air, was all that there was to break the monotony of the surroundings. His house was a military fortress of the backwoods, an arsenal supplied with the means of defense against a merciless foe, with portholes on every side from which to meet the attacks of the enemy. And thus it is that Irish John Lewis and his five sons planted a colony of their own in the Western wilderness, carved out of the forest both fame and fortune for themselves and posterity, and established beyond the Blueridge a distinct branch of the Lewis family.

Distinct and disconnected as this may seem to have been at first, however, as will be seen from the pages further on, the intermarriages between their posterity and the posterity of the other branches have been so numerous that they have, to a great extent, merged into each other.

2. Samuel Lewis oldest son of John Lewis and Margaret Lynn, born 1716, died unmarried. He was a captain in the old French War. His brothers, Andrew, William, and Charles were members of his company, and all three were wounded at Braddock's defeat.

2. Thomas Lewis, second son of John Lewis and Margaret Lynn, was born 1718. He married Jane, daughter of William Strother of Stafford county, Virginia, in 1749, and had thirteen children: First John, born 1749, died single; second Margaret Ann, born 1751, married first, a Mr. McClanahan, second Wm. Bowyer; third Agatha, born 1753, married first, Captain John Frogg, and second, John Stuart; fourth Jane, born 1755, married Thomas Hughes; fifth Andrew, sixth Thomas, both died young; seventh Mary, born 1762, married John McElhany; eight Elizabeth, born 1765, married Thomas M. Gilmer, and was the mother of George Rockingham Gilmer who was twice governor of Georgia, and many years a member of Congress from that state; ninth Ann, born 1767, married first, A. M. Douthat, second, Mr. French; tenth Frances, born 1769, married Layton Yancy; eleven

Charles, born 1772, married Miss Yancy; twelve Sophia, born 1775, married John Cathrae; thirteen Wm. Benjamin, born 1778, married Miss M. Hite.

Thomas Lewis was surveyor of Augusta county, Virginia. Was a member of the House of Burgesses, was a member of the Virginia convention of 1776, and was one of the commissioners of Confederation of 1777 to treat with the Indian tribes who had been defeated at the battle of Point Pleasant.

Of the foregoing sons of Thomas Lewis, all except the two youngest, were officers in the Revolutionary army. John, Andrew and Thomas, Jr., were with Washington through his most important campaigns and are frequently mentioned in his reports, and John and Thomas were at the surrender of Cornwallis. Captain McClanahan, first husband of Margaret Lewis and Captain Frogg, first husband of Agatha Lewis, were both killed at the battle of Point Pleasant.

General Andrew Lewis, third son of John Lewis and Margaret Lynn, was born in Ireland 1720 and came with his parents to America in 1732.

It will be seen from the foregoing dates that Andrew Lewis entered upon frontier life at the age of twelve and for more than forty years was engaged in a ceaseless struggle, a warfare that was as incessant and of longer duration than the "War of the Roses." The first twenty years of the active life of Andrew Lewis was mainly spent in defending his father's home, his mother and sisters from the predatory attack of the savages, and extending the same aid to other frontier settlements; and then in the service of his country, still under the English dominion, in the numerous Indian wars, and the old French war; and lastly as an officer in the patriot army, in the war for Independence.

It is not claimed that there was any formidable contest in the Continental Congress for commander in chief of the American armies, nor would any one underrate either the military ability or prestige of General Washington, but it is an historical fact that many of the members (John Adams at their head), were favorable to General Lewis for that position. The long military service of Lewis, culminating as it had done in the great victory of Point Pleasant over the combined tribes of northwestern Indians, led on by British influence in 1774, marked him as a leader eminently fit to take charge of the armies; but there was no discount on the record of Washington, and with the political influence of the East Virginia Lewises, Mr. Jefferson and the Lees, with all of whom he was allied by blood or marriage, it was not difficult to forecast in advance and plainly see upon whom the lot would fall. On the other hand, General Lewis was nearing sixty and already broken down in health, while Washington was only a little the rise of forty and in the full vigor of manhood.

From Lippencott's "Gilmers Georgians," and the "History of Augusta County, Virginia, by J. L. Peyton, the following extracts are taken:

"General Andrew Lewis was engaged in all of the Indian wars down to the Revolution, participated in the war of 1755 between France and Great Britain, was an officer at the battle of Fort Du Quesne, or Braddock's defeat, and was the commanding general of the Virginia troops at the battle of Point Pleasant on the 10th of October, 1774. In 1774 he was a member of Virginia Assembly, and was a member of the Committee, together with Patrick Henry, Richard Henry Lee, George Washington, and Thomas Jefferson, appointed to prepare a plan of defense. An Indian war being apprehended, Governor Dunmore appointed General Andrew Lewis of Botetourt county, then a member of the assembly, to the command of the Southern Division of the forces raised in Botetourt, Augusta, and the adjoining counties east of the Blue Ridge. The troops rendezvoused at Camp Union, now Lewisburg, in Greenbriar county, Virginia.

"On the 11th of September, 1774, General Lewis with eleven hundred men took up his line of march through the wilderness, and after a march of one hundred and fifty miles, on the 30th of September, they reached Point Pleasant at the junction of the great Kanawha and the Ohio, where on the 10th of October the battle was fought and the victory won.

"His first important service after the commencement of the

Revolution was to drive the Scotch Governor Dunmore, and his Tory adherents from the State of Virginia.

"General Washington, with whom Lewis had been at Fort Necessity, and under whom he had served in various capacities, had formed a very high estimate of his ability and character, and in a letter under date of October 15, 1778, in respect to his services, remarks: 'If Congress is not convinced of the impropriety of a certain irregular promotion, they are the only set of men that require additional proof of the error of their measure.'

General Lewis' services, after driving Dunmore from the State, were confined principally to the defense of the country bordering on the Chesapeake Bay. His iron constitution, however, having given way to the strain of long military services, having been constantly at the front and in the saddle for more than forty years, he resigned his commission in 1778, and set out for home, but died on his way before reaching it, in Bedford county, Virginia.

"In the beautiful valley of the Roanoke river, then Botetourt, but now Roanoke county, Virginia, a few miles west of where the town of Salem now stands, was the home of General Andrew Lewis, and there his remains still rest, marked by a simple marble slab."

2 General Lewis married Miss Elizabeth Givens of Augusta county, Virginia, in 1749, and had issue as follows:

    3 ¹Captain John Lewis married Patsy Love of Alexandria.

    3 ²Thomas married Miss Evans of Point Pleasant.

    3 ³Col. Samuel of the United States army died in Greenbriar county, unmarried.

    3 ⁴Col. Andrew of the United States army resided at Bent Mountain, Virginia, born 1759; married Eliza, daughter of John Madison, Montgomery county, Virginia; died 1844.

    3 ⁵Annie married Rowland, son of John Madison.

    3 ⁶William, born 1764, married Lucy, daughter of John Madison; he married second, Nancy McClanahan.

3 Captain John Lewis, oldest son of General Andrew Lewis was
an officer in his father's command at Braddock's defeat
where he was taken prisoner and carried to Quebec, thence
to France. The following are his children: Andrew, Samuel,
Charles, and Elizabeth.

   4 ²Samuel Lewis, second son Captain John Lewis and Patsy Love, married Miss Whitley.

   4 ³Charles Lewis, third son of Captain John Lewis and
Patsy Love, married a daughter of General Abraham
Trigg of Virginia.

   4 ⁴Elizabeth Lewis, daughter of Captain John Lewis and
Patsy Love, married three times, first, a Mr. Luke,
second, a Mr. Ball, and third, a Mr. Alexander Marshall. Issue: Jane married Charles T. Marshall.

3 Wm. Lewis, son of General Andrew Lewis, had eleven chil-
dren: Andrew, Agatha, Sallie, Bettie, Lucy, Wm. Lewis,
Jr., General John W. Lewis, Dr. Charles Lewis, Ann, Mary
Jane, Pauline.

   4 Sallie Lewis married Mr. Fleming and died in Huntsville,
Alabama, in 1865.

   4 Bettie married Mr. Beale, whose daughter married a Mr.
Norville of Huntsville, Alabama.

   4 Lucy married John Bowyer of Fincastle, Virginia.

   4 William Lewis, Jr., died in Mississippi, leaving nine children.

   4 General John Lewis married Susan Bowyer in 1831 and
moved to Alabama. He lost two sons in the war between the States, 1861-5. General Lewis was a man
of considerable ability. He was a member of the Legislature of Alabama and general of Militia. He moved
to Texas in 1842.

   4 Dr. Charles Lewis was killed in a rencounter in the
streets of Mobile.

   4 Ann married a Mr. Bradly and in 1873 lived in San
Antonio, Texas.

134

4 Pauline, married a Mr. Christian and died in Tuscumbia, Alabama, in 1876.

2 Col. Wm. Lewis, fourth son of Irish John Lewis of Augusta county, Virginia, born in Ireland in 1724, married Ann Montgomery and left eight children: Margaret, born 1756; John, born 1758; Thomas, born 1761; Alexander, born 1763: William I., born 1766; Agatha, born 1774; Elizabeth Montgomery, born 1777; Charles W., born 1780. Colonel Lewis was an officer under General Braddock and was wounded at his defeat. He was an elder in the Presbyterian church, and known as "Civiliser of the border." Governor Gilmer says of him: "Though as powerful in person and as brave in spirit as his brother, Andrew, he was less disposed to seek fame by the sacrifice of human life." He resided at the "Old Sweet," which property he owned, and which was one of the most celebrated watering places of the mountains of Virginia.

Of the children of Colonel Wm. Lewis, we will mention briefly, John, William I., and Elizabeth Montgomery. For a more complete history of this family, whose name is legion, the reader is referred to Peyton's history of Augusta county, Virginia.

3 John Lewis, oldest son of Colonel Wm. Lewis, born 1758. He married first a daughter of Colonel Wm. Thomson of South Carolina, 1788, by whom he had two children, second, Mary Preston, daughter of Colonel Wm. Preston of Montgomery county, Virginia, 1793, by whom he had ten children. Miss Preston was a sister of Governor Preston and aunt of Governor McDowell of Virginia. Major Lewis resided at the "Old Sweet" Springs, the home of his father, where he died, 1823. The names of Major Lewis' children by both wives follow: Eugenia Ann, born 1789; Sophia, born 1790; Susannah Preston, born 1794; Mary, born 1795; Wm. Lynn, born 1799; John, born 1801; Ann Montgomery, born 1802; Sarah Elizabeth, born 1806; Margaret Lynn, born 1808; John Benjamin, born 1810; Thomas Preston, born 1812; Polly Dora, born 1817.

3 John Lewis entered the Continental Army, at the age of eighteen as lieutenant and came out with the rank of major. He passed the winter at Valley Forge with Washington in 1777, between whom a warm personal friendship existed; and Governor Gilmer says that he threw down and out-jumped General Jackson until the future hero of New Orleans had the greatest admiration for him.

Ann Montgomery Lewis, daughter of Major John Lewis and Mary Preston, married the Honorable John Howe Peyton of Augusta county, Virginia, 1821, and left issue.

3 Colonel Wm. I. Lewis, son of Colonel Wm. Lewis and Ann Montgomery, born 1766, died 1828. He married Elizabeth Cabell of Nelson county, Virginia, but left no issue. Colonel Lewis was a man remarkable for his talents and acquirements, fond of literary pursuits and a student of history, and being possessed of ample fortune, he had every means at his command for gratifying his bent of mind. His residence, seven miles east of Lynchburg, Virginia, on James river, was situated on the top of Mt. Athos overlooking that stream, at the foot of which, and in the bend of the river lay one of the most princely estates in eastern Virginia. He and his wife are buried on the top of this mountain five hundred feet above the river. He was elected to Congress one term, 1815-1817, and was defeated for governor by one vote, at a time when the governors were elected by the Legislature. Colonel Lewis bequeathed his entire estate to his niece, Ann Trent, who married Judge John Robertson of Richmond, Virginia.

3 Elizabeth Montgomery Lewis, daughter of Colonel William Lewis of Sweet Springs and Ann Montgomery, his wife, born 1777, married Colonel John Trent of Cumberland county, Virginia, and had three children: Eliza Trent, Ann Trent, and John Trent, M. D.

4 Ann Trent married Judge John Robertson of Richmond, Virginia, and, as before stated, became the heiress of her uncle, Wm. I. Lewis, and succeeded to the Mt. Athos property.

Judge Robertson was perhaps one of the most unique characters of his age and generation. A lineal descendant of the Princess Pocahontas, he possessed to a wonderful degree all of the peculiarities for which her descendants are remarkable, gifted, brilliant and eccentric. He was also a man of learning and a lawyer of rare attainments who ranked among the brightest lights of the profession. He was elected to Congress one term, but he was a man of too much independence of thought to be confined within party lines, and he never pursued politics. He was appointed judge of the chancery court of Richmond when that court was first created by the Legislature in the early forties, which position he held until that court was abolished by the Constitution of 1851. It was the writer's rare good fortune to have been thrown much with Judge Robertson when quite young, as his vacations were always spent at his Mt. Athos home which adjoined my mother's plantation. When Mr. Lincoln was elected in 1860 his anticipations in regard to the future of parties and the country were prophetic. In a series of letters written for the Richmond Enquirer in November and December of that year he foreshadowed coming events with almost mathematical precision. He declared that after March 4, 1861, and so long as the Black Republican party was in power, their platform would be the Constitution of the United States. And in reference to the campaign speech of Wm. H. Seward, delivered at Rochester, New York, in which Seward declared that slavery "Must and shall be abolished," he said: "Slavery, like all things else human, will have an end, but if that end is brought about in the way indicated by Mr. Seward, it will be when the Potomac becomes a sea of blood and its departed waves give way for the passage of the enemies of God and man." Judge Robertson spent the remainder of his life after the war an unreconstructed rebel, constantly refusing to avail himself of any of the supposed benefits of amnesty, holding that as he had done nothing for which pardon should be asked, it would be inconsistent to accept forgiveness. His exact age at the time of his death is not known, but it is certain that he was over eighty. He died in 1870.

The children of Ann Lewis Trent by her marriage with Judge Robertson were:

5 [1] Powhattan, married and has issue. Resides in Culpepper county, Virginia.
5 [2] Elizabeth, married a gentleman by the name of Barksdale of Richmond, he belonged to the numerous family of that name who were engaged in the manufacture of flour and owned the most extensive mills of Richmond. They left issue.
5 [3] Boling, never married.
5 [4] Ann, and [5] Gay, the two youngest, both died young.

2 Colonel Charles Lewis, youngest son of Irish John Lewis, was killed at the battle of Point Pleasant, October 10, 1774. He was a favorite in the army and one of the most skillful officers in border warfare. He married Miss Murray of Bath county, Virginia, and left issue.

DU BREUIL.

Among the many hundred names who protested against the errors and crimes of Rome, and alligned themselves under the banner of Protestantism, none were more conspicuous than that of du Breuil; and of those who shared the fortunes of "Harry of Navarre" and followed the black plume in the thickest of the conflict, none were more constant in their devotion, or more daring in their deeds; but unlike Harry none of them ever swerved from that devotion, either from fear of assassination or in the hope of wearing a crown.

A Frenchman never does anything by halves, and when he once entered the Protestant ranks, he espoused the cause with his whole soul. Never in the history of the world were such religious persecutions known as those waged against the French Huguenots, but in spite of all the powers of Rome, French Protestantism went steadily on, and when at last its followers were compelled to flee for their lives, France lost her best population; but French Protestantism was scattered throughout the civilised world.

Such having been the history of the French Huguenots in their native France, with more or less severity for more than a century, it is not strange that patriotism should have been one of their leading characteristics, and that they should have been the champions of human liberty wherever they went. The du Breuils were no exception to the rule.

The historian has been compelled to deal with this subject from a general standpoint. It has been impossible for him to even refer to the parts taken by individual participants; every Huguenot was himself a hero, and furnished abundant material for a volume. Biographers have commemorated the deeds of a few of the leaders, but it has been reserved for the genealogists, whose province it is to deal with individuals, to commemorate the heroism of the rank and file. By way of illustration we will mention the hairbreadth escape, after relentless pursuits, of one of those devoted heroes. Many, however, did not succeed in escaping, but were captured and suffered long terms of imprisonment, or were put to death. This is only a sample. They were pursued as felons, hunted as beasts of prey, and tortured, mentally and physically, as only a relentless priesthood could do.

From Bishop Meade's "Old Churches and Families" we make the following extract, from notes written at the base of the ancestral tree of the Dupuy family, volume 1, page 468:

"Bartholomew Dupuy, born 1653, entered the army at 18, and was promoted to an office at an early age. He was assigned to duty in the household of the king, in which capacity he was entrusted with orders bearing the signature of his sovereign.

"One of these papers was the means of saving this officer from arrest, and most probably from death. But a short time before the revocation of the edict of Nantes he married a countess, Susannah Lavillon, and retired to his villa for a short respite from his military duties. Very soon after his retirement they were called upon by one of the king's messengers who informed them of the revocation, and further that he had been sent by the king from motives of esteem, to save him and his wife from the impending fate, and urged their renunciation of the Protestant faith. Dupuy asked for a few hours for consideration. In the meantime he disguised his wife in the livery of a page, and mounting two horses started at midnight for the frontier of the kingdom. They traveled in this way 'fourteen or eighteen days' and although stopped almost daily, they always escaped by exhibiting the king's signature. Upon reaching the German border they sang the praise of God in the fourteenth Psalm, and offered up prayers and thanksgiving to their great deliverer for their escape from a cruel death. They remained in Germany fourteen years, then stayed two years in England, from whence they came to America in 1700, and settled in Manakintown, on James river, having been preceded by the du Breuils and other Huguenot settlers, ten years previously.

190

LEWIS AND KINDRED FAMILIES.

So far as is known this was the only family of du Breuils among the Huguenot settlers; indeed the proofs are conclusive, as the name of du Breuil is extinct, and the name of Dibrell, which took its place, is confined to the descendants of the only son of Dr. Christopher du Bruil of France, but more recently of Manakintown.

DR. CHRISTOPHER DU BREUIL.

(Pronounced "du Bray.")

Of this great ancestor of the Dibrell family, very little is known. It is known, however, from the records, that he was among the Manakintown settlers, and hence, among the Huguenot refugees. Mr. Charles Lee Dibrell in his manuscript says of Dr. du Breuil: "Among the Manakintown settlers was Christopher du Breuil, a physician, who died in the year 1729. Nothing more is known of him than that it was said that he was eminent in his profession. Beyond him it is impossible to trace our genealogy on the paternal line. We will therefore consider him the vine from which so many branches of the Dibrell family have sprung." After the death of Dr. du Breuil his widow married a Huguenot named Labsiraira (pronounced Lubarier), by whom she had one or more sons and probably daughters, of whom, however, so little is known that an intelligent account cannot be given.

From the library of universal knowledge the following extract is taken:

"Both Charles V and Frances I proceeded at once to execute the articles of the peace of Cressy relating to the extirpation of heresy in their respective dominions. Charles ordered certain doctors of the University of Louvaine to draw up a confession of faith which he required all of his subjects in the Netherlands to accept under the penalty of death. To show that he was in earnest he caused Peter du Breuil, a Calvinistic preacher, to be burned to death in the market place; February, 1545."

191

From the "Dictionnaire Historique et Heraldique de la Noblesse Francaise," by D. Demailhao—Paris, 1895—first volume, page 583, we find that as early as 1413 Jean du Breuil was mentioned as one of the large land holders of France, and that in 1545 the same reference is made to Antoine du Breuil, with description, respectively, of their Arms which will be found described hereafter.

The birth of Dr. du Breuil occurred about 1680, after three generations had passed through the storms of civil and religious strife which had shaken France from center to circumference; many in the meantime had followed Harry of Navarre on bloody fields of carnage, and some had witnessed the massacre of St. Bartholomew. It is not strange, therefore, that from such an ancestry a race of patriots should have descended, or that men and women who had sprung from the loins of such heroes should make their mark in whatever sphere their lots chanced to be cast.

From the records of the church of the French refugees at Manakintown we learn that "Jeane Antoine du Breuil, son of Christoffe du Breuil and Marianne his wife, was born May 15, 1728, and on the first of August following, was baptised by Mr. Masons, was presented by Antoine Benin, and Elisabeth Dutoi was grandmother." The foregoing extract is signed by Jeane Chastain, clerk, and is taken from the historical collections, volume V.

From the foregoing sketch two deductions necessarily follow: First, as Mr. Charles Lee Dibrell's manuscript says that Antoine Dibrell was born a month after the death of his father, and the record says that he was born 1728, it follows that Dr. Cristopher du Breuil died in 1728 instead of 1729; second, if Elizabeth Dutoi was Antoine's grandmother, then the maiden name of Dr. du Breuil's wife, "Marianne," was Dutoi, but if grandmother should read "godmother," then the deduction would fail; but it must be remembered, that in the baptism of infants the Roman Catholic Church instituted the office of godfather and godmother, and that with the exception of the Church of England, which was a very slight remove from the mother church.

this office was abandoned by all the Protestant churches, and it is not to be presumed that the French Huguenots, who had been the special victims of Romish persecutions, would perpetuate a Romish custom which all of the other Protestant churches, except the established church of England, had abandoned, and the conclusion is almost inevitable that grandmother is here used in the sense of consanguinity, and not in place of godmother, as I find it transcribed the same way in three instances by different persons, and it seems hardly probable that a mistake was made in transcribing it.

But the inquiry may be made, What has become of the Dutoi family? They have gone into the wastebasket, so to speak, just as the du Breuils did, with the difference that it is not known what other name was adopted in its stead. The truth is that these exiles were in a transition state from French to English, or American, and comparatively few of them retained their original name. Outraged, disgusted and heartsick, they sought to forget their native land and the very names by which they had been known. Some adopted their equivalent in an English translation; thus L'Oiseai became Bird; Le Blanc, White; Le Noir, Black; Le Roy, King; while others were changed to suit the sound, and still others dreadfully vulgarized. Thus, Conde became Cundy; Couquerell, Cockerell; Drouet became Drewet; De Aeth, Death; Huyghens, Huggins or Higgins; and Braufoy, Broffy. And doubtless, Dutoi, gave way to some other name the connection of which has been lost sight of.

There is a tradition that the maiden name of Marianne du Breuil, was Le Grande, and this name has been perpetuated in some of the Dibrell families, but this is a mere tradition, without foundation.

MANAKINTOWN SETTLEMENT.

A short sketch of this settlement, where Dr. du Breuil is first found, will not be amiss at this time:

"All the countries of Europe had opened their arms, so to

speak, to these fleeing exiles and nothing less could have been expected from Virginia than the warmest hospitality.

"In 1690 so many Huguenots had settled on the south bank of James river, in Henrico county, about twenty miles from where Richmond now stands (Henrico then embraced both sides of the river at that point), and which was known as Manakintown, from the tribe of Indians which had occupied that section, that the assembly passed an act giving them a large tract of land along the river as their possession, exempting it from all taxes, state and county, for seven years, and then extending the privilege indefinitely; and here they rested for a time worshiping with an entire freedom of conscience, without restraint or dictation from any source, until such time as they grew so much in numbers that it became necessary for them to spread out and seek their fortunes in different parts of the country.

"The names of the families still remaining in Virginia, who derive their descent from these Huguenots are, Marye, Fontaine, Dupuy, Harris, Sublett, Watkins, Markham, Sully, Chastain, Duval, Bondurant, Flournoy, Potter, Michaux, Pemberton, Munford, Hatcher, Jaquiline, Bernard, Barrond, Latane, Moncure, Agie, Amouet, Chadouin, Dibrell, Moxie, Pasteur, Perron, Thweatt, Manry, Boisseau, Fouche, Lanier, Leneve. There are doubtless others who might be added." (Meade's "Old Churches and Families," volume I, page 468.)

DIBRELL FAMILY.

Dibrell, originally French, and spelled du Breuil, was among the oldest and most prominent Huguenot families. In Virginia, however, it became thoroughly anglicised, and for more than a hundred and fifty years, and for six successive generations, it has been spelled Dibrell. As was referred to under the head of du Breuil, this is one of the instances of the general change of names which resulted from the conditions surrounding the French Huguenots in America. The purely English rendition of the name by the first Anthony Dibrell has stripped it of all complications and made it purely American.

As before stated, Dr. Christopher du Breuil, which name became changed to Dibrell, was the original head of the family in America. It is generally accepted that he was born in France and with his parents fled from that country towards the close of the seventeenth century, in consequence of the relentless war which had been waged by the government and the Romish church against all Protestants.

The du Breuils like the Dupuys and the other names mentioned in the Manakintown settlement, did not come directly to America, but refugeed first to Holland, then to England, and afterwards to America; and it is a notable fact that only one of the name was known among the Manakintown settlers.

There are no records to show that Dr. du Breuil left any other child than Anthony, who was the great ancestor of the Dibrell family in America.

We learn from the records of the church of the French refugees at Manakintown, known in English church history as Parish of King William, that Jean Antoine du Breuil, son of Christoffe du Breuil and Marianne his wife, was born May 15, 1728, and baptised first of August following. This is none other than Anthony Dibrell, whose name has become changed, as we have seen, from du Breuil to Dibrell, as almost all the names of the Manakintown settlers had undergone radical changes, owing to their changed condition in the colonies.

ANTHONY DIBRELL.

The father of Anthony Dibrell having died previous to his birth, and his mother having married the second time and died soon thereafter, Anthony was left to be raised by strange hands.

It is not known what the financial condition of Anthony Dibrell was when his parents died, but it is known, when he started out in his early manhood, he was on his own resources without money. There is one fact, however, that stands forth most prominently and speaks for itself; whatever the early opportunities of Anthony Dibrell may have been, he not only proved himself equal to the battle of life, but from his first appearance upon the arena he was acknowledged the full peer of his fellows, and established his claim, in spite of adverse fate, to a lineage that placed him in the front rank of the best names of the seventeenth and eighteenth centuries. Left an orphan when so young that he had no distinct recollection of either of his parents, raised by an unlettered Frenchman (by the name of Benning), and turned loose upon the world penniless, he married before he was thirty years old, in one of the wealthiest and most aristocratic families of Virginia.

The father-in-law of J. M. McAllister, Charles Lee Dibrell, in his manuscript so frequently referred to, gives the following items of the early life of Anthony Dibrell: "About one month after the death of Christopher du Brueil, Anthony, his only child, was born. It is supposed that Dr. du Breuil died poor, and left his wife without the means of educating their son. After his death, how long it is not known, his widow married a Huguenot named Labairaire (pronounced Lubarier) by whom she had a son or sons, and probably daughters, of whom too little is remembered to justify any remarks about them. Shortly after or before the marriage of the mother of Anthony to Labairaire, he then a small boy, was given up to a man named Benning who treated him with great cruelty and raised him in profound ignorance. Having finished his term of apprenticeship with Benning, he turned his attention to procuring an education and having equipped himself for the battle of life, started out to measure lances with others of his generation."

Mr. Charles Lee Dibrell further says of Anthony Dibrell: "In person my grandfather was about five feet seven inches in height, weight about 140 pounds, dark complexion, dark eyes and hair, aquiline nose, and prominent forehead. My recollection of him is distinct, although I was little more than eight years old when he died."

In 1756, at about the age of twenty-eight, Anthony Dibrell married Miss Elizabeth Lee, at the house of John Fearn, in Buckingham county, Virginia. Her sister, Leeanna, having become the wife of John Fearn twelve years previously. At this point in the history of the Dibrell family it becomes necessary, in order to make the complete history intelligent, to introduce a sketch of the Lee family.

As the du Breuils preceded the Dibrell family, and as a reference to their history was necessary to an introduction to the Dibrell history, reference to the history of the Lee family at this point is necessary to a clear understanding of Dibrell history.

LEE FAMILY.

The best authenticated English history informs us that Launcelot Lee entered England with William the Conqueror in 1066. He was originally from London, France, and was the founder of the Lee family in England from which the Virginia family is said to have descended. After the battle of Hastings, when the estates of the native English nobility were divided among the followers of William, a fine estate in Essex was bestowed upon him. Lionel Lee, a lineal descendant of Launcelot, who was Earl of Litchfield, raised a company of gentlemen cavaliers, at the head of which he accompanied Richard Coeur de Leon in the third crusade in 1192. For gallant conduct at the siege of Acre, he was made Earl of Litchfield, and another estate was bestowed upon the family called Ditchley. The armor worn by Lionel Lee was placed in the horse armory in the tower of London (see Guilliam's complete Heraldry). Richard Lee, a descendant of his, accompanied the unfortunate Earl of Surrey in his expedition against the Scotch border in 1542. Two of the family were knights companion of the garter, and their banners surmounted by the Lee Arms, were placed in St. George's Chapel, Windsor Castle. The Arms consisted of a shield, band scimiter, battled and embattled; crest a cloist visor, surmounted by a squirrel holding a nut; the motto, "Non incantus future" (see memoirs of 1776, by Henry Lee).

It is true that Dr. Edmund Jennings Lee, author of "Lee of Virginia," does not embrace this part of Lee history in his work. Dr. Lee is eminent authority, but it is nevertheless true that he discards much authentic history because it is not confirmed by family records which have come into his possession, although it is an established fact that the history in question is based upon the most reliable authority.

198

LEWIS AND KINDRED FAMILIES.

RICHARD LEE.

The first Richard Lee of American history was born in Shropshire, England, towards the end of the sixteenth century. He was member of the privy council of Charles I, and during the reign of that monarch, 1641, he emigrated to Virginia. He was first attorney general of Virginia, he was secretary of the colony with Sir William Berkley, and was conspicuous in all colonial affairs.

After the death of Charles I, and during the Protectorate of Cromwell, Lee was conspicuous in his adherence to Charles, though sufficiently cautious to avoid a conflict. Berkley and Lee declared allegiance to Charles II, and invited the fugitive royalist to come to Virginia and live; more than a hundred of his adherents did come, and Charles was ultimately invited to Virginia as its ruler. Upon the death of Cromwell, Berkley and Lee declared in favor of Charles II, as King of England, Scotland, France, Ireland and Virginia, whom they had proclaimed king two years before, in consequence of which the motto was added to the Virginia Arms, "En dat Virginia quintum." Until after the union of England and Scotland it was changed to "En dat Virginia Quartum," and from this incident in colonial history Virginia became known as the "Old Dominion," which proud distinction she still enjoys.

This Richard Lee had six sons and two daughters, John, Richard, Francis, William, Hancock, Charles, Betsy and Anne. Only three of these sons, Richard, Hancock, and Charles, left descendants in Virginia. Nothing is known of the marriage or descendants of the daughters.

The maiden names of very few of the wives and mothers of this period of our history have been retained, and like General Robert Lewis, Augustine Warner, and many others contemporaneous with them, the maiden name of the wife of the first Richard Lee has been lost to history and tradition, except that her given name was Anna; and until very recently, there was nothing known of the history of any of his sons except Richard and

199

Hancock, but in the last few years, through the persistence of some of the descendants and family connections, with the aid of wills and other court records, church registers and tomb-stones, many of the descendants of Charles, the youngest son, have been traced, and two families, the Fearns and Dibrells, known to have belonged to the Lee family, have been enabled to trace themselves directly from this Charles Lee.

As the Lee family has been taken up wholly with reference to the Fearns and Dibrells, only that branch from which they descended will be considered.

The three sons of Richard Lee, who left descendants in Virginia, Richard, Hancock and Charles, and who established families, were known respectively as the Shropshire or Stratford, Ditchley, and Cobbs Hall lines, these names having attached to their respective estates.

COBBS HALL.

This was the name of the residence located on the estate bequeathed by the first Richard Lee to his son Charles. The history of this estate is not known, nor is it known how the first Richard Lee came into possession of it. It is known that the name of Cobbs was one of the earliest of the colonial names, that they were in Virginia more than twenty years previous to the arrival of Richard Lee, and it is quite certain that this ancestral mansion was built by some one of the name and came into possession of Richard Lee, either by purchase or some matrimonial alliance, almost certainly the latter, as Lee in all probability would not have retained the name of strangers to be handed down to his descendants if it had come into the family by purchase.

Cobbs Hall stands to the Lee family identically as Warner Hall does to the Lewis family, and the Lees who have descended from that branch, are known as "the Cobbs Hall Lees," as the Eastern Virginia Lewises are known as those of "Warner Hall."

Leading up to the history of the Fearn and Dibrell families

it becomes necessary to publish the wills of several members through three generations of the Cobbs Hall Lees, as it is in the will of the first Charles Lee that we obtain the first and only clue to the respective heads of the Fearns and Dibrells, Leanna and Elisabeth Lee.

WILL OF THE FIRST CHARLES LEE,

"Youngest son of the first Richard Lee, and grandfather of Leeanna Fearn, and Elisabeth Dibrell.

"Northumberland county, Virginia, July Ye 13, 1700. I, Charles Lee, being in perfect health and strength of memory. do make this my last will and testament. Test, I give and bequeath my soul to my blessed Redeemer Jesus Christ, assuredly trusting, in and by His meritorious death and passion, to receive salvation, and my body to be disposed of as my loving wife shall . . . not doubting, but at last both body and soul will be renovated and glorified. Next, I give to my son Thomas all my land on Rappahannock riverside, had by my wife, as also five hundred acres left me by Walter Jenkins, to him and his heirs male. One featherbed, and further a child's part of my negroes, cattle and household stuff, and in case of his death without heirs, to be divided among my other children. Next, I give and bequeath to my son Charles the six hundred acres whereon I now am, a featherbed and furniture, a child's part of my negroes and cattle with other household stuff, and in case of his death before age, to be equally divided among the other children. Next, I give and bequeath to my daughter Leeanna Lee, that two hundred acres of land had out of brother Hancock's tract, a child's part of my negroes, with cattle and other household stuff; the sheep of her mark, which is two crops, and a slit in one ear, and in case of her death before age, to be divided amongst my other children. Next, I give and bequeath to my daughter Elisabeth, a child's part of my negroes and cattle, with other household stuff. The half of my white servants, and in case of her death before age to be equally divided among my other children.

"Lastly. I give and bequeath to my loving wife all my bedding not set down, and an equal part of my negroes and cattle, the half of my white hands, with a child's part of my other household stuff. My part of the mill, and all my sheep and hogs. Whom I make executrix of this, my last will and testament.

"As witness my hand and seal the day and year above written. CHARLES LEE."

"Die. December, 1701. Then Mr. John Tuberville, for Mrs. Elizabeth Lee, executrix of Captain Charles Lee, deceased, motioned the county court of Northumberland, for a probate to be granted of this will, and the court perused the will and were of opinion that, as well ye words of as the subscription to the said will, are his own hand, written by himself, and doe therefore grant to her, the said Elizabeth, probate of ye said will.

"Test.

"THE HOBSON, Clerk of Court."

"Die. January 21, 1718. The original will attested of Captain Charles Lee, was presented to ye court by Richard Lee (ye records where it was recorded, being burnt with the office). On the said Richard Lee's motion, it was again admitted to record.

"Test.

"RD. LEE, Clk. of Court."

From the foregoing will it will be seen that Charles Lee, youngest son of the first Richard, had two daughters, Leeanna and Elizabeth. These names in connection have never before been known in the Lee family, nor is it known from whence they were derived. It is presumable, however, that Elizabeth was named for her mother, Elizabeth Medstand, but as to the combination of Leeanna, we are left to conjecture. It will be noted that the name is a combination of two separate and distinct names, Lee and Anna, and it is doubtless from the name of the wife of the first Richard Lee, who was named Anna, that the name was derived. Charles Lee evidently sought to perpetuate the memory

202

of his mother in the name of his oldest daughter, which he could not do by merely calling her Anna, as she would then have been only Anna Lee, but he conceived a thought much more comprehensive and called her Leeanna, and prefixing it to his own name, made it Leeanna Lee.

In my search for the ancestry of Leeanna and Elisabeth Lee, I had opened correspondence with all of the genealogists of the Lee family. Mr. Cassius F. Lee of Alexandria, Virginia, being recognized as authority, I was persistent in my search through him. We differed very widely as to the proper method of obtaining the desired information, in consequence of which our correspondence ended rather abruptly. It transpired, however, that Mr. Lee was in very poor health and died soon thereafter. Dr. Edmund J. Lee of Philadelphia, administered upon his effects and succeeded him as family genealogist. Dr. Lee was a brother of Mr. Cassius Lee, and as executor of his brother came into possession of all his effects and correspondence, my letters being among the latter.

Finding from my correspondence with his brother that I was inquiring very anxiously for the history of Leeanna and Elisabeth Lee, Dr. Lee thought that he had found the ladies for whom I was inquiring in the daughters of the first Charles Lee, and, as he was preparing for publication a history of the Lee family, he opened correspondence with me, but the information he had was only what I was already in possession of from "Hayden."

It will be seen that the will of the first Charles Lee was written July 13, 1700, and that his daughters, Leeanna and Elisabeth, were born previous to that time, and from other records it is shown that they were several years old when their father died; so that it followed as a matter of necessity that they belonged to a generation preceding the Leeanna and Elisabeth for whom I was searching, as Leeanna Lee had married John Fearn, in 1744, and Elisabeth Lee had married Anthony Dibrell in 1756, and both of them had raised large families of children; therefore it became necessary to make further search.

Up to this time nothing had been ascertained except that Leeanna and Elisabeth were family names in the Cobbs Hall line, and although Charles Lee of Cobbs Hall left but two sons, and Leeanna Fearn and Elizabeth Dibrell necessarily belonged to the same generation as their children, these names could not be found in their wills.

"WILL OF THE FIRST THOMAS LEE,

"Oldest son of the first Charles Lee, and grandson of the first Richard Lee, and father of Leeanna Fearn and Elizabeth Dibrell.

"In the name of God, amen. I, Thomas Lee, being in good health, mind and memory, do make and appoint this my last will and testament.

"I give and bequeath my soul to God who gave it, hoping in and through the merits of my blessed Lord and Savior Jesus Christ to receive remission of all my sins. My body to the ground, to have a Christian and decent burial.

"I give my son William Lee all my land where William Rankins and Richard Weaver now live, to him, and the heirs of his body forever.

"I give unto my sons, Thomas, Richard and Charles, all the tract of land whereon I now live, to be equally divided between them, to them and the heirs of their body lawfully begotten, forever.

"I give and bequeath to my son John, all that tract of land on ye head of Currotomson river, which I had of my wife, where Harvey now lives, to him and his heirs forever. Provided the child my wife goes with be not a boy, which if it be, then my will is that the said land be equally divided between them and the heirs of their bodies forever.

"I give and bequeath unto my wife one-fourth part of my personal estate, during her natural life or widowhood, but if she should intermarry, then to have but one child's part. also my will is, that she have the liberty to dispose of her fourth part to such of her children as she shall think proper, at her decease, provided she lives unmarried.

"My will is that my estate be kept together until my children come to lawful age or marriage.

"My will is that my loving brother, Major Charles Lee, my good friend, William Nicholas Martin, and my loving wife, be executors of this, my last will and testament, and that my son, William Lee, when he arrives at the age of one and twenty, be allowed to be one of my executors.

"My will is that my present estate, after my wife's part it taken out, be equally divided between *all my children*.

"I give and bequeath unto my son, William Lee, my Phillips' English Dictionary.

"I do ordain and appoint this my last will and testament, revoking all previous wills by me heretofore made. As witness my hand and seal, this 16th day of June, 1733.

"THOMAS LEE.

"WILL OF THE SECOND THOMAS LEE.

"Son of the first Thomas, grandson of the first Charles, great-grandson of first Richard, and brother of Leoanna Fearn and Elizabeth Dibrell.

"In the name of God, amen, December 1, 1758. I, Thomas Lee of the colony of Virginia, in the county of Lancaster, and Parish of Christ Church, being very sick and weak in body, but a perfect mind and memory, thanks be to God for it however, calling to mind the mortality of my body, and knowing that it is appointed unto all men once to die, do make and ordain this my last will and testament, that is to say, principally and first of all, I recommend my soul into the hands of God that gave it, and my body to the earth, to be decently interred, at the discretion of my executors hereafter named, not doubting but that at the general resurrection I shall revive again by the mighty power of my blessed Redeemer. And as to such worldly estate as it has pleased God to bless me with in this life, I give and dispose of the same in manner and form following:

"After my just debts and funeral charges are fully paid and satisfied, then I give and bequeath to my daughter Mary Lee, one negro boy named Dick, that I had from my brother Richard Lee, to her and her heirs forever.

"I give and bequeath unto my brother John Lee, one negro woman named Cate, that I had by my brother Richard Lee, to him and his heirs forever, and as I owe Richard Blade some money it is my will and desire, that it shall be paid out of the money that William Griggs owes me, and the remainder of the money derived from William Griggs, I give and bequeath to my brother John Lee, to him and his heirs forever.

"Then I give and bequeath unto my two children, Mary Lee and George Lee, to them and the heirs of their body forever, all the rest and residue of my estate, both real and personal, of what nature or kind soever, but in case my children should die without heirs lawfully begotten of their body, then I give and bequeath to my loving wife, Lucy Lee, all the estate I had by her and the increase, and one negro woman named Felicy, and likewise my chair, and two horses, and the explanation of the testament. And in case of the death of my two children, Mary Lee and George Lee, without heirs lawfully begotten of their body, I give and bequeath to my brother, Charles Lee, all the tract of land I now live on, to him and his heirs forever.

"I give and bequeath unto my brother John Lee, all of the land I have in White Chapel Parish, to him and his heirs forever, in case my two children, Mary Lee and George Lee, should die without heirs lawfully begotten of their body.

"I give and bequeath unto my brother Charles Lee, one negro fellow named Aaron, in case my children should die without heirs, lawfully begotten of their bodies, to him and his heirs forever.

"I give and bequeath unto my loving wife, Lucy Lee, one-half my stock, and household furniture, in the case of the death of my children without heirs lawfully begotten of their bodies, and in the case of the death of my two children, Mary Lee and George Lee, without heirs lawfully begotten of their bodies, I give and bequeath all the rest of my negroes not before mentioned, to my brother John Lee, to him and the heirs of his body forever, and my will and desire is that my brother John Lee may work the negroes he now has upon the land I now live on, as long as he lives single, and have the profits of the land I now live on and the negroes, as long as he lives single, and in case of the death of two children Mary Lee and George Lee, without heirs lawfully begotten of their bodies, my will and desire is, that my estate be kept together until forty pounds current money of Virginia be raised, and that money I give and bequeath to my sister Elisabeth Dibrell's eldest son to him and his heirs lawfully begotten of his body forever, and in case he dies without such heirs, then the forty pounds, current money to be equally divided between my two brothers, Charles Lee and John Lee.

"I do hereby nominate, constitute and appoint my loving wife, Lucy Lee, executrix, as long as she lives a widow and no longer, also Charles Lee, Eppa Lawson, and George Currell, executors of this my last will and testament, revoking and disannulling all other will or wills, by me heretofore made. In witness whereof I have hereunto set my hand and seal the day and year first above written.   "THOMAS LEE.

"Signed, sealed and delivered, in presence of Benj. Kelly, James Sarasty, Charles Lee, G. Currell."

"At a court held for Lancaster county, on the 16th day of March, 1759, this will was proved in open court, by the oaths of Charles Lee, George Currell, and Benj. Kelly, witnesses thereto, and ordered to be recorded.

"Teste.
"THOMAS EDWARDS, Jr., C. Clk."

A train of ideas may be traced from the foregoing wills. For the first time in the history of the Lee family, the names

of Leeanna and Elizabeth appear in combination in the will of
the first Charles Lee. These were the names of his only daughters, and from that fact it was almost a matter of necessity
that the names should be traced in this line.

The will of the second Charles Lee has not been published
in these pages, as there was nothing in it, or in any of the records growing out of it that could possibly shed light upon the
names that we were in search of.

The will of the first Thomas Lee, however, opened up new
thought for reflection. He names his five sons and provides for
them specifically but makes no mention of his daughters. It is
clear, however, that he had daughters, as he mentions in a general way, that his personal estate shall be divided equally among
"all my children." Had there been no daughters this provision
would have been unnecessary, as his personal estate, as well as
his real estate, would have been divided among his sons.

It is a well-known fact that testators at this period of the
country's history, gave their lands to their sons as also an equal
proportion of their personal estate, and hence the names of the
daughters were rarely ever mentioned; but in this will of the
first Thomas Lee we have proof conclusive that he had at least
one daughter and almost certainly several others.

The second Thomas Lee, son of the first Thomas, aforesaid,
mentions his sister Elizabeth Dibrell in his will, and Mr.
Charles Lee Dibrell in his Mss. which are the highest record authority, mentions Leeanna who married John Fearn, and still
another sister who married a gentleman by the name of Bates,
whose descendants are not known.

A singular coincidence occurs in connection with the will
of the first Thomas Lee, written July 16, 1733. At that time
he refers to an unborn child, whose name, of course is not mentioned in the will, but about twenty-two years thereafter, Elizabeth Lee married Anthony Dibrell, and the second Thomas Lee
refers to her as his sister, Elizabeth Dibrell.

Taking all the foregoing circumstances into connection, together with names and dates, there can be no doubt that the

unborn child mentioned by the first Thomas Lee in his will, was Elizabeth Lee who married Anthony Dibrell in 1756.

LEEANNA AND ELIZABETH LEE.

These names form a separate chapter in "Lee history." There is no doubt that the genealogists of the Lee family had lost sight of these two ladies, but Leeanna and Elizabeth had not lost sight of the Lees, nor did the country lose sight of them or their descendants.

When Napoleon Bonaparte was inquired of in regard to his ancestry, he replied that he himself was the head of his own ancestral line, and the ancestry of the Bonapartes dated from his advent upon the stage of history. The same may be said of Leeanna and Elizabeth Lee. They were not heroines in the common acceptation of the term, but they were heroic mothers, who, like the Spartan mothers, bid their sons go forth and fight the battles of life and make a history for themselves.

As has been seen, Leeanna Lee married John Fearn, and Elizabeth married Anthony Dibrell, and for four generations these names have left their impress upon the history of the times. As jurists, diplomats, scholars, masters of the various professions, or in whatever capacity they have been called to act they have proven themselves equal to the occasion, and at all times the peers of their fellows.

That Elizabeth was the daughter of the first Thomas Lee, referred to in his will as then unborn, is conclusively proven. That she married Anthony Dibrell about 1756, is also proven by the reference made to her in the will of her brother Thomas in 1758, and that she was married to Anthony Dibrell at the house of John Fearn, in Buckingham county, Virginia, in 1756, is proven by the Mss. of Mr. Charles Lee Dibrell.

That Leeanna Lee was a sister of Elizabeth Lee, and consequently a daughter of the first Thomas Lee, is proven by the Mss. of Mr. Charles Lee Dibrell, the concurrent history of both the Fearn and Dibrell families, and the generally accepted and unbroken traditions for four generations.

The records of Middlesex county, Virginia, show that Leeanna Lee was married to John Fearn, December 31, 1744. The Manuscripts of Mr. Charles Lee Dibrell shows that John Fearn and his wife, Leeanna, removed to Buckingham county previous to 1756, and that Elizabeth and another sister accompanied them, and that Elizabeth was married to Anthony Dibrell at the house of John Fearn, in the above named year. So that nothing can be more conclusively proven than that these ladies were sisters, and that they were the daughters of the first Thomas Lee, granddaughters of Charles Lee of Cobbs Hall, and great-granddaughters, of Richard Lee, secretary of the colony, and first attorney general of Virginia.

As set forth in the outset, reference to the Lee family was taken up as an interlude to the Dibrell family, as it was necessary to show the descent of the maternal head of this family, and therefore it will be pursued no further.

Dr. Edmund Jennings Lee, author of "Lee of Virginia," has published a very exhaustive history of the Lee family, and from that volume may be derived all necessary information in regard to the Lees. Dr. Lee, however, knew nothing of the Fearns and Dibrells, and for this reason we have inserted this sketch of the Lee family from which branch they were descended. We will now return to the Dibrell family proper.

ANTHONY DIBRELL.

We now return to Anthony Dibrell, the first of the name in America, and so far as is known, in the world; indeed, it is believed to be a fact that he was the author of the name as well as its first possessor, the general change of names on the part of the Huguenot exiles having given rise to almost every conceivable variety, resulting from translation, similarity of sound or peculiar fancy.

Having already laid the foundation of his fortune which was added to by his marriage, he became a large land holder, in Buckingham, where he continued to live and raise his family, his home being on what is known as Walton's fork of Slate river.

Four children were born to Anthony Dibrell and Elizabeth Lee, two sons and two daughters; Charles, Leeanna, Judith and Anthony.

In 1770, Mrs. Elizabeth Dibrell, first wife of Anthony Dibrell, died at the age of 36, having been married only 14 years. After the death of his first wife, Anthony Dibrell married the second time, Miss Magdaline Burton. There were no children by this marriage. Anthony Dibrell died in 1800, aged 73 years. His second wife survived him, having died in 1806.

CHARLES DIBRELL.

Charles Dibrell was the oldest son of Anthony Dibrell and Elizabeth Lee. He was born in Buckingham county, October 24, 1757. He married first Miss Burton of Buckingham, and second, Miss Patterson of the same county. He had eight children by the first wife; John, Elizabeth, Polly, Leeanna, Anthony Judith, Charles and Joseph. By the second marriage he had four children; Patterson, Panthea, Elvira, and Agnes. This Charles Dibrell born 1757, is the "oldest son of my sister Elizabeth Dibrell," referred to in the will of her brother, Thomas Lee, written 1758. This son, Charles Dibrell, oldest son of Anthony Dibrell and Elisabeth Lee, removed to Madison county, Kentucky, in 1782, where all of his first wife's children were born, except John and Elizabeth, who were born previous to his removal.

Mr. Charles Lee Dibrell says of him: "After his first wife's death he moved to Wayne county, Kentucky, and settled on the Cumberland river, ten miles from Monticello, where I visited him in 1810, when on my way to Nashville. His first wife was amiable and affectionate, and breathed her last in his arms."

Mr. Charles Lee Dibrell does not state it as a fact that this Charles Dibrell came back from Kentucky to Virginia in after life, but the trend of his article is such that the conclusion is inevitable. He says he married first Miss Burton of Buckingham, and removed to Kentucky; that all of his first wife's children except two, were born in Kentucky. He certainly came back to Buckingham to marry the second time, and his return to Kentucky is not noted. Besides Mr. C. L. Dibrell's wife, who was never in Kentucky, knew him well, and loved him very much, and her acquaintance with him was necessarily in Virginia. There is no doubt, however, that he returned to Kentucky, where some of his older children resided, and ultimately to Tennessee, as we find him in 1832 at Sparta, Tennessee, the home of his son Anthony.

Like his brother, Anthony, he was a Revolutionary soldier, as shown by the records in the war office at Washington, by the Pension records, and numerous affidavits.

A partial history only of the descendants of this Charles Dibrell has been obtained, as we have found it next to impossible to secure information in regard to them.

I have found them in almost all of the Southern States and some of them scattered North, and their lives have invariably proven their superiority, but strange to say, nothing like a complete line of them has ever been obtained by anyone so far as is known. Charles Dibrell had five sons and seven daughters, and doubtless there are hundreds of his descendants scattered through the country who have been lost to genealogists, and know nothing of their antecedents, and are almost unknown to each other. Of course, there are exceptions to this general statement. The descendants of this Anthony Dibrell, son of this Charles, and the Shrewsburys who married his daughters Elizabeth and Polly, are to some extent traceable, but there are so many breaks even in those lines that it would be impossible to construct a family tree.

Of the children of Charles Dibrell, we have found it impossible to obtain record evidence or even reliable tradition of all of their marriages.

His son Anthony, born June 4, 1788, married Miss Millie Carter and settled at Sparta, Tennessee. Another son Charles married Miss Mitchell, and died in the Indian Territory. Another son married Miss Lee Haley. Panthea Dibrell, daughter of Col. Charles Dibrell, by his second marriage, married Nathaniel Bramlett. Polly, another daughter married Nathaniel Shrewsbury and Elizabeth married Drury Shrewsbury. Leeanna Dibrell, daughter of Col. Charles Dibrell, married George G. Gibbs, and Judith Dibrell married a gentleman by the name of Poston.

4 ANTHONY DIBRELL.

Anthony Dibrell, second son of Col. Charles Dibrell by his first wife, Miss Burton, was born in Madison county, Kentucky, June 4, 1788, and died in Sparta, Tennessee, January 25, 1875, in the eighty-seventh year of his age. He married Millie Carter, by whom he had ten children, six sons and four daughters. The oldest son Edwin, died in infancy. Montgomery C. Dibrell, born March 6, 1813, married first, Mary E. Carter, second, Mary E. Eastland; Charles Crockett Dibrell, born September 15, 1817, married Miss Mary E. Jenkins; Joseph Dibrell born July 20, 1820; George G. Dibrell, born April 12, 1822, married Miss Mary E. Leftwich; William C. Dibrell, born July 2, 1829, married Margaret E. Jenkins; Elizabeth N. Dibrell, born March

18, 1815, married Charles J. Sullivan; Lucinda A. Dibrell, born August 28, 1824, married James G. Hood; Sarah B. Dibrell, born February 20, 1827, married John W. Whitfield; Martha F. Dibrell born October 21, 1834, married Jasper N. Bailey.

Anthony Dibrell was among the earlier settlers of Tennessee having settled in White county at a very early period in the history of the State. He was one of the sturdy citizens of that section, and for a long time was clerk of the court. He raised a large family, and his sons and grandsons have proven themselves worthy of their ancestry.

5 GEN. GEORGE G. DIBRELL.

General George Dibrell was a son of Anthony Dibrell, grandson of Col. Charles Dibrell, and great-grandson of Anthony Dibrell and Miss Elizabeth Lee. He was born April 12, 1822, married Miss Mary E. Leftwich, to which marriage was born nine children, seven sons and two daughters: Waman L., December 3, 1844; Joseph A., November 3, 1845; James, January 8, 1852; Jefferson, 1856; Frank, 1858; Stanton William Crockett, May 7, 1864; Mary Lou, and Emily died in infancy.

Waman L. Dibrell married Evelyn Morgan; Joseph Dibrell married first, Bertha Brewster, second, Dora Taylor; James Dibrell married Dora Jett; Jefferson Dibrell married Cora Taylor; Frank Dibrell married Louisa Rhea; Stanton Dibrell married Lizzie Cary; Mary Lou Dibrell married James T. Officer. William Crockett Dibrell married Catherine Stratton.

6 WILLIAM CROCKETT DIBRELL.

William Crockett Dibrell is the son of General George Dibrell and is a merchant in Nashville, Tennessee, of the firm of Murray, Dibrell & Co. He was born May 7, 1844, and married Catherine Stratton, of that city. Their oldest son, George Stratton Dibrell, born August 22, 1870, married Bessie Murray,

November 11, 1897. Mary Leftwich Dibrell, daughter of William Crockett and Catherine Stratton Dibrell, was born May 14, 1876. Catherine Stratton Dibrell, daughter of George Stratton and Bessie Murray Dibrell, and granddaughter of William Crockett Dibrell, was born 1898.

General George Dibrell was one of the leading men of Tennessee covering the period preceding the war between the States, as well as during the war and for twenty years thereafter.

When the stormclouds of civil war burst in 1861, George Dibrell, true to his antecedents, was found upon the Southern side. East Tennessee did not present an unbroken front at that time, but owing to political complications, the leaders were very much divided. Andrew Johnson and Thomas R. R. Nelson, two of the most prominent men of the day, opposed secession bitterly. Johnson had been governor of the State, and was then in the senate of the United States. Nelson, one of the greatest lawyers of his time, while he did not hold an office, swayed a powerful influence. Johnson went over, horse, foot and dragoon, to the Federal side, and while Nelson did not do so, he accepted a parole of honor under the pledge of remaining at home and taking no active part on either side.

William G. Brownlow, editor of the Knoxville Whig, and a Methodist preacher withal, who swayed the riff-raff of East Tennessee illiteracy and preached a mixture of politics and religion to the mountain element from Chattanooga to Bristol and from the North Carolina to the Kentucky line, also espoused the Federal cause. With these three leaders, two of them old-line Whigs, and the other, Johnson, a leading Democrat, East Tennessee was the scene of contending factions, so that it was but little less than martyrdom for an East Tennesseean to espouse the Southern cause. There were, however, many brave spirits who, regardless of financial interest or personal safety, chose to fight under the Southern flag, among whom was George Dibrell.

Raising a regiment of cavalry from among the yeomanry of the Cumberland mountains, after having served some time as a private, he offered their services to the Confederate government, and pitching, as it were, into the thickest of the fight, he rose steadily by promotion until he was made brigadier-general of cavalry. General Dibrell's command played a conspicuous part in many of the active engagements of the war, and when at last the fates had doomed the failure of the Confederacy, it fell to their part to act as a body guard of the Confederate government when Richmond was evacuated.

What has been said of East Tennessee at the breaking out of the war, and the consequences which followed during the war as a result of contending political factions and a deep-seated difference of opinion in regard to secession, conveys but a faint idea of what followed after the war had closed. Brownlow, with all of the intensity of hate that could possibly possess the soul of a political preacher, was made military governor, and the Confederate soldier who dared to go back home when the war was over, took his life in his own hands. It is a fact, strange and contradictory as it may seem, that fighting was going on in East Tennessee among local factions two years after the war had closed. It was no crime, in the opinion of Brownlow's followers, to kill an ex-Confederate. The courts consisted entirely of South-haters, and juries were made up from among the ignorance of the mountains, so that it was next to impossible to obtain the conviction of any one charged with committing an outrage against an ex-Confederate. But if a conviction was obtained, William G. Brownlow hastened to pardon the convict.

The state of affairs in East Tennessee at this time reads like a romance, and is difficult to believe. James W. Sheffy, a distinguished Virginia lawyer, in a speech delivered at Bristol, on the Virginia side of the town, with impassioned eloquence, "thanked God that he was in Virginia, but as much as he thanked God that he was in Virginia, he thanked Him more that he was not in Tennessee, and still more that he was beyond the reach of Brownlow."

In this state of affairs it fell to the lot of George Dibrell and other leading men to rescue that section from the grasp of what was no less than a lawless element. East Tennessee was composed of three congressional districts, the First, Second and Third, all of which were solidly Republican and solidly lawless in their tendencies, while the remainder of the State, though differing very much, was virtually under the heel of the lawless element.

When the crucial time came, when it was an absolute necessity to break this power, it fell to the part of every law-abiding citizen to play his full part in the effort, and it was at this juncture that George Dibrell proved himself, in peace as he had in war, equal to the emergency, and broke the backbone of the Republican party in the Third district of Tennessee.

General Dibrell was the standard-bearer of the Democratic party in the congressional race of 1874, and led the party to victory. He was elected to Congress for five successive terms, and might have represented his district indefinitely, but voluntarily retired from politics. At the time of his death (May 9, 1888). he was most prominently mentioned for the Democratic nomination for governor of Tennessee, which he would doubtless have received had he lived, but he died a few weeks before the convention met. In the preceding gubernatorial convention he received five hundred votes.

Remarks of Rev. Dr. Kelly at memorial meeting on the occasion of the death of General Dibrell, from the Nashville American, May 10, 1888: "Tennessee to-day mourns the loss of one of her noblest sons.

"General George G. Dibrell died at his home in Sparta, White county, yesterday afternoon, full of honors and in his sixty-seventh year.

"He was a man among men, the soul of honor, one whose word was never lightly given, but once passed, was to be relied on as the unchangeable truth. . . . He joined the Confederate army at the beginning of the war as a private, served as lieutenant colonel of the 25th Tennessee Infantry one year, and then organized the Eighth Tennessee Cavalry, of which he was colonel. He was promoted to be brigadier-general, and served under Generals Forrest and Wheeler, surrendering his division at Washington, Georgia, on May 9, 1865. After the war he again engaged in farming and mercantile pursuits, until 1874, when he was elected to Congress, and served five successive terms, after which he declined to allow the use of his name again.

"He was a candidate for the Democratic nomination for governor in 1886, receiving at one time more than five hundred votes. He was also a member of the constitutional convention of 1870.

"No man had more friends than General Dibrell, and none deserved them more. His friendship was of that enduring kind which Shelly describes

> " 'A star
> Which moves not 'mid the heavens alone,
> A smile among dark frowns—a gentle tone,
> Among rude voices, a beloved light,
> A solitude, a refuge, a delight.'

"An honored and honorable citizen is gone; a brave soldier is at rest; a loving father has left the home circle to mourn his irreparable loss. By his bier the people of his beloved State stand uncovered and say in reverent tones, 'Peace to his ashes.' "

Crockett and William Dibrell were two other sons of Anthony Dibrell, and like their brother, George Dibrell, were staunch Southern men, having linked their fortunes with the Confederacy. I mention these brothers together because they were so long associated together in business. Previous to the war they were merchants and partners at different places in Texas, and after the war they were wholesale boot and shoe merchants in New Orleans and Galveston. William Dibrell has long since been dead, and Crockett, if living, is a very old man.

5 ELIZABETH DIBRELL.

This daughter of Col. Charles Dibrell married Drewry Shrewsbury, and had issue in part as follows: Anne, married

Joseph Gingry; Mary, married Hezekiah Bradbury; Charles, never married; Judith, married Charles J. Love; Martha, married her cousin, Edwin Dibrell, who was a son of Anthony Dibrell and Wilmuth Watson, of whom more will be said under the proper head.

Polly Dibrell, another daughter of Col. Charles Dibrell, married Nathaniel Shrewsbury, who was most probably a brother of Drewry. Their marriage took place in Madison county, Kentucky, but we have no account of their descendants.

4 JUDITH DIBRELL.

Daughter of Col. Charles Dibrell by his first wife, Miss Burton, married a gentleman by the name of Poston, about whose descendants, however, nothing is definitely known, except one son, Charles Dibrell Poston, and his identity seems to have been one of the casualties that appear to bid defiance to fate, and perpetuate names in spite of adverse fortune.

5 Charles Dibrell Poston, one of the most remarkable characters of his age, was born in Hardin county, Kentucky, and died in Phoenix, Arizona, the latter part of June, 1902, when nearing his eightieth year. Extracts from the Washington Evening Times, written at the time of his death, give some idea of the character of the man, the life that he led, his rare attainments and eccentricities. A press dispatch from Phoenix, Arizona, dated July 2, 1902, in that paper, is as follows:

"One of the noteworthy men of the West died here the other day, after a career with many remarkable characteristics. Charles D. Poston, pioneer, traveler, poet, author, diplomat, breathed his last here where he had made his home during the latter years of his life. He had nearly attained his eightieth birthday. For twenty years his life had been a solitary one, though his bent figure was well known in Phoenix.

"The Legislature of Arizona had voted him a pension of $35 per month, he being the only beneficiary of that nature. The reasons for this bestowal were enumerated by the last Legislature. The act recites:

" 'Charles Dibrell Poston, January, 1854, prospected the A. J. O. mines in what is now Pima county, Arizona, and in the same year, organized in said mines the first mining company to invest capital, and to do development work on mines in what is now Arizona after its transfer to the United States under the Gadsden purchase, and was from 1856 to 1861 deputy clerk and recorder of Dona Anna county which then embraced all Arizona, and in 1863 gave Arizona her name, and obtained President Lincoln's signature to the act, that, together with the then delegate to Congress from New Mexico, he had drawn and obtained congressional enactment thereof, creating the Territory of Arizona, and in 1864 was elected the first delegate to Congress from Arizona, and from 1867 to 1880 was register of the United States land office of Arizona, and from the above and many other well known facts, Charles Dibrell Poston, among all other pioneers was pre-eminently the moving spirit, and in fact, may be truly said to be the father of Arizona.' The last check from the Territorial auditor was found in the pocket of the stricken pioneer.

"Notwithstanding his loneliness and everything that might have marked him as a recluse, there were evidences of a time of mental vigor and ability. There were heaps of papers mainly comprising matter descriptive of Arizona's early days, and evidently prepared for the Arizona Historical Society, of which he had been founder and first president. There were a few copies of a volume of poems, several small volumes he had written upon his travels in Europe and in the Orient, and many references to magazine and newspaper articles, one of them of considerable length, on 'The Building of a State in Apache Land,' having been published in the Overland Monthly. He had written voluminously, as well upon philosophical and religious subjects. He had his own modified form of Theosophy, and had conceived the idea that it was the same form of religious worship practiced by the prehistoric Toltecan inhabitants of Arizona. Near Florence,

Arizona, rises a conical hill of considerable height, solitary on the plain, not far from the ruins of CasaGrande, and itself covered with potsherd, and with the ruins left by a forgotten people. For more than thirty years this hill has been known as 'Poston's butte.' Around and up the butte, at considerable expense, Poston had built a road. Upon the summit it was his dream to erect a temple, from which the deity should be worshipped with solemnity on the uprising of the sun, to him the glorious manifestation and representative of Celestial Omnipotence.

"Poston was a native of Hardin county, Kentucky. At twenty-two he was admitted to the bar and practiced for several years in his native State, and in Washington. He outlived the wife and several children of an early union. A daughter married Dr. Benjamin F. Pope of the regular army. Pope won distinction as the chief surgeon of the Fifth army corps in the advance on Santiago, and died at his post in the Philippines, with the rank of deputy surgeon general. Mrs. Pope died on the Pacific while returning home with her husband's remains. After several years in Washington, Chas. Dibrell Poston went to California as a gold seeker, and later from Guaymas, he headed a party into the land acquired by the Gadsden purchase. He was back again soon, conducting operations for a mining company he had organised in New York. At the outbreak of the civil war the Union forces abandoned the Southwest. Poston was compelled to leave mining property on which $1,000,000 had been spent, and joined the Federal army as an aide on the staff of General Heintzelman. A couple of years later he was sent back to the Southwest with a commission from President Lincoln as superintendent of Indian affairs. At the same time he served as recorder of the region which embraces Arizona. After securing the organization of the new Territory and serving as its first delegate in Congress, he went abroad. For a while he was associated with several New York papers. One of his experiences was a trip to China, with his friend J. Ross Browne, as accredited agent of the United States, bearing despatches to the Chinese Emperor. Again he turned towards the Sunset land, to take charge of the United States land office at Florence. Later he had an appointment as special agent of the government along the Mexican border. His last official place was that of agent of the Agricultural Bureau of the Interior Department of Arizona.

"It was Poston's wish that his last resting place be the summit of the butte that bears his name. It is not improbable that the Historical Society will some day remove his remains to the site of the projected temple of the Sun."

3 LEEANNA AND JUDITH DIBRELL.

3 Leeanna Dibrell was the oldest daughter of Anthony Dibrell and Elisabeth Lee. She was born 1759 in Buckingham county, Virginia, and previous to 1780, she married Michael Jones of that county, and had ten children; Anthony, Elizabeth, Mary or Polly, Michael, Judith, Charles, Sarah or Sally, Martha and Margaret.

Very little is known definitely of the descendants of Michael Jones and Leanna Dibrell. It is a fact, however, that the name of Jones, in Buckingham and surrounding counties, who have descended from this couple, is legion, to say nothing of the descendants of the daughters who have intermarried with other names.

William D. Jones of Buckingham, one of the children above named whose home was at the historic yet unpretentious village of the New Store, left a number of descendants. One of his daughters, Mary, married a cousin, Richard Dibrell of Richmond, Virginia, of whom more will be said under another head, and a son, Mr. Monroe Jones, was for a long time associated with Mr. Dibrell in business under the firm name of Dibrell & Jones.

As will be seen there are at this point two branches of the Dibrell family united, and under the head of Anthony Dibrell, brother of Leeanna Dibrell Jones, more will be said of Richard and Mary Jones Dibrell.

It is to be regretted that so little has been collected of this branch of the Dibrell family. Every effort has been put forth and every means exhausted to obtain data in regard to them, but it has been in this as in many other cases utterly impossible to obtain information.

Between the lack of interest, loss of data, and a still more objectionable feature, the idea that genealogy is undemocratic and hence unpopular, genealogy is made a difficult task from start to finish.

I do not mean to suggest that this last charge applies to this branch of the Dibrell family, as I have never found any of the name or connection that were not proud of their ancestry or who did not delight in perpetuating their lines of descent, but it is nevertheless a fact that men and women, whatever their antecedents or preferences may be, are more or less under the influence of a class of humanity that delights to sneer at anything that rises above the level of the common herd, to which, as a general rule, they themselves belong.

3 JUDITH DIBRELL.

Judith Dibrell, second daughter of Anthony Dibrell and Elisabeth Lee, was born in Buckingham county, 1760, married David Patterson of that county, about 1780. David Patterson and Judith Dibrell, had twelve children; Samuel, Thomas, Peter, John, David, Charles, James, William, Agnes, Elizabeth or Betsy, Sarah or Sally, and Judith.

David Patterson and his wife, Judith Dibrell, both lived to a very old age, their married life having run through a period of more than sixty years. There was very little difference in the dates of their deaths.

As in the case of Leeanna who married Michael Jones, very little is definitely known of the marriages or descendants of this large number of children, but as there were eight sons it can be readily seen that the name of Patterson who have descended from this marriage are very numerous.

In this as in every other instance, I have employed every effort and exhausted every means of obtaining information, but for the reasons suggested in the case of Michael Jones and Leeanna Dibrell, I have been unable to follow the different lines. I have, however, obtained through the assistance of Mrs. Abraham, whose first husband was Dr. Lafayette Dibrell, and who married secondly Mr. John Abraham of Buckingham county, Virginia, and who now resides in Richmond, the descendants of Elizabeth Lee Patterson, daughter of David Patterson and Judith Dibrell.

4 ELIZABETH LEE PATTERSON.

Elizabeth Lee Patterson, better known in her girlhood days by the pet name of "Betsy," as noted above, was among the children of David Patterson and Judith Dibrell, married William Lewis, son of Owen Lewis of Nelson county, Virginia, and grandson of Planter John Lewis of Albemarle, of the Zachary Lewis line. They had three children, all daughters, Judith Dibrell, Sarah and Elizabeth Lee.

5 Judith Dibrell Lewis married Edward H. Mosely of Buckingham county, Virginia, Sarah Lewis married a Mr. Morris, and Elizabeth Lewis married a Mr. Thomas of Nelson county, Virginia.

5 JUDITH DIBRELL LEWIS.

Judith Dibrell Lewis, daughter of William Lewis and Elizabeth Patterson, married Edward H. Mosely of Buckingham county, Virginia. Mr. Mosely was a brother of Alexander Mosely, who, for so many years was editor and proprietor of the Richmond Whig. They had three children, all daughters—Sarah Ann Lewis, Mary Elizabeth, and Virginia Edward.

6 SARAH ANN LEWIS MOSELY.

Married first, Dr. Lafayette Dibrell, a son of Mr. Charles Lee Dibrell and consequently a relative of Miss Mosely. Dr. Dibrell, who was in very poor health at the time of his marriage, lived but a few months thereafter; they left no children. Miss

Mosley married the second time, Mr. John Abraham of Buckingham county, Virginia. By this marriage there was one son—Rev. W. Y. Abraham of Richmond, Virginia. Mrs. Abraham also lives in Richmond with her son.

A more extended notice will be given Dr. Dibrell under the head of his own immediate line, and also of Mrs. Abraham, under the head of the Lewis family.

7 The Rev. Wyckliffe Yancy Abraham, only son of Sarah Ann Mosely, by her second marriage, was born in Rockbridge county, Virginia, whither his parents had removed from Buckingham, about 1850 or 1851, and is hence the rise of fifty years of age. He was educated at Richmond College, graduated in a theological course at the Baptist Theological seminary, located first at Greenville, South Carolina, but afterwards removed to Louisville, Kentucky. He married first, Miss Annie Broadus, daughter of Dr. Broadus, President of the Seminary at that time. Mr. Abraham's first wife died about 1895, and he married the second time, Miss Laura Christian of Buckingham county, Virginia, December, 1900. He had by the first marriage, two children—John a young man, twenty-five or six, in business in Richmond, Virginia; and Annie Louise, eight or ten years of age.

6 MARY ELIZABETH MOSELY.

Mary Elizabeth Mosely, daughter of Edward Mosely and Judith Lewis, married the Rev. Thomas N. Johnson, a distinguished Baptist divine of Virginia, who filled some of the most important stations within the bounds of the State, was a power, so to speak, in Baptist circles, and wielded a religious influence which but few men ever did. He lived to a ripe old age, was minister of the gospel for more than half a century, and was above eighty when he died. They had five children, Sarah Louisa, Thomas Edward, Ella, Lafayette Dibrell and Mary Lewis.

7 Sarah Louisa Johnson, daughter of the Rev. Thomas N. Johnson and Mary Elizabeth Mosely, married the Rev. William Shipman, of Nelson county, Virginia. Mr. Shipman was also a

Baptist minister, who has filled many important stations in the State, among others, Salem, Virginia, Halifax Court House, Virginia, and one of the Richmond churches. Among their children are the Rev. Thomas Shipman, a bright light in the galaxy of Baptist divines, and Miss Ella, a young lady of rare attainments, and a graduate of Hollins Institute.

7 The Rev. Thomas Shipman, though barely out of the twenties, has risen rapidly in his denomination, has filled important stations, one in Kentucky, one in Savannah, and when last heard from, was in Roanoke, Virginia.

In tracing genealogy it is strange to note how different families will run into each other, but we are compelled to note at the same time the old adage, "that birds of a feather will flock together," and while there is sometimes a contradiction of this adage, where emotional and erratic young people fly off at a tangent and defy the natural laws of affinity, the exceptions are very rare.

We find in the foregoing lines where the name of Lewis, Lee, du Breuil and others of equal rank and distinction have become almost indiscriminate by intermarriages.

SECOND ANTHONY DIBRELL.

3 Anthony Dibrell, the second of that name in America, was the son of the first Anthony Dibrell and Elizabeth Lee. He was born in Buckingham county, Virginia, May, 1763, being the youngest of four children, before mentioned. Although a boy at the breaking out of the Revolution, being only 13 years old, he enlisted in the army in 1778, at the age of 16, and was actively engaged until the close of the war, doing much military service, and actively participated in the battles of Guilford Court House and Yorktown. We have no record of his life between the close of the war and the date of his marriage, an interval of seven years. He died 1816.

In 1790 Anthony Dibrell married Miss Wilmuth Watson, of Amherst county, Virginia, daughter of James Watson of that county. For about a year the young couple remained in Amherst, where the first child, Charles Lee Dibrell, was born, after which, Anthony with his young wife, just 16 years old, returned to his native county of Buckingham. To this couple were born 13 children, six sons and seven daughters, as follows:

Charles ·Lee, born October 3, 1791; James Watson, February 9, 1793; Edward, born September 19, 1794; Elizabeth Nicholas, born March 16, 1798; Martha Rookings, December, 1799; Leeanna, October 2, 1801; Francis Watson, born June 18, 1803; Anthony, born August 19, 1805; Judith Ann, born June 26, 1807; Catherine, born July 15, 1809; Wilmuth Watson, born May 20, 1811; Matthew Watson, born October 22, 1813; Collins died in infancy.

Following is a brief record of the boy career of Anthony Dibrell as a Revolutionary soldier, and as brief as it is it contains volumes· when the dates are considered. It will be considered that he was born in 1763, and his first enlistment being in 1778, he was only 15 years old, and was only 19 years old when Cornwallis surrendered.

As the result of a correspondence with the War and Interior Department, I received the following from the Commissioner of Pensions.

"Department of Interior, Washington, D. C., April 26, 1892.

"Sir: In reply to your request for a statement of the military history of Anthony Dibrell, a soldier in the Revolutionary war. You will please find below the desired information as contained in application for Pension, on file in this bureau, by his widow.

"He enlisted twice, 1778 and 1781, and was a private in Captain John Mosely's company, and his regimental commanders at different times, were Colonel John Cabell and Colonel John Harper.

"The last service is not clearly stated and may have been more than one enlistment. He was engaged in removing stores and was in North Carolina part of the time.

"He was engaged in the battle of Guilford Court House, and at the surrender of Cornwallis at Yorktown.

"His residence at the time of enlistment was Amherst county, Virginia.

"Remarks: Widow's maiden name was Wilmuth Watson to whom the soldier was married in November, 1790.

"Very respectfully,

"D. D. MURPHY,

"Acting Commissioner."

From the sworn statement of David Patterson, John Thomas and others on file in the Pension office, Anthony Dibrell served three months under Captain John Mosely of Buckingham county, Virginia, at Albemarle Barracks, as a lieutenant or ensign guarding prisoners taken at the defeat of Burgoyne at Still Water in the State of New York. This service began in February, 1778, before Anthony had completed his fifteenth year.

John Thomas of Buckingham county, made oath that he was a captain in Colonel Taylor's regiment of guards at Albemarle Barracks, and at the expiration of that service which was three months, "I made out the pay roll for Captain Mosely myself."

David Patterson and John Patterson, both of Buckingham county, Virginia, made oath that in addition to the foregoing service, "Anthony Dibrell and many others were ordered by Colonel John Cabell to remove the military stores from Scott's Ferry to New London, Bedford county, Virginia, and that he was also sent to Cumberland Courthouse, Pr. Edward, and Louisa counties to meet the enemy. Further; that said Anthony marched from the county of Buckingham early in the month of February, 1781, to the State of North Carolina and was in the battle of Guilford Court House, March 15, 1781; that he continued in General Green's army some time after the battle of Guilford. I also distinctly remember that in the month of September, 1781, the said Anthony Dibrell went to Yorktown, where he remained until the surrender. of Lord Cornwallis and the British army."

It is a matter of family history related by Anthony Dibrell to his sons and many friends, that he was brought off the battlefield of Guilford, wounded or exhausted, by the celebrated Peter Francisco.

Peter Francisco was doubtless one of the most celebrated private soldiers of the Revolutionary war. His antecedents are unknown and were doubtless very little known to himself. He was, however, believed to be of Portuguese origin, and was a protege of Judge Edmund Winston, of Buckingham county, Virginia.

This incident of Francisco in connection with Anthony Dibrell gives the author an opportunity, as it is also a pleasure, to make a brief reference to this grand old hero, who seems to have almost passed out of history, and indeed to have been lost to memory. This phenomenal character and brave patriot seems to have been specially fitted for the age in which he lived, and to have filled a niche which, but for him, would have remained a vacuum. A reference to Peter Francisco at this point is by no means a digression from the history of Anthony Dibrell; it will be remembered that Judge Edmond Winston and the first Anthony Dibrell lived in the same county, attended the same court, and were on terms, not only of friendship, but intimacy. Peter Francisco was a protege of Judge Winston, and young Anthony the boy soldier, not fifteen years old when he left the paternal roof in defense of his country, was a son of Judge Winston's special friend. Anthony, a mere strippling, strong alone in a brave heart and unswerving patriotism, Francisco fully developed, of wonderful physical ability and herculean strength, it was to be expected that young Dibrell, as far as could be among soldiers, should be the special charge of Peter Francisco.

Owing to his wonderful prowess, dauntless courage, and superhuman strength, Francisco was allowed by his commanding officers to play the part of a "Free Lance." He was indeed an independent command, solitary and alone by himself. Wherever he went he crippled the enemy and his blows were of the more telling than those of a whole regiment. The sword that he wielded could not be handled by an ordinary man, and its length was such, that, single handed he was invincible, and he often proved an overmatch for two or three. Frequently overpowered by numbers and captured, he invariably escaped, and the theory that two armed men are sufficient to guard one man who is not armed, in his case, was contradicted, for on more than one occasion he disarmed one, killed the other, and walked away free.

On the return of peace Peter Francisco returned to his home, the old Winston homestead, one mile east of the New Store, a village in Buckingham county, Virginia, situated on the old stage thoroughfare between Lynchburg and Richmond. He was as remarkable in peace as he was in war. As a soldier he loved to fight, as a citizen he was not only peaceable, but a "peacemaker." Among the many anecdotes related of Francisco is that of a man who was ignorant of his character and who had become offended with him. This man in his haste and heat of passion, early one morning before breakfast, hastened to Francisco's home to demand satisfaction. The mansion and its surroundings like most residences of that period of Virginia history, had very spacious grounds. The house set back from the main thoroughfare nearly a hundred yards, while the inner inclosure gave ample space for a smaller yard. The irate visitor had ridden inside the larger inclosure and called Francisco out, who employed every possible means to pacify his visitor, enticing him away from the house in the meantime, so as to avoid disturbing the family. When they had gotten to the outside inclosure and all pacific means had failed Francisco took his visitor at arm's length and lifted him from his horse and set him over the fence. Bewildered at the way in which he had been handled, in his amazement, he stood silent for a few moments, then told Francisco if he would hand him over his horse he would go home; with some assistance from the horse he was landed on the same side of the fence with his rider, and the difficulty was settled.

Peter Francisco married a widow West (whether he had previously married is not known), and so far as is known he left no children. One of his stepsons, John William West, formerly of Buckingham county, Virginia, and afterwards of Bedford, was personally known to the author. From this source much information has been obtained of the life and character of this Revolutionary patriot. Mr. West always spoke in the most affectionate terms of his stepfather.

Late in life he was appointed sergeant-at-arms to the Virginia House of Delegates, in which position he remained until his death in 1836. He was buried with military honors in the public cemetery at Richmond, Virginia, and thus he continued in death as he had been in life, "guest of the State."

There is little known of the history of Anthony Dibrell after the close of the Revolution, as his life subsequent to that time was strictly that of a private citizen. We have no record of him from 1781, until 1790, at which time, as we have before seen, he married Miss Wilmuth Watson of Amherst county, Virginia, and during the short life that he spent thereafter in agricultural pursuits, he transferred to a large family of children the duties and priviléges of perpetuating family history. He died in 1816, aged 53 years.

4 CHARLES LEE DIBRELL.

Charles Lee Dibrell was the oldest son of Anthony Dibrell and Wilmuth Watson. He was born October 3, 1791, in Amherst county, Virginia and was raised in Buckingham to which county his father returned soon after his marriage. Here he was educated and spent the first few years of his early manhood. About 1820 he commenced business in Lynchburg, Virginia, where he was quite successful as a merchant and large operator in the tobacco trade, and in 1823 married Miss Mary Jane Lambeth of Campbell county, Virginia. About 1835 Mr. Dibrell purchased a popular watering place as a summer resort in Botetourt county, Virginia, which had been previously owned by a German by the name of Dagguer, and hence known as Dagguer's Spring, but after the property was purchased by Mr. Dibrell they became known as Dibrell's Springs, which name they still retain. These springs are about sixty-five miles west of

Lynchburg, near James river and the Richmond and Allegheny railroad which has been recently built; and it was here for about ten years, at this beautiful mountain resort, hedged in by peaks on every side, a bold and beautiful sulphur spring, gushing from the base of Garden Mountain, that Mr. Dibrell entertained from lower Virginia, and States farther south and north those who were in search of health among the mountains. Among the distinguished visitors at Dibrell Springs, I have often heard Mr. Dibrell describe in his own language, the visit of Van Buren and party, in 1838, which was quite an event in those days, when a trip from Washington to Virginia Springs would require as much time as it would now to visit the Valley of the Congo.

Having acquired interests in the Warm Springs of Bath county, Virginia, and subsequently in Richmond, he sold Dibrell Springs in 1842, and after spending one season at the Warm Springs, he opened the Powhattan House in Richmond, Virginia. This house was located on Broad street adjacent to Capitol square, and owing to its surroundings, its location was one of the most desirable in the city, but owing to gross mismanagement, however, it had been allowed to fall into disrepute. Under the management of Mr. Dibrell the Powhattan House was restored to its former prestige and became again one of the leading hotels of Richmond.

Having spent five years in Richmond as proprietor of the Powhattan, he returned to Lynchburg, where he first commenced his business career, and it is a very singular coincidence that, after an eventful business life running through more than thirty years, and at different localities, several hundred miles apart, he should have closed active business life at the same place that he begun it.

In 1847 Mr. Dibrell took possession of one of the best known houses in Lynchburg, which had been kept by the venerable Robert Morris, who belonged to a preceding generation, and subsequently by Paul Jones, who died in Atlanta in 1876. It is said to have been in this house that the gifted and erratic Maj. Tom Rudd, for many years the representative from Campbell in the Legislature, sang "Show pity, Lord" when the stars fell in 1833. This house was opened under the name of Dibrell's Hotel, and it is yet a landmark in Lynchburg, though it has ceased to be a hotel for more than forty years.

It was at this house that a new epoch in Mr. Dibrell's life took place. On the 23d of December, 1850, Mary Jane Dibrell, consort of Mr. Charles Lee Dibrell, breathed her last. It is not too much to say that she was the mainspring of Mr. Dibrell's life; she was in the habit of saying jocularly, that she had kept him alive for thirty years, and in this there was more truth than poetry. There is no doubt that she was indispensable to his vitality, and in her death he not only lost his right arm, but lost the vital force which gave activity to his very being.

Mrs. Dibrell was a woman of rare characteristics, possessing at one and the same time the most tender, affectionate and womanly traits, and yet the rare power to command obedience and respect. Gen. John Echols of the Confederate army, who was afterwards vice president of the Chesapeake and Ohio railroad, was a nephew of Mrs. Dibrell, and from him it was my pleasure to hear the highest encomiums paid her character. As a culmination of what he had to say, "not even his own mother had been so true and disinterested in her friendship or had more to do in shaping the better traits of his character than Mrs. Dibrell."

In 1853 Mr. Dibrell retired from active business life, and in 1859 went to Texas. Two of his married sisters, Mrs. Simons and Mrs. Gary, settled in Texas in early life and raised their families there. The three surviving sons of Mr. Dibrell, Charles Lee, Jr., James Watson and John Meredith also cast their lots in the Lone Star State. Mr. Dibrell was not a stranger in Texas; as has been seen two of his sisters had preceded him and their families had grown up with the country, while three of his sons were already there. Sam Houston a native of Rockbridge county, Virginia, who was afterwards governor of Tennessee, the leader in the Texas struggle for independence and hero of San Jacinto, was governor of Texas, at that time.

Houston was an old personal friend of Mr. Dibrell of bygone days and welcomed him, as it were, with open arms, and gave him an appointment in the State Department. At the close of the war, however, with Houston dead, and Texas in the hands of unscrupulous adventurers, Mr. Dibrell found himself without a position, and as almost all the southern people, without money.

In the dilemma above described, Mr. Dibrell instinctively turned his face eastward and sought the scenes of his early manhood. His older son had left Texas with the army and after the war had not returned, and his only surviving daughter was still a resident of Virginia. For a man of his age, then 74, and the country all torn up by the wreckage of war, this was no small undertaking. Fifteen hundred miles of travel over roads that had been torn up by military operations, and through a country that had not been restored to business methods, is indeed a task that would command all the strength and energy of a much younger man, but there is nothing that so buoys the human mind as the hope of returning to the scenes of its childhood.

About the first of October, 1865, Mr. Dibrell started upon this homeward journey, and in his enfeebled condition made the trip as it were, by relays. Coming first to Galveston, he rested for some time with his nephew, Mr. Thomas A. Gary, then with a desperate effort he came on to Huntsville, Alabama, where his relative Mrs. Moore, took charge of him and detained him for several weeks, thence he came on to Virginia, where with another nephew, Mr. Edward Echols of Balcony Falls, he remained some time.

It was at the house of Mr. Echols, twenty-eight miles from Lynchburg, at the point where James river passes through the Blue Ridge, that I found Mr. Dibrell on my way from Baltimore in January 1866. He was but a few miles from my home at that time, as I was merchandising at Buffalo Forge, in Rockbridge county, Virginia, but he was too feeble to travel. After resting a few days, however, Captain Echols brought him to my house in his carriage, but he did not survive many weeks after his arrival. Having accomplished the one object most dear to his

234

heart, the return to the home of his childhood, the land he so much loved, and being surrounded by those who loved him most, being with two of his children, my wife and his oldest son, Charles Lee Dibrell, Jr., the latter having been left in Virginia by the war, it seemed that he regarded his mission as completed, and quietly passed away February, 1866, in the seventy-fifth year of his age. Owing to the difficulties in transportation, there being no railroad between that point and Lynchburg, the waterway being closed by ice, and the mountain roads impassable, it was impossible to carry out the wishes of his children, in taking his remains to Lynchburg, and he was therefore buried at Falling Springs Cemetery, ten miles from Lexington, Virginia, full in sight of the Blue Hills of his nativity, among which he delighted to roam in his boyhood days.

Charles Lee Dibrell, and his wife, Mary Jane Lambeth, had eleven children, four of whom died in infancy. Those who survived, were Lafayette, Elizabeth, Mary Jane, Frances Ann, Charles Lee, James Watson and John Meredith.

5 DR. LAFAYETTE DIBRELL.

Lafayette Dibrell was the oldest child of Charles Lee Dibrell and Mary Jane Lambeth. He was born in Lynchburg, Virginia, in 1824. The circumstance attending the visit of Gen. Lafayette to America about this time, bringing more vividly to mind the patriotic services of that officer in our struggle for independence, gave rise to the naming of many hundreds of children for him, and this accounts for the name of the oldest son of Mr. Charles Lee Dibrell. Mr. Dibrell's father, the second Anthony Dibrell, had seen service with Lafayette, had been with him at Yorktown, and the name of the "Marquis De Lafayette," had been a household word in the Dibrell family for nearly half a century, and hence it is not strange that they should have perpetuated his name.

Lafayette Dibrell was principally educated in Richmond, Virginia, and was graduated from the Medical College of that city in the class of 1845, carrying off the honors of the institution. He was valedictorian of his class, and few men ever entered the medical profession with brighter prospects. In 1846 Dr. Dibrell married Sarah Ann Mosely of Buckingham county, Virginia, and established himself in the practice of medicine at Mount Vinco, in that county, but consumption had marked him for a victim and he was compelled to retire from the practice a few months after his marriage. Leaving Buckingham he came to Lynchburg and spent the last weeks of his life at his father's house, "Dibrell's Hotel." He was buried at the Presbyterian Cemetery in that city.

5 ELIZABETH DIBRELL.

Elisabeth was the oldest daughter of Charles Lee and Mary Lambeth Dibrell. She was born in New London, Virginia, March 23, 1833. Her early life was spent in Richmond, where her father resided for a number of years, and later in Lynchburg to which place he removed in 1847. She was a lady of rare gifts and attainments, with a disposition at once attractive and lovely, but like her older brother, Dr. Lafayette Dibrell, consumption had set its seal upon her early life, and after battling with the fell disease for twelve years, she finally fell a victim to it in the summer of 1862, in the twenty-ninth year of her age.

Being the oldest daughter at the time of her mother's death, she became in every essential sense of the word, a mother to her younger brothers, and was to them indeed everything that a mother could be. She was not so situated that she could have them at all times with her, but she saw to it that they always had a mother's care and attention. For five or six years previous to her death, and up to within a few months of that sad event, she had been engaged in teaching both academics and music, and it is rarely ever that one is found who gave such general satisfaction in this most difficult position, to both pupils and parents, and in many a Virginia family is to be found a "Lissie Dibrell" in token of the ardent love and affection borne for her while living and in perpetuation of her memory after death.

236

5. MARY JANE DIBRELL.

Mary Jane Dibrell was the second daughter of Charles Lee Dibrell and Mary Jane Lambeth. She was born March 11, 1835 at Dibrell's Springs, Botetourt county, Virginia. Her early childhood was spent at this place and in Richmond, and her early womanhood in Lynchburg, Virginia. Her early life was very bright and promising; beautiful, vivacious and intellectual, she was the center of attraction. It fell to the lot of but few to be so fortunately and advantageously situated as was Molly Dibrell, but, "all things sweet are fleeting, the sweetest still the fleetest," and thus it was in the life of Molly Dibrell. To one without philosophy, and to whom religious thought was a stranger, it would have seemed that "unmerciful disaster had followed fast and followed faster" upon her footsteps, and to one to whom philosophical training and religious conceptions had not been the predominant feature of life, her song might have been like that of Poe, and her hope might have been one melancholy dirge. But Molly Dibrell was of a very different cast of mind from that of Edgar Allen Poe; she was no less poetical, but much less erratic. She was imaginative but not a victim of vagaries. While Poe dreamed of a "Distant Aiden where he should clasp a radiant maiden whom the angels name Lenore," she had a sure anchor of hope that she would in a "Distant Aiden" meet and clasp all of her loved and lost, and above all meet him who had redeemed and saved her. As confidently and as hopeful as she looked upon the hereafter, life was bright and beautiful to her. Bereft of her mother at a very tender age, and seeing a delightful household scattered as a consequence, hers was a religion that repined not at adverse conditions, but wrested victory from defeat, and enabled her in the darkest hours, to see by faith the silver lining of the cloud which for a moment obscured her vision. She died in the autumn of 1856. For some time previous to her death she had been betrothed to a Lynchburg gentleman, prominent in business and social circles, who at the time of her death was absent in New York, in the interest of his firm. I know that the cold world cannot understand and does not appreciate, such devotion, and will give a smile of incredulity at the bare mention of the fact, but it is nevertheless true that this gentleman never left his room after returning home and learning of her death, until he was carried to his grave.

5. CHARLES LEE DIBRELL, Jr.

Charles Lee Dibrell, Jr., was the second son of Charles Lee Dibrell, Sr. He was born the 19th of July, 1840, at Dibrell's Springs in Botetourt county, Virginia. His early childhood was spent in Richmond, and later in Lynchburg. His early education was obtained in these cities. After the death of his mother, and the retirement of his father from business, he obtained a position in Blacksburg, Montgomery county, and afterwards in Christiansburg, the county site. In 1859 he turned his face to the southwest and cast, as he believed, his fortune, in the "Lone Star State," entering active business life in mercantile pursuits, but the rude hand of war was destined to change all of his plans, and before he had become well settled in his new home, the bugle blast called him to the field. As Virginia was destined to be the battleground between the sections, the Southern troops were hastened forward to the front, and Mr. Dibrell, with what was afterwards known as the Fourth Texas Regiment, under command of the gallant John B. Hood, contrary to all his preconceived ideas or plans, found himself back in Virginia.

During 1861, and until the latter part of 1862, Mr. Dibrell followed the fortunes of the Fourth Texas Regiment, anxious for the fray and fearful, lest the war would be over before they reached Virginia. They were permitted to know very soon something of its realities, and before a year had passed they were fully convinced that they had not been slighted by the authorities, but that they had been allowed a full participation in passing events, indeed, to their entire satisfaction. In the series of battles from June 26th to July 2d, inclusive, Mr. Dibrell's regiment was constantly engaged; its Maj. Bradfute Warwick was killed, Captain Bain commanding his company was severely wounded, and, indeed, the entire regiment, under command of the brave but reckless Hood, was cut to pieces.

After this series of battles had been fought and the seige of Richmond raised, Mr. Dibrell's military services underwent a change. His captain who was severely wounded was taken to the house of Mr. Edwin Dibrell, an uncle of Mr. Charles Dibrell, and the latter detailed to attend him. The operations of the army were changed in another direction, and the main body under Gen. Lee proceeded north by way of Burkville, Orange Courthouse and Culpepper to meet Gen. Pope who had started on another "on to Richmond," by the same route that McDowell first undertook.

Mr. Dibrell obtained a transfer from the Fourth Texas Regiment to the Partisan Rangers under command of "Harry Gilmer," and during the years 1863, 1864, 1865, to the close of the war, was in all of the partisan warfare of Northern Virginia, the operations of which frequently extended into Maryland and Pennsylvania, and more than once under the very spires of Washington City. He was with the Southern troops at Magnolia Station, on the P. W. & B. road between Baltimore and Philadelphia, in 1864 when Gen. Patterson was captured. He was with the army at the burning of Chambersburg, and the entire detachment under command of Gen. Bradley T. Johnson barely escaped capture from the pursuit of Averill's cavalry which followed. The Federal cavalry continued to pursue and harass the Confederates through the valleys of Virginia, when at Mount Jackson bridge the Confederates took a stand and gave battle repulsing the Federals, and gaining time by this means to fall back in better order. It was at this engagement that Mr. Dibrell was severely injured, having received a gunshot wound through the lungs. Maj. Gilmer carried Mr. Dibrell to the nearest farmhouse on his own horse and under his immediate supervision, not knowing but that he was leaving him with strangers. He requested that special care and attention be given him at his own expense, and that the enemy be warned, should they advance, that whatever treatment was meted to Dibrell would be received by their prisoners which had fallen into his hands. As a matter of fact, however, the enemy did not advance; they had gotten enough in their engagement at Mount Jackson Bridge.

Major Harry Gilmer was very fond of Mr. Dibrell who came up to the full measure of his idea of a dashing cavalry officer, and at no time did he fail to give full expression of his appreciation. His charge, however, to the people in whose hands he left Mr. Dibrell, was needless, though Maj. Gilmer was not aware of this. Mount Airy is the most celebrated body of land in the Shenandoah valley, embracing a thousand acres of bottom land in one body on the Shenandoah river seventy-two miles northeast of Staunton. On an elevation overlooking this vast estate and at the base of Massanuttin mountain was the palatial home of John G. Meem of Lynchburg, Virginia, whose son, Gen. Gilbert Meem married a sister of General Jordan who was chief of Gen. Beauregard's staff. At the time spoken of Mount Airy was occupied by the family of Gen. Meem, while the wife and sister of Gen. Jordan, were among the visitors at the home. These were all intimate friends of the Dibrell family in Lynchburg, Virginia, and Mr. Dibrell so far as being left among strangers was in the house of his friends. There was no surgeon at hand nor was there any doctor nearer than five miles across Massanuttin mountain. The battle occurred after eight o'clock at night in December, 1864, and by the time Mr. Dibrell had been carried to Mount Airy, it was after ten o'clock at night. Notwithstanding the hour of night, nor the fact that the thermometer was hovering around zero in this mountain pass, Miss Betty Jordan and Kate Riley of Winchester, crossed the mountain having to wade several swollen streams to get a doctor to attend Mr. Dibrell. This is only another instance of the self-sacrificing devotion of Southern women when the needs of the Southern soldier required it. Mr. Dibrell recovered from his wounds in time to return to his post before the collapse of the Confederacy. When the surrender took place he was in the mountains of Virginia very far removed from the base of operation and therefore he did not hasten to some nearby headquarters to obtain a parole or to seek the benefits of amnesty, but like Jubal Early, Bob Toombs and a few others, he enjoyed while living the rare distinction of "never having surrendered."

After the close of the war Mr. Dibrell returned to his friends in Campbell county, Virginia, who were delighted at the privilege of having him back alive. In 1871 Mr. Dibrell formed an association with the Pullman Palace Car Company, and was assistant superintendent of the lines between Lynchburg and Vicksburg, and was subsequently assistant superintendent and receiving cashier for that company at New Orleans. Subsequently Mr. Dibrell was general southern agent for the Richmond & Danville railroad, with headquarters at Augusta, Georgia, and it may be said that this was the turning point in the life of Mr. Dibrell. It is proper to say, however, in this connection, that no single individual in the soldier life or in the discharge of the duties thereof, ever commanded a higher regard from his superior officers than did Mr. Dibrell. Major Harry Gilmer, in his account of his military operations in the valley of Virginia and elsewhere, pays him the highest commendation for gallant services.

In 1878, Charles Lee Dibrell, Jr., married Sally Lou, daughter of the Hon. Henry Russell of Augusta, Georgia. They have only one child, a daughter, Mary Lee Dibrell, a bright and beautiful young lady of about sixteen years, who is now nearing graduation in the Nashville schools.

For a number of years Mr. Dibrell was connected with the Southern Express Company at Augusta, Georgia, of which he was auditor up to the time of his death, with headquarters temporarily at Memphis but afterwards at Chattanooga. He died October, 1895, and was buried in the Russell burying ground in Augusta, Georgia.

MISS SALLY R. DIBRELL.

Mr. Charles Lee Dibrell, Jr., married Sally Russell of Augusta, Georgia, November, 1878. Miss Russell was a daughter of Mr. Henry Russell, one of the most prominent citizens of that city, who was at one time its mayor, and at all times a leader in its affairs. Miss Russell was one of a large family of daughters noted for their beauty and accomplishments. One of the sisters married Mr. Gregg Wright, son of Gen. Wright of the Confederate army, and up to the time of his death was editor of the Augusta Chronicle; and the older daughter married Col. E. W. Cole of Nashville, Tennessee, one of the leading railroad magnates of his day who was withal a capitalist who engaged in the largest ventures; possessed of a fine executive ability and of a large fortune, he was a recognized leader in financial affairs. Some of the most important railroad schemes were worked out as a result of his rare abilities. The Nashville, Chattanooga and St. Louis system as also the East Tennessee, Virginia and Georgia, it may be said, were his handiwork. He was president of both of those companies.

Col. Cole was twice married. By the first marriage he left descendants and by the second marriage with Miss Russell he had two children, a son and a daughter. The son, Mr. Whiteford Russell Cole, is a young business man of Nashville, he has recently married and has bright prospects before him; and a daughter, Miss Anna Cole, who is just blooming into womanhood.

RUSSELL.

It is proper that I should briefly note at this point a sketch of the Russell family. I do this for several reasons. First, it is a family that has made its mark and left its impress upon the times covering the period of its history; second, its individual members have led lives and played a part which entitle them to special notice; and, third, it is a family to which Mr. Dibrell was specially endeared, and which entertained for him the highest appreciation.

The Hon. Henry Russell, as has been before stated, was a landmark in the history of Augusta. He was not a politician by profession or even by preference, but drawn into the maelstrom by the force of circumstances and what was believed to be the best interest of the city, he accepted the situation, and without being sullied in the dirty stream, he did much to rectify and overcome the practices which render politics odious.

Mr. Russell very early in life married. Martha Danforth, and commenced business in Augusta, Georgia, as cotton factor. They had but two sons, William and James. William married Miss Pullen of Lagrange, he fell into bad health early in life and was compelled to retire from business. James for a long time associated with his father in the cotton business, subsequently removed to Atlanta where he has been engaged as commission merchant for ten or twelve years. He resides with his family on West North avenue in Atlanta. One son, and a beautiful and accomplished daughter, contribute to the happiness of the household.

I omitted to mention the name of their oldest son, who had been so long dead that he had passed for the time out of my memory.

Maj. Whiteford Russell, oldest son of Hon. Henry Russell and Martha Danforth, married in early life, and when the war between the States broke out, leaving a young wife and two small girl children, he marched to the front and into the thickest of the fight. He was killed in one of the early engagements leaving a widow and two little children.

Mr. Henry Russell left seven daughters, all of whom were estimable and accomplished. They were social leaders in Augusta society, and their father's house might be said to have been headquarters for social gatherings. Their oldest daughter married Col. Cole of Nashville, another married Mr. Gregg Wright of the Augusta Chronicle. The third daughter Ella Russell, was perhaps the best married young lady of her age and generation, having been wooed and won by a young Hebrew banker, prominent in social and financial circles by the name of Cohen. The parents of both parties opposed the union, hence they took matters into their own hands, and crossed the river into South Carolina where they were married by a justice of the peace, and when they had returned to the home of the bridegroom's father, it was ascertained that the proceeding did not meet the approval of the old Hebrew, hence they were conducted down to the Synagogue where the marriage ceremony was performed by the Rabbi; then returning to the home of the bride's father it was found that neither of preceding marriages met his approval, and in true Methodist style they were accompanied by their friends to St. John's Church where they were married by a Methodist preacher in accordance with the regulations of the church. By this time the young people had gotten somewhat used to getting married, and doubtless settled down to the belief that they were well married. They have spent their married life in Augusta, Georgia, where they have reared a large and interesting family.

The marriage of Miss Sallie Lou Russell to Charles Lee Dibrell, Jr., has already been noted.

Another daughter, Miss Nodie Russell, married, first, a Mr. Davies, and, second, a Mr. Hammond; they reside in Augusta.

The youngest daughter, Miss Irene Russell, while traveling in Europe met among the Alps an adventurous young man of wealth and position by the name of Washburn, from Chicago. It is not known whether this was a case of love at first sight, but be this as it may, their acquaintance and friendship at least ripened into love, and upon the return home to America, they were married. One little boy has blessed their union, and it does by no means overdraw the subject to say that they give every evidence of a happy life.

FRANCES ANN DIBRELL.

Frances Ann, the third and youngest daughter of Charles Lee and Mary Lambeth Dibrell, was born May 2, 1837, at Dibrell's Springs, Botetourt county, Virginia. Her early life was spent in Richmond and Lynchburg at which places her father was engaged in business at different times. She lost her mother at a very tender age, and spent her early womanhood with her relatives. On the 18th of August, 1857, she was married to J. M. McAllister of Campbell county, Virginia, and it is not over-stepping the proprieties of a volume devoted to genealogy, to say that they have spent 44 years of a happy married life, a length of time rarely allotted to any couple, of a continued married life.

Under the head of the McAllister family a more extended account will be given of her and her descendants.

[Since the above was written, Mrs. Frances Ann McAllister has passed into the "Great Beyond." No language can do justice to her memory. Her life and character are written upon the hearts of those who knew and loved her in life, and can only be revealed, as the "Ages of Eternity Roll." A loved and loving wife, and devoted mother, a sincere and disinterested friend, a devout, pure-minded, blood-washed and life-long Christian, she has gone to her God.—AUTHOR.]

5 JAMES WATSON DIBRELL, JR.

James Watson Dibrell, Jr. ("Wattie Dibrell"), the third son of Charles Lee Dibrell, and Mary Jane Lambeth, was born December 25, 1842, at Dibrell's Springs, Botetourt county, Virginia. His early life was spent in Lynchburg, where he was for the most part educated. "Wattie Dibrell" was a wonderfully bright youth and attracted all with whom he came in contact. In 1856 a gentleman by the name of Church formed a very warm attachment for him and insisted that his father allow him to send him to his old home, Munson, Massachusetts, to be educated, but he fell a victim to a severe attack of typhoid fever which left the effects of its ravages upon him to such an extent that he was compelled to return home. The result of this spell was such that curvature of the spine followed which gave rise to a serious deformity from which he never recovered. In 1860 he went to Texas with a view to growing up with the country, but before he had time to settle squarely down to business, the war clouds burst forth with all their fury, and with all true Southerners he took the field, and though extremely delicate, being scarcely more than an invalid, he was in the saddle during the entire war.

When the war was over, having gone into the service with what was already believed to be a shattered constitution, having been the victim of a very severe affliction when a boy, he came out of the army, penniless, homeless, and as far as human sight could go, friendless; for whatever friends he had were either too far away to render him any assistance, or in the same sad plight as himself. And thus it was, with four of the best years of his early manhood spent in the service of the Lost Cause, and consequently lost, he began life in 1865 at the age of twenty-three; and as the sequel has shown, battled against adverse fate and proved himself a genuine hero. His success was not what the world would call brilliant, but it was truly wonderful, because it was in the face of apparently insurmountable difficulties, which were overcome by the most persistent energy of life and tenacity of purpose. He was in the United States Mail service from 1878 until his death, February, 1896, and during that time performed the duties of his position under physical difficulties which none but a hero in the fullest sense of the term would dare to undertake.

In 1871 James W. Dibrell was married to Miss Marza Dalton, a daughter of a truly historic Texas family, and resided in Galveston, Texas, up to the time of his death.

James W. Dibrell and Marsa Dalton had six children, two sons and four daughters: Mary Lee, James Watson, Geneva, Marsaline, Charles Granger, and Frances Zelma.

Mary Lee and Marsaline both married but died without issue. Geneva married Robert Sholes and resides at a railroad station between Houston and Galveston at which he is depot agent; they have one child, a daughter.

6 JOHN MEREDITH DIBRELL.

John Meredith Dibrell, the youngest of the sons of Charles Lee Dibrell and Mary Lambeth who survived infancy, was born in Richmond, Virginia, February 21, 1845. His early boyhood was spent in Lynchburg and vicinity. At the age of fourteen he went with his father to Texas, and spending a few years in the mercantile establishment with his relatives, Crockett and William Dibrell, the entire drift of his life was changed. The war between the states broke out at this time, and young Dibrell, like every one else of his age in whose veins coursed Southern blood, responded to the first buglecall. It is true that he was only sixteen, but nevertheless he entered the cavalry of Colonels Terry and Lubbock, and continued in the service until the close of the war.

When the war had ended, John M. Dibrell commenced business at Calvert, Texas, where he became established and made many friends. In 1874 he married Lella Preston, of Calvert, a descendant of the celebrated Virginia family of that name. He was very prominent and popular in his county, and as a consequence was entrusted with positions of honor and trust. At the time of his death he was sheriff of his county. In July, 1877, John M. Dibrell died suddenly at his home in Calvert, in the thirty-third year of his life. He left only one child, a daughter named Minnie Lee. His widow married a second time an excellent gentleman by the name of Bingham, by which marriage she has several children. They reside in Beaumont, Texas, about one hundred miles east of Houston.

6 Minnie Lee Dibrell has developed into a beautiful woman, attractive and very popular. She married William Dixon, a resident of South Carolina, afterwards of Atlanta, Georgia, and more recently of Beaumont, Texas.

EDWIN DIBRELL.

4 Edwin Dibrell, third son of Anthony Dibrell and Wilmuth Watson, was born September 19, 1794, in Buckingham county, Virginia. He married in Nashville, Tennessee, his cousin, Martha Shrewsbury, daughter of Drewry Shrewsbury and Elizabeth Dibrell. They had nine children: James Anthony, born August 15, 1817; Elizabeth Watson, born October 8, 1819; Richard Henry Lee, born April 30, 1820; Letitia Perkins, born December 20, 1824; Mary Jane, born June 6, 1828; Martha Sophronia, born May 7, 1831; Charles Drewry Shrewsbury, born September 30, 1834; Edwin, date of birth not obtained; and Virginia, born October 1, 1840.

Edwin Dibrell settled in Nashville, Tennessee, early in life, and during his residence there married, and it was there that all of his children were born. While he was not in politics, he was nevertheless an intimate friend of James K. Polk, and when Mr. Polk was advanced to the Presidency in 1844, and inaugurated March 4, 1845, he gave Mr. Dibrell an important appointment in Washington. This was something of a turning point in Mr. Dibrell's history. He never returned to Nashville.

When Mr. Polk's term of office had expired and he was succeeded by General Taylor, who was elected by the Whig party, Mr. Dibrell was superseded by one of Taylor's choice, after which time he made his home in Richmond, Virginia.

6 DR. JAMES ANTHONY DIBRELL

Oldest son of Edwin Dibrell and Martha Shrewsbury, was born at Nashville, Tennessee, August 15, 1817, and died at Van Buren, Arkansas, July 23, 1897, aged nearly 80 years.

He married Anne Elizabeth Pryor, daughter of Nicholas B. and Sallie M. Pryor, of Van Buren, Arkansas, and had the following children: Angela Medora, born December 9, 1841; James Anthony, born August 7, 1844, who died July 9, 1845; James Anthony, born August 20, 1846; Thomas Henry, born September 19, 1849, died July 19, 1853; Anne Eliza ("Missie"), born January 1, 1852; Sarah Susan, born November 10, 1856; Edwin Richard, born October 21, 1858; Richard Griffith, born July 24, 1860; Mattie or Mathew Shrewsbury, born December 3, 1866.

Dr. James A. Dibrell, after graduating in medicine, settled in Van Buren, Arkansas, early in life, married and raised his family there.

Following will be found some of the notices of Dr. Dibrell's death, from the Van Buren Daily Venture and the Times-Democrat, of Fort Smith:

From the Van Buren Daily Venture: " 'Earth to earth and dust to dust' has been said over the remains of Dr. James A. Dibrell, and his body has been consigned to its last resting-place in the city of the dead. Many were the tears that fell in grief at the loss of this venerable man.

"The funeral sermon was preached at the Presbyterian church by the Reverend Tucker, in which he spoke feelingly of the saintly life of the deceased. The sermon finished, the beautiful burial service of the Masons was read, and all that was mortal of Dr. James A. Dibrell passed from sight to be seen no more on earth."

Then follows a memorial of his Masonic lodge, delivered by the Worshipful Master, H. C. Johnson:

"My Brethren: I have called you to assemble in the character of Masons, to pay the last tribute of our esteem to an honored citizen, a devoted Mason, a devout Christian. And when we say that he shone with a lustre that marked his consequence among men, that as a citizen he was widely and well known; that he proudly unfurled the Christian banner in early life, and that he wore the badge of a Mason with credit to himself and 'honor to the institution,' there is little more to be said.

"What a glorious record to be inscribed to his memory! An honored and beloved citizen; a faithful and devoted Mason; a sturdy and devout Christian.

"And now, with sorrowing hearts, my brethren, let us lay to rest all that is mortal of our deceased brother, Dr. James A. Dibrell, and may we emulate his many virtues!"

From the Fort Smith News-Record: "Dr. James A. Dibrell died at his home in Van Buren this morning at the ripe age of 79.

"Dr. Dibrell was one of the most prominent citizens of this section of the state, and was likewise a man eminent in his profession. He came to this part of the state nearly sixty years ago, and with the exception of a brief period when he was absent in the army, has resided at his present home in Van Buren during the entire time.

"He at once took the foremost place in the medical fraternity, and held it without intermission. He was zealous in the performance of his professional duties, and was ever ready to respond to the call of those who needed his services.

"He practically died in harness, and died a martyr to the profession to which he devoted three-score years of his long, honorable and useful career.

"Dr. Dibrell leaves three sons and four daughters to mourn his death. His sons are Dr. James Dibrell, of Little Rock, and Drs. Edward and Matthew Dibrell, one of whom was associated with him in later years. His son, Dr. James Dibrell, of Little Rock, is a distinguished member of the medical fraternity, with a professional reputation nearly as widespread as that of his deceased father. His other two sons are likewise highly respected socially and professionally, and have inherited much of their father's zeal, and have made enviable reputations in the practice of their profession. In short, the dead physician's sons will do much toward keeping alive the memory of their deceased and worthy father.

"Three of Dr. Dibrell's daughters reside in this city. They

are Mrs. Dr. Duval, Mrs. George T. Sparks, and Mrs. Dr. Hines. The fourth daughter, Mrs. Irene Shipley, lives in Van Buren.

"Dr. Dibrell's death removes from the medical fraternity of this state one of its oldest and most distinguished members, and one whose loss will be lamented by thousands who knew the aged physician during the years of his long residence in Van Buren and the country tributary."

6 ¹Angela Medora Dibrell, oldest daughter of Dr. James A. Dibrell and Eliza Pryor, born December 9, 1841; married Dr. Elias Rector Duval of Forth Smith, May 8, 1860, and had the following children: Annie Medora, born February 20, 1861; Eliza Rector, born August 8, 1863; Benjamin Taylor, born February 7, 1872; Dibrell Legrand, born October 10, 1874; Angela Medora, born August 29, 1880.

6 ²Dr. James Anthony Dibrell, son of Dr. James A. Dibrell, of Van Buren, Arkansas, grandson of Edwin Dibrell and Martha Shrewsbury, and great-grandson of Anthony Dibrell and Wilmuth Watson, was born August 20, 1846. He has been for a number of years, and is now, president of the medical department of the University of Arkansas, located at Little Rock. He married Miss Riordan, of Little Rock, the marriage having taken place in Philadelphia October 3, 1876. Miss Riordan was a daughter of Lambert J. and Priscilla A. Riordan, of Little Rock, Arkansas. Mrs. Dibrell died March 4, 1899. Issue: John Raleigh Dibrell, born September 24, 1877, and christened by Rev. Thomas B. Welch, of the Presbyterian church. He is now a physician at Little Rock, Arkansas.

6 ³Anne Eliza Dibrell, daughter of Dr. James A. Dibrell, born January 1, 1852, married George Thomas Sparks, a banker of Fort Smith, Arkansas, March 11, 1879. Issue: Mitchell Bennett Sparks, born Fort Smith, Arkansas, February 16, 1881; James Dibrell Sparks, born Fort Smith, June 1, 1883; George Thomas Sparks, born Fort Smith, Decem-

ber 27, 1886; Medora Duval Sparks, born Fort Smith,
September 20, 1889.

6 ⁴Sarah Susan Dibrell, daughter of Dr. James A. Dibrell,
was born November 10, 1856. Married George Franklin
Hines, a physician of Fort Smith, Arkansas, October 4,
1883. Issue: Dibrell Pryor Hines, born Fort Smith, November 17, 1884; Mary Russell Hines, born Fort Smith,
November 4, 1886; Irene Gregory Hines, born Fort Smith,
September 26, 1890.

6 ⁵Edwin Richard Dibrell, son of Dr. James A. Dibrell, was
born at Van Buren, Arkansas, October 21, 1858. Married
Estelle Tucker, daughter of Sterling H. Tucker, of Chicago, Illinois. No issue. He is a physician at Little Rock,
Arkansas.

6 ⁶Irene Griffith Dibrell, youngest daughter of Dr. James A.
Dibrell, born July 4, 1860. Married Albert B. Shibley,
son of Henry Shibley, and resides at Van Buren, Arkansas. Issue: James Albert Shibley, born Van Buren, Arkansas, July 24, 1882; Emily Pryor Shibley, born March
5, 1885; Sue Edna Shibley, born November 16, 1887; Minerva Boyd Shibley, born June 26, 1890; "Missie" Sparks
Shibley, born February 17, 1893.

6 ⁷Matthew Shrewsbury Dibrell, youngest son of Dr. James A.
Dibrell, born December 3, 1862. Married Eula Jane Pierce.
Issue: Attilla Pryor Dibrell, born Van Buren, January
5, 1898. Matthew Shrewsbury Dibrell is a physician at
Van Buren, Arkansas.

5 RICHARD HENRY LEE DIBRELL.

Second son of Edwin and Martha Shrewsbury Dibrell, born
April 30, 1820, married his cousin, Mary Jane Jones, daughter
of William D. Jones, a merchant of "New Store," Buckingham
county, Virginia.

Mr. Dibrell went into business in Richmond, Virginia, early
in life, and under the firm name of Dibrell & Jones, they were

extensive and successful commission merchants for a number of years. They made tobacco a specialty, and commanded the trade of all lower Virginia. Mr. Richard Dibrell had four sons and three daughters. A son and daughter, James and Mary Lee, met death in a tragic manner. James, when a boy of about fifteen, was drowned while bathing in the Falls of James River, and Mary Lee, who had but recently married a gentleman by the name of Apperson, came to her death from burning, her clothing having caught fire from an open grate. His oldest son, William, was educated in Germany, and afterwards settled down in Richmond in the tobacco business with his father.

6 Alphonso Dibrell, second son of Richard Henry Lee Dibrell, and Richard Lewis Dibrell, a younger brother, engaged in the tobacco business in Danville, Virginia, under the firm name of Dibrell Brothers. Alphonso died unmarried, but the business was continued by Lewis Dibrell under the same firm name.

6 Lewis Dibrell is still in the tobacco business in Danville and has been successful in business, he married and has an interesting family.

Having met Mr. Dibrell, and having corresponded with him from time to time for several years, and having known his father and mother, brothers and sisters, for a number of years I have felt a peculiar interest in all of them, and take great pleasure in making this brief reference to Richard Lewis Dibrell, and only regret that I have not sufficient data to give the lineage of his wife and to refer intelligently to his children. This reference to them, however, will suffice to direct the attention of the searcher after genealogical history and enable them the better to reach a more extended data.

Mr. Dibrell had three daughters, the older Mary Lee, having come to a tragic end—having been burned to death. The other two daughters, Bettie Von Gronin and Kate Mieure, were bright and beautiful girls, and attractive and accomplished young ladies. The names that I have mentioned in regard to

those young ladies, however, are names that are attached to them
as children, and I do not know that they retained them after
they were grown up. I think it doubtful that Bettie retained
the name of Von Gronin, or that Kate retained the name of
Mieure, as when I saw them later in life they seemed to have
no recollection of either. They both made advantageous marriages, and one of them resides in Henderson, North Carolina,
and the other, near Burkville, Virginia.

4 ELIZABETH NICHOLAS DIBRELL.

4 Elizabeth Dibrell was the oldest daughter of Anthony
Dibrell and Wilmuth Watson. She was born in Buckingham
county, Virginia, March 16, 1798, and died at New Madrid,
Missouri, October 16, 1861. She married Archibald Hatcher in
May, 1818, in Buckingham county, Virginia. Archibald
Hatcher was born in Bedford county, Virginia, March 15, 1789,
and died in Lafayette, Indiana, March 1, 1845. He removed
from Lynchburg, Virginia, to Lafayette, Indiana, in 1837, and
became the first mayor of the city of Lafayette in 1838. Archibald Hatcher and Elizabeth Dibrell had nine children:

5 ¹Robert A. Hatcher the eldest, born in Lynchburg.

5 ²James Watson Dibrell Hatcher, born in Lynchburg, July 25,
1820, and died in Lafayette, Indiana, August 28, 1839.

5 ³Charles E. Hatcher born in Lynchburg, August 6, 1823, died
in Lafayette, Indiana, September 7, 1839.

5 ⁴William Henry Hatcher born in Lynchburg, December 28,
1829, died in Lafayette, Indiana, February 25, 1869.

5 ⁵Richard Hatcher born in Lynchburg, died in Missouri.

5 ⁶Fanny Hatcher married Alphonse Laforge, and was living at
last accounts at New Madrid, Missouri.

5 ⁷Maria Hatcher married Edward Barroll, married a second
time a Mr. Adams, and died in Missouri, 1869.

5 ⁸Elizabeth Hatcher married Morris Simons, and at last accounts they were living in Goliad, Texas.

5 ⁹Mary Hatcher never married, and at last accounts was living in New Madrid, Missouri.

5 ¹⁰William Henry Hatcher was married to Sarah Eliasbeth Early, born at Terre Haute, Indiana, September 18, 1837, the marriage having taken place at St. Louis, Missouri, in St. Paul's church, by the Rt. Rev. Cicero Stevens Hawks, Bishop of Missouri, February 16, 1860. She died at Paris, France, February 3, 1883, leaving issue:

6 ¹Louisa Hatcher, born in Lafayette, Indiana, February 26, 1861, married December 27, 1884, at Lafayette, Indiana, Senho Jose Coelho Gomes, secretary of the imperial Brazillian legation to the United States (who died in Rome, Italy while secretary of the Brazillian legation to the Vatican, in 1893).

6 ²Robert Stockwell Hatcher, born in Lafayette, Indiana, February 15, 1865; married in Lafayette, Indiana, April 22, 1889 (by the Rt. Rev. David Buel Knickerbocker, P. E. Bishop of Indiana), Georgia Hatcher Stockton.

Robert Stockwell Hatcher is a son of William H. Hatcher, of Lafayette, Indiana, hence a grandson of Archibald and Elisabeth Dibrell Hatcher, and a nephew of Robt. A. Hatcher, above referred to. He was born February 15, 1865, at Lafayette, Tippecanoe county, Indiana; attended public school at LaFayette, Philadelphia and Boston; accompanied his family to Europe in 1877; remained five years and a half pursuing his studies in France, Italy and Germany, and acquiring the languages of those countries; student in 1878 at the Parisian Lycee de l'Ecluse; studied and traveled in Italy during 1879 and 1880; in later years lived in Munich, and was in 1881 pupil at private school for boys in Dresden, Germany. In 1882 received instruction from private tutors in Berlin; traveled in Germany, Austria and Switzerland, and returned to Paris, remaining there until February, 1883, when, owing to the sudden death of his mother in that city, he sailed for America. At Washington, District of Columbia, studied law in the office of Hon. Rudolph Claughten, and took a course in law at Columbian University. Admitted to the bar in Indiana in 1895. Married April 22, 1889, at LaFayette, Indiana, to Miss Georgia Hatcher Stockton, and in the same year revisited Paris, accompanied by his wife. After further travels in France, Belgium, Germany, Holland, England, Ireland, Scotland and Wales, returned to the United States in September, 1890. In the following year was a member of the staff of the Chicago Tribune. In 1892, visited California. In 1893 was elected president of the Tippecanoe Republican Club, of LaFayette, Ind. Appointed in 1895 by the Secretary of State of Indiana as a member of the State Commission to confer with the naval authorities concerning the heraldic furnishing and decorating of the then newly commissioned United States battleship "Indiana." Elected in the same year reading clerk of the Indiana State senate, serving throughout the fifty-ninth General Assembly. By senate concurrent resolution number twenty, was appointed to investigate the origin and history of the seal of the State of Indiana, and directed to report to the Legislature as to the advisability of altering the same. (See Report of R. S. Hatcher, Com'r, spread of record in senate and ordered printed March 18, 1895). As special correspondent of the Indianapolis News in Central America, toured with his wife through British Honduras, Spanish Honduras and Guatemala. In December, 1895, was recommended by the entire Indiana Republican delegation of the United States House of Representatives, for reading clerk of the House; received the appointment, serving throughout the 54th Congress. (See Cong. Dict. 1897.) Upon the temporary organization of the Republican National Presidential Convention held in St. Louis in 1896, was recommended by the Republican National Committee for temporary reading clerk, and approved by the latter. Was unanimously elected permanent reading clerk of that body upon the permanent organization of the convention. (See official proceedings of the 11th Republican Convention, St. Louis, 1896.) Commissioned by Postmaster-General James A.

Gary, May 1, 1897, secretary of the United States delegation to the Fifth Universal Postal Congress held in Washington, District of Columbia, in the summer of 1897, and at the opening session was, upon motion of M. Edouard Hohn, director-general of the International Bureau of the Universal Postal Union of Berne, Switzerland, unanimously chosen secretary of the entire Congress, the proceedings of which were conducted exclusively in French. Was officially thanked on the closing day for his efficient services, and presented by the Dean of the Congress, on behalf of the international delegates present, with a beautiful silver platter as a token of esteem. Was created by the President of Venezuela, November 30, 1897, in recognition of services rendered to the Venezuelan delegates to the Postal Congress, Knight Commander of the Order of Bolivar, the Liberator, and decorated with the cross and placque of that order. Appointed by the Postmaster-General and the Director of the Mint jointly to design the medal in silver presented by the United States government to the members of the Universal Postal Congress, and at the request of the Treasury Department personally supervised its preparation, in conjunction with Chief Designer and Engraver Charles E. Barber, of the Philadelphia mint. Is a student of heraldry, numismatics and genealogy. Compiled the history of the family of Early in America. His investigations concerning the seals or coats of arms of the American States resulted in the United States government re-engraving the coats of arms upon the notes issued by national banks located in fourteen different states, Alabama, Arkansas, California, Delaware, Iowa, Maryland, North Carolina, New York, Ohio, Utah, Vermont, Wisconsin, Wyoming and the District of Columbia, which bank notes had borne for more than thirty years obsolete or inaccurate devices. (See correspondence of the Comptroller of the Currency and the Chief of the Bureau of Engraving and Printing, Washington, District of Columbia, 1892-1896.) Organized the Tippecanoe Historical Society, of LaFayette. Formed the valuable archaeological exhibit known as the "Hatcher Collection," in Purdue University, LaFayette, Indiana, unearthed in the vi-

cinity of the Wabash river, upon the former site of Fort Ouia-
tenon, of the period of the French occupation. Assisted Hon.
Wm. H. English, democratic candidate for the vice-presidency
of the United States in 1881, in preparing his history of the
Northwest Territory. Was several times elected honorary vice-
president for Indiana of the general society of the Sons of the
American Revolution. Was elected delegate from Indiana to the
Seventh Continental Congress of this society, held in Richmond,
Virginia, in 1896. Was appointed by the same society held in
Pittsburgh, Pennsylvania, in 1901, a member of the National
Press Committee. In 1899 made a trip with his wife to Porto
Rico and Venzuela, visiting Caracas on a mission for the United States Superintendent of Foreign Mails and in the interest of
a firm of New York publishers. In same year was appointed by
the Secretary of the Interior at the request of Hon. Binger Her-
mann, commissioner of the general land office, an assistant chief
of division in the general land office in Washington. In 1900 was
appointed by the acting Secretary of War, Hon. George P. Mei-
klejohn, translator of languages for the War Department, at
first in the Bureau of Insular Affairs, and later in the office of the
chief signal officer of the army. Was appointed, through the
United States commission, to the Paris Exposition of 1900, one
of the eight delegates to represent the government of the United
States at the International Congress for the amelioration of the
condition of the blind, held in Paris in 1900. Was the first secretary for Indiana appointed by the Society of Colonial Wars.
Was a member of the society of the War of 1812 and of the Huguenot Society of America. Was elected a member of the New
York Genealogical and Biographical Society, and honorary vice-
president of the Historical Society of Alabama. In 1893 was
made a thirty second degree Mason (Indiana Consistory Scot-
tish Rite). In 1890 was a made Knight Templar in Coeur de
Leon Commandery, New York City. In 1902 engaged in jour-
nalism. Mr. Hatcher now resides in Washington, District of
Columbia, 1119 K Street.

5 MARIA HATCHER BARROLL.

5 Maria Hatcher Barroll, daughter of Archibald and Elisabeth Dibrell Hatcher is thus sketched by United States Senator
David Turpie, of Indiana, in a letter to Mr. Stockwell Hatcher,
under date of September 29, 1902:

"Dear Sir: I enclose a slight sketch of recollection of your
aunt, Mrs. Barroll. She was one of the finest characters I ever
knew. Miss Maria Hatcher was a young lady of handsome appearance, of elegant manners, and of many graceful and useful
accomplishments. She was a good musician, sang and played
with much taste and feeling. Her voice was a contralto of singular sweetness and purity and of considerable strength and volume. In fair weather a great deal of her time was devoted to the
garden and to the care and culture of plants and flowers. She
was very fond of the rose—and, what was regarded as a little
curious she gloried in having the largest sunflower and the most
gaily tinted hollyhocks in the neighborhood. Her conversational
powers were of the first order, very swift and brilliant in repar-
tee, as a raconteur, quite remarkable. She was a constant reader,
and that of books of the gravest characters—history, theology,
mental and moral philosophy—though she also kept pace with
the lighter literature of that time and was familiar with the contents of 'The Lady's Companion,' and what she called the 'cook-
ery bookery.' Her gifts of wit, humor and fanciful invention were
often used in the way of pasttime and amusement. Walter Scott's
novels were then in the full flush of fashion and favor. She used
to playfully select from their pages sobriquets, which she applied
to the young gentlemen of her acquaintance. One was Captain
Waverly, another was Prince Charles, a third was Dominie
Sampson, and yet another was County Guy.

"Once at an evening party she was requested to sing. She
responded with the well known and then popular ballad in which
the following words occur:

"The village maid steals through the shade
To greet her lover nigh,

LEWIS AND KINDRED FAMILIES.

The lark his lay, who trilled all day,
   Sits hushed, his partner nigh
Bee, bird and bower confess the hour
   But where is County Guy?"

"The young gentleman just named and known in her circle was present, and a listener. He was not an adept in literature, but was a man of easy fortune who lived in the county not far from town, much given to bee culture, and skilled in ornithology. When he heard, therefore, in thrilling musical tones, the mention of the bee and the bird, he somehow conceived the idea that Miss Hatcher had improvised these lines, by way of chafing him upon the subject of his favorite pursuits. He was somewhat offended until one of her friends led him up to the piano, and showed him in Scott's ballad the printed lines just as they were sung.

"Miss Hatcher was a general social favorite, frequently toasted as the belle of Lafayette. Yet with all her gaiety and cheerfulness she was a woman of deep religious feelings and convictions—a regular attendant upon the services of St. John's church, and a member of the Choir as punctual in the performance of her duties as the rector. We were glad to see her in her place knowing that the music under her charge could not be a failure. During the church festivals, Christmas and Easter, she was always very much in request, and she took also a large and generous part in work of private benevolence and charity. Often she left her father's house, and going to some neighbor's dwelling of her acquaintance, she watched for many hours over a sick child in the cradle while its weary mother rested and slept."

6 HARRY H. BARROLL.

Commander Barroll of the United States Navy, whose name heads this paragraph, is a son of Mrs. Maria Hatcher Barroll and, hence, grandson of Archibald and Elizabeth Dibrell Hatcher, great-grandson of Anthony Dibrell and Wilmuth Watson, and great-great-grandson of Anthony Dibrell and Elizabeth Lee. He is a graduate of the Naval Academy at Annapolis, and has done regular service in the United States Navy having been promoted from time to time until he was retired as commander.

I regret that I have not been able to learn more of the life and services of Commander Barroll. As before stated I am informed that he had been retired for several years. I am not informed however, as to the grounds upon which his retirement was based. It is hardly possible that he was retired on account of age, as a comparison of dates would not bear out that conclusion, and, hence, the conclusion is almost inevitable that his retirement resulted from meritorious services.

5 ROBERT ANTHONY HATCHER.

Robert A. Hatcher was the oldest child of Archibald and Elisabeth Dibrell Hatcher, and should have been taken up in regular order in the list of their children. He was born in Lynchburg, Virginia, and early in life removed with his parents to Lafayette, Indiana, and subsequently, after his father's death, made his home in New Madrid, Missouri, at which place he practiced law successfully until the breaking out of the war in 1861.

Robert A. Hatcher was distinguished for his strict integrity, adherence to duty, and devotion to principle. He was emphatically a gentleman of the proverbial "Old Virginia" type. He never swerved from the traditions of his fathers. Of the scores of testimonials which have come from various sources we have only space for the following, written by General Alexander P. Stewart, on whose staff he served during the war between the States. We select this from among other testimonials because of the high character of its source, and the intimacy that existed between General Stewart and Major Hatcher. The testimonial is in the form of a letter written by General Stewart to Mr. Robert Stockwell Hatcher, a nephew of Maj. Robert A. Hatcher:

"Dear Sir: Yours of the second instant forwarded from Chattanooga, Tennessee, has been received, and it gives me pleasure to have an opportunity to bear testimony to the excellent qualities of your uncle Robert A. Hatcher of New Madrid, Missouri. He was a man of fine abilities and good common sense, faithful to every trust and duty, thoroughly reliable and of the highest order of honesty and integrity. He was an admirable soldier, brave as a lion, and apparently utterly devoid of fear both as a man and a soldier; and I may add, as a Christian he commanded the highest respect and the utmost confidence of all who knew him. In every way you could take him he was a man of unexceptional character."

The following is a notice of Major Robert A. Hatcher from the Congressional Directory, Forty-Third Congress, First Session, Washington, D. C., 1876:

"Robert A. Hatcher of New Madrid, Missouri, was born in Lynchburg, Virginia, February 24, 1819; was educated at private schools in Lynchburg; studied law and was licensed to practice in Kentucky; removed to New Madrid, Missouri, in 1847, and has there followed the practice of his profession ever since; was for six years circuit attorney of the Tenth judicial circuit of Missouri; was a member of the State Legislature in 1850-1851; member of the State Convention in 1862, and a member of the Confederate Congress in 1864-65; was elected to the Forty-Third Congress as a democrat receiving 13340 votes against 4,594 cast for his opponent. And was re-elected to the Forty-Fourth Congress as a Democrat, receiving 19,087 votes without opposition."

In the above notice from the Congressional Record Major Hatcher's Confederate service is not referred to except that he was elected to the Confederate Congress of 1864-65, when as a matter of fact, he left New Madrid in the service of the Confederate government in 1861, and remained in the field until he was elected to Congress in 1864. Indeed he was elected to Congress from the field and by the votes of the Missouri soldiers who were in the field.

It was in November 1864 that Major Hatcher stopped for a day's rest at my house in Virginia on his way from 'the army in Tennessee, to Richmond after he had been elected to Congress, only a few months previous to the collapse of the Confederacy, and this was the first respite that he had taken from field duty since hostilities commenced.

Extracts from columns of newspaper published in Charleston, Missouri, contributed by J. J. Russell, law partner of Mr. Hatcher:

"Robert A. Hatcher was born in Buckingham county, Virginia, February 24, 1819. He removed to Hickman, Kentucky, in 1841. He was married May 11, 1842, to Miss Mary E. Marr, the mother of his now bereaved children. His wife died on the second day of July, 1872, and on the 20th of January, 1875, he was married to Miss Eudora Forbes, who is now a grief-stricken widow. Major Hatcher died at Charleston, Missouri, December, 1886.

"Mr. Hatcher began the study of law under Judge E. I. Bullock in 1844, and soon afterwards entered into the active practice of his chosen profession. In 1848 he removed with his family to New Madrid, where he made his home until the year 1876, when he removed to Charleston, Missouri, where he resided until his death.

"During the late war Mr. Hatcher sympathized with the South and took up arms in the cause to which he believed duty called him. When once enlisted he showed the same qualities that have ever characterized him in private life, honesty of purpose, courage to do his duty, and fidelity to every trust. He was, during the greater part of the war, a major under General A. P. Stewart, and was with him in some bitter and hardfought battles. General Stewart, in his official report of the battle of Chickamauga, now published in book form, wrote in high praise of Major Hatcher as a good and valiant soldier, and for the valued assistance rendered him in that battle.

"Major Hatcher has also held many high offices of honor and trust in private life, and in no case has he ever violated any of them but has honestly, earnestly and faithfully done his whole duty.

"He was at one time a member of the State Legislature from New Madrid county. He was for several years circuit attorney of the Tenth judicial circuit, was a member of the Confederate Congress and for six years representative in the United States Congress from this district. He was for several years one of the curators of the State University.

"Major Hatcher may properly be counted among the pioneers at the bar in Southeast Missouri. He practiced in this circuit when it was more than 100 miles to travel to some of the courts, and on horseback the best means afforded for traveling. It was in the days of Judge Hough and when such men as General Watkins, General English and Greer Davis were his associates at the bar. He was then considered the peer of the best, and has ever since held a high place in his profession."

Major Robert A. Hatcher was twice married leaving issue only by his first wife. His first wife was a Missouri lady, and his second wife was of Glensfalls, New York. By the first marriage there were several children, among whom was Mr. James Hatcher, who followed his father during the stirring scenes of the Civil war, was with him in camp and on the march, and when Major Hatcher was elected to Congress his son James still followed the fortunes of the army, following Hood in his ill-fated attempt to cut off the supplies of the Federal army then enroute to Savannah, he was with Hood at Franklin, Tennessee, where the Confederate army was severely repulsed, and afterwards at Nashville, where the defeat was so decisive that General Hood was compelled to retrace his steps, as best he could into Dixie land.

A daughter, Miss "Florrie" Hatcher by the first marriage died in Washington, District of Columbia, a few years ago.

6 Mrs. Wilkie of Longwood, Florida, is a daughter of Mrs. Maria Hatcher Barroll, and hence a granddaughter of Mrs. Elizabeth Dibrell Hatcher. Major Hatcher died at Charleston, Missouri, and was buried at the home of his widow in Glenfalls, New York, in 1886.

4 JUDITH DIBRELL.

Judith Ann Dibrell, daughter of Anthony Dibrell and Wilmuth Watson, born June 26, 1807, married also Archibald Hatcher, who was a nephew of the gentleman of the same name that married her sister Elizabeth. They had no children. After the death of Mr. Hatcher she married a second time—Judge Simons of Texas. There were no children by this marriage. Morris Simons, a son of Judge Simons by a former marriage, married Elizabeth Hatcher, who was a niece of his stepmother and daughter of Archibald and Elizabeth Dibrell Hatcher.

4 JAMES WATSON DIBRELL.

James W. Dibrell, son of Anthony Dibrell and Wilmuth Watson, born September 19, 1794, married first Lettitia Perkins, second Sallie Brown. These ladies were respectively of Buckingham, and Amherst county, Virginia. There was no issue left by either marriage. Mr. Dibrell's first wife was a descendant of Leeanna Lee who married John Fearn, and as Mr. Dibrell was a descendant of her sister Elizabeth, he and his wife were consequently related.

The obituary of Mrs. Lettitia Dibrell, nee Perkins, was published in the Virginia Press, March 1, 1822, which stated that she departed this life on Monday night, February 25, in the twenty-third year of her age.

Mr. Dibrell married second Sallie Brown of Amherst county, Virginia; a lady of highest social standing and family connections. His second wife survived him several years, though the condition of her health was such that she had been an invalid for some time previous to his death.

4 MARTHA BROOKINGS DIBRELL.

Martha Brookings Dibrell, daughter of Anthony Dibrell and Wilmuth Watson, born December, 1799, married Dr. Ezekiel

266

Gilbert of Amherst county, Virginia, and with her husband set-. tled near Peddlar Mills of that county where he practiced medicine successfully for about thirty years. They left two sons and three daughters, Dr. Charles Anthony Gilbert, Benjamin Rush Gilbert, Anna, Mattie and Kate.

Dr. Gilbert died comparatively young, and his son, Dr. Charles Anthony Gilbert succeeded him in the practice.

5 Dr. Charles Anthony Gilbert, born about 1825, married Miss Bettie Templin, who was a great-niece of Anthony Wayne, better known as "Mad Anthony of the Revolution." It was to this Anthony that General Washington gave the order to "storm Stony Point," and when asked if he could do it, replied that he would "storm hell" if General Washington gave the order.

Dr. Charles Anthony Gilbert removed to Missouri in 1870, where he again took up the practice of medicine with much success. His first wife died shortly after leaving Virginia, and he married the second time; the issue by the second marriage is unknown. By the first marriage of Dr. Gilbert with Miss Templin there were three sons and a daughter, Robert, Charles, William, and Fannie.

6 Robert and Charles Gilbert have married and raised families in Missouri. William is unmarried. He is quite a success-. ful traveling salesman for a St. Louis drug house. He has visited Atlanta on business occasionally, and been a guest at my house. William Gilbert gives very positive evidence of being a successful business man, and withal a courteous, affable gentleman, who sustains well the character of the family from whom he is descended.

5 Benjamin Rush Gilbert, the younger son of Dr. Ezekiel Gilbert, born 1833, and educated at Emory and Henry College, Va., was a worthy scion of the lineage to which he belonged. It was not the fortune of Mr. Gilbert to be financially successful. He was too cautious and conscientious to engage in reckless speculation, too hospitable and generous to hoard his means, and dispensing as he did his charities with a liberal hand, there was not much left to make up a bank account; nevertheless, he provided

comfortably for his family and raised his children in a way to command the respect of those around them. He was twice married, first to Miss Nannie Logwood of Bedford. There was no issue to this marriage; second, he married Virginia Rucker of Campbell county, Virginia. By this marriage there were three children, two sons and a daughter; Walter Bryan, Earnest, and Elizabeth Dibrell. Walter married and resides in Philadelphia; Earnest is also married and resides in Manchester, Virginia; "Lizzie Dibrell" married a druggist in Lynchburg, Virginia, and resides in that city. The gentleman she married was named Hale.

5 Anna Gilbert married Mr. George Phillips of Amherst county, Virginia. They had three daughters, one of whom died young, the other two at last accounts were not married. They were all very bright and highly educated. Kate Gilbert married a Mr. Bailey, and had one son, Mattie Gilbert, never married.

4 ANTHONY DIBRELL.

Anthony Dibrell, one of the younger sons of Anthony Dibrell and Wilmuth Watson, was born August 19, 1805. He was married in 1832 to Miss Marietta Howlett of Chesterfield county, Virginia. They had nine children, six sons and three daughters: Edwin, born June 1833, and died 1834; Willie Anna, born June 1835, married to Thomas R. Moore of Petersburg, Virginia, in January, 1855, died February, 1872, leaving no children; Marietta, born June 1837, married E. S. McArthur November, 1856; Thomas Mieure, born June, 1839, died 1858; Anthony, born March, 1842, married to Miss Chambliss in 1870, and died April, 1893; Watson S., born June 1844, married twice, first, to Miss Hoages in 1870, then to Miss Saunders both of Norfolk; Edward, born 1847, married Miss Steinbach of Petersburg, and died March, 1877, leaving no children; Julia, born July, 1850, died October, 1874; James Anderson, born February, 1853, died August, 1864.

5 Marietta McArthur, daughter of Anthony Dibrell and

LEWIS AND KINDRED FAMILIES.

Marietta Howlett, resides in Leesburg, London county, Virginia. She has five children; Estelle, born 1857, died 1861; Edwin D., born 1860, never married; Mary E., born 1862, married Dr. A. Penuelin in 1887, one child, a daughter born 1890; Minnie B., born 1865, died in 1899; Marietta, born in 1871, died in 1875.

4 Anthony Dibrell was graduated from the University of North Carolina, studied law and was admitted to the bar in Lynchburg, Virginia, but having embraced religion in 1828, the entire trend of his life was changed. He then studied for the ministry, and was received on trial in the Virginia conference in 1830. For a quarter of a century he was one of the brightest stars in that constellation of brilliant intellects where such men as Bascomb, Rosser, David S. Dogget and William A. Smith held spellbound admiring thousands by their inapproachable reasoning and eloquence. They were indeed the bright particular stars of the Methodist Episcopal Church South.

Mr. Dibrell had the reputation of making a specialty of the "Thunders of Sinai," the awful consequences of a broken law and an offended God; but this did not result from his lack of appreciation of a God of love and mercy. His line of thought and teaching was that God's love and mercy were shared by the obedient children, while the disobedient were banished from his presence by their disobedience, and choosing to wander into a far country away from God, they were permitted to feed the flocks of strangers and to live on the husks that the swine would not eat, but when they came to themselves and made the resolution "I will arise and go to my father," the Father was always ready to receive them with open arms.

The Rev. Anthony Dibrell was one of the delegates from the Virginia conference to the Convention of 1844 which met in Louisville, Kentucky. It was at this convention, which embraced all of the annual conferences in the Southern States, that the division of the church was effected, and all of the Southern conferences withdrew from the Methodist Episcopal Church and formed themselves into a separate organization, which has been ever since known as the Methodist Episcopal Church South. Mr.

269

Dibrell was a member of every succeeding general conference from that time until his death. At the general conference at Columbus, Georgia, 1854, he declined the nomination for bishop, and but for his untimely taking off, he would have doubtless been compelled to yield his objections and to have accepted the office.

4 Leeanna Dibrell, born October 2, 1801, married a gentleman by the name of Staples, in Amherst county, Virginia. They had sons and daughters, but little is known, however, of their descendants. One of their sons, George Staples, removed to Texas.

4 Frances Watson Dibrell, born June 18, 1803, married a gentleman by the name of Hendrix, and removed to Alabama. They left a number of sons and daughters, who still reside in that State and have descendants.

4 Catherine Dibrell, born July 8, 1809, married Thomas Mieure, of Richmond, Virginia, but left no children.

4 Wilmuth Watson Dibrell, born May 20, 1811, married a gentleman by the name of Gary. They removed to Alabama, and subsequently to Texas. They left a number of sons and daughters. Their oldest son, Thomas Anthony Gary, and one of his brothers, were successful merchants at different places in Texas. He was afterwards prominent in politics as a Democrat, and was appointed by Mr. Cleveland during his first administration postmaster of Galveston. He was succeeded by a Republican during Mr. Harrison's administration, and removed to Washington, District of Columbia, where he has remained ever since.

Mr. Gary, with his family, resided in Galveston for a number of years, and when I visited that place in 1885, I had the pleasure of spending a day at his house. He has an interesting family, which then consisted of his wife and one daughter. A son, who was at the military academy at West Point, was necessarily absent. A very singular incident in connection with the appointment of Mr. Gary's son to the military academy is that it was procured through the then representative in Congress of the Galveston district, Tom Ochiltree, a Republican of reconstruction proclivities, with whom Mr. Gary had been for years politically antagonistic; but while the political antagonism between the two was strong, their personal feelings were very kindly. I do not know whether young Gary graduated or not. I have had no information from him since that time. The daughter referred to, a bright and beautiful young woman, and very proficient in music, has since made her mark in Washington society. In correspondence with the family it has been learned that Mr. Gary is permanently, and believed to be prominently, located in Washington, in some government connection. Through Mr. Robert Stockwell Hatcher it is learned that he is yet in Washington and permanently located.

THE FEARN FAMILY.

This is among the older Virginia families, and also has an English history extending very far back.

Walker Fearn, who was minister to Greece during Mr. Cleveland's first administration, writes me that he found at Athens a marble slab with the name "William Fearn, Captain H. M. S. Unity, native of London, who died at Porto Leone 1687." Mr. Fearn adds that before leaving Athens, in 1889, he had the marble carefully fixed in the English church at that place.

From the church registry of Gloucester we learn that John Fearn was married to Mary Lee in that county, December 31, 1687, and that Thomas Fearn, son of John Fearn and Mary Lee, was baptized November, 1688.

In 1644, John Fearn was married to Leeanna Lee in Middlesex county, Virginia, December 31; and with the death of William Fearn in Athens in 1687, the marriage of John Fearn to Mary Lee in Gloucester county, Virginia, the same year the baptism of their son Thomas Fearn in 1688 and the marriage of John Fearn to Leeanna Lee, in Middlesex county, Virginia, December 31, 1744, we have three generations of the Fearn family, covering about one hundred years. While we have not the record proof of the direct line of descent from the first William Fearn, the facts go to show not only the existence, but the standing and importance of the Fearn name from a very early period of English history, and prove the descent from John Fearn and Mary Lee through their son Thomas.

It will be seen that John Fearn married Mary Lee, November, 1687; that his son, Thomas Fearn, was baptized in 1688, and that John Fearn married Leeanna Lee in 1744, which show them conclusively to be in direct succession. So we take John Fearn and Mary Lee, married 1687, as the progenitors of the Fearn family in Virginia.

LEWIS AND KINDRED FAMILIES.

Much has been said in regard to the descent of Leeanna Lee, and no little controversy has grown out of it. Dr. Edmund J. Lee, author of "Lee of Virginia," could not be induced to locate her or give to her a well-defined descent, but contents himself with saying that "there is a tradition in the families of Dibrell and Fearn that Leeanna was a daughter of Thomas and granddaughter of Charles, the youngest son of Colonel Richard Lee, the emigrant, but unfortunately, no authentic proof of this tradition has been discovered." He does not even recognize her as a member of the Lee family, but speaks of her as "an unconfirmed traditional sister of Elizabeth Dibrell," who is proven by the records to have been the daughter of Thomas Lee. He even refuses to admit her marriage to John Fearn, and indeed leaves her very existence in doubt, when as a matter of fact the records of Middlesex county, Virginia, prove most positively that she was married to John Fearn, December 31, 1744. The manuscript of Mr. Charles Lee Dibrell shows beyond a doubt that she was a sister of Elizabeth Dibrell, and unbroken tradition through four successive generations confirms the same. Dr. Lee is undoubted authority when he makes an assertion, but he has the faculty of leaving the reader in doubt by declining to make an assertion, in which he certainly is overcautious, when the proofs are so well founded.

There is the most undoubted proof, as has been seen, that Leeanna Lee was a descendant of Colonel Richard Lee, the emigrant, through his youngest son, Charles; that she was the sister of Elizabeth Lee Dibrell; that she married John Fearn, of Middlesex county, Virginia, and was the ancestor of the Fearn family of America. As is shown under the head of the Dibrell family, and also that of Lee, by the most conclusive record evidence, Elizabeth Lee, who married Anthony Dibrell, was the daughter of Thomas Lee, and we now turn to the train of circumstances which inseparably connect Leeanna with her and prove them to have been sisters.

Mr. Charles Lee Dibrell, who was a grandson of Elizabeth Lee, in his manuscript, says that they came to Buckingham county together; that his grandparents were married at the house of Leeanna Fearn, and that they were sisters; that this was not a mere tradition but a recognized fact. Mr. George R. Fearn, of Dallas, Texas, who is a lineal descendant of John Fearn, in a letter to me confirms Mr. Dibrell's statement, and Mrs. Cole, of Alabama, in a letter to me in 1892, states that she recollected distinctly that her mother always spoke of Anthony Dibrell and Elizabeth, his wife, as uncle and aunt. Mrs. Cole was born in 1810, while her mother's birth was as early as 1775, and was hence nearly thirty years old before either Anthony Dibrell or Leeanna Fearn died.

The exact date of the removal of John Fearn from Middlesex to Buckingham county is not known, but it was between 1744 and 1756, as on the first named date he was married in Middlesex, and on the latter date Anthony Dibrell and Elizabeth Lee were married at his house in Buckingham.

4   Thomas Fearn, oldest child of John Fearn and Leeanna Lee, was born October 24, 1745, and died October 4, 1805. According to two of his grandchildren, Mrs. Eliza Cole, of Gunter's Landing, Alabama, and Mr. George Fearn, of Dallas, Texas, he married three times, first a daughter of Chancellor Creed Taylor of Virginia; second, a widow Allen, nee Miss Coleman; and third, Mary Burton, daughter of Dr. Robert Burton, May 5, 1785. She was born in 1751 and died in 1845, aged 94 years. By the first marriage he had one daughter, who died unmarried. By the second marriage he had two daughters, both of whom married and left issue. Thomas Fearn by his third marriage had seven children, five sons and two daughters, as follows: John, Thomas, Robert, George, Richard, Leeanna Lee, and Mary. Of Richard, George and Mary we have partial data, which we trust will serve to give clews to many other members of the family, by means of which they will be enabled to complete their family history.

From all the data that I have been able to obtain, Thomas Fearn was the only son of John Fearn and Leeanna Lee, whose descendants are known. There were four daughters, however, concerning whom there is very little data. From an entry among the papers of Mr. Charles Lee Dibrell, it appeared that John Fearn was married a second time to Eliza Winfree. From the parish register kept by William Douglas, rector of the parish from 1750 to 1797, this entry is found, but there is no further data in regard to the marriage.

5 Richard Lee Fearn was the youngest son of Thomas Fearn and Mary Burton. From his son, Mr. Walker Fearn of New Orleans, we obtained much valuable information. He says: "My father, Dr. Richard Fearn of Alabama, was the youngest of four brothers, Thomas, Robert, George and Richard, and was born near Danville, Spottsylvania county, Virginia, in 1804. He was a graduate of Chapel Hill University (the University of North Carolina), and afterwards in medicine at Philadelphia, with the highest honors of his class. He removed to Huntsville, Alabama, about 1830, and there married Mary Jane Walker, daughter of Hon. John William Walker, formerly of Virginia, who presided over the constitutional convention for the admission of Alabama into the Union, and was afterwards United States senator from that State. His sons, Pope, Richard and Percy, were respectively Confederate States secretary of war, chief justice of the Supreme Court of Alabama, and members of Congress.

"Shortly after my birth, 1832, my father, Dr. Richard Lee Fearn, settled in Mobile, where he died in 1868. His oldest brother, Thomas Fearn, of Huntsville, Alabama, was also a distinguished physician. He died about 1864 at home. His wife was a Shelby of Tennessee. Dr. Thomas Fearn left a large family of daughters, two of whom, Mrs. Steele and Mrs. Garth, still live in Huntsville, as also Berenice, who never married. Another daughter, Mrs. Sarah Barrett, widow of Hon. W. S. Barrett, lives on her plantation at Shellmound, Sunflower county, Mississippi. My father's older brothers, George and Robert, are also dead."

6 Hon. Walker Fearn, from whom the foregoing quotation is taken, was born in Huntsville, Alabama, 1832. He married Miss Fannie Hewett, of Louisville, Kentucky, and wrote me in 1892 that he had three living children, the oldest, a daughter,

Mary, was then with him in Chicago, where he was stationed as director of the foreign department of the Columbian Exposition. His two sons, Parey and Hewett, were civil and mining engineers, and were holding good positions in Costa Rico. It is a singular fact that among all the criticisms in regard to Mr. Fearn, the most formidable that has ever been brought to bear was that his scholarship was too extensive. There can be no doubt that he was one of the ripest scholars and most profound lawyers of his age and generation, and has held many positions of honor and trust. During Mr. Cleveland's first administration he was Minister to Greece, from 1885 to 1889. It was while in Athens that Mr. Fearn very strangely came across the tombstone of a hitherto unknown ancestor in the person of William Fearn, who had been in command of H. M. S. Unity, and having died, was interred in Athens.

6 Eliza Frances Coles of Alabama, under date of July 28, 1892, writes: "John Fearn and Lreanna Lee were my great-grandparents. Their oldest son, Thomas Fearn, was my grandfather. He married three times, first a daughter of Chancellor Creed Taylor, of Virginia; second a widow Allen, nee Miss Coleman, and third, Mary Burton, daughter of Dr. Robert Burton, May 5, 1785. My mother, Mary Fearn, daughter of Thomas Fearn and Mary Burton, married Dr. James Patton, of Danville, Virginia." Mr. Thomas Fearn Patton, of New Orleans, is a son of Dr. James Patton, of Danville, Virginia, and a brother of Mrs. Coles. A postscript to Mrs. Cole's letter, signed Paulina Fearn, speaks of Mrs. Coles as "our grandmother." The writer is evidently a young lady, but she does not say whose daughter she is, nor how she got to be Mrs. Cole's granddaughter. Evidently, some Fearn, "in search of a wife," married his cousin Coles.

5 Mr. George R. Fearn, a lawyer of Dallas, Texas, has given me much general information. He was a son of Thomas Fearn and Mary Burton. Mr. Walker Fearn speaks of him as his cousin, and he is most probably the son of George Fearn, who died in Jackson, Mississippi.

6 Mary Lee Patton, daughter of Dr. James Patton and Mary Burton Fearn, granddaughter of Thomas Fearn and Mary Burton, and great-granddaughter of John Fearn and Leeanna Lee, married George Taylor Swann, and her daughter, Mary Lee Swann, married William Jasper Brown at Jackson, Mississippi.

Berenice Fearn forwarded me several years ago from her father's records the following list of the children of John Fearn and Leeanna Lee: Thomas, born October 24, 1745; Elizabeth, who married William Perkins; Sallie, who married a Bates, by whom he had two sons and four daughters; Jane, who married Hansford Young; and a daughter, who married Samuel Putney.

8 From Mr. John B. Cannon, of Franklin, Tennessee, I have the following: "I am the great-grandson of the late Governor Newton Cannon, of this State. My paternal grandmother was Miss Perkins, a daughter of Samuel Perkins, of this county, and a granddaughter of Elizabeth Lee Fearn and Col. Samuel Harding Perkins, and a great-granddaughter of Leeanna Lee, who married John Fearn." Brought down, we have Elizabeth Lee Fearn, daughter of John Fearn and Leeanna Lee, married Col. Samuel Harding Perkins. Samuel Perkins, son of Col. Samuel Harding Perkins and Elizabeth Lee Fearn, removed to Williamson county, Tennessee, married and had issue, and a daughter of Samuel Perkins, of Williamson county, Tennessee, married a son of Governor Cannon of that State, and Mr. John B. Cannon, from whom this data is obtained, is a grandson of this couple. From this and like data furnished in these pages, hundreds will be enabled to complete their genealogical line, if they will only avail themselves of the opportunity.

From Mr. Wm. J. Brown, of Jackson, Mississippi, the following is obtained: "Mary Lee Brown, daughter of William Jasper Brown, Jr., and Jane Lile (Swann) Brown, granddaughter of George Taylor Swann and Mary Lee (Patton) Swann, great-granddaughter of Dr. James D. Patton and Mary Burton Fearn, great-great-granddaughter of Thomas Fearn and Mary Burton, his third wife, and great-great-great-granddaughter of John Fearn of Buckingham county, Virginia, and Leeanna Lee."

Brought down, we have Thomas Fearn, son of John Fearn and Leeanna Lee, born October 24, 1745, married (third wife) Mary Burton, May 15, 1785; Mary Burton Fearn, daughter of Thomas Fearn and Mary Burton, married Dr. James D. Patton, of Danville, Virginia; Mary Lee Patton, daughter of Dr. James D. Patton and Mary Burton Fearn, married George Taylor Swann; Jane Lile Swann, daughter of George Taylor Swann, and Mary Lee Patton, married William Jasper Brown, Jr., of Mississippi; Mary Lee Brown, daughter of the last named couple.

From the foregoing the Fearn family, so far as can be ascertained, may be summed up as follows: William Fearn, who died in Athens, Greece, 1685, probably born about 1635; John Fearn, who married Mary Lee in Gloucester county, Virginia, in 1687, born about 1665; Thomas Fearn, son of John Fearn and Mary Lee, born in Gloucester county and baptized 1688, and John Fearn, son of Thomas Fearn and Mary Lee, who married Leeanna Lee in Middlesex county, Virginia, December 31, 1744. These four names show the successive generations of the Fearn family, from about 1650 until the close of the eighteenth century.

Newton Cannon Perkins is in the regular line of succession from John Fearn and Leeanna Lee, through their daughter, Elizabeth Lee Fearn, who married Col. Harding Perkins. He is a cotton factor in Memphis, Tennessee. He was born January 31, 1865, and is much interested in the Fearn family. From him much valuable information may be obtained in regard to the history of the Fearns.

7 Helen Fearn Grace, of Yazoo City, Mississippi, is also a descendant of this line. She married Thomas Grace, Jr., of that place, and had issue as follows: Walter Anderson, born June 1, 1882; Thomas, born August 30, 1884; Mary Fearn, born July 14, 1886; Helen Grace, born September 11, 1888; Edward Lee, born February 16, 1890; Bessie Fearn, born August 2, 1892. All of these children were living August 29, 1902.

It will be seen, from the numbering of the generations, as

stated above, that I have taken John Fearn and Mary Lee, of Gloucester county, Virginia, married December 31, 1687, as the progenitors of the Fearn family of Virginia, hence John Fearn, who married Leeanna Lee, would be third in line of descent.

THE COBBS FAMILY.

This is one of the oldest names known to English history, and while they were among the earliest emigrants to America, until the last few years their early history was wholly unknown. Burke's Heraldry gives the name of Cobbs from Devonshire, Lancaster, London, and northern England.

As early as 1613, only six years after the settlement of Jamestown, Joseph Cobbs is registered as landing at Yorktown on the "Treasurer." His wife with her two children, Benjamin and Joseph Jr., came over in the "Bonnie Bess" in 1624. The arrival of Ambrose Cobbs in Virginia is not definitely known, but he appears on the land books in 1635. Ambrose and Joseph Cobbs were no doubt brothers. Joseph came over 1613, and received land grants in 1635 and 1637. The time when Ambrose arrived is also doubtful, but he received land grants in 1635, or about the same time that Joseph did.

Robert Cobbs appeared in 1651, as church warden, and his name also appears on the records of York county in the same year. In 1667 Robert Cobbs appears as justice of the peace for York county, and in 1681 he appears as one of the county commissioners. In 1682 he is high sheriff of the county. He died intestate in the same year, and his son Edmund administered on his estate.

This Edmund Cobbs, who administered on his father's estate in 1682, died 1692 or 1693. He left a will, but no sons, and it would seem no living children. He mentions his son-in-law, Matthew Pierce, and makes bequests to him, but provides that his entire estate shall be divided among his three brothers, Ambrose, Robert and Otho.

It is not positively known whether Robert Cobbs, the father of Edmund and his three brothers, who died in 1682, was the son of Joseph or Ambrose, but as the name Ambrose is perpetuated in the line, and Joseph is not, we are led to conclude, almost necessarily, that he was the son of Ambrose, and must so take him up.

Ambrose, Robert and Otho Cobbs were sons of the first Robert Cobbs, as described in the will of their brother, Edmund, and we are again brought face to face with the three-brother theory, and left to select from these three, upon the best testimony, the head of the Cobbs families.

From the foregoing we reach the following conclusions as inevitable results: Ambrose Cobbs, emigrant, born about 1590, came to Virginia about 1613. Robert Cobbs, son of Ambrose Cobbs, born about 1620. Robert Cobbs, son of the above Robert and brother of Edmund, born about 1660.

Thomas Cobbs, John Cobbs and Robert Cobbs, who appear upon the records of Henrico and Goochland from 1736 to 1750, son of the second Robert Cobbs, were born about 1706, 1708 and 1710, respectively, and are heads of three lines of that name throughout the United States.

Goochland county was taken off from Henrico, which accounts for the three brothers appearing at different times on the records of the two counties.

4 JOHN COBBS, OF GOOCHLAND.

As this ancestor is the head of the most numerous branch of the name, his line will be first taken up. He appears upon the records of Goochland with his wife, Susanah, as early as 1736, and at different times thereafter until 1750, after which he appears on the books of Goochland as John Cobbs of Albemarle.

In 1750, John Cobbs of Goochland purchased five hundred acres of land of James Neville, said land being located in Albemarle county on the south side of Fluvanna, or James river.

The name of John Cobbs appears upon the records of Albemarle county at different times, until 1760, after which all trace of him is lost. In 1761, that portion of Albemarle lying on the south side of James river was cut off and the county of Buckingham formed out of it. The records of Buckingham were destroyed by fire in 1867, and, hence, all trace of John Cobbs of Goochland was lost. There is no doubt that his will was recorded in Buckingham, but was destroyed with the other records. It has been by the most patient and persistent labor running through a number of years that these record proofs have been brought out and this long-neglected name unearthed, as it were, and rescued from oblivion. John Cobbs had three sons, Samuel, Edmund and John.

The fact that Robert Cobbs, the second of the name in America, born 1620, was justice of the peace and high sheriff is proof that he was more than peer of his surroundings, as these positions could be held at that time by none but the best class of citizens. Justice of the peace in 1650 was a position equally as honorable and important as judge of the Supreme Court at the present day.

As persistent as the authors of these sketches have been in their search for information, it was not until within the last few years that they knew of the existence of any of the Cobbs name mentioned in the preceding line, and in reporting the lineage of the name to the American ancestry, he stated that Samuel Cobbs, his great-grandfather, was from Wales; while as a matter of fact, the great-grandfather of Samuel Cobbs was born in Virginia; but in this he was in advance of the majority of Americans, who at that time did not know who their great-grandfathers were. As much as has been ascertained in regard to the Cobbs name in the last few years, a volume of unwritten history doubtless lies yet undeveloped, hidden away, so to speak, in the archives of the country, or lost in extinct church registries and neglected graveyards.

Two of the oldest and most distinguished families in Virginia, Lee and Randolph, had each a branch that was known by the name of Cobbs. The estates which they owned had either been inherited from some one of the name or the manors named in honor of some intermarriage, the record of which has long since been lost and all of the events passed out of the memory of all the families.

Richard Lee came to Virginia in 1641, and Henry Randolph the head of that family in America, came to Virginia in 1643, so that it is clear that the Cobbs family had become settled in the colony before the Lee or the Randolph family came over. The Cobbs Hall Lees and the Randolphs of Cobb were as distinctive designations as Smith of Purton or Lewis of Warner Hall.

5 SAMUEL COBBS.

Samuel Cobbs and his two brothers, Edmund and John, are known from the best record evidence to have been residents of Louisa county, Virginia. Samuel was doubtless the eldest of the three brothers, and as he was the immediate ancestor of one of the authors of these sketches, his line will be first treated of.

Samuel Cobbs' will, written September, 1758, and probated November 20 of the same year, is recorded in the clerk's office of Louisa county, Virginia. From this will we learn the following facts: First, his wife, Mary Cobbs, survived him; second, he left three children, Robert, Jane and Judith; third, that he had two brothers, Edmund and John; fourth, that after providing for his wife and children, he bequeathed to his brothers jointly one thousand acres of land in Bedford county, Virginia; fifth, that from a special provision of the will disposing of such property as came to him from his wife, in the event of the death of his children without issue, the fact is established that his wife was Mary Lewis, daughter of Robert Lewis, for a long time a citizen of Louisa county, but more recently of Belvoir, Albemarle county. Samuel Cobbs was married about 1750, and left when he died as before stated, three children. His daughter Jane married a gentleman named Waddy. They had one child, who survived them both. This child has a son named Samuel, and was raised by his grandmother Cobbs; but there is no trace to be had of him after his maturity. Judith, the younger daughter, never married. She died in early life.

6 ROBERT COBBS.

Robert, so far as record evidence goes, was the only son of Samuel Cobbs and Mary Lewis. He was positively a unique character, in his day and generation. Descended from a distinguished line of ancestry, whose lives for centuries had been inseparably connected with that of their country's history, both in England and America, he was at the same time plain in his manners and unassuming in his bearing. The inheritor of large estates, and raised in wealth and luxury, he was among the first to take the field, though quite young, in defense of his country, and braving the hardships of war, he remained at his post until the close of the struggle. Calm and dignified at all times, yet positive in his convictions, and fearless in maintaining them, he steered clear of politics and never allowed himself to be drawn into its arena. Nevertheless, he was a positive Jeffersonian in political opinions. He belonged to the Church of England, as that expression is understood, but was emphatically a non-conformist. Scrupulously conscientious and always ready for every good word and work, he submitted to no earthly dictation and in the language of the immortal Crittenden, "bowed to none but God." As illustrative of his character, as well as what was supposed to be his eccentricities, an incident in his life, which was to become part of his history, may be mentioned. One of his most reliable managers, who had been in charge of his home plantation for a number of years, was taken sick with fever. Mr. Cobbs had been called away from home on business, and when he returned he ascertained that the doctor had given the patient up to die. He declared, however, that he could not give up Bosher—for that was his name—and hastening to the house of his faithful manager, he called them all to prayer. This was a new departure, for with all of his sterling virtues, he was not in the habit of praying publicly, and every one was struck with astonishment. He prayed most fervently, assuring the divine Master that Bosher was an indispensable factor in the general make-up of human society; as husband, parent and citizen, true to every trust and faithful to every pledge. His death would deprive the community of one whose place could not be filled; and he enumerated a long list, calling them by name, all of whom could be spared, and none of them missed, and presented them in a lump, as it were, as an offering, or sacrifice, in place of Bosher.

We have always regretted that a stenographic report could not have been taken of that prayer. It afforded much amusement to his best friends and most ardent admirers, and even to his children and grandchildren, who never had the slightest conception of its import. Nor will we say that he himself fully understood it; but whatever opinion may be entertained in regard to it, two things are certain: the author of the prayer was in earnest, and Bosher got well; and even now, after the lapse of more than a century, the story of the prayer of "Robin Cobbs" for the recovery of Bosher is told in many Virginia homes; and truly may it be said that the author of that prayer, without pretension or ostentation, put his trust in God.

This volume might be filled with anecdotes of this Revolutionary patriot, but the scope of the work is such as to render all historical or biographical references very brief.

Robert Cobbs was born in 1754, in Louisa county, Virginia. He entered the Revolutionary army from Louisa county, enlisting in the regiment of his uncle, Charles Lewis. The records show that he married in Louisa after the return of peace, and was a citizen of that county until 1788, when he removed to Bedford county, Virginia, where he inherited large landed property from his father's estate. His Revolutionary services have always been treasured as a sacred legacy by his children and grandchildren, and his widow was awarded a pension within the memory of the author, but, being a very young man, and his rank being only that of captain, no account is to be found of him in the condensed historical events of the war. The records, however, furnish ample testimony of his rank and services, and Brock's Historical Collections make frequent mention of him, and others, that together with Charles and Nicholas Lewis, he took the oath of allegiance to Virginia under the colonial government in 1776. His services were principally with Gates and Green in the Carolinas, and more conspicuously at the siege of 1781 and the battle of Guilford courthouse, at which place family tradition informs us, as senior captain he commanded his regiment.

About 1795, Robert Cobbs removed to Campbell county, Virginia, where he also owned valuable estates. He did not, however, part with his Bedford property, but owned it at the time of his death, after which, upon the division and settlement of his estate, it became the property of his son, Charles Lewis Cobbs. He gave to his Campbell county home the name of "Plain Dealing," indicative of his methods of doing business, and at this place, about twenty-five miles nearly due south of Lynchburg, about two miles from the Durham railroad, six miles from Brook Neal, and a few miles from "Red Hill," the home of Patrick Henry, on the Staunton, or upper waters of the Roanoke, Robert Cobbs spent the remainder of his days.

Robert Cobbs died 1829, and the records of Campbell county show the settlement and disposition of his estate. His widow survived him about twelve years, spending her entire widowhood with her daughter, Sarah White, who married Captain William C. McAllister, where she died in 1842, and was buried by the side of her husband at the old homestead. This old burying ground has proved an exception to most of the private cemeteries, which fall into disuse and neglect, and are lost sight of. Although it has passed into the hands of strangers, it has been kept enclosed, and while the graves of these old people are not marked, they are not forgotten, their grandchildren having arranged to reclaim them.

Robert Cobbs, married Anne G. Poindexter, daughter of John Poindexter, of Louisa county, Virginia, and to this couple were born nine children:

7 ¹John Poindexter Cobbs married Jane Garland, daughter of David S. Garland, of Amherst county, Virginia, who was for many years a member of Congress from his district.

7 ²Mary Lewis Cobbs married first, William Armistead of Char-

lotte county, Virginia, and second, William McLean, D. D.,
M. D., of the same county.

7 [3]Robert Lewis Cobbs, never married.

7 [4]Samuel Cobbs, never married.

7 [5]William Cobbs, married Miss Marianne Scott, of Bedford
county, Virginia.

7 [6]Charles Lewis Cobbs, married Anne Scott, of Bedford
county, Virginia.

7 [7]Sarah White Cobbs, married Captain William C. McAllister,
of Campbell county, Virginia.

7 [8]Anne Elizabeth Cobbs, married Joel Motley, of Nottoway
county, Virginia.

7 [9]Meriwether Lewis Cobbs, never married.

Dr. John Poindexter Cobbs, oldest son of Robert Cobbs and
Anne Poindexter, was born May 27, 1785. He graduated from
Hampden-Sidney college in 1808, and from the medical college
at Philadelphia in 1810. Commenced the practice of medicine at
New Glasgow, Amherst county, Virginia, immediately after his
graduation. This was a small town about twenty miles northeast of Lynchburg, which at the time was the center of wealth
and learning, the home of the Garlands, the Crawfords and the
Pendletons; and it was here that he married Miss Jane Garland,
the daughter of David S. Garland, who then represented the district in Congress. She belonged to one of the most distinguished
families in Virginia, at a time when that State embodied the
great bulk of the distinguished names of the country. The Garlands had been more than a century distinguished in the leading
professions, and had held positions in colonial history and subsequent to the Revolution. Her mother, a Miss Meredith, a name
no less distinguished, was the niece of Patrick Henry.

Dr. Cobbs subsequently removed to Nelson county, Virginia,
which county he represented in the Legislature for a number of
years. He also continued the practice of his profession while
he remained in this county, but in 1836, foreseeing the great
wealth to be developed in the Northwest, he made investments in

the northern part of Indiana, Milwaukee, and other places, preparatory to removing from Virginia.

Dr. John Cobbs had five children, three sons and two daughters: Jane, married a gentleman by the name of Thwing; Robert, never married, was born in Nelson county, Virginia, about 1818, and died in Atlanta, Georgia, about 1895; John, married, but whom is not known, and died in Colorado; Garland, never married, born about 1830; Mary, married (1) Thomas Stewart, one of the proprietors of the Chicago Times-Herald, and (2) Dr. Fravel.

8 Jane, oldest child of John Cobbs and Jane Garland, was born 1813, and about 1830 was married to a gentleman named Thwing, as above mentioned. She lived to a very old age, having died about 1895, at the home of her son, Franklin Thwing, in Chicago. She had four children: Franklin, Jane Henry, Virginia Garland and Sarah Florence.

9 Franklin Thwing, son of Jane Cobbs Thwing and grandson of Dr. John P. Cobbs, married Miss Elizabeth Ogden Smith, and resides in Chicago. They have three children: Franklin Thwing, Jr., Harriet Ogden and Ellen.

9 Jane Henry Thwing, oldest daughter of Mrs Jane Cobbs Thwing married Horace G. Smith and resides in Denver, Colorado.

9 Virginia Garland married S. J. Peterson Halstron of Sweden. They do not retain the latter part of the name in ordinary use, as it is so strongly foreign, but in legal transactions, and in all matters of record they perpetuate the full name. They are known socially as Peterson, legally they are known as Peterson Halstrom. They have five children: Jane Garland, Virginia Garland, Charles Henry, Mary Lewis Loring.

10 Virginia Garland Peterson great-granddaughter of Dr. John P. Cobbs, born 1863, married Arthur St. M. Claflin, formerly of Boston, but now of Chicago. They have two children, both boys: Henry and Aubrey. Mr. Claflin is a great-nephew of President Pierce.

7 Mary Lewis Cobbs, born June 11, 1787, and married

William Armistead, 1806. She married second, John McClean, M. D., D. D., about 1820. By her first marriage she had three sons, and by the second marriage she had two, but no daughters.

8 Dr. John O. Armistead, born 1807, died 1873. He married Miss Elizabeth Jennings of Charlotte county, Virginia, about 1830. They had five daughters, no sons: Mary Susan, Sarah Ann, Emma, "Bettie" and Henrietta.

9 Mary Susan Armistead married Frances Thornton of Buckingham county, Virginia. They had several children.

9 Sarah Ann Armistead married a relative, James Armistead, of Charlotte county, Virginia. They removed to Bedford county. Mr. Armistead left her a widow, and her oldest son having died, she removed to San Francisco, where an uncle, Samuel McLean, resided.

9 Emma Armistead, born 1837, married a gentleman named Scott. They had several children. They removed to Palestine, Texas.

9 "Bettie" and Henrietta never married. "Hettie" died young.

8 William B. Armistead, after varied business ventures settled in Nashville, Tennessee. He married Miss Woods of that city and merchandised there successfully for a number of years. They had three sons and several daughters: Robert married Miss Hunphous of Clarksville, Tennessee; William, who is engaged in the insurance business in Nashville, and James who married Miss Washington of that city. One of Wm. B. Armistead's daughters married Dr. Hughes of Birmingham, Alabama, who was postmaster of that city for eight years. Another married a man named Johnson who is a large business operator of that city.

8 Robert Armistead never married, he died young.

7 ROBERT LEWIS COBBS.

Robert Lewis Cobbs was born December 25, 1789. He graduated with distinction from Hampden-Sidney in the class of 1809, and from the Jefferson Medical College of Philadelphia in 1811. He practiced medicine with his brother, Dr. John P. Cobbs, in New Glasgow, Amherst county, Virginia, and in January, 1813, he traveled on horseback across the mountains to join Jackson at Nashville, Tennessee, who was then preparing for his campaign against the Indians and British. He was United States surgeon in all of the campaigns, up to the close of the war at New Orleans, after which he returned to Nashville, studied law with his relative, General Wm. White, which profession he followed for 25 years. He was a member of the Constitutional Convention of Tennessee of 1834, and was at one time attorney-general of the State. In 1827-8 he revised the laws of the State. He never married. He retired from practice in 1843, and spent the remainder of his days in quiet, at the home of his sister, Mrs. Sarah White McAllister in Virginia. He died 1856 on presidential election day, Tuesday after the first Monday in November. His last words were: "I must get up and vote for Filmore."

7 Samuel Cobbs was born in Campbell county, Virginia, July 14, 1796. When the war of 1812 broke out he was 16 years old. He obtained the appointment of first lieutenant and was ordered to the northern frontier. He was in all of the principal engagements along the lakes, and was severely wounded at the battle of Lundy's Lane and reported among the dead. He was mourned as such at home, and preparations for his funeral were being made when he appeared in person and stopped the proceedings. He afterward joined an expedition against the Indians in Florida, fell a victim to fever, and died in South Georgia 1817, aged 21 years.

7 William Cobbs was born in Campbell county, Virginia, March 2, 1792, and died about 1852, aged about 60 years. He married Miss Marianne Scott and only one child, a girl, blessed their union. Wm. Cobbs fell into bad health early in life and, hence, was very little known to the public. He purchased the home of Thomas Jefferson in Bedford county, "Poplar Forest," where he spent his entire life.

8 Emerly Cobbs, born at Poplar Forest about 1820, mar-

ried Edward Sextus Hutter 1840. Mr. Hutter was from Easton, Pennsylvania, was a graduate of the Naval Academy at Annapolis, and a brother of Major Hutter, then paymaster of the United States army. They had seven children, three sons and four daughters:. Imogene, William Cobbs, George E., Christian Sextus, Nannie, Charlotte. Imogene Hutter died in girlhood.

9 Wm. Cobbs Hutter, born 1842, entered the naval academy, from which he resigned in 1861 to take part in the war between the States. He was killed in the naval engagement in Hampton Roads, March, 1862. He never married.

9 George E. Hutter, born 1852, is unmarried. He graduated from the naval academy and was for some time lieutenant in the United States navy, but was incapacitated for duty from injuries received on a man of war.

9 Christian Sextus Hutter, was born 1862, and in 1886 married Miss Ernistine, daughter of Mr. James M. Booker of Lynchburg, Virginia. He resides at the old homestead, "Poplar Forest," and is engaged in business in Lynchburg.

9 Nannie Hutter married a lawyer named Griffin of Bedford City.

9 Emma Cobbs Hutter married a gentleman named Logwood and resides in St. Louis, Missouri.

9 Charlotte S. Hutter married her first cousin, Major J. Risger Hutter. They reside at the old Hutter homestead near Lynchburg, Virginia.

7 SARAH WHITE COBBS.

Was born February 12, 1798 at "Plain Dealings," Campbell county, Virginia, and married Captain Wm. C. McAllister of the same county. Their remains are buried at the old McAllister burying ground at the old home, seven miles east of Lynchburg, where they spent their entire married life. Her descendants will be noticed under the head of McAllister family.

7 CHARLES LEWIS COBBS.

Was born at Campbell county, Virginia, March 12, 1800. He married Miss Ann Scott of Bedford county, and had seven children: William, Scott, Maria Louisa, Nannie, Harriet, Mary Lewis, and Emma. He removed to Indiana in 1848.

8 Louisa Cobbs married James Slaughter of Bedford and had one son, Joseph, who went to Kentucky; and several daughters, one of whom, Harriet, married a Marsh, of Campbell county. The others never married.

8 Nannie Cobbs married a gentleman named Cox. They had several children, but only two of them married. The others died young—fell victims to consumption.

9 Fannie Cox, the oldest of Nannie Cobb's children, married a Hawkins. She was left a widow when still young, her husband having met his death by accidental shooting. She did not survive him very long. They left three children, all daughters. They grew to be very pretty women, and were very bright. One of them married a gentleman named Hurt.

9 Powhattan Cox married a Miss Moorman and resided near Lynchburg.

8 Mary Cobbs married a gentleman in Indiana by the name of Kabler. They had known each other in Virginia. She died without issue.

8 Harriet Mary Lewis and Emma never married, nor did William or Scott, so far as is known.

7 ANN ELIZABETH COBBS

Was born in Campbell county, Virginia, 1802, and died in Amelia county, 1886, aged 84 years. She married Joel Mottley of Nottaway county, Virginia, and had five children, all sons: Robert Cobbs, John Lewis, Meriwether Cobbs, Joel Wm. and Charles Adolphus.

8 · Robert Cobbs Mottley was born 1824, graduated from

Hampden-Sidney in 1845, and from the Medical College of Pennsylvania in 1847. He located in the practice of medicine in his native county. He married Miss Indiana Vaughan of Amelia and had six children.

9 Elizabeth, only daughter of Dr. Mottley, never married.

9 Robert Milton Mottley, oldest son of Dr. Robert Cobbs Mottley, never married.

9 John Egbert Mottley, married Miss Lee of Buckingham county, Virginia, where he resides.

9 Jefferson Davis Mottley, married his first cousin, Miss Bayley of Amelia county. Wirt and William Henry, younger sons of Dr. Mottley, are neither married, so far as is known.

8 John Lewis Mottley was born in Nottaway county, 1826. He married Anna, daughter of Miles Gill, of Amelia county, and had nine children: Mary Elisabeth, John Meriwether, Joel William (the last two twins), Emma Lewis, Sarah Roberta, Alice Armistead, Anna Atkinson, Charles Adolphus, and Robert Miller.

9 Mary Elisabeth Mottley, married Wm. Vaughan, December 9, 1891. They reside in Nottaway county.

9 Emma Lewis Mottley married C. Butler of Amelia, May 7, 1882.

9 Sarah Roberta Mottley married James M. Wooten, December, 1889. They have one child and reside in Prince Edward.

9 Alice Armistead Mottley married Henry W. Hubbard, December 1, 1880. They have seven children.

9 Anna Adkisson Mottley married Samuel Hubbard of Prince Edward, April 27, 1887. She died 1889, leaving two children.

9 John Meriwether Mottley died in Danville, Virginia, April 29, 1890.

9 Charles Adolphus Mottley is unmarried. He is engaged in merchandising in Richmond, Virginia.

9 Joel William, and Robert Miller Mottley are unmarried. They are engaged in business in West Virginia.

8 Meriwether Cobbs Mottley, born 1828, was never married. He spent his early life in merchandising. He entered the Confederate army in 1861, broke down in the disastrous retreat from Cheat Mountain and never recovered from the effects. He died a few years after the war.

8 Joel Wm. Mottley, born 1835, never married. He spent four years in the Confederate army, and after war went to Texas where he met his death by cowardly assassination.

8 Charles Adolphus Mottley, born 1838, never married. He entered the Confederate army in 1861, and died a few months thereafter in Richmond, Virginia.

7 Meriwether Lewis Cobb, youngest child of Captain Robert Cobb, was born March 4, 1805. He never married. He graduated from Hampden-Sidney, 1825, and from the Medical College of Pennsylvania in 1827. He located in the practice of medicine in Surry county, Virginia. He died 1828.

5 JOHN COBBS.

John Cobbs was the son of John Cobbs of Goochland, and the younger of the three brothers who appear on the records of Louisa county, Virginia. His name first appears on the records in the will of his brother Samuel who bequeaths one thousand acres of land to him and his brother Edmund, situated on Ivy Creek in Bedford county, Virginia, and, as illustrative of the obscurity with which the early life of John Cobbs seems to have been surrounded, and the difficulties attending the efforts to trace him, it may be mentioned in this connection that, while Edmund settled on this land, and, as shown by the settlement of his estate in 1799, more than forty years after the execution of the will of Samuel Cobbs, was still in possession of the entire 1000 acres, which was distributed among his children, there is nothing on the records of Bedford county to show how Edmund got into possession of the whole, or that John Cobbs ever transferred his portion to any one.

The first that we see of John Cobbs on the record, after

he is mentioned in the will of his brother Samuel, is in Granville county, North Carolina, in a deed to land purchased by him from Wm. Moore in 1769. This purchase is made just before his marriage to Mildred, daughter of Howell and Mary Lewis, and is witnessed by Thomas Cobbs, Howell Lewis and Mary Lewis, and his marriage took place September 6, 1769, after which he disappears from the records again until 1784, when he reappears on the records of Goochland county, Virginia, from which county he originally came, in the payment of taxes on property in that county. In this entry he is described as John Cobbs of Georgia, and finally by deed of gift on record in Washington county, Georgia, we find him described as John Cobbs of Columbia county, Georgia, deed bearing date August 1791. His descendants are noticed under the head of Howell Lewis, whose daughter, Mildred, he married 1769.

5 EDMUND COBBS

Is the son of John Cobbs of Goochland county, Virginia, and a younger brother of Samuel Cobbs, who married Mary Lewis, that is, he was one of the three sons of John Cobbs—Samuel, Edmund and John. Edmund Cobbs first appears on the records in the will of his brother Samuel on record in Louisa county, Virginia, in which Samuel bequeaths to his two brothers, Edmund and John, 1,000 acres of land jointly, located on Ivy creek in Bedford county, Virginia, and in the division of Edmund Cobbs' estate in 1799, this identical land, which we find described in the will of Samuel Cobbs in 1758, is described as part of his estate. A curious fact connected with this bequest of Samuel Cobbs to his brothers is, that there is nothing on record to show that John Cobbs ever transferred his interest in this land to any one, and no record evidence as to how Edmund Cobbs ever came into possession of the whole of it. Perhaps it was a case of "squatter sovereignty."

Edmund Cobbs died intestate and his estate was divided between his widow and ten children, as follows: Mrs. Sarah

Cobbs widow, and Elisabeth who married William Tompkins; John Cobbs, Reuben Cobbs, Edmund Cobbs, Samuel Cobbs, Waddy Cobbs, Jeffry Cobbs, Wm. Cobbs, and Judith, now married to John Staples. Edmund Cobbs married Sarah Lewis, daughter of "Planter John Lewis" of Albemarle county, Virginia, who is distinctly referred to in his will as "Sarah Cobbs." Of the ten children of Edmund Cobbs we have not been able to obtain data of any of them but John Lewis, Waddy and Edmund. Five sons and two daughters have been entirely lost sight of and their descendants have no doubt lost sight of their line of descent.

6 JOHN LEWIS COBBS.

John Lewis Cobbs was the oldest son of Edmund Cobbs and Sarah Lewis. His name appears with that of his mother as a witness to the inventory and appraisement of his father's estate in 1799. He married first Miss Susannah Hamner, daughter of Nicholas Hamner of Albemarle county, Virginia, and second, he married Mrs. Judith (Price) Noel. Issue by first marriage:

7 [1]Nicholas Hamner Cobbs married Lucy Henry Landonia Cobbs.

7 [2]Elizabeth Cobbs married Junius A. Clay.

7 [3]Sarah Lewis Cobbs married Captain Henry Jones.

7 [4]John Lewis Cobbs married Mary Bolling and had one child, Bolling Cobbs.

7 [5]James Madison Cobbs married first Eliza Alexander, second, Celeste Slaughter.

7 [6]Damarius Cobbs married Jesse Alexander Barton.

7 [7]Cary Ann Cobbs.

7 [8]Agnes Cobbs married Dr. John Slaughter.

7 [9]Anne Hamner Cobbs married Baker Davidson.

    Issue by second marriage with Mrs. Noel:

7 [10]Virginia Cobbs married Charles William Price.

7 [11]Thomas Nelson Cobbs married first Mary Bedford Averill,

second, Louisa Taylor, third, Sarah Taylor, fourth, Margaret Bedford.

7 [13]Amanda Cobbs married John Lackland.

7 Nicholas Hamner Cobbs, the oldest son of John Lewis Cobbs, born in Bedford county, Virginia, February 5, 1796, married Lucy Henry Landis, daughter of Edmund Cobbs of the same county. She was his first cousin and at one time his pupil when he was principal of New London Academy. They had issue as follows:

8 [1]George Washington.

8 [2]Robert Addison married Elizabeth Storrs; no issue.

8 [3]Susan Hamner married Rev. John Marsh Mitchel and left one child, a daughter.

8 [4]Mary Lee Cobbs.

8 [5]John Lewis Cobbs married Dorothy Evans Peagues.

8 [6]Richard Hooker Cobbs married Frances Ann Avery.

8 [7]Martha Smith Cobbs married John Alexander Elerbe.

8 [8]Leighton Cobbs.

8 [9]Charlotte Walker Cobbs married Nicholas Cobbs Elerbe and had issue.

8 John Lewis Cobbs and Dorothy Evans Peagues had seven children as follows: Nicholas Hamner Cobbs, John Lewis Cobbs, Christopher Claudius Cobbs, Lucy Hamner Cobbs, Leighton, Bessie Evans, and Edward Elerbe Cobbs.

9 John Lewis Cobbs, son of John Lewis, and grandson of Bishop Nicholas Hamner Cobbs, married Ida Woodfin. Issue: John Lewis Cobbs, Isabel Cobbs, Woodfin Cobbs, Nicholas Hamner Cobbs.

9 Christopher Claudius Cobbs, son of John Lewis Cobbs, and grandson of Bishop Nicholas Hamner Cobbs, married Annie Westcote and had issue as follows: Mary Ella Cobbs, Christopher Claudius Cobbs, Dorothy Cobbs, fourth name illegible.

9 Edward Elerbe Cobbs, son of John Lewis Cobbs and Dorothy Peagues, and grandson of Bishop Nicholas Hamner Cobbs,

married Edith Harter, and have one son, John Hunter Cobbs.

8 Richard Hooker Cobbs, son of Bishop Nicholas Hamner Cobbs, married Frances Ann Avery and had issue as follows:

9 [1] John Hunter Cobbs.

9 [2] Richard Hooker Cobbs married Lida Tunstal.

9 [3] Francis Avery Cobbs married first Eleanor Randolph, second Fanny Jones.

9 [4] Ann Cobbs married Hollinswink.

9 [5] Mary Elerbe Cobbs married Edwin S. Jack.

9 [6] Lucy Landon Cobbs married Nathaniel Lane Castleman.

9 [7] Edith Hamner Cobbs married Armistead Inge Selden.

9 [8] William Addison Cobbs married Mary Stringfellow.

9 Richard Hooker Cobbs, son of Richard Hooker Cobbs and his wife Frances Ann Avery, and grandson of John Lewis Cobbs, married Lida Tunstal and had issue: Augusta Cobbs, Richard Hoker Cobbs, John Cobbs, Wyley Tunstal Cobbs (last two twins).

9 Francis Avery Cobbs, son of Richard Hooker Cobbs and Frances Ann Avery, married first Eleanor Randolph, second, Fannie Jones, and have one son, Richard Hooker Cobbs.

9 Ann Cobbs, daughter of Richard Hooker and Frances Ann Avery, married Charles Stolenwert. They have one child, Edith Manson Stolenwert.

9 Edith Manson Cobbs, daughter of Richard Hooker Cobbs and Frances Ann Avery, married Armistead Inge Selden. They have one child, Frances Selden.

10 William Addison Cobbs, son of Richard Hooker Cobbs and Frances Ann Avery, grandson of John Lewis Cobbs, and great-grandson of Bishop Nicholas Hamner Cobbs, married Mary Stringfellow. They have one child, William Addison Cobbs.

8 Charlotte Walker Cobbs, youngest daughter of Bishop Nicholas Hamner Cobbs, married Nicholas Cobbs Elerbe. Is-

sue: Clarence Heber Elerbe, Irene Semple Elerbe.

9 Irene Semple Elerbe married Dr. William Bonnel Walker, who occupies a chair in the medical department of the University of the South. No issue.

As has been seen, Bishop Cobbs was born in Bedford county, Virginia, February 5, 1796. He was educated in the best schools of Virginia, and began his active life as an educator. One of his first positions was as principal of New London Academy, but he soon turned his attention to the ministry, and one of his earliest ministerial charges was in his native county at St. Stevens Church, twelve or fifteen miles west of Lynchburg on the old Forest Road, and he continued in the service of this parish until he was called to build up some other weak point in the diocese. There are hundreds now living in Bedford and adjoining counties whose parents and grandparents were led to the Christian altar and baptized into the church by the Reverend Nicholas Cobbs and whose marriage ceremonies he performed and at whose funeral rites he officiated. Mr. Cobbs served a number of other parishes in the diocese of Virginia during his ministry, and his success in building up the church, not so much upon a financial as a spiritual basis, was marked in every field.

The Reverend Nicholas Hamner Cobbs was ordained bishop at Philadelphia, and installed at once Bishop of the Diocese of Alabama. The services of Bishop Cobbs after his promotion to the Episcopacy were even more marked than they were during his ministry. His manner and methods, however, were ever unostentatious, and being actively engaged in the labors of the diocese he devoted very little time to literary work, and left little for publication except sermons. He died in Montgomery, Alabama, in 1861, at the age of sixty-five. His widow and a large family of children survived him.

John Lewis Cobbs was the only one of Bishop Cobbs' sons who ever engaged in public life, and he seems to have been literally dragged into it. He was for a number of years a dry goods merchant in Montgomery, but after the close of the war between the states and the restoration of Alabama, he was called from his retirement and made treasurer of the state.

7 Sarah Lewis Cobbs, daughter of John Lewis Cobbs and his wife Susannah Hamner, married Captain Henry Jones and had issue:

    8 [1]Susan Adeline Jones married William Harris Lee.

    8 [2]Edwin Nicholas Jones.

    8 [3]Mary Ann Sarah Jones.

    8 [4]Agnes J. Jones.

    8 [5]Elizabeth Amanda Jones.

    8 [6]John William Jones married Sallie Williams Andrews.

8 Susan Adeline Jones, daughter of Sarah Lewis Cobbs and Captain Henry Jones, married Wm. Harris Lee and had issue:

    9 [1]Wm. Henry Lee married Bettie Murrell. Infant child, died.

    9 [2]Mary Ella Lee married Harold Peters Read.

    9 [3]Jones Edwin Lee married Sarah Virginia Lee.

    9 [4]John Addison Lee married Elizabeth Fitzgerald.

    9 [5]Sarah Elizabeth Lee.

    9 [6]Samuel Custis Lee married, first, Martha Gowings, second, Sarah Lewis Jones.

9 Mary Ella Lee and Harold Peters Read had issue: Annie Belle Read, and infant name unknown.

9 James Edwin Lee, son of Susan Adeline Jones and Wm. Harris Lee, and grandson of Sarah Lewis Cobbs, married Virginia Lee and had issue: Ada Arnold Lee, Sarah Elizabeth Lee, Edwin Cecil Lee, Caroline May Lee, Wm. Howard Lee, Samuel Hunt Lee, Gilmore Thomas Lee, Kirtley Lee, Booker Lee, Susan Adeline Lee, Robert Fitzhugh Lee.

9 John Adison Lee and Elizabeth Fitzgerald had issue: William Otway Lee, Harriet Fitzgerald Lee, Thomas Fitzgerald Lee, Samuel Lee.

9 Samuel Custis Lee, son of Wm. Harris Lee, and grandson of Sarah Lewis Cobbs, by his second marriage with Sarah Lewis Jones had one child, Annie Stewart Lee.

8 John Wm. Jones, son of Captain Henry Jones and Sarah Lewis Cobbs, married Sallie Williams Andrews and had issue: Sarah Lewis Jones married Samuel Custis Lee; Charles Wm. Jones married Mrs. Adeline Booker; Ettie Vernon Jones, Mary Henry Jones, Helen St. Clair Jones, Agnes Surrenia Jones, Fannie Elisabeth Jones, James Nicholas Jones.

7 JAMES MADISON COBBS.

Madison Cobbs was the second son of John Lewis Cobbs and his wife Susannah Hamner. He was born 1798 in Bedford county, Virginia, where he spent his boyhood and early manhood. Early in life he made Lynchburg his home, where he engaged in merchandising, selecting the dry goods trade as his line, operating at different times individually, or under the firm name of Cobbs & Armistead, or Cobbs, Armistead & Henderson.

Mr. Cobbs was a model of the old-school gentleman, and was a contradiction to the generally accepted idea of the dry goods merchant. No one ever thought of questioning his integrity, and his reputation for the most scrupulous veracity was everywhere recognised. At the breaking out of the civil war he suspended business, but resumed again at its close, but soon found that any kind of success depended upon the adoption of methods wholly foreign to his convictions and at war with the teachings of a lifetime, and hence he retired from business.

Mr. Cobbs married his cousin, Eliza, daughter of Sarah Lewis Cobbs and John Alexander, and had issue:

8 ¹Sarah Hamner Cobbs married Thomas McNeil.
8 ²Margaret Gwatken Cobbs married Thomas Knight Scott.
8 ³Edward Alexander Cobbs; no record.
8 Sarah Hamner Cobbs, daughter of James Madison Cobbs, married Thomas McNeil, had issue as follows: Ralph McNeil, Eliza Cobbs McNeil, Edward Parkinson McNeil, Virginia McNeil, James Alexander McNeil, Henry McNeil.

8 Margaret Gwatken Cobbs, daughter of James Madison Cobbs, married Thomas Knight Scott, had issue as follows;

    9 [1] Jessie Scott married Dr. Charles Montgomery. They have infant child.

    9 [2] Eliza Huxley Scott married Grecian Nixon.

    9 [3] John Goodwin Scott.

    9 [4] Helen Nelson Scott.

9 Elisa Huxley Scott, daughter of Margaret Gwatkin Cobbs, and granddaughter of James Madison Cobbs, married Grecian Nixon, and had issue: Pope Nixon, Thomas Scott Nixon, Margaret Cobbs Nixon.

7 Damarius Cobbs, daughter of John Lewis Cobbs, married Jesse Alexander Burton and had issue as follows:

    8 [1] Margaret Macon Burton married James Samuel Mackey.

    8 [2] Susan Hamner Burton married James Booker Nolin.

    8 [3] Elisabeth Clay Burton married James Samuel Mackey.

    8 [4] John Madison Burton married Ella Wilson Berry.

8 Margaret Macon Burton, daughter of Damarius Cobbs and her husband, married James Samuel Mackey and had issue as follows:

    9 [1] Alfred Price Mackey married Mary Julia Lackey.

    9 [2] Lelia Mitfone Mackey married Charles Price Nowlen.

    9 [3] Alexander Burton Mackey married Agnes Locket Morton.

    9 [4] James Merton Mackey married Elizabeth Macon Davis.

    9 [5] Mary Damarius Mackey married Venable Watkins Davis.

    9 [6] Carrie Cobbs Mackey.

9 Alfred Price Mackey and Mary Julia Lackey, had issue: Price Armstrong Mackey, Margaret Macon Mackey, Alfred Baxter Mackey.

8 Susan Hamner Burton, daughter of Damarius Cobbs, and her husband James Booker Nowlin had issue:

    9 [1] Charles Price Nowlin married Lelia Mitford Mackey.

Issue: Virginia Margaret Nowlin, Ross Booker Nowlin, James Samuel Nowlin.

9 ²Virginia Susan Nowlin.

9 ³John Burton Nowlin married Roberta Ellis Hall.

9 ⁴Jesse Graham Nowlin.

8 John Madison Burton, son of Damarius (Cobbs) Burton, and grandson of John Lewis Cobbs, married Ella Wilson Berry and had issue: Mabel Burton, Edith Burton, George Lewis Burton, Ruth Burton, John Marvin Burton.

7 Ann Hamner Cobbs, daughter of John Lewis Cobbs and his wife Susannah Hamner, married Baker Davidson and had issue: two daughters, marriage of one unknown, the other married William Lackland and had issue: Nannie Lackland, Thomas Cobbs Lackland.

7 Agnes Cobbs, daughter of John Lewis Cobbs, married Dr. John Slaughter. Issue: Susan Slaughter, marriage unknown.

7 Virginia Cobbs, daughter of John Lewis Cobbs by his second marriage, married Charles William Price and had issue as follows:

8 ¹Virginia Price married William Black.

8 ²Mary Price married Travis Alexander; issue: Lena Alexander, Daisy Alexander.

8 ³Ida Price married Allen Barnes.

8 ⁴Olivia Price.

8 ⁵Charles William Price.

8 ⁶Willie Price married Dr. Doubleday.

7 Thomas Nelson Cobbs, son of John Lewis Cobbs by his second marriage, married first Mary Avery and had issue: infant, daughter dying at birth; by second marriage with Miss Louisa Taylor, one son, Wm. Byars Cobbs married a Henley; issue: Marion Cobbs; by third marriage with Sarah Taylor, one son, Charles Price Cobbs.

6 Waddy Cobbs is one of the three sons of Edmund Cobbs and Sarah Lewis who has not been entirely lost to history. He married Miss Margaret Gwatkin and they had ten children

whose names have all been preserved, and the marriages of four are matters of record, but we have no account of the descendants of any except Sarah Lewis and Eliza Frances. The names of the children of Waddy Cobbs and Margaret Gwatkin follow:

7 [1] Charles Gwatkin Cobbs married Ann Cobbs.

7 [2] Sarah Lewis Cobbs married John Alexander.

7 [3] Mary Caloway Cobbs married Hartwell Eppeo.

7 [4] James L. Cobbs.

7 [5] Lemira Cobbs.

7 [6] Eliza Frances Cobbs.

7 [7] Martha Cobbs.

7 [8] Catherine Cobbs.

7 [9] Nancy Cobbs.

7 [10] Emily Cobbs married a Mr. Nelson.

7 Sarah Lewis Cobbs married John Alexander and had issue:

8 [1] Charlotte L. Alexander married John F. Sale.

8 [2] Sarah Ann Alexander married Dr. Thomas H. Nelson.

8 [3] Mary Glenn Alexander married Dr. William Davis.

8 [4] John D. Alexander married Mary Pannil.

8 [5] Olivia Alexander married first Robert Camm, and second, Edwin R. Page.

8 [6] Eliza Alexander married James Madison Cobbs.

8 [7] Susan Alexander married James Van Hoose.

8 [8] Robert Alexander.

8 [9] Edward Alexander.

8 [10] Roberta Alexander married a Mr. Hilton.

8 Sarah Ann Alexander and Dr. Thomas H. Nelson had issue:

9 [1] Charles Sumerious Nelson, single.

9 [2] John Alexander Nelson, single.

9 [3] Hugh Nelson, single.

9 [4] Wm. Steptoe Nelson, single.

9 [5] Eliza K. Nelson married Dr. James A. Boyce.

9 [6] Thomas Walker Nelson married first Lelia McDaniel, second a Miss Morison.

9 [7] Charles Kenlock Nelson married Etta Scott.

9 [8]Helen Lewis married J. N. Early.

8 Mary Glenn Alexander and Dr. William Davis had issue:

9 [1]Mary Caloway Davis married Governor Wm. Dunington Bloxham. He was a member of Congress from Florida and twice governor of the state.

9 [2]Sarah Ann Davis.

9 [3]Elisa Davis married Isham Miller Blake.

9 [4]Katherine Davis.

9 [5]John Alexander Davis.

9 [6]Edward Micajah Davis.

9 [7]William Davis.

9 Mary Callaway Davis and Governor Bloxham had issue: Wm. Davis Bloxom, Martha William Bloxom.

9 Elisa Davis and Isham Miller Blake had issue:

10 [1]Mary Alexander Blake married Walter James Glenn.

10 [2]Annie Blanche Blake.

10 [3]Joe Clifton Blake.

10 [4]Lewis Gwynn Blake.

10 [5]Miller William Blake married Nancy Graves.

10 [6]Katherine Byrd Blake.

10 [7]John Cromartis Blake.

10 Mary Alexander Blake and Walter James Glenn had issue: William Dunnington Glenn, Bloxham Glenn, Anna Blanche Glenn, George Baxton Glenn, William Bloxham Glenn.

6 Edmund Cobbs was the third son of Edmund Cobbs and Sarah Lewis, in the order named in the settlement of the estate, and grandson of John Cobbs of Goochland county, Virginia. He married Miss Elizabeth Manson of Bedford county, Virginia, which was also his native county. He owned a large plantation seven or eight miles west of Lynchburg on the Lexington turnpike, where he resided and raised his family. They had issue as follows:

7 [1]Lucy Henry Landonia Cobbs married Bishop Nicholas Hamner Cobbs.

7 [2]Eleanor Cobbs married Oliphant. Issue: Lucy Oli-

phant, and Mary Oliphant who married a Martines.
Issue: Louise Martines, George Martines.

7 ³Mary Adeline Cobbs married Henry Landon Davies.

7 ⁴Frederick Augustus Cobbs.

7 ⁵John Cabell Cobbs.

7 Mary Adeline Cobbs and Henry Landon Davies had issue:

  8 ¹Elizabeth Read Davies married Montraville Whitson Gudger.

  8 ²Virginia Washington Davies married William Swearingen.

  · 8 ³Tamerlane Wm. Whiting Davies married first Susan Clayton, married second Nettie Alice Galanus.

  8 ⁴Mary Landon Davies married a Hensley.

  8 ⁵Letitia Terry Davies.

  8 ⁶Charlotte Wilson Davies.

  8 ⁷Addison Meriwether Davies married Mary Anna Townes.

  8 ⁸Charlotte Davies married first Edgar A. Murrell, second McFadden Alexander Newell.

8 Elizabeth Read Davies, daughter of Adaline Cobbs, and granddaughter of Edmund Cobbs and Elizabeth Manson, married Montreville Whitson Gudger and had issue as follows: Montraville Love Gudger, Annie Dillard Gudger, Mary Landon Gudger, Rosa Gudger, Bettie Cazine Gudger married J. G. Gilbert, Frances Gudger married S. P. Bolin, James Gallatin Gudger, Charles Meigs Gudger.

8 Tamerlane William Whiting Davies, daughter of Adaline Cobbs and Landon Davies, married and had issue as follows: Clayton Davies, Addison Davies, Nicholas Hamner Davies, John Davies; and by second marriage with Nettie Alice Galanus, Annie Lucile Davies.

8 Charlotte Davies married first Edgar A. Murrell and had issue: Wm. Henry Murrell, Cornelia Cobbs Murrell married Wm. Henry Fields; and second she married McFadden Newell and had James Alexander Newell, Josephine Cushing Newell.

8 Addison Meriwether Davies and Mary Ann Townes had issue as follows: Landon Townes Davies, Addison Meriwether Davies, Bedford Dispatch Davies, Constant Machen Dandridge Davies, Joseph Tamerlane Davies, Mary Pearl Breckenridge Davies, Francis Huntington Davies, Mary Frances Davies.

7 John Cabell Cobbs, son of Edmund Cobbs and Elisabeth Manson, married Martha Broadnax Carter. Issue: Ann Elisabeth Cobbs, Editha Lee Cobbs, Nicholas Hamner Cobbs, Susan Landonia Cobbs, Lucy Landonia Cobbs married John Marshall Steptoe, Martha Cabell Cobbs, Richard Wilmer Cobbs married Georgie Smith.

8 Lucy Landonia Cobbs and Marshall Steptoe had issue: Hampden Early Steptoe, Pattie Wilmer Steptoe, Mary Grace Steptoe, Lucy Cabell Steptoe, Marshall Steptoe, Aurie Marshall Steptoe.

9 Richard Wilmer Cobbs and Georgie Smith had Winston Cobbs, John Cabell Cobbs, Richard Wilmer Cobbs.

4 THOMAS COBBS.

Thomas Cobbs of Goochland, Hanover and Albemarle counties, Virginia, Granville county, North Carolina, and Columbia county, Georgia, was born early in the eighteenth century, the exact date not definitely known. Goochland county, Virginia, was no doubt his native county. As is seen, he was so migratory in early life that it is something like chasing a wil-o'-the-wisp to try to keep up with him. He was fourth in line from Ambrose Cobbs, the emigrant, and was a son of the second Robert Cobbs and was a brother of the third Robert of Henrico and John of Goochland.

The records place Thomas Cobbs first in Goochland until 1750, after which he appears on the fee books of Goochland as "Thomas Cobbs of Hanover." He subsequently removed to that portion of Albemarle county which lay on the south side of

James river, which was cut off to form the county of Buckingham, and afterwards to Granville county, North Carolina, on the records of which county he appears for several years prior to and after 1769. He next appears on the records of Columbia county, Georgia, where he evidently spent the remainder of his life, having lived to an incredible old age. He first appears on the Goochland records prior to 1735, and is reputed to have been born 1708 or 1710, and as he died in 1832, he was more than 120 years old. Tradition says that he was an officer in the Revolution, but this is not probable, as he was over 65 when the war broke out. The tradition doubtless had its origin in the fact that he had a son of the same name who was an officer in the army.

5 Thomas Cobbs, son of the above Thomas, was an officer in the Revolution. He married and left issue but nothing is known of them except one daughter, Nancy, who married William Smith of Prince Edward county, Virginia, and was the ancestor of General E. Kirby Smith of the Confederate Army. Their children were Robert H., Napoleon B., Catherine, Nancy, Julia, James, Sterling and Mary.

5 John Cobbs, son of Colonel Thomas Cobbs, seems to have been more fully identified with his father than any of his children. Indeed it seems that old Thomas was a sort of migratory specimen for a number of years, from Goochland to Hanover, to Albemarle, to Granville, North Carolina, until he finally settled down in Columbia county, Georgia, in the latter part of the eighteenth century; and it seems, so far as the records show, that John is the only one of his sons that kept up with him. There is no doubt that this is the John Cobbs whose name appears as witness to a deed of gift executed by John Cobbs conveying land and negroes to his children in 1791. This John Cobbs signs his name to that instrument as "John Cobbs, Jun.," while the maker of the instrument is described as John Cobbs the elder, but they are clearly not father and son, as John Addison Cobbs is named in the deed as the son of John Cobbs the "elder." There is no doubt that this John Cobbs left a number of sons, as there are

many descendants of Thomas Cobbs scattered throughout Georgia and Alabama, but there is only one whose name has come down in history, and we have no well authenticated line of descent from him.

6 Thomas W. Cobb was the son of the abovenamed John Cobbs, and grandson of Thomas Cobbs of Columbia county, Georgia. The paradox in the difference in name of father and son is quite apparent. The father of Thomas W. Cobb, in a sworn statement to a court paper in 1796, signed his name "Cobbs," as maker of the instrument; and the ancestor of another line of the Cobbs family in Georgia, whose descendants sign their names "Cobb," in an instrument referred to above, executed in 1791, describes his children as Cobbs, and signs his name Cobbs. If there was ever any reason for the change it has never been suggested. The name of Cobbs has been unsullied as to reputation, remarkable for high character and integrity, and distinguished for learning throughout their history, which makes the change still more unaccountable. All of the other branches so far as known, have retained the original spelling. Nothing but the merest caprice can account for the change.

It is asserted historically that Thomas W. Cobb was educated by his grandfather, old Thomas Cobbs, when nearly one hundred years old, against the remonstrances of his friends; but, true to the characteristics of his name, he persisted, and lived to see his grandson in the United States senate from Georgia.

Thomas W. Cobb studied law with Wm. H. Crawford, and was eminent in his profession. He represented his district in the lower house of Congress, and was also chosen United States senator from Georgia. Cobb county was named in honor of him. Mr. Cobb was also appointed one of the Superior Court judges for Georgia and resigned his seat in the Senate to take his seat on the bench.

It is not known who Thomas W. Cobb married, nor is there any definite data in regard to his children. There is no doubt, however, that Thomas Cobbs of Columbia county had other sons, and that a numerous descent has sprung from this head of the family who have chosen to write themselves "Cobb" instead of "Cobbs." There are a great many in Georgia and Alabama who spell their name "Cobb," who, from neglect or indifference, have lost all trace of their ancestry, and know nothing of their line of descent. Unlike the Frenchman that Mark Twain tells about, they are perfectly satisfied about their fathers, but are anxiously inquiring about their grandfathers.

Judge Cobb of Alabama who represented the Tuskegee district in Congress for a number of years is of this family. The late Henry W. Grady and the widow of Governor H. Y. Atkinson, are also descended from the same branch, but the descent is sustained only by tradition, but it is well sustained in both families, and supported by family records.

ROBERT COBBS OF HENRICO.

Robert Cobbs was the third son of the second Robert Cobbs of York, grandson of the first Robert, and great-grandson of Ambrose the emigrant. He was the younger brother of John and Thomas Cobbs of Goochland county, Virginia, and appears on the deed books of Henrico from 1744 to 1748. His will is not recorded in Henrico, and there is no doubt that he removed to Chesterfield, or some adjoining county. There were many of the name in Chesterfield, doubtless descended from this ancestor. The Randolph manor, known as "Cobbs," was in Chesterfield, and the Randolphs of Cobbs were intimately associated, if not connected, with this branch of the family.

Chancellor Cobbs of Alabama is descended from this branch. From Chancellor Cobbs we have the following verbatim account of his family. Beyond this he knew nothing: "My father was born in Manchester, Virginia, 1777. His name was Thomas and he had a brother John. He married three times, the names of his first two wives were unknown. His third wife

310

was a widow Hopkins, nee Miss Boone. He removed to Raleigh, North Carolina, and was at one time mayor of the city. He afterwards removed to Alabama where he spent the remainder of his life."

Chancellor Cobbs, when I saw him, 1894, was a well preserved man of about 65. He was a ripe scholar, an eminent lawyer, and profound jurist. He was at the time presiding over the chancery court of Birmingham, Alabama. In my general search for information I was thrown into correspondence with -Thomas D. Cobbs of Houston, Texas, a son of Chancellor Cobbs of Alabama, a lawyer of high standing, eminent in his profession. He was then general counsel for the Houston & Texas Central railroad.

SAMUEL COBBS OF AMELIA.

Samuel Cobbs was the first clerk of Amelia county, Virginia, when it was first laid off in 1735. He was an appointee of the crown and was sent from Williamsburg to take charge of the office. He continued clerk of the county until he died 1757. It does not appear that this Samuel Cobbs was in the same line of descent as Thomas, John and Robert of Goochland and Henrico, but it is reasonably certain that he descended from the same common ancestry; from either Ambrose or Joseph of York, who were the original emigrants; and this conclusion is confirmed by the fact that he comes from the same locality, and the same characteristics are shown in all of his recorded writings. While the date of his birth is not definitely shown, the records show that he was born prior to 1700. He makes a bequest to a grandson in 1757, and states that he had been married nearly forty years, from which it follows that he was over sixty at the time. The will of Samuel Cobbs bears date June 27, 1757, and was probated July 28, following. He left his entire estate to his widow, Edith Cobbs, but mentions his two sons, Samuel and John Catlin. The records show that John Catlin Cobbs remained in Amelia and married there, but there is no account of any descendants. Samuel Cobbs returned to Williamsburg as shown by the records. In the will of his mother, Edith Cobbs, probated August 27, 1761, all of the property left by the elder Samuel, in the town of Williamsburg, was bequeathed to her son Samuel, and he appears on the records of Amelia as Samuel Cobbs of Williamsburg. There is no account of any of his descendants. He was probably born about 1740, as he was a minor at the time his father's will was made.

Samuel Cobbs was an officer in the Revolutionary Army and appears on the land books as Lieutenant Samuel Cobbs, as having received land grants in consideration of military services.

Mrs. Edith Cobbs mentions in her will two unmarried daughters, Theodocia and Judith, and a granddaughter Rachel Booker; a grandson, Samuel Cobbs, is also mentioned.

THOMAS COBBS.

Thomas Cobbs appears on the records of Albemarle in deed book 2, August 11, 1760. His will is also on record in which he names two sons and one daughter, Thomas and Charles Cobbs and Mary Campbell. His two sons are named as executors. His will was probated June 11, 1761.

Thomas Cobbs, the son of above Thomas and executor of his father's will, appears on deed book 12, page 508, Albemarle county, Virginia, May 11, 1797. Thomas Cobbs and Mary his wife convey certain lands to ———— Garth in Albemarle county and commission is appointed by the county court in 1802 to obtain Nancy Cobbs' alienation of dower.

Charles Cobbs, another son of the above Thomas Cobbs, appears on the records of Albemarle, deed book 2, page 272, in a deed from William Walton to Charles Cobbs, both of Albemarle. Charles Cobbs married a daughter of this William Walton and removed to Campbell county, Virginia, where his will is on record. He left a large family of sons and daughters, but they seem to have lost all trace of their ancestry beyond Thomas Cobbs of 1760. There can be no doubt that they descended from the same line of the other Cobbs of which we have been treating, but they have lost the connecting link.

MERIWETHER FAMILY.

Stereotyped family history informs us that during the reign of Charles II, three brothers, Nicholas, Charles and David Meriwether left Wales and emigrated to the colony of Virginia. Whether there were three or more is not important. It is certain that Nicholas came, and as he will furnish more material than we can handle we will content ourselves with him for the present.

Nicholas Meriwether was born in Wales toward the close of the sixteenth century and died December 19, 1678. He was the father of Nicholas, the present subject of our sketch, and the other two traditional brothers.

Nicholas Meriwether, son of the above-named Nicholas, was born in Wales, 1647, and died in Virginia 1744. He married Elizabeth Crawford, daughter of David Crawford of New Kent county, Virginia, and had children as follows: William Meriwether, David Meriwether, Thomas Meriwether, Nicholas Meriwether, Elizabeth Meriwether, Sarah Meriwether, Mary Meriwether, Jane Meriwether.

The Meriwether family, confined to Nicholas and Elizabeth Crawford, would furnish material in itself to make up an ordinary library. I will therefore attempt only a partial sketch of the family, confining myself to the descendants of Jane, who has been already disposed of under the head of her husband, Col. Robert Lewis of Belvoir, and David, who married Ann Holmes.

2 David Meriwether, son of Nicholas Meriwether and Elizabeth Crawford, born about 1685, married Ann Holmes, daughter of George Holmes, and had children as follows: Thomas, Francis, Nicholas, Ann, Sarah, David.

Genealogists differ as to whether Thomas Meriwether, who married Elizabeth Thornton, was a son of David or William Meriwether. I have, however, selected David, as the weight of evidence seems to be in his favor.

314

8 Thos. Meriwether, oldest child of David Meriwether and Ann Holmes, born 1714-15, died 1756. He married Elisabeth Thornton and had children as follows: Nicholas, Francis, David, Mary, Elizabeth, Sarah, Ann, and Lucy Meriwether, born February 4, 1752. She married first, Col. William Lewis and was the mother of Meriwether Lewis, of whom mention is made on another page. She married second, Col. Marks, an officer of the Revolutionary army. She died September 8, 1837, in her eighty-sixth year; Mildred, Thomas, and Jane—as Governor Gilmer calls her, "Pretty Jane Meriwether." She married Samuel Dabney; she was the recognised beauty of the circle in which she moved, very pretty, very rich, and very much courted. Her sphere was necessarily wide.

William, youngest son of David Meriwether and his wife, Ann Holmes, born December 25, 1730, in Louisa county, Virginia, married Martha Cox Wood and had eight children, among whom was David Wood Meriwether who was born in 1756 and married Mary Lewis, daughter of John Lewis of Spottsylvania county, Virginia. He moved to Kentucky, and died in 1795.

The following notes on the Meriwether family will be necessarily desultory, as the names are so numerous that it is impossible in the space allowed to take them up in regular order. They will be for the most part confined to the descendants of Thomas, James and William Meriwether, sons of David Meriwether and Ann Holmes his wife:

4 Frank Meriwether, born October 31, 1787, was a son of Thomas Meriwether and Elisabeth Thornton, married Martha Jamison, and from this marriage ten children resulted three sons and seven daughters: Thomas, Valentine, Nicholas, Mary, Mildred, Elisabeth, Lucy, Margaret, Nancy and Sarah.

(This member of the Meriwether family, being included in Governor Gilmer's book as one of the North Georgia settlers, was doubtless among the pioneers of Broad river, and in further confirmation of this, it may be mentioned that two of his children, a son and daughter, married a daughter and son of Governor Mathews.)

4 David Meriwether, third son of Thomas Meriwether and Elizabeth Thornton, born September 2, 1739, married Mary Harvie. They had only two children, a son and a daughter: Lewis B. Meriwether married Elizabeth Johnson, and Mary married Benjamin Taliaferro. (David Meriwether was also one of the Broad river Colony mentioned by Governor Gilmer in his "North Georgians," and it is recorded in the history of Georgia Methodism, that the first conference held in the State was at the house of David Meriwether in the forks of Broad river, 1784.)

4 Mary Meriwether, daughter of Thomas Meriwether and Elizabeth Thornton, born April 4, 1742, married Peachy R. Gilmer of Albemarle county, Virginia. They had two sons and four daughters: Thomas Gilmer, George Gilmer, Mary Peachy, Lucy, Elizabeth and Francis, who married Richard Taliaferro.

5 Thomas Gilmer, son of Mary Meriwether and her husband Peachy R. Gilmer, born about 1765, maried Elizabeth Lewis daughter of Thomas Lewis, and granddaughter of Irish John Lewis of Augusta county, Virginia. They had eight children: Peachy Ridgway Gilmer, Thomas L. Gilmer, Mary, John, Wm. B., Charles Lewis, Lucy Anne, and George Rockingham Gilmer, who married Elisa Frances Grattan. (This family was also among the pioneers of Broad river, having left Virginia with the general exodus of the Meriwethers, just after the close of the Revolution, and the last-named son, George Rockingham Gilmer, represented his district in Congress for many years, and was twice Governor of Georgia. A more extended notice of him will be given in the closing pages of the Meriwether family.)

4 Elizabeth Meriwether, daughter of Thomas Meriwether and Elizabeth Thornton, born March 3, 1744, married Thomas Johnson of Louisa county, Virginia, known as "Sheriff

Tom." They had a large family of children, among whom
were Mary who married Henry Winston, Elizabeth who
married the Rev. John Poindexter, Rebecca who married Joseph Winston, Lucy who married Wm. Quarles, Sarah who
married Richard Overton, and Nanny who married Charles
Barrett.

4 Sarah Meriwether, daughter of Thomas Meriwether and Elisabeth Thornton, born November 26, 1746, married Michael
Anderson and had five children. No marriages recorded.

4 Ann Meriwether, daughter of Thomas Meriwether and Elizabeth Thornton, born May 1, 1750, married Richard Anderson
and had seven children.

5 David Meriwether Anderson, son of Ann Meriwether and Richard Anderson as above, married first, Susan Moore, and second, Mrs. Mary Walker Leitch. Issue by first marriage:
Ann, Catherine, Richard, Lucy Jane, Elizabeth Moore, Lewis; no children by second marriage.

6 Ann Anderson, oldest daughter of David Anderson and Susan
Moore, married William Porter and had two children: Helen
Porter, and J. Meriwether Porter.

6 Lewis Anderson, son of David Anderson and Susan Moore,
ried Eliza M. L. Leitch and had six children: Susan Moore,
David Johnson, Nannie, Margaret, Ellen Overton, and Warner Lewis.

7 J. Meriwether Porter, son of Ann Anderson and William Porter, married Mary Boothe and had three children: Nannie,
Kate and Nellie.

7 Susan Moore Anderson, daughter of Lewis Anderson and Eliza
Leitch, married John R. McMurdo and had a number of
children, but the names of only three have been obtained:
Eliza, Susan and John, Jr.

5 Elizabeth Anderson, daughter of Ann Meriwether and Richard
Anderson, married Waddy Thomson. This Waddy Thomson was the son, by a former marriage, of the first Waddy
Thomson of Albemarle county, ·Virginia and whose second
wife was Mary Lewis, widow of Samuel Cobbs and daughter

of Robert Lewis of Belvoir. Mr. George Woods Meriwether
of Louisville, Kentucky, says in his sketch of the Meriwether
family, that Waddy Thomson, whom he describes as Waddy
Thomson of South Carolina, whose son was in Congress a
number of years from that State, and also minister to Mexico, was the same that married Elizabeth Anderson. He died
in Greenville, South Carolina, at an advanced age, in 1845.
This settles the identity of Waddy Thomson of South Carolina who was minister to Mexico, as the grandson of Waddy
Thomson who married Mary Lewis Cobbs.

4 Lucy Meriwether, daughter of Thomas Meriwether and Elisabeth Thornton, married first, Col. Wm. Lewis, second, Col.
Marks. Her descendants by her first marriage are noted under the head of the Lewis family. Col. Wm. Lewis being one
of the sons of Robert Lewis of Belvoir. By her second marriage Lucy Meriwether had two children: Dr. John Marks
and a daughter named Mary who married a gentleman named Moore. Mary Moore and her husband removed to Texas
and left issue. Among them were Hon. George Fellows,
chief justice of the State, and others.

4 Mildred Meriwether daughter of Thomas Meriwether and
Elisabeth Thornton, married John Gilmer and had eight
children: Thomas, Nicholas, George, Francis, David, Harrison, Sarah, Elisabeth and James.

4 Jane Meriwether, youngest child of Thomas Meriwether and
Elisabeth Thornton, who has already been mentioned, irreg-
ularly, is taken up again to supply omissions. She was born
April 3, 1757. Her mother provided wholly for her in her
will. She having been born after her father's death, was
not provided for in his will. Mrs. Elisabeth Thornton Meriwether, after the death of her first husband, married Col.
Robert Lewis of Belvoir. As before stated, "Pretty Jane
Meriwether" married Samuel Dabney, and had eleven children: William, Samuel, Thomas, George, Elisabeth,
Charles, Frank, Richard, Mildred, Edmund and John Dabney.

3 James Meriwether son of David Meriwether and his wife, Ann Holmes, born June 1, 1729, married Judith Hardenis Burnly. They had three children, General David Meriwether being the oldest.

4 General David Meriwether was born in Louisa county, Virginia, 1754, died in Clark county, Georgia, 1832. He married Miss Frances Wingfield of Wilkes county, Georgia, in 1782. They had eight children: John who lived in Alabama; Major James who married several times and his daughter Fannie married Thomas W. Cobb who was in the United States Senate, and for whom Cobb county was named; Dr. Wm. Meriwether, Fannie, George David, Thomas, Judith who married Rev. Mr. Henning, some of whose descendants are now living in Memphis, Tennessee. David Meriwether entered the Revolutionary army in the Virginia Continental line and continued in active service, except when in captivity, until the close of war. He participated in the battles of Monmouth, Trenton, Brandywine, Germantown, and the seiges of Savannah and Charleston. He was twice elected to Congress and was appointed to fill an unexpired term in the United States Senate. He was appointed by the President of United States in conjunction with General Jackson, to treat with the Southern Indians, and held many other positions of trust and honor.

5 James Meriwether, second son of General David Meriwether, married and with his family removed to Tennessee near Memphis. He was commissioned under the general government to make treaties with the Creek and Cherokee Indians. He represented his district in Congress before leaving Georgia.

5 Dr. Wm. Meriwether, third son of General David Meriwether, married a Miss Malory and left a son and daughter. He gave up medicine on account of health, studied law and was admitted to the bar.

4 James Meriwether, second son of James and Judith Burnly Meriwether, born 1776, married Sarah Meriwether, a rela-

tive and had six children, only one of whom left issue. Wm. Meriwether of Louisville, Kentucky, was his grandchild.

4 Wm. Meriwether, third son of James and Judith Burnly Meriwether, married a Menslow and left six children.

5 David Meriwether, second son of Wm. Meriwether, last named, was born in Louisa county, Virginia, October 30, 1800. He removed to Kentucky in early life and his first business venture was in the fur trade, which he conducted with energy, and in which he was eminently successful. When yet a young man he entered politics as a Democrat, and between 1832 and 1883 he was thirteen times elected to the Kentucky Legislature, becoming speaker of the House in 1859. He was in the Constitutional Convention of 1849, and upon the death of Henry Clay, was appointed by Governor Powell to fill his unexpired term in the United States Senate; under President Pierce's administration he was territorial governor of New Mexico from 1853 to 1857. He married Sarah Leonard of Massachusetts, and had seven children: Catherine, William Augustine, Orlando Raymond, James Beverly, Elisabeth, Mary, David.

6 [1]Catherine H. B. Meriwether, daughter of Governor David Meriwether married Edmund A. Graves of Lebanon, Kentucky. Issue: Edmund A. Graves of San Jose, California; William, Charles, John.

6 [2]Wm. Augustine Meriwether, oldest son of Gov. Meriwether married first, Lizzie Morselle, second, Mrs. Julia Morselle Tryon.

6 [3]Orlando Raymond Meriwether married Rebecca Owen.

6 [4]James Beverly, third son of Gov. David Meriwether married, first, Martha Reid, and second, Rebecca Reider.

6 [5]Elisabeth Winslow Meriwether married John Williams.

6 [6]Mary Leonard Meriwether married John Bartlett.

6 [7]David Albert Meriwether married Alice Armistead and had one child—Dixie.

3 William Meriwether, son of David Meriwether and Ann Holmes, married Martha Cox Wood of Louisa county, Vir-

ginia, and had eight children: Elisabeth married Nicholas Meriwether and died November 27, 1784; Martha married George Meriwether and died 1786; David Wood Meriwether, born 1756, died 1797, married Mary Lewis, daughter of John Lewis of Spottsylvania county, Virginia; Mary (Lewis) Meriwether, died 1801.

4 William Meriwether, second son of William and Martha Cox Meriwether, born 1757-8, married Sarah Oldham, May 24, 1788, and died June 26, 1814. His wife died 1830. Mildred, Sarah, Valentine, and Ann, were the other four.

5 Sarah Lewis, youngest daughter of David Wood Meriwether and Mary Lewis, born September 9, 1794, married first David Farnsly, January 2, 1814, and second Ebenezer Williams, September 3, 1832, and died 1854. By her first marriage she had six children and by her second marriage she had two, Leah Anne, and Sarah Ebenezer.

6 Leah Ann Williams, oldest daughter of Sarah Lewis Meriwether and Ebenezer Williams, married Charles Pawson Atmore and had six children: Wm. Ebenezer, Charles Pawson, Mary Lloyd, Cary, George Williams and Annie, born December 8, 1858, married Paul Caine, December 1880.

7 Annie Atmore, Great-granddaughter of David Wood Meriwether and his wife Mary Lewis, married Paul Caine of Louisville, Kentucky, and have two children, Sidney Atmore and Idelle Meriwether, born respectively, June 26, 1883, and August 3, 1884.

2 Nicholas Meriwether son of Nicholas Meriwether and Elizabeth Crawford was born 1699 and married Mildred Thornton. The exact date of his death is not known. We learn, however, from the will of his father that he died previous to the making of that instrument, December 12, 1743, as he is referred to in that, as "Nicholas Meriwether, deceased," and one negro girl is bequeathed to his daughter Mildred. There is very little known of the children of this marriage, except the above reference to Mildred, and from tradition, and numerous records, which go to confirm same, that he had

a son Thomas who married Jane Lewis, daughter of Robert Lewis of Belvoir.

3 Thomas Meriwether, son of the above-named Nicholas Meriwether, was born about 1725, and married Jane, eldest daughter of Col. Robert Lewis of Belvoir. That this Thomas Meriwether was the son of Nicholas and Mildred Thornton is shown by the most conclusive proofs: First, the elder Nicholas makes no mention of any sons except William, David, and Nicholas. David had no son Thomas, and William's son Thomas married Elizabeth Thornton, so that this Thomas had nowhere else to look for his paternity; second, these three sons of Nicholas Meriwether and Elizabeth Crawford being the only males of this generation of the Meriwether name, it necessarily follows that this Thomas was the son of Nicholas Meriwether and Mildred Thornton. That this Thos. married Jane Lewis of Belvoir is equally clear, as there was only one other of the name in the Colony at the time and he married Elizabeth Thornton. It is only necessary to show that Jane Lewis married a Thomas Meriwether, and this is abundantly proved by the will of her father and that of Samuel Cobbs who married her sister, and who refers to her as the wife of Thos. Meriwether; and, finally, Thomas Meriwether and Jane his wife join in a deed to Charles Lewis of Albemarle, conveying land in 1766. So that it is clearly shown that the only two Meriwethers of this generation, by the name of Thomas, married respectively Elizabeth Thornton and Jane Lewis. Some of the descendants of Thomas Meriwether and Jane Lewis have been obtained and herewith given.

3 Thomas Meriwether and Jane Lewis had the following: Wm. Meriwether, born 1751; Robert Meriwether, born 1752; Thomas Meriwether, born 1754; and Mary, Jane, Elizabeth, Nicholas and Richard, younger children, date of birth not given.

4 Wm. Meriwether, son of Thomas Meriwether and Jane Lewis, born 1751, had issue as follows: Thomas, born 1781; Fran-

cis, born 1785; Matilda, born 1790; Lucinda, born 1800; Jane, born 1783; William, born 1792; Robert, born 1795.

5 Robert Meriwether, son of the last-named William, and grandson of Thomas Meriwether and Jane Lewis, married Martha Fuqua Baker and had issue as follows: Francis Meriwether, born 1824; Martha Meriwether, born 1827.

6 Martha Meriwether, daughter of Robert Meriwether and Martha Fuqua Baker, and great-granddaughter of Thomas Meriwether and Jane Lewis, was born 1827 and married David W. Lewis and had issue as follows: Fannie Grattan Lewis, born 1852, married H. H. Perry of Georgia. Martha Whitten Lewis, born 1855, married Luther B. Ramsauer, Georgia; Anna, born 1857, married Wm. Garrett; Willie Wells, born ———, married James H. Littlefield of Texas; Mary Reagan, born 1862, married W. F. Crussell of Georgia.

The children of Thos. Meriwether will be found with those of Jane Lewis.

This short sketch of the Meriwether family has not been from lack of material. As stated in the outset, this family furnishes enough material for a library. It would have been impossible, however, in a work of this scope, to have taken up and followed out all of the lines, and to have attempted it would have destroyed all interest in a general review of the leading members of the family. Enough has been given to preserve the general features of a family history and to assist any one in search of information in working out their lines. The line of Jane Meriwether, daughter of Nicholas and Elizabeth Crawford, has been run down to completion under the head of her husband, Robert Lewis of Belvoir, and the lines of David and the second Nicholas have been followed up as far as information could be obtained. We will now conclude this sketch with a notice of George Rockingham Gilmer and Meriwether Lewis, either one of whose lives furnishes a family history, in itself of which any family should be proud: .

GENEALOGIES OF THE

GEORGE ROCKINGHAM GILMER.

This member of the Meriwether family was descended on all sides from one of the most distinguished connections of his day and generation. The Gilmers being leaders in Virginia, politically and professionally, united with the Meriwethers, and then added to that the sturdy Scotch-Irish characteristics of Irish John Lewis, and you have something of the make-up of George Rockingham Gilmer. His grandfather, Peachy Ridgway Gilmer, born about 1735, married Mary Meriwether, daughter of Thomas Meriwether and Elizabeth Thornton, born April 4, 1742, and their son Thomas, father of George Rockingham Gilmer, married Elizabeth Lewis, daughter of Thomas Lewis, and granddaughter of Irish John Lewis of Augusta county, Virginia, thus combining, as above stated, the elements going to make up his remarkable character.

At what time Governor Gilmer came to Georgia is not definitely known. He may have been a native Georgian as many of his Meriwether kin came to Georgia at the close of the Revolution, and he was born about 1790. Be this as it may, he was a Virginian by blood, and a thorough Georgian by adoption. He represented his district in Congress for many years and was twice governor of the State. He was an extreme Whig which party had succeeded the Federal party, and the antagonism between them and the Democratic party, and especially General Jackson, was intense. In this antagonism Governor Gilmer shared, and at times "out Heroded Herod." He fought Jackson's Administration with all of the vigor of his bright mind, and when his logic and reasoning powers failed to check the admirers and followers of Jackson, he would turn loose upon them his ridicule and sarcasm in which he excelled. For ridicule "Nancy Hart" was his model. Nancy was a Revolutionary heroine, whose devotion to the cause of freedom was equaled by few and surpassed by none; but she was red-headed and cross-eyed and utterly regardless of all of the conventionalities of life and many were the deeds of heroism that she performed, and many times the Tories were made to stand in mortal dread of "Nancy Hart." On the occasion of a band of Tories raiding through North Georgia, a party of three stopped at her house. She was alone, and they ordered her to prepare supper for them which she proceeded to do. When they sat down to eat she seised a musket and ordered them to surrender. As she had the "drop on them" and being cross-eyed, they did not know which one she was pointing at, all of them threw up their hands. She stood guard over them all night and next morning carried them off, prisoners to the camp of the patriots.

In order to curry favor with General Jackson after he became president, there was always some member of the House offering some resolution appealing to his vanity, one of which was, that all of the vacant niches in the rotunda of the Capitol be filled with paintings of the different battles he had fought. To this Governor Gilmer made no objection but offered an amendment, reserving one place for a painting of Nancy Hart crossing Broad river with her clothes in one hand and a musket in the other, marching three Tory prisoners to the camp of Capt. Cook. It is needless to say that the resolution was killed.

The political school to which Governor Gilmer attached himself, rapidly become more and more unpopular, and while his party embodied hosts of the best element of the country, controlled to a large extent by the giant mind of Henry Clay, yet the rank and file drifted away from the teaching of the fathers, and Governor Gilmer's success and even usefulness was materially crippled thereby. It will be remembered that Kentucky was always a Whig State until after the war, and that Tennessee voted against Polk (her own son), for President.

MERIWETHER LEWIS.

Meriwether Lewis has been sketched and the story of his expeditions fully told under that head of the Lewis family, and the result of that expedition has told its own story and become part of American history, but why it should ever have become known in history as the expedition of Lewis and Clark passes comprehension, and proves that history is no bar to fiction, but often serves as a basis upon which to build it. The expedition was in no sense the Expedition of Lewis and Clark, but the expedition of Meriwether Lewis. It is true that Clark was with Lewis and that he was a commissioned officer, but he was there by the permission of Lewis—simply as commandant of the privates.

Mr. Jefferson had just effected the Louisiana purchase, but that did not reach to the Pacific and the only means of accomplishing this end was by discovery and occupation. And to this end he turned his attention at once. In his letter appointing Lewis to carry his plans into execution, under date June 20, 1803, he uses this prefatory language: "Your situation as Secretary of the President of the United States has made you acquainted with the object of my confidential message to congress, of January 18, 1803. You have seen the act and you are appointed to carry its provisions into execution." Clark's name was at no time mentioned in connection with the expedition. So broad was the authority given Lewis that he was authorized to name his successor so that, in the event of his death, no confusion would result, and Clark could not have succeeded to the command unless named by Lewis. Therefore, Clarks name has no legitimate connection with it.

CAPTAIN WILLIAM CLARK.

Far be it from the authors of this history to detract either from the merits or fame of Captain Clark, or to fail to mete out to him the just mead of praise to which he is entitled. Indeed, every one connected with that expedition is entitled to all praise, from Lewis down to the humblest private, and while the names of only two are perpetuated in history, they were all a band of heroes. It was only with reference to the strict historical text that I was referring. The reader is cited to the appointment of, and instructions to, Lewis by Mr. Jefferson under head of "Lewis family."

There is no doubt that there was Congressional recognition of the services of Captain Clark after their return, which necessarily connected Clark with the expedition, but until it had been completed, "Lewis" was the only name known.

McALLISTER FAMILY.

In the list of American families there are very few whose history antedates that of McAllister or whose descendants have better reason to hold in high esteem than those who have come down in that line, for they have back of them an ancestry whose lives were remarkable mostly for the performance of worthy deeds; or whose ancestral record has been better maintained by those following in succession. Many, it is true, have fallen short of the true standard, but as a rule, with a steady of purpose, like the needle to the pole, in every generation, they have left "footprints upon the sand of time."

The McAllisters are descended from McAllister McDonalds, the progenitors of the McAllisters, who flourished about 1263, who traced back to Somerled, Thayne of Arguyle and first Lord of the Isles, who was son of Magnus, sometimes called "Barefoot," King of Norway. They were also maternally descended from a sister of Robert Bruce (The Bruce) who married a Highland Chief of that name. The family crest is an upraised arm and hand with a cross, crosslet, fitchel and the motto: "Pes Mane Pes Terras."

The McAllisters were not among the early settlers in the colonies, as it was well up in the eighteenth century when they made their appearance on this side the Atlantic. But while Pennsylvania was yet a wilderness, two traditional brothers (some say three but the authors were never able to find the third), came over from Scotland. These were Archibald and Hugh McAllister who landed at Philadelphia 1732. Archibald took up lands and settled in Cumberland county, Pennsylvania, which then embraced all of the territory west of the Susquehanna river. Hugh McAllister came farther south and settled in Maryland where the town of Cumberland was afterwards built.

Archibald McAllister located at Big Spring, near where the

town of York now stands, and with his wife, who came from Scotland with him, spent their lives at that place, where they raised their family. They had six sons and two daughters: John McAllister, Richard McAllister, James McAllister, Archibald McAllister, Daniel McAllister, Andrew McAllister, Mary McAllister, Jean McAllister.

It is not intended to trace the descendants of Archibald McAllister further than to give brief sketches of a few of them whose names belong to history, as Miss Mary McAllister one of his descendants, and daughter of Mr. James H. McAllister of Harrisburg, Pennsylvania, has published a complete history of all of the generations.

2 Col. Richard McAllister was no doubt the most conspicuous of Archibald McAllister's sons. He commanded a regiment under Washington's immediate command, and was with him in all of the principal engagements of the Revolution. Col. Richard McAllister had ten children, as follows:

3 ¹Jane, born March 3, 1750, married Robert White of Georgetown, District of Columbia.

3 ²Abdiel, died single. He served with Arnold at the siege of Montreal and Quebec, was taken prisoner and paroled.

3 ³Mary McAllister, died single.

3 ⁴Archibald McAllister, born 1756, married Elizabeth Carson and had six children. He served in the Revolutionary army with the rank of captain.

3 ⁵Mathew was born May 4, 1758, died in Savannah, Georgia. He married Maria Hannah Gibbons and was the father of Mathew Hall McAllister of whom more will be seen hereafter.

3 ⁶Nancy married Patrick Hays.

3 ⁷Elizabeth married a cousin, John McAllister, and removed to Tennessee.

3 ⁸Sarah, born April 28, 1765, married John Orme. She was the grandmother of Dr. Orme of Atlanta.

3 ⁹Richard, born August 28, 1763, died in Georgia.

3 ¹⁰Margaret, born February 23, 1767, died single.

3 [11]Jessie, born February 23, 1768, married and had several children.

John McAllister who married Elizabeth McAllister, daughter of Col. Richard McAllister, was doubtless the grandfather of Judge Wm. McAllister of Nashville, Tennessee. It is true that Judge McAllister says that his grandfather married a Miss Aikin, but he says that he was from Taseytown, Maryland and as this is the locality in which John McAllister resided, and the records show that he was a widower when he left there for Tennessee, his marriage with Miss Aikin was no doubt a second marriage.

Another circumstance goes to confirm this conclusion. Judge McAllister spells his name with one "l," and the records show that this John McAllister did the same, notwithstanding the fact that his first wife who was his first cousin, spelled her name with two "l's," and his father-in-law, Col. Richard McAllister, who was his father's brother, spelled his name with two "l's." This incident goes to show how easily families may lose their identity, as Judge McAllister is still at sea as to his ancestry back of his grandfather.

Many of the relatives of Judge McAllister are to be found in Tennessee and many of the name doubtless belonging to the same family, are scattered over Kentucky, Missouri, and other States, but so negligent have the American people been in keeping up with their family lines that the great majority have lost all clue to their ancestry. The wife of General Humphrey Marshall of Kentucky, member of the United States Congress from that State, and also of the Confederate Congress, and general in the Confederate army was a McAllister.

Mathew McAllister, fifth child of Col. Richard McAllister, as before stated, was born May 4, 1758, and removed to Savannah. He left a number of sons and daughters who have not only scattered throughout Georgia, but their descendants may be found from New York to California.

4 Mathew Hall McAllister, was a son of Mathew McAllis-

ter and Mariah Gibbons, born and raised in Georgia, and educated in the best schools. He chose the law as his profession and soon forged to the front, both at the bar and in politics, but as he belonged to the old Whig party, which was then fast losing popularity in the South, it generally fell to his lot to lead a forlorn hope. He led his party in a number of campaigns in Georgia, and while he always acquitted himself creditably, no human power could withstand the current that had set in and that bore Democracy on to victory. Too firmly fixed in his political opinions to think of changing them and too conscientious to falsify his convictions, seeing no probability of a change in Georgia, he turned his face to the setting sun and the Golden Gate, and cast his lot in California. This was in 1850, when the gold fever was at its height. McAllister was no gold-hunter in the ordinary sense of the term; yet he knew full well that amid the flow of prosperity he would doubtless share his part.

Mathew Hall McAllister went to the front of the bar upon his arrival in California, for his reputation had gone before him, and he was soon elevated to the Supreme bench of the State. His career as an attorney and also as jurist, after going to California, was to say the least, brilliant, far outshining any political fame that he could have won in Georgia, even if he had been successful. He had four sons: one graduated from West Point and was an officer in the United States army; his other sons were lawyers; two of them were Supreme Court Judges in California, and the fourth, the eccentric Ward McAllister, came east and became a well known figure in New York society.

Ward McAllister needs no eulogy from me, much less does he stand in need of any introduction to the public. His reputation was public property for twenty years before he died. He made it so. He did not seek popularity or notoriety, but while he very successfully avoided the first he could not escape the latter. He was accused of toadying to the moneyed aristocracy of New York for gain; he neither toadied nor sought to profit by his connection with society. He was a man of ample means and his family the social equal of the wealthiest nabobs of Europe or America, but he loved the best in everything, and sought it among the wealthy. His book, "Society as I found it" doubtless gave him more notoriety than anything else, or everything else put together.

HUGH McALLISTER.

It is passing strange that ancestral lines, though of so much importance, often involving financial interests of vast proportions are so lightly esteemed and allowed to pass from the memory of the descendants, and sometimes to become entirely obliterated in so short a time.

Hugh McAllister came over from Scotland in 1732, the same year that Archibald came over, and like Archibald landed at Philadelphia. As the sequel shows, they both penetrated the forest, but cast their lots in different localities. There can be no doubt that these two Scotchmen were brothers, as undisputed family history says "two brothers came over together," but before the third generation had came upon the scene the descendants of each had entirely lost sight of each other. The descendants of Hugh did not know what had become of Archibald, and the descendants of Archibald only knew that their ancestor had a brother who came over from Scotland with him, and did not even know his name, but had a family tradition that he had "gone South," when in fact he had only crossed the Maryland line from Pennsylvania, and then two brothers had raised their families within less than one hundred miles of each other. It must be considered, however, that a hundred miles at that time meant five days of laborious travel, through dense forest, over which roamed hostile Indians and presented much greater difficulties than crossing the Atlantic now.

Hugh McAllister, as has been seen, came over from Scotland 1732, landing in Philadelphia and, as tradition says, "came South," but as the sequel shows, settled in western Maryland where the town of Cumberland now stands. Here he spent his entire life and raised his family, among whom were four sons: Hugh, William, John and James. While these sons doubtless participated in the Revolution, nothing is known of their war history, except John, and only the record of his enlistment and commission is known. Of John McAllister more will be said hereafter. William McAllister married and left descendants. General Robert McAllister of New Jersey, who was an officer in the Federal army during the war between the States, was a grandson of Hugh McAllister and son of William McAllister; a daughter of General Robert McAllister married Governor James H. Beavers of Pennsylvania and resides at Bellfont, Centre county, Pennsylvania, and another, Mrs. J. H. Baldwin, resides at Edgwood Park, Aleghenny county, Pennsylvania.

2 John McAllister, son of Hugh McAllister, was born at Cumberland, Maryland, about 1745, and died in Campbell county, Virginia, 1821. In a list of officers in Col. Thomas Hartley's Pennsylvania battalion, dated Middlebrook, 17th June, 1777, captain Archibald McAllister's name appears; date of commission, April 18, 1777.

In the same list John McAllister's name is mentioned as quartermaster. His commission is dated April 17, 1777.

2 John McAllister came South at the close of the American Revolution and purchased lands in Campbell county, Virginia, as early as 1787, on what was known as Falling river. He married Miss Elizabeth McReynolds of that county, by whom he had five children, all sons: Joseph, John, James, William and Thomas. John McAllister's will, dated April 14, 1818, was probated at Campbell Courthouse, June 6, 1821.

3 [1]Joseph McAllister born 1783, married Miss Helen, a relative, and about 1830 emigrated to Western Kentucky. They had two sons, Shepard and William.

3 [2]John McAllister married Miss Moors, emigrated to Indiana and then to Illinois. They had a family of four: Thomas Bell and Christopher, and two daughters. John McAllister was a lawyer of brilliant promise.

3 [3]James McAllister married Miss Hopkins of Bedford county, Virginia. He died young. They had one son, John Hopkins McAllister. He was living in Virginia as late as 1872. His mother had died a short time previous to that time.

3 ⁴William C. McAllister, born 1789, died 1841, aged 52. He
married Miss Sarah White Cobbs, daughter of Captain Robert Cobbs of Campbell county. Wm. C. McAllister was active and prominent both in political and judicial life. He
represented his county in the Legislature from time to time.
His will is probated at Campbell Courthouse, June, 1841.
William C. McAllister and Sarah White Cobbs had only
two children to reach adult age, Robert Cobbs and John
Meriwether.

4 ¹Robert Cobbs McAllister was born May 3, 1830, in Campbell county, Virginia. He selected medicine as his profession, graduating from the Richmond Medical College 1857.
He married Miss Moore of Appomattox county, Virginia.
They never had any children. Dr. McAllister practiced his
profession in Campbell and Appomattox counties, Virginia,
until 1878, at which time he removed to Morgan county,
Tennessee, where he had practiced with remarkable success
for 26 years. He has been in active and successful practice for 47 years, and is now nearing his 75th birthday.

4 ³John Meriwether McAllister, born October 3, 1833, in Campbell county, Virginia, married Miss Frances Ann Dibrell, daughter of Mr. Charles Lee Dibrell of Lynchburg,
Virginia, August 18, 1857. He chose the law as his profession, attending the Lexington Law School, then Washington
College (now Washington and Lee University), graduating
in the class of 1856. But before he had fairly gotten settled down in his profession the rude hand of war changed all
of his plans, and he drifted into railroad operations, making
his headquarters at Atlanta, Georgia. John Meriwether Mc-
Allister and Frances Ann Dibrell had eight children, but
only two lived to be grown, Frances Elizabeth and Robert
Lewis Dibrell. [Mr. J. M. McAllister who assisted so materially in the compilation of "Genealogies of the Lewis and
Kindred Families" died March 9, 1906, while the book was
being printed.—L. B. T.]

5 Frances Elizabeth McAllister known among her friends as
"Lizzie McAllister," was an intellectual star of the bright-

est magnitude, but with no physique to sustain it. She graduated with honors from the best schools in Georgia. She took to literature, wrote character and dialect stories successfully, and became widely and favorably known as a writer of short stories. She married Dr. Wm. H. Leyden, December 8, 1897, whom she survived several years. They left two children, Estelle Dibrell, and John McAllister, though his mother, after his father's death, added to his name "Wm. Herring." She died May 18, 1901.

5 Robert Lewis Dibrell McAllister was born in Atlanta, Georgia, December 2, 1872. Was educated in the Atlanta Schools, graduated from Auburn College, Alabama, and the University of Virginia, and chose the law as his profession, which he has followed, with varying success, since he left the University. He holds at present an official position with the Supreme Court of Georgia. He married Miss Sarah Elizabeth Smith of St. Louis, a lineal descendant of Professor Cooper, for a long time president of the University of South Carolina, who was favorably mentioned in English history, and was a personal and intimate friend of Thomas Jefferson. R. L. D. McAllister and his wife "Bessie" Smith have three bright children, Lesesne Meriwether, Dorothy Lee, and Robert Lewis Dibrell, Jr., aged respectively: seven, five and three; also, Cornelia, aged three months, a bright blue-eyed little cherub.

The McAllister family has been taken up in this volume only because of the intimate association and connection of one of its branches with the leading names which go to make up the record, as it would have been impossible otherwise to show intelligently what these connections were. No attempt has been made to give the genealogy of the family, except that of John McAlister, the son of Hugh McAllister, as any attempt to give a full genealogy would have been futile. Miss Mary McAllister, direct descendant of Archibald, who is thoroughly posted on that line, having published their genealogy, it would be needless to attempt to enlarge or improve on it, while the other branches seem to have utterly neglected all attempt to keep alive anything like a family history. Even Mrs. Governor Beavers and Mrs.

Baldwin, descendants of Hugh McAllister, through his son William, ladies of position and family pride, could not be induced to become interested in genealogical work.

While I have dealt with Hugh McAllister, the head of this branch, as the brother of Archibald, there is no record evidence of this fact, and Miss Mary McAllister in dealing with the line of Archibald does not accept Hugh as a brother of the latter, but the identity of the date of their arrival in America, the generally accepted tradition in the family of Archibald which has been accorded all the sanctity of family history, that he did have a brother who came over with him, all point unmistakably to Hugh McAllister as the brother of Archibald.

The identity of John McAllister, son of Hugh, has been definitely settled by the pension records, which locate him, at time of death, in Campbell county, Virginia.

BOULTON FAMILY.

The emigrant of the Boulton family came from near Birmingham, England, and settled in Virginia prior to the Revolutionary war. It is claimed on what is believed to be reliable family history, that he was of the same family as Matthew Boulton, the noted scientist and mechanic of Soho, near Birmingham, a younger brother or son of Matthew Boulton. This claim is strengthened by the fact that the spelling of the name is identical with that of Matthew Boulton, while there are other Boltons in the United States from Bolton, England, who spell their names "Bolton."

Matthew Boulton belonged to a very old family, entitled to coat armor, and was for some time high sheriff of Staffordshire. He was born September 8, 1728. The manufactory at Soho, near Birmingham, was erected by him, and in its operations he employed nearly a thousand persons. As the improver of the steam engine, of the apparatus for raising water and other fluids, and in the manufacture of our copper, and some of our silver coin, he has immortalized his name. He made nearly all the large pennies used in England, during the latter part of the reign of George III, known as "Boulton pennies," and were in size as large as a silver dollar. His life was an uninterrupted application to the advancement of the useful arts, and to the promotion of the commercial interests of the country. Mr. Boulton died at Soho, August 17, 1809, and was interred at Handsworth, being followed to the grave by 600 of his workmen who had each a silver medal presented to him, which had been struck for the occasion. The manufactory was sold many years ago, the present owners not being named Boulton, but the property is still known as the Boulton Estate. Andrew Carnegie, the well known philanthropist, said of Matthew Boulton in a piece printed in the Globe-Democrat of St. Louis, April, 1905: "It may be doubted whether there is on record so charming a business connection as that of Matthew Boulton and James Watt; in their own increasing close union for twenty-five years, and at its expiration, in the renewal of that union in their sons under the same title, in their sons' close union as friends, without friction, as in the first generation; in the wonderful progress of the world resulting from their works; in their lying down side by side, in death upon the bosom of mother earth in the quiet church-yard as they had stood side by side in life. In the sweet and precious influences which emanate from all this, may we not gratefully make acknowledgment, that in contemplation thereof, we are lifted into a higher atmosphere, refreshed, encouraged, and bettered by the true story of men like ourselves, whom, if we can never hope to equal, we may at least try in part to imitate."

The progenitor of the Boulton family in America, was presumably Rice.

1 Rice Boulton came to Virginia before the Revolutionary war and settled near Petersburg, where he married a Miss Talley of French descent. As did many of the early settlers of Virginia, Rice Boulton turned his attention to raising and shipping tobacco. He was also a splendid blacksmith. He was a man of great muscular strength, always coming out "best man," in any pugilistic encounter.

He was taken prisoner during the Revolutionary war by the British soldiers, and the causes leading up to his being taken prisoner, as related by his descendants, are as follows: "Several Red Coats came to his shop to have their horses shod; and while there began making use of profane epithets calling him a rebel, etc. One of them reached for the sledge-hammer and he seeing and realising their intention, smote the side of the face and one ear off of one of them with the red-hot iron he had prepared to make the nails for shoeing their horses." This happened near the close of the Revolutionary war, so that he was soon released.

Although we have not obtained a complete record of his children, we will present the record of those we have, that others may add to them. They are as follows:

2 [1]William Boulton went south and settled in Mississippi, or Louisiana. We have no further trace of him.

2 [2]John Boulton married in Owen county, Kentucky, name of wife unknown. They were parents of one child, Mary Boulton.

2 [3]Robert Boulton, of whom we have no record except that he had his foot knocked off by a cannon ball in the war of 1812.

2 [4]Mary Boulton married —— Morton and lived in Tennessee. They had a son, Robert Boulton Morton a dentist.

2 [5]Joel Boulton married a lady of Owen county, Kentucky.

2 [6]Rice Boulton, born near Petersburg, Virginia, December 23, 1787, served nine years apprenticeship as blacksmith, during these years, he spent his spare hours studying, thereby acquiring the rudiments of an education. He obtained the best education the schools of that day could give him and was afterwards taught mathematics by private teachers. He was a noted mathematician being often called upon to solve problems no one in his vicinity could solve. He emigrated to Mason county, Kentucky, in company with Ned and Jack Robinson where he married October 20, 1814, Eliza Pepper, born September 17, 1798, daughter of Jesse Pepper and Elizabeth (or Betsey) Lamkin. Elizabeth Lamkin's mother's maiden name was Munday. She was a sister to John Munday, who owned a grant of several thousand acres of land in Kentucky, which he bequeathed to his niece, Betsey (Lamkin) Pepper. Upon this land a silver mine was afterwards discovered. Her brothers were: Peter Lamkin, went to South Carolina, where he died unmarried, leaving a large estate; James Lamkin lived in Lynchburg, Virginia; Lewis Lamkin lived in Versailles, Woodford county, Kentucky, single; Jesse Pepper had two brothers named Elijah and William all from Virginia. Jesse Pepper's children were (1) Elkanah Pepper, born before 1798, married Miss King of Mason county, Kentucky, and had two daughters. Charlotte married Anderson, Elizabeth married Augustus

Hargett. (2) Eliza Pepper, born 1798, as before stated married Rice Boulton. (3) James S. Pepper, born about 1800, married Lydia Worthington. Their children were: Elizabeth married Dr. Bailey; Ann married Samuel Mannen; Fannie married Thomas Victor, brother to Dr. S. B. and William Victor late of Columbia, Missouri; Laura Pepper married Perry Bateman; Maria Pepper married Warder Victor. (4) Abner Pepper married Miss Murrell of near Washington, Mason county, Kentucky. (5) Alfred Pepper married Miss Snyder. (6) William Pepper, died in 1832, with cholera. (7) Amanda Pepper died young in Mason county, Kentucky.

2 *Rice Boulton was a prominent educator having taught public school, composed and taught vocal music. He was sheriff of Mason county, Kentucky, for several years. He owned a farm bordering on the Ohio river in Mason county, Kentucky, and was engaged extensively in raising and shipping tobacco; in its cultivation he employed many slaves. His wife was a woman of fine executive ability, rare mental attainments and a devoted Christian. Rice Boulton and his wife left Kentucky for Missouri in March, 1853. He died in Boone county, Missouri, March 17, 1866 and his widow May 31, 1884. They were buried in the family burying ground on the farm then owned by their son Judge J. A. Boulton.

Children of Rice and Eliza Boulton all born in Mason county, Kentucky.

3 ¹Peter Lamkin Boulton, born September 14, 1815, engaged in shipping tobacco from Augusta, Bracken county, Kentucky, in partnership with his brother James, where he married June 13, 1839, Ann Eliza Baker, born in spring of 1823. He went from Kentucky to Caldwell county, Missouri, where he owned and cultivated a farm of 400 acres. He died in fall of 1883, and was buried near Cameron, Clinton county, Missouri. His widow, was living in Kansas City, Kansas

with her youngest daughter Tillie, but while on a visit to Cameron, Missouri, died August, 1901.

3 ³Jesse Augustine Boulton, born May 19, 1817, married near Georgetown, Kentucky, October 17, 1839. Mary Hannah Smith, daughter of Levi Todd and Mary (Emerson) Smith. They moved to Boone county, Missouri, where she died February 27, 1846. He married second, April 7, 1847, near Maysville, Kentucky, Clarissa Dixon Perrine, daughter of Robert and Betsey Crane (Loyd) Perrine.

Judge J. A. Boulton was educated at Bacon College, Georgetown, Kentucky. His life was devoted to teaching and farming. He was principal of the first Academy for young ladies in Columbia. He was curator of Christian Female College, and served two terms as judge of the county court in the 70's. He became a member of the Christian church, was baptised October 26, 1834. He held the office of Sunday School Superintendent and elder in Columbia, Oakland and Virden, Illinois. After his children were all educated, his sons having become professional men and his daughter having married and gone to Illinois, he sold his farm three miles north of Columbia and went to Virden, Illinois in 1888, to be near his daughter, but having property in Columbia, returned to Columbia in 1896 and remained for two years, when he went back to Virden, Illinois, where he died January 28, 1902 and was buried in Litchfield, Illinois. His widow is now living at Virden, Illinois. She is a woman whom to know is to love, being possessed of a sweet disposition and fine intelligence.

3 ³James William Boulton, born March 26, 1821, baptised March 3, 1838, died March 13, 1849. He and his brother, P. L. Boulton, shipped tobacco from Augusta. He was buried in Augusta by the Odd Fellows, having been a member of that order for several years.

3 ⁴John Rice Boulton, born February 20, 1823, was baptised March 18, 1838, and united with the Christian Church. His afterlife has been devoted to the cause of Christ, having

been elder, deacon and Sunday School Superintendent. He went to Missouri from Kentucky in 1844, but returned to Kentucky the same year. Went back to Missouri in 1853, and engaged in teaching school at Bonne Femme, Boone county, Missouri. He was a valued instructor and mathematician. He married December 25, 1855, Margaretta Estes, daughter of Berkeley and Malinda Estes, born December 25, 1837. Although he had studied surveying and dentistry, he was engaged after marriage in farming and fruitgrowing on their homestead adjoining her father's, now known as the "Fair View Fruit Farm." It can emphatically be said of him he was honest and upright in all his dealings with his fellowmen and a devoted conscientious Christian gentlemen. He is now in his eighty-third year and almost blind. One of the truly noble and good; content in his devotion to his family, religion and books, never aspiring to a public career, although eminently fitted to hold positions of trust for his country. He has laid up for himself an everlasting inheritance, which fadeth not away, and will certainly be able to hear the welcome plaudit, "Well done thou good and faithful servant, enter thou into the joy of thy Lord," when the final summons shall come. His wife was educated at Christian Female College during the presidency of John Augustus Williams, a member of the Christian church and an industrious energetic woman, devoted to her family and home. They now reside at 605 Elm street, Columbia, Missouri, and December 25, 1905, celebrated their golden wedding, all of their children and grandchildren being present, excepting their son, W. W. Boulton. Mrs. Boulton was sixty-eight years of age upon their 50th wedding anniversary.

5 5 Alfred Elkanah Boulton, born November 7, 1825, baptized March 18, 1838, in Mason county, Kentucky. He went from there to Columbia, Missouri, in 1854 and practiced dentistry until 1857 when he went to Roanoke, Missouri, where he continued the practice of dentistry. He was a vio-

linist of superior merit and his violin has been preserved in the family as a souvenir. He died December 25, 1859, and was buried in Roanoke, Missouri.

3 ⁶Amanda Frances Boulton, born April 29, 1829. She was a gifted musician and a most attractive beautiful young lady. She married October 22, 1850, John Murphy, a tobacco commission merchant of New Orleans, in partnership with his brother, Joseph Murphy and Mr. Crafts. They spent their winters in New Orleans and summers in Dover, Kentucky. She died with yellow fever in New Orleans, August 20, 1853, and was buried there.

3 ⁷Elizabeth Lamkin Boulton, born November 9, 1831, married December 20, 1859, George Smith, a painter. They lived in Columbia, Missouri, until 1865 or 6, when they moved to Litchfield, Illinois, where he died April 12, 1887, and his wife September 25, 1900. They are buried in Boone county, Missouri in the family burying ground on the Judge J. A. Boulton farm.

3 ⁸Mary Eliza Boulton, born May 2, 1834, died in Mason county, Kentucky, August 4, 1844 with scarlet fever.

3 ⁹Edwin Ruthven Boulton, born April 27, 1840, died August 10, 1844, with scarlet fever and was buried in Mason county, Kentucky.

Children of P. L. and Ann E. Boulton:

4 ¹Lucy M. Boulton married first, at her grandfather's in Buchanan county, Missouri, —— Goodwin. She married, second, at her father's home in Caldwell county, Missouri, James Squires of Kansas City, Kansas. She died about the year 1901 and is survived by her husband and an adopted daughter, Mrs. Lula Garniere of Kansas City, Kansas.

4 ²William Boulton, married a widow named Merritt, nee Bush. He served in the Union army during the Civil war and was a farmer for several years in Caldwell county; now resides in Colorado.

4 ³Charles Boulton married Winnie ——, now living in Oklahoma.

4 ⁴Isophene Boulton married ——Swaggard.

4 ⁵Mary Boulton married Joseph Pope, lived several years after marriage in Caldwell county, Missouri, and went from there to Colorado. Resides now in Seattle, Washington. Has one child named Clara, several younger, names unknown.

4 ⁶John Boulton married Alice Bush, sister to his brother William's wife. Place of residence, Colorado.

4 Their seventh and eighth children were twins and were born and died in Caldwell county, Missouri.

4 ⁹Annie F. Boulton, born in Caldwell county, Missouri, in 1854, educated at College in Kidder, Missouri. A faithful member of the Christian Church, ever ready to do for the good of others, both temporal and spiritual. She married Dr. W. F. Waite, and they reside in Kansas City, Kansas, and have a daughter, Mary Valentine Waite.

4 ¹⁰Effie Boulton, unmarried; residence Colorado.

4 ¹¹Henry Boulton married in Holt county, Missouri, Lydia Davis. When last heard from they were living on the old home place in Caldwell county, Missouri. He died February, 1905.

4 ¹²Abraham Lincoln Boulton married and name of wife is unknown; died several years ago.

4 ¹³Homer Boulton.

4 ¹⁴Tillie Boulton married ——Thomas and resided after marriage in Kansas City. They left there in May, 1905, for her husband's health and now reside in Polo, Missouri. Their children are: Erwin Boulton Thomas; Genevieve Thomas; and Theodore Thomas, aged respectively, 10, 8 and 2 years.

4 ¹⁵Infant, died young.

Children of Judge J. A. Boulton, by his first marriage with Mary H. Smith:

4 ¹David Rice Boulton, born October 30, 1841. Educated at Missouri State University; served in Confederate army of the Civil war taking part in several of the hard-fought battles. He married near Shreveport, Louisiana, Obera Cave,

sister to Fannie who married Gilmer. They went to Missouri in 1865 and purchased a fine farm five miles east of Columbia, where they lived until 1874 when they went to Marysville, California. He died in California and his widow is now living in Oakland, California.

4 ²Mary Alice Boulton, born October 23, 1844, married May 6, 1864, Captain Monroe Bateman of Kentucky. For his services in the Union army he is now drawing a pension. Mrs. Bateman is an alumna of Christian Female College, a tender-hearted, sympathetic woman, faithful wife and devoted mother. They now reside three miles north of Columbia, Missouri on the farm bequeathed to her by her grandparents.

4 ³Infant, died young.

Children of Judge J. A. and Clarissa D. Boulton (by second marriage).

4 ⁴Leverett Boulton, died young.

4 ⁵Robert Perrine Boulton, born June 29, 1854, in Boone county, Missouri; graduated from Missouri State University, was professor in Christian University, Canton, Missouri; is now president and manager of the Litchfield Herald, Litchfield, Illinois. He married Kate Elliott, a most attractive, interesting young lady of Litchfield, Illinois. No issue.

4 ⁶Lillie Frances Boulton, born July 25, 1857, in Boone county, Missouri; educated at Christian Female College; a young lady of rare musical attainments, attractive personality and engaging manner, she made many friends. She married at the home of her parents in Boone county, Missouri, J. H. Darneille of Chatham, Illinois, in 1886. She and her daughter, Jessie Clara Darneille, now reside with her widowed mother in Virden, Illinois.

4 ⁷Walter Emmett Boulton, born in Boone county, Missouri, April 6, 1861; a graduate of the Missouri State University, also a graduate of the Bible College of Kentucky. He is an able and distinguished minister of the Christian church,

having been located in Missouri, West Virginia, Kentucky, and is now in Caldwell, Idaho, preaching and conducting the dairy business. He married in Holt county, Missouri, Drusa Hunter. Their first child, Charlotte, died young. Names of younger children, Ellen and Roberta.

4 ³Payne Augustine Boulton, born in Boone county, Missouri, August 18, 1863. He received three diplomas from the Missouri State University, afterwards spent one year in Paris, studying the languages, and then attended Chicago University. His untiring zeal in the pursuit of an education eminently fits him to hold the most important positions in after life. He married Claire Carpenter of Holden and they now reside in Holden, Missouri, where he is principal of the high school. They have a daughter named Ruth, and a son named Philip Augustine.

4 ³John W. Boulton, born July 21, 1866, educated at the Missouri State University, is now an eloquent and able preacher of the Christian church in Holden, Missouri. He married in Columbia, Missouri, June 6, 1888, Jessie Boulton Evans, daughter of Major Frank D. Evans. Their children are: Clara, Reid, Louise, Allen and John P.

Children of John R. and Margaretta Boulton all born in Boone county, Missouri:

4 ¹Lura May Boulton, born February 11, 1858; educated by private teacher and at Missouri State University. Became a member of the Christian church in September, 1872. Taught school in the counties of Boone, Holt and Nodaway in Missouri. She married March 4, 1885, Robert Thomas Tandy, son of Adrian and Mary Tandy, Elder J. W. Mountjoy performing the ceremony. She is a devoted mother, faithful wife, and conscientious Christian, of modest, retiring disposition, always preferring others to herself. She was the first person to suggest to the Louisiana Purchase Exposition officials the celebration of a "Lewis Day," and served on the executive committee for Lewis Day, September 23, 1904. She is a member of the Vir-

ginia Historical Society, the State Historical Society of Missouri, the Loyal Lewis Legion, and is now engaged in the work of genealogical research and compilation of family genealogies and has lately been appointed representative for Missouri, of the Genealogical Association of New York City.

4 ²Malinda Estes Boulton, born February 2, 1861, resided in Boone county, and Columbia, Missouri, until she married February 14, 1900, Matthew Fountain, born in Boone county, February 20, 1849, but removed to the far west with his parents when eight years of age. He has owned property in Washington and Idaho, but they were living on a fruit farm near Chico, California, where he died very suddenly September 24, 1905. In all the vicissitudes of life she has proven herself a faithful devoted sister, daughter and wife, patient in affliction and ever ready to help others in time of trouble. Having become a Christian in early life she has ever lived true to the faith. No children. Since her husband's death she has returned to Columbia, Missouri, to reside.

4 ³Mary Eliza Boulton, born December 21, 1862, died September 2, 1865.

4 ⁴Frances Elizabeth Boulton, born July 21, 1864. She was reared to womanhood on the farm of her parents and when they removed to Columbia in 1887 she came with them and was married May 4, 1893, to John F. Evans, brother to Major F. D. Evans of Columbia. They have two children: Lucile Evans, born January 15, 1894; Edna Proctor Evans, born April 16, 1896.

4 ⁵Clara Annie Boulton, born September 2, 1866, died October 16, 1878.

4 ⁶William Walter Boulton, born October 31, 1871, married 1st October 13, 1897, Ella Brook of St. Louis. He married second May 14, 1902, Lillie Helwig. They now reside at St. Louis, Missouri. He possesses an ingenuity akin to his distinguished relative Matthew Boulton. When a

mere child he could invent and make almost any toy, with which he wished to play. Has always been able to understand, and explain to others, the most intricate machinery and may be designated as a natural mechanic. When manufacturing and repairing bicycles in Columbia, Missouri, he earned the sobriquet of "Fix It," by being able to repair anything of the most delicate workmanship. After travelling extensively finally decided to locate in St. Louis in the photograph business, but on account of poor health and confinement decided to change and is now superintendent of the Landan Cabinet Company, North Commercial street, St. Louis, Missouri.

4 [7]Eulalia Mabel Boulton, born June 21, 1880. She came to Columbia when quite young and received an excellent education in the schools of Columbia. She resides with her parents, 605 Elm street, Columbia, and by her vivacity and tender, affectionate care for her aged parents, is the pet of the family, unmarried.

4 [1]James William Smith, only child of George and Elizabeth Smith, born in fall of 1860, died young, buried in Boone county, Missouri.

Children of David R. and Obera Boulton:

5 [1]Carrie Lou Boulton, born in Louisiana; came to Missouri when quite young, went to California with her parents in 1874 or 5, where she married ——— Richardson. They are now living near Sacramento, California. Parents of several children, names unknown.

5 [2]Arthur Hodge Boulton, born in Boone county, Missouri, married in Marysville, California, Nellie Rainey. He is a successful dry goods merchant of Marysville. They have no children but by their affable, loving manner gain the affections of the children with whom they are associated.

5 [3]Emerson Boulton, born in Boone county, Missouri, married in California, name of wife unknown. They now reside in San Francisco, California, where he is a druggist.

5 ⁴Jessie Boulton, born in Boone county, Missouri; now married and living in California.

5 ⁵Emma May Boulton, born in California, died in Marysville when young.

Children of Mary A. and Captain M. Bateman, born in Boone county, Missouri:

5 ¹Clarence Bateman, died young with smallpox.

5 ²Newton Bateman, died young with smallpox.

5 ³Ruth Adrian Bateman, died young with smallpox.

5 ⁴Mary Monroe Bateman, born ————, educated at Christian College, Columbia, Missouri; married February 20, 1889, Andrew Winn, then a dry goods merchant of Columbia, but now connected with a men's clothing establishment of Columbia. They are the parents of three children named respectively, Mary Monroe, Martha Linton and Earl Browning Winn.

5 ⁵Jesse Oren Bateman, born ————, now a valued employee of the Columbia postoffice, unmarried.

5 ⁶Clinton C. Bateman, born ————. He held a position in the postoffice of Columbia until January, 1903, when he left Columbia to take an important position in the United States Department of Agriculture, Washington, D. C. He married Anna Louise Johnston, daughter of Honorable R. W. Johnston of Arlington, Virginia, July 29, 1904. Issue, a son, born Friday, August 11, 1905.

5 ⁷Clara Roberta Bateman, born ————, educated at Christian College; married in the First Christian Church, Columbia, Herbert J. Corwin, February 28, 1900. He is a minister of the Christian church, then located at Montgomery City, Missouri, now of California, Missouri.

5 ⁸Gertrude Bateman, born ————, educated in Columbia, unmarried.

Children of R. T. and L. M. Tandy, born in Boone county, Missouri:

5 ¹Herbert Leroy Tandy, born May 9, 1886, a noble boy be-

loved by all who knew him; died in Columbia, Missouri, January 6, 1898.

5 [2]Francis Lewis Tandy, born October 17, 1887; baptized by Elder C. H. Winders, pastor of the First Christian Church, Columbia, Missouri, October 25, 1905; now a student in Columbia High School. His first business venture is the raising of fine poultry. He is a fine mathematician and possessed of considerable inventive ability.

5 [3]Ruth Estes Tandy, born February 5, 1891, will graduate from the grade school next year. She is desirous of preparing herself to fill the vocation of teacher in after life; baptized October 4, 1905, by Elder C. H. Winders, pastor of First Christian Church, Columbia, Missouri.

5 [4]Mary Elizabeth Tandy, born December 18, 1892. She has a talent for painting and drawing which gives promise of an excellent artist. Baptized October 4, 1905.

5 [5]Excell Boulton Tandy, born February 1, 1895.

5 [6]Margaretta Tandy, born December 6, 1896.

5 [7]Mabel Estelle Tandy, born December 8, 1898.

5 [8]William Berkeley Tandy, born March 6, 1902, died August 5, 1903. His short life taught volumes in the pure unselfish love, which only these angels on earth can manifest, and drew our hearts though bleeding and broken nearer to the God of Love.

ESTES FAMILY OF VIRGINIA.

The ancestor of the Estes family was from Dover, England. The progenitor of that line of the Estes family, who settled in Spottsylvania county, Virginia, is not known, but he was probably a brother to John Estes who married Nancy Montigue, as the families are known to have been closely related. Richard Estes is the first of this line known to the authors and he was living in Virginia during the Revolutionary war. Mr. Charles Estes in his Estes Genealogies makes this Richard a son of Bartlett Estes, who was a younger brother of Middleton, hence a grandson of John Estes and Nancy Montigue, but this is a mistake, as proven by the date of the birth of his son, Berkeley Estes, who married Malinda, a daughter of Middleton Estes. Berkeley Estes was born April 9, 1797, and Middleton Estes, December 11, 1782, and they are known to have been second cousins. This Richard was married about the close of the Revolutionary war to Catherine Carleton, daughter of Ambrose Carleton of Spottsylvania county, Virginia, as shown by the Spottsylvania records.

The records in the Record and Pension Office, War Department, Washington, D. C., show that one "Richard Estes, served as a private in Captain John Spottswood's Company of Foot, Tenth Virginia regiment, commanded by Colonel John Green, Revolutionary war. He enlisted February 19, 1778, to serve one year, and his name last appears on a muster roll dated at Middlebrook, March 4, 1779, which shows that he was discharged February 17." Given by authority of the secretary of war, Washington, D. C. We have no proof that this Richard was the person referred to in the records of the War Department but it is quite probable he was.

Children of Richard and Catherine (Carleton) Estes, all born in Spottsylvania county, Virginia:

351

2 [1]Ambrose Carleton Estes, born September, 1780, married in Spottsylvania county, Virginia, Margaret Brock. They emigrated to Missouri where they died and are buried at "Bonne Femme," Boone county, Missouri.

2 [2]Richard Estes emigrated to Boone county, Missouri, where he died unmarried. A part of the land, now the University campus, was given by Richard Estes, toward securing the location of the University in Columbia.

2 [3]Polly Estes married in Spottsylvania county, Virginia, William Carter, where they both died leaving no children.

2 [4]Frances Estes married Nathan Johnson of Spottsylvania county, Virginia. They had no children but left a large inheritance to their nieces and nephews.

2 [5]Catherine Estes married ——— Kale.

2 [6]George Estes married, name of wife unknown. She died soon after their marriage leaving no issue.

2 [7]Nancy Estes married ——— Rowe.

2 [8]Berkeley Estes, born April 9, 1797, in Spottsylvania county, Virginia, married February 5, 1826, his second cousin, Malinda Estes, in Clark county, Kentucky. She was a daughter of Middleton and Elisabeth (Adams) Estes, born September 2, 1805. They moved from Kentucky to Missouri in 1830, settled on a farm three miles east of Columbia where she died April 28, 1838. He married, second, April 25, 1839, Mary Truitt of Callaway county, Missouri. He was one of the pioneer settlers of Boone county, a very successful man, owning several tracts of land and many slaves, and lived in one of the first brick houses built in Boone county. Ever ready to do his part toward the development of the country and the advancement of education, he contributed three hundred dollars toward securing the location of the University in Columbia. He was in the War of 1812; although too young to participate in active warfare, assisted in transferring baggage and was present on muster days. After coming to Missouri was captain of a company which met once a month to practice. He died

July 29, 1869, and was buried in the family burying
ground on his homestead, by the side of his first wife. His
second wife died soon afterwards, and was buried near him.

2 ⁹Sarah Estes, born 1804, married Marshall Johnson, brother
to Nathan who married her sister Frances. They lived
and died in Spottsylvania county, Virginia.

Children of Ambrose Carleton Estes, who married Margaret Brock:

3 ¹Joseph Estes, born July 4, 1820; married January 6, 1852,
in Boone county, Missouri, Susan Bedford, daughter of
Stephen and Elizabeth (Robinson) Bedford. He was a
farmer and owner of fine stock. He lived two miles southwest of Columbia where he and his wife died and are buried
at Bethel cemetery.

Children of Catherine and ——— Kale:

3 ¹Louisa Kale married Zachary Taylor who wrote in the Pat-
ent or Pension Office, Washington, D. C. He died in
Spottsylvania county, Virginia, at his uncle Nathan's.

3 ²Mary Kale married Enoch Hardin of Stafford county, Virginia.

3 ³Julia Kale married Robert Alexander.

3 ⁴William Kale married and lived in Owen county, Kentucky.
They had a daughter who married a Mr. Herndon, and one
who married ——— Todd.

3 ⁵John Kale went to Texas and married there. He now resides
at Livingston.

Children of Nancy Estes and ——— Rowe:

3 ¹Martha Rowe married James T. Williams of Richmond, Virginia.

3 ²Nancy Rowe of Spottsylvania county, Virginia, unmarried.

3 ³Bettie Rowe married Zachary Rawlings, both of Spottsylvania county, Virginia.

3 ⁴George Rowe married first Miss Daniels, married second
Miss Hughes.

Children of Berkeley and Malinda Estes:

3 ¹Anderson Estes, born in Clark county, Kentucky, October
26, 1826, died September, 1827.

3 [3]Catherine Elizabeth Estes, born September 18, 1829, in Kentucky, married in Boone county, Missouri, January 26, 1853, Reuben Hume, son of Lewis and Henrietta (McBaine) Hume, whose ancestry is given in the Hume Genealogy. She died July 8, 1856.

3 [3]Martha A. Estes, born September 21, 1832, died young.

3 [4]Sarah Frances Estes, born February 18, 1835, married as his second wife, her brother-in-law, Wm. Allen Park, February 2, 1869. He died May 20, 1874, and she died August 8, 1875. They are both buried at the family burying ground on the farm of her brother Richard.

3 [5]Margaretta Estes, married John Rice Boulton, whose descendants are given in the Boulton family on page 346 in this book.

Children of Berkeley Estes and Mary (Truitt) Estes, born in Boone county, Missouri:

3 [6]George Washington Estes, born June 30, 1840, died young.

3 [7]Mary Eliza Estes, born May 20, 1843, married January 19, 1865, William Allen Park, a dry goods merchant of Columbia, Missouri. She died March 31, 1866, leaving a daughter, Mary Eliza Park, one month old, who died with consumption when eighteen years of age.

3 [8]William Berkeley Estes, born May 7, 1845, married December 22, 1868, Martha Dinwiddie, daughter of Samuel and Patsey Dinwiddie of Boone county, Missouri. He is a very industrious successful business man. They are now living on one of the best farms in Boone county, which he owns, besides property elsewhere.

3 [9]Richard Samuel Estes, born May 27, 1847, married April 6, 1869, Cordelia V. Carlisle, daughter of John and Margaret Carlisle, of Boone county, Missouri. He, like his brother is one of Boone county's representative citizens and a successful farmer, living on his father's old homestead, whose kindness and devotion to his family and all small children is proverbial.

Children of Sarah Estes who married Marshall Johnson, all born in Spottsylvania county, Virginia:

3 ¹Amanda Johnson married G. Smith, a dentist of Spottsylvania county, Virginia.

3 ²Joseph W. Johnson, unmarried.

3 ³Edgar Marshall Johnson married first Miss Farrish, of Caroline county, Virginia, married second May T. Landam.

3 ⁴Richard J. Johnson, ⁵Sarah Ann Johnson, twins. R. J. Johnson married Margaret Jarrell and his sister Sarah married her brother, Robert H. Jarrell, of Spottsylvania county, Virginia. R. J. Johnson was a soldier in the Confederate army of the Civil war, having taken part in the hard-fought battles of Virginia.

3 ⁶Berkeley Estes Johnson, born in Spottsylvania county, Virginia, married in Joplin, Missouri, Margaret Wise. They now reside at Kirkwood, Missouri. He graduated as civil engineer at the University of Virginia, and now holds an excellent position in St. Louis, Missouri.

Children of Joseph and Susan (Bedford) Estes, born in Boone county, Missouri:

4 ¹Ella Estes married Bingham Johnston, son of Jacob and Pauline Johnston of Boone county, Missouri. She died in St. Louis, Missouri, aged about 43 years.

4 ²Fannie Estes, unmarried.

4 ³Ambrose J. Estes married Foster Denny, daughter of Alexander Denny of Roanoke, Missouri.

4 ⁴Bedford Estes married a widow Metcalf, of St. Louis, Missouri.

4 ⁵Joseph Estes, Jr., married Mary Pierce.

Children of Catherine E. Estes and Reuben Hume:

4 ¹Louella Hume, born February 12, 1854, married Nathaniel Torbett of Boone county, Missouri.

Children of Sarah F. Estes and Wm. Allen Park:

4 ¹A son, died in infancy.

4 ²Berkeley Estes Park, born August 19, 1871, died November 2, 1871.

4 ³Allen Park, born December 27, 1873, married Mary Lynes,

daughter of Jackson and Ella Lynes, and niece of Sallie Lynes, who married John W. Beasley of Boone county, Missouri. They now reside in Tahlequah, Indian Territory, where he is a banker.

Children of Wm. B. and Martha Estes, born in Boone county, Missouri:

4 [1] James W. Estes, born July, 1870, married Effie Lynes, sister to Allen Park's wife. He now owns and operates a grist-mill in Warsaw, Missouri.

4 [2] Berkeley Estes married Ola May Turner, daughter of M. A. and Nannie (Carlisle) Turner. He is now a member of the firm of the Taylor-Estes Lumber Company, Columbia, Missouri.

4 [3] Annie Belle Estes married Joseph L. Lynes, son of Wm. and Elizabeth (Douglas) Lynes of Boone county, and a cousin to her brother James' wife. They have a son named Leland Estes. They live on a fine farm near her father.

4 [4] Samuel Estes, living with his parents, unmarried.

4 [5] Nettie Pearl Estes, born March 15, 1880, educated at Christian Female College, Columbia, Missouri, unmarried.

Children of Richard S. and Cordelia Estes, born in Boone county, Missouri:

4 [1] John S. Estes, born March 28, 1870, single.

4 [2] William Estes married Louise Lynes, daughter of Jackson and Ella Lynes. They now reside in Indian Territory.

4 [3] Birdie May Estes, married Baxter Turner, son of George Turner of Boone county, Missouri. Reside in Indian Territory.

4 [4] Lillie Blanche Estes married Robert McHarg. Reside at Harg, Boone county, Missouri.

4 [5] Richard Estes, Jr.

4 [6] Margaret Estes.

4 [7] Lollie Estes.

4 [8] Reasin Estes.

4 [9] Nannie A. Estes.

Children of Richard J. Johnson and Margaret (Jarrell) Johnson:

4 [1]Annie Pauline Johnson married Hill Weaver. They are the parents of three children.

4 [2]Cora Lee Johnson married William Mitchell. They have several children.

4 [3]Arthur Johnson married Lizzie Hamilton.

4 [4]John E. Johnson, died, aged 19 years.

4 [5]Ambrose Hill Johnson, unmarried.

4 [6]Laura Leta Johnson married Arnett Jacobs.

4 [7]William Estes Johnson married Fannie Wade.

4 [8]Richard S. Johnson married Margaret Wilson.

4 [9]Joseph Berkeley Johnson.

4 [10]Katie Pearl Johnson, died young.

4 [11]Amanda Louise Johnson.

4 [12]Stella Watson Johnson.

4 [13]Infant, died.

The first three above were born in Spottsylvania county, Virginia, and came with their parents to Boone county, Missouri, where the others were born and all are now living.

Children of Berkeley E. and Margaret (Wise) Johnson:

4 [1]Margaret Maud Johnson, born in Joplin, Missouri, married in Kirkwood, Missouri, in summer, 1905, Robert Bruce Brown, youngest son of ex-Governor' B. Gratz Brown. They reside in New York City.

4 [2]Blanche Virginia Johnson, aged 16 years, born in Kirkwood, Missouri.

4 [3]Grace Lucile Johnson, born in Kirkwood, Missouri, aged 14 years. They are with their parents at their elegant suburban home in Kirkwood, Missouri.

Children of Bingham and Ella (Estes) Johnston:

5 [1]Estes Johnston, born in 1884 in Boone county. Lived for several years with his parents in St. Louis, now with Parker Furniture Company, Columbia, Missouri.

5 [2]Jacob Johnston, born in Boone county, Missouri.

5 [3]Ambrose Johnston, born in Boone county, Missouri.

5 [4]Bingham Johnston, Jr., born in Boone county, Missouri.

5 [5]A son, born in St. Louis, died young.

Children of Ambrose J. and Foster (Denny) Estes, born in Boone county, Missouri:

5 ¹Zannie May Estes, born 1885. Educated at Christian College, now living with her parents on their large farm six miles south of Columbia.

5 ²Joseph Estes, unmarried.

5 ³Denny Estes.

5 ⁴Ambrose Estes, Jr.

5 ⁵Elizabeth Estes, born 1899.

4 Joseph Estes, who married Mary Pierce, has a daughter named Mary Susan Estes, born in Boone county, Missouri. A son, born in summer of 1905.

Children of Louella Hume, who married Nathaniel Torbett, born in Boone county, Missouri:

5 ¹Infant, dead; ²Catherine Torbett, twins. Katie died, aged about 7 years.

5 ³Reuben Hume Torbett (called Bud), unmarried.

5 ⁴Henrietta Wilson Torbett married —— Tomlinson. They have a daughter, Ecce Tomlinson.

5 ⁵Ecce Gladys Torbett married her second cousin, Dr. Charles Hume. Reside at Columbia, Missouri. They have a son, Frank Monroe Hume.

5 ⁶Natalie Torbett.

5 ⁷Agnes Torbett.

5 ⁸C. C. Torbett, Jr.

5 ⁹Rex Gerald Torbett.

Children of Allen and Mary (Lynes) Park, born in Boone county, Missouri:

5 ¹Lynes Park.

5 ²Allen Park, Jr., living with their parents in Tahlequah, Indian Territory.

4 Birdie May Estes who married Baxter Turner, has a daughter, May Turner.

4 Lillie Blanche Estes, who married Robert McHarg, has a son, Robert McHarg, Jr., nearly two years old.

ESTES FAMILY OF VIRGINIA AND KENTUCKY.

Since Mr. Charles Estes, of Warren, Rhode Island, has published a genealogy of the Estes family in the United States we will only give a brief sketch of that line of the Estes family which settled in Spottsylvania county, Virginia, and emigrated from there to Kentucky.

1 ¹John Estes came from England and settled in Virginia. He married Nancy Montigue. We have no record proof of when nor where this marriage occurred, but their children were born in Spottsylvania county, Virginia. Mr. Charles Estes in his "Estes Genealogies," states they were the parents of eight children which will be given below:

2 ¹Middleton Estes, born December 11, 1782, in Virginia, married in Lexington, Kentucky, Elizabeth Adams, daughter of Captain Adams, of Orange Courthouse, Virginia. The greater part of their married life was spent in Clark county, Kentucky, but at what date they emigrated to Kentucky is not known.

2 ²John Estes, born ————; went to Clay county, Missouri.

2 ³Abraham Estes, born in Virginia, September 25, 1787, died September 11, 1825, married· December 24, 1813, Beulah, daughter of Whorton and Margaret (Gatewood) Schooler, born April 22, 1787, died February 10, 1854. Abraham's vocation was agriculture. One Abraham Estes served in the volunteer militia under Captain Bledsoe in War of 1812, and was probably discharged early in April, 1814, on account of disability, and placed on Kentucky roll in 1816. He is doubtless the person whose record is given here.

2 ⁴Clement Estes, born ————, married first Sarah Adams, married second Miss Wilson.

2 ⁵Bartlett Estes married near Mt. Sterling, Kentucky. When last heard from was at Liberty, Clay county, Missouri.

2 ⁶Elisabeth Estes married her cousin, Spencer Estes.

2 ⁷Nancy Estes married William Estes, brother to Spencer.

2 ⁸Polly Estes married Mr. Robinson.

Children of Middleton and Elizabeth (Adams) Estes, all born in Kentucky:

3 ¹Jackson Estes, no record.

3 ²Clement Estes, no record of birth or marriage. Went to Henry county, Kentucky.

3 ³Malinda Estes, born in Clark county, Kentucky, September 2, 1805, where she married February 5, 1826, her cousin, Berkeley Estes, born April 9, 1797, who was a son of Richard and Catherine (Carleton) Estes of Spottsylvania county, Virginia. They moved to Boone county, Missouri, during the summer of 1830, where she died April 28, 1838, and was buried in the family burying ground on their homestead, three miles east of Columbia. Their descendants will be given in lineage of Richard Estes of Spottsylvania county, Virginia.

3 ⁴Nancy Estes, born ————, married in Clark county, Kentucky, John Gwynn of Henry county, Kentucky. He died in Henry county, Kentucky, in 1837, and his widow came to Boone county, Missouri, the following year and settled on a farm near her sister, Malinda Nancy Gwynn, and died June, 1869, and is buried in Columbia, Missouri.

3 ⁵Jeptha Estes, born in Clark county, Kentucky, and went to Missouri.

3 ⁶Henry Estes married his cousin, Caroline Lighter, nee Estes, daughter of Clement Estes.

3 ⁷Abraham Estes went to Owen county, Kentucky.

3 ⁸Sarah Estes married Peter Fore.

3 ⁹Lucy Estes married ———— Gwynn, brother to John, who married her sister Nancy.

3 ¹⁰John Estes married first Frankie Atkins, and second Mary ————. They lived in Terre Haute, Indiana, Columbia, Missouri, and then in Texas.

3 ¹¹William Estes, born in Lexington, Kentucky, April 27,

1820, married in New Liberty, Kentucky, September 30, 1841, Malinda C., daughter of B. R. Davis.

3 ¹²Joseph Estes, born in Kentucky, came to Boone county, Missouri, and married Ann Palmer. No issue. He died soon after marriage.

3 ¹⁶Frances Estes married a Mr. Green of Kentucky.

Children of Abraham and Beulah (Schooler) Estes, born in Kentucky:

3 ¹Nancy Estes, born May 1, 1815, married September 25, 1829, John Ballenger.

3 ²Martha (called Patsey) Estes, born July 2, 1818, died June 8, 1859, married August 8, 1833, Preston Hedges, and lives at Hedges Station, Clark county, Kentucky.

3 ³John W. Estes, born March 13, 1823, married in Winchester, Kentucky, December 18, 1850, Mary J. Stiff, born June 28, 1822, died June 26, 1875, daughter of Frederick and Mary (Clinkenbeard) Stiff.

Children of Clement, son of John and brother to Middleton Estes, who married first Sally Adams, married second Miss Wilson:

3 ¹Letitia Estes married John Gwynn.

3 ²Caroline Estes married first ———— Lighter, and second her cousin, Henry Estes.

3 ³Abner Estes.

3 ⁴Clement Estes.

3 ⁵Jeptha Estes.

3 ⁶John I. Estes.

Children of Polly Estes who married a Robinson:

3 ¹Benjamin Robinson, born in Kentucky, married Maria Young of Kentucky, and moved to Boone county, Missouri.

3 ²Nancy Robinson married Nathaniel McFarlane and moved to Henry county, Kentucky.

3 ³Margaret (called Peggy) Robinson married William Whiting, moved to Henry county, Kentucky.

3 ⁴Matilda Robinson married Jacob Gecoby.

Children of Nancy Estes, daughter of Middleton Estes, who married John Gwynn:

3 ¹Lucy Ann Gwynn, born in Henry county, Kentucky, moved with her mother to Boone county, Missouri, where she died young.

3 ²Sarah Elizabeth Gwynn, born in Henry county, Kentucky, February 9, 1826, died in Boone county, Missouri, January 13, 1891, buried in Columbia cemetery.

3 ³Casandra Gwynn, born in Henry county, Kentucky, March 6, 1829, moved to Boone county, Missouri, married Edward Dailey of St. Louis. He died in 1881 or 1882 and is buried in Columbia. His widow is now a resident of Columbia.

Children of John and Frankie (Atkins) Estes, grandchildren of Middleton and Elizabeth:

4 ¹Lewis Estes married May ———, of Cincinnati, Ohio. They have a daughter, Mable Clare Estes.

4 ²James Estes.

4 ³Margaret Estes.

4 ⁴Laura Estes.

Children of John Estes and his second wife, Mary ———:

4 ⁵Charles Estes.

4 ⁶Emma Estes.

4 ⁷John Estes, Jr.

Children of William and Malinda C. (Davis) Estes, born in New Liberty, Kentucky:

4 ¹Sallie F. Estes, born July 28, 1844.

4 ²Elizabeth A. Estes, born December 16, 1846.

4 ³Annie M. Estes, born November 22, 1850.

4 ⁴Benjamin D. Estes, born November 5, 1853.

4 ⁵Absalom A. Estes, born June 26, 1856, died July 29, 1884.

4 ⁶William Albert Estes, born November 9, 1858.

4 ⁷Samuel W. Estes, born October 22, 1860.

4 ⁸Katie M. Estes, born July 3, 1863, died June 20, 1880.

4 ⁹John M. Estes, born April 10, 1866.

Children of Nancy Estes who married John Ballenger of Kentucky:

4 ¹Mary Ballenger married September 4, 1861, James Stiff.

4 ²Sarah Ballenger married May 23, 1876, Benjamin Stiff, of Clintonville, Kentucky.

4 [3]Martha Ballenger married March 10, 1870, Jasper McDonald. Reside at Clintonville, Kentucky.

4 [4]Nancy Ballenger married May 16, 1879, James Haggard. They reside in Paris, Kentucky.

Children of John W. and Mary J. (Stiff) Estes of Winchester, Kentucky:

4 [1]James T. Estes, born January 23, 1856, married in Paris, Kentucky, July 29, 1879, Laura, daughter of Larkin and Hannah (Hildreth) Dawson, born January 14, 1859. They live near Clintonville, Kentucky. Issue: A daughter, Ada Pearl Estes, born January 13, 1884.

4 [2]William C. Estes, born November 19, 1858, married in Paris, Kentucky, August 11, 1881, Mattie, daughter of David Davis and Martha (Dawson) Davis, born January 14, 1862. Reside at Winchester, Kentucky. Their children are: Lynn Smith Estes, born May 1, 1884; John Davis Estes, born September 22, 1889.

4 [3]Evaline Estes, born July 16, 1860, married June 19, 1889, George W. Dawson.

4 [4]Frederick Abraham Estes, born November 17, 1861, married December 20, 1888, Sarah Kennedy. Resides on a farm near Clintonville, Kentucky.

4 [5]Mary Beulah Estes, born April 11, 1863, married October 13, 1889, Harlan Kennedy of Clintonville, Kentucky.

4 [1]Lewis Robinson, son of Benjamin and Maria (Young) Robinson, married Ann Campbell. They lived on a farm southeast of Columbia until his death, about seventeen years ago. She is now living with her son.

Children of Casandra and Edward Daily of Boone county, Missouri:

5 [1]John Thomas Daily, born February 24, 185—, married in 1877 or 8, Josie Fleming of Boone county, Missouri. He is now a farmer living near Harg, Boone county, Missouri. Their children are: Madge F. Dailey, William Dailey, Cassie Dailey, born in summer of 1891.

5 [2]Mary C. Dailey, born January 30, 1857.

5 [3]Cora F. Dailey, born May —, 1859, Columbia, Missouri.

5 [4]Emma Florence Dailey, died young.

5 [5]James Dailey, now of Montana.

Children of Lewis and Ann (Campbell) Robinson, born in Boone county, Missouri:

5 [1]Harvey Robinson married Miss McClure of Boone county. She died soon after marriage and he is now living with his widowed mother, ten miles northeast of Columbia, Missouri.

5 [2]Edward Robinson married Nannie Miller of Callaway county, Missouri. He died April 26, 1905, leaving no children.

5 [3]John Robinson, a physician of McAllister, Indian Territory, married a widow of that place.

5 [4]Clara Robinson, unmarried.

5 [5]Clark Robinson, graduated in law at Missouri State University, now teaching in Boone county.

LEWIS AND KINDRED FAMILIES.

1. JOHN LEWIS, OF HANOVER COUNTY, VIRGINIA.

John Lewis, Sr., emigrated from Wales to Virginia. He was born about 1640. It is not known whom he married. He died in Hanover county in 1726, where his will is on record. In his will he mentions the names of his six children, as follows:

2 [1]Mrs. Rebecca Lindsay, born about 1677.
2 [2]Abraham Lewis, born about 1679.
2 [3]Sarah Lewis, born about 1681.
2 [4]Mrs. Angelica Fullelove, born about 1683.
2 [5]David Lewis, born about 1685.
2 [6]John Lewis, Jr., born about 1687.

2 David Lewis, Sr., fifth child of John Lewis the emigrant, born about 1685 in Hanover county, Virginia, married first about 1717, Miss Terrell, daughter, it is said, of Joel Terrell. She died in 1734. The name of his second wife is not known by whom he had no issue. About the year 1750, David Lewis moved from Hanover and settled in Albemarle county, Virginia. Albemarle was then a new county, having been carved out of Goochland. In 1753 he married his third wife in Albemarle county. She was the widow of Dr. Hart, of Philadelphia, whose maiden name was Mary McGrarth. Her sister, Elisabeth McGrarth, married John Lewis, Jr., David's brother. David Lewis was engaged to be married the fourth time, but died very suddenly just before the nuptials in the year 1779. His will was probated at the September term of the Albemarle County Court in 1779. Joel Lewis, John Martin, James Lewis and Talliaferro Lewis were his executors.

Children of David Lewis and Miss Terrell his first wife:
3 [1]Williaim Terrell Lewis, born 1718, married 1739 Sarah Martin, resident of Surry county, North Carolina.
3 [2]Susannah Lewis, born 1720, married Alexander Mackey.

They moved to Rutherford county, North Carolina, where she died in 1784.

3 [3]Hannah Lewis, born 1722, married James Hickman.

3 [4]Sarah Lewis, born 1724, married Abraham Musick. They both died near Florissant, St. Louis county, Missouri.

3 [5]David Lewis, Jr., born 1726, married first, Rebecca Stovall, married second, Elizabeth Lockhart. He died near Spartansburg, South Carolina, in 1787, his wife in 1796.

3 [6]John Lewis, born 1728, died 1784; married first, Sarah Talliaferro; married second, Susan Clarkson.

3 [7]Joel Lewis, born 1730; married first, Mary Tureman; second, Mrs. Gordon; third, Lucy Daniels. He was born in Hanover, moved to Albemarle and afterwards to Spottsylvania county, where he died in 1813.

3 [8]Anna Lewis, born 1753, married; first, Joel Terrell; second, Stephen Willis. She died in Rutherford county, North Carolina, July 2, 1835.

Children of David and Mary (Hart) Lewis:

3 [9]Elisabeth Lewis, born 1754, married John Martin.

3 [10]Col. James Lewis, born 1756, married; first, Lucy Thomas; second, Mary Marks.

3 [11]Miriam Lewis, born 1759, married Col. Gabriel Madison.

This chapter will contain only the descendants of Hannah Lewis, third child of David Lewis, and Miss Terrell, who married in 1744, James Hickman, of Culpepper county, Virginia, where they resided until 1784, when they moved to what is now Clark county, Kentucky. James Hickman was born in 1724 and died in Clark county, Kentucky in 1816. Hannah, his wife, died in the same county in 1822, lacking only four months of being 100 years old. She was a pious member of the Baptist church.

Children of James and Hannah (Lewis) Hickman:

4 [1]Susannah Hickman, born 1745, married James Browning.

4 [2]David Hickman, born 1749, married Clara McClannahan.

4 [2]Anna Hickman, born 1754, married Stephen Holladay.
4 [4]Rev. Henry Hickman, born 1755, married Phebe Eastham, died in Fayette county, Kentucky, in 1804.
4 [5]Eleanor Hickman, born 1756, married Joseph Hill, of Virginia, and moved to Kentucky.
4 [6]Gen. Richard Hickman, born 1757, married Lydia Calloway.
4 [7]James Hickman, born 1760, married Elisabeth Bryan.
4 [8]Joel Hickman, born 1761, married Frances Garetta Wilson.
4 [9]Hannah Hickman, born 1765, married George Hill.

4 Susannah Hickman, oldest child of James and Hannah (Lewis) Hickman who married James Browning was born in Culpepper county, Virginia in 1745, and died in Harrison county, Kentucky, leaving five children, namely:

5 [1]Caleb Browning, married Anna ————, and died in Pendleton county, Kentucky. Their children are; Nancy, Sallie, James and Caleb Browning.
5 [2]Mary Browning, married Talliaferro Browning and died in Pendleton county, Kentucky.
5 [3]Col. James Browning, born Oct. 2, 1768, married 1795, Jane Morrow, born January 4, 1778. They settled in Clark county, Kentucky, where he died July 7, 1825, and his widow June 4, 1864. Mrs. Browning's parents, James and Elizabeth (Frame) Morrow, moved from Virginia to Kentucky about 1775.
5 [4]Micajah Browning, married Sarah Brown.
5 [5]Ann Browning, married Mr. Overall, and resided near Cynthiana, Kentucky.

Children of Col. James and Jane (Morrow) Browning:
6 [1]Elisabeth Browning, born March 1, 1796, married James Grimes.
6 [2]Hickman L. Browning, born November 9, 1798, died young.
6 [3]Mary L. Browning, born October 22, 1800, married Daudridge Holladay in 1826.

6 [4]Lucinda B. Browning, born June 22, 1803, married John Headley, October 7, 1828.

6 [5]Matilda Browning, born September 27, 1805, died young.

6 [6]Franklin M. Browning, born June 11, 1808, married Cynthia Grimes.

6 [7]James B. Browning, born August 17, 1811, married Christina Fonda. Their children are Jane, Alice, James and Gertrude Browning.

6 [8]William Perry Browning, born October 13, 1813, married Emeline Armstrong. They had three daughters, Anna, who married Mr. Butler, Bettie and Charlotte.

6 [9]Dr. Milton A. Browning, born April 13, 1816, married Mary J. Starr, July 2, 1851, resides near Laomi, Illinois.

6 [10]Edwin C. Browning born April 24, 1819, married Lucy Blaydes, November 8, 1842, resides at his father's old home in Clark county, Kentucky.

6 [11]Martha J. Browning, born November 11, 1822, and Fauntleroy Jones, of Clark county, Kentucky, in 1841, P. O. Jones, Nursery, Kentucky.

Children of John and Lucinda E. (Browning) Headley:

7 [1]James B. Headley, married Mary Thomas, one child, Julia P. Headley.

7 [2]John M. Headley.

7 [3]Charlton Headley, killed at Hartsville, Tennessee, belonged to Eighth Kentucky Cavalry, Col. Clark's Regiment.

6 [6]Franklin M. Browning, born June 11, 1808, married Cynthia Grimes, their children are as follows:

7 [1]Mary A. Browning, married Cyrus Blackburn, of Havilandville, Kentucky.

7 [2]Nancy J. Browning, married William Parker Morgan, of Pendleton county, Kentucky.

7 [3]Lucinda Browning, married Jacob Hall.

7 [4]Sallie Browning, married N. B. Aulick, of Kentucky.

7 ⁵James Browning, married Hester King, of Cynthiana, Kentucky.

7 ⁶William Browning, married Addie Blackburn.

7 ⁷Thomas Browning, married Hannah Echle.

7 ⁸Edwin B. Browning, of Havilandville, Kentucky.

7 ⁹David P. Browning, an artist, Havilandville, Kentucky.

6 ⁷James B. Browning, born August 17, 1811, married Christina Fonda; their children are Jane, Alice, Jennie and Gertrude.

6 ⁸William Perry Browning, born October 13, 1813, married Emaline Armstrong, they had three daughters, Anna, who married Mr. Butler, Bettie and Charlotte.

6 ⁹Dr. Milton A. Browning, born April 13, 1816, married Mary J. Starr, July 2, 1851, resides near Laomi Illinois.

6 ¹⁰Edwin C. Browning, born April 24, 1819, married Lucy Blaydes, November 8, 1842, resides at his father's old homestead in Clark county, Kentucky.

7 ¹Lizzie B. Browning, married Jacob Embry.

7 ²James Browning, married Anna Capps, Athens, Kentucky.

7 ³Blaydes Browning.

7 ⁴Woodson Browning.

7 ⁵Perry Browning, married Dixie Woodford, Athens, Kentucky. Their children are Edwin, Edna, Willie and Lucy C. Browning.

6 ¹¹Martha J. Browning, born November 11, 1822, married Fauntleroy Jones, of Clark county, Kentucky, in 1841.

7 ¹Mary Jones, married John W. Moore.

7 ²Dr. Francis Jones, Pine Grove, Kentucky.

7 ³Willie Jones, died.

7 ⁴Judge Lewis H. Jones, attorney-at-law, Winchester, Kentucky.

7 ⁵Bettie Jones.

7 ⁶Alice Jones, married Louis Woodford, of Pine Grove, Kentucky, in 1877.

Children of Micajah Browning, son of Susan Hickman and James Browning, who married Sarah Brown, daughter of Judge James Brown, of Bourbon county, Kentucky.

6 [1] Tabitha Ann Browning, married Capt. Elijah O. Bannon, of near Lexington, Kentucky. He was high sheriff of Fayette county, Kentucky.

6 [2] and 6 [3] Twins died, aged twenty-five years.

6 [4] Hon. Orville Hickman Browning, born 1806, in Harrison county, Kentucky, he located in Quincy, Illinois; was a lawyer of national reputation, married Eliza Caldwell, left no children, except an adopted daughter, Elisa Skinner, he died in Illinois, August 10, 1881.

6 [5] Marcus Elliott Browning, born 1807, married a Miss ——— Reese and was one of the chief clerks of the Northern Bank of Lexington, Kentucky.

6 [6] Milton Davis Browning, born in 1809, married Miss ——— Brown and was a lawyer of high standing in Burlington, Iowa.

6 [7] Zelinda Field Browning, born 1813, died 1817.

6 [8] Ann Davis Browning, born 1819, married Dr. William Robertson, whose first wife was Jane Madison, daughter of Mariam Lewis and Col. Gabriel Madison, of Jassamine county, Kentucky. Dr. Robertson resided many years in Fayette county, Kentucky, but finally settled near Rock House Prairie, Buchanan county, Missouri.

6 [9] Elizabeth Brown Browning, born 1822, died in 1836.

4 David Hickman, oldest son of James and Hannah (Lewis) Hickman, born in Culpepper county, Virginia, in 1749, and moved to what is now Bourbon county, Kentucky, in 1784, he married in 1771 Clara McClanahan, of Virginia; he died in Bourbon county, Kentucky, in 1825.

Children of David and Clara (McClanahan) Hickman:

5 [1] Peggy or Margarett Hickman, born in Culpepper county, Virginia, in 1772, married James Hutchinson, and died in Missouri in 1844.

370

5 [2]Anna Hickman, born in 1775, married William Markham and resided in Bath county, Kentucky, where she died childless in 1856.

5 [3]Hon. John Lewis Hickman, was born in 1777 and died near Paris, Kentucky, in 1849. He was sheriff of his county for many years; also member of Senate of Kentucky. The greater part of his life was spent on a farm, he married in 1811 his cousin, Elizabeth Hickman, daughter of Gen. Richard Hickman.

5 [4]Nancy Hickman, born 1779, married John Buford, of Versailles, Kentucky.

5 [5]Agnes Hickman, born 1781, married Joseph Bledsoe, they settled near Lexington, Missouri.

5 [6]Col. Thomas Hickman, born 1782, married Sarah Pruett in 1808, they were both members of the Christian church, and both died in Bourbon county, Kentucky, in 1854, he served as a soldier, fighting the Indians about the lakes.

5 [7]Lieut. James Hickman, born in Bourbon county, Kentucky, in 1784, a graduate of Princeton College. He was connected with the regular army of the United States for sometime. He was a merchant at Old Franklin, Missouri. He married Sophia Woodson, daughter of Josiah Woodson, of Goochland county, Virginia, in 1817 and died in Boone county, Missouri, in 1826, Mrs. Hickman's sister is the mother of Mrs. John J. Crittenden.

5 [8]Capt. David McClanahan Hickman, born in Bourbon county, Kentucky, in 1788, emigrated to Missouri in 1823, and settled on a farm on the two-mile Prairie, Boone, county, Missouri, where he died, June 14, 1857. He married first Eliza Keller Johnston, daughter of Capt. William Johnston and Rachel Spears, in 1818; second, Cornelia Ann Bryan in 1829.

5 [9]Lucy Hickman, born 1789, married Mason Moss, she died in 1841 and her husband in 1838..

5 [10]William Hickman, born 1792, died in Bourbon county, Kentucky, in 1845, married Mary Tureman.

Children of James and Margarett (Hickman) Hutchinson:

6 [1] Lewis Hutchinson, married Miss ——— Adams. They resided in Pittsburg, Pennsylvania.

6 [2] James Hutchinson, Jr., lived near Boonville, Cooper county, Missouri.

6 [3] Nancy Hutchinson.

6 [4] Margarett Hutchinson, married; first, William Johnston and second, Leonard, of Cooper county, Missouri.

6 [5] Eliza Hutchinson, married John Lewis Hickman, her cousin, and son of Col. Thomas Hickman and his wife, Sarah Pruett, of Bourbon county, Kentucky. They resided near Boonville, Missouri. The other children were: [6] David, [7] Thomas, [8] John, [9] Clara, [10] William, [11] Mary who married Henry Buford, [12] Benjamin Hutchinson of Pittsburg, Pennsylvania.

Children of Hon. John Lewis Hickman and Elizabeth (Hickman) Hickman:

6 [1] Catharine C. Hickman, married 1812, James K. Marshall, a lawyer, and after practicing law several years, turned his attention to farming and merchandising, died 1828.

6 [2] Richard Hickman, born 1813, died 1833.

6 [3] Edward L. Hickman, born 1815, died 1833.

6 [4] Lydia E. Hickman, born 1817, married in 1834, Richard P. Shelby, son of Gen. James Shelby, of Fayette county, Kentucky, and grandson of Gov. Shelby. They had three children, all died young except James, who married in 1855; moved to Missouri, where he died in 1856, leaving an infant son, who has since died.

6 [5] Margarett Hickman, born 1819, married in 1837, William H. Shackleford, a merchant of Richmond, Kentucky, afterwards at Paris, Kentucky, she died in 1844.

6 [6] John Lewis Hickman, Jr., born 1821, a farmer, married in 1844, Adelia Edwards.

6 [7] David H. Hickman, born 1823, died 1849, single.

6 [8] Caroline P. Hickman, born 1829, married William Duke, a

farmer in 1847, Mr. Duke was a soldier in the Mexican War.

Children of John and Nancy (Hickman) Buford:

6 ¹Helen Buford, married Mr. Johnson, one of her daughters, married J. G. Morrison.

6 ²Col. Buford.

6 ³Gen. Napoleon Buford, an officer of the Civil War, died from wounds received, or was killed in battle during the latter part of the War. He was forty-two years of age and was made a Major-General on the very day he died.

Children of Joseph and Agnes (Hickman) Bledsoe:

6 ¹Hiram Bledsoe, married Susan Hughes. Capt. Bledsoe, served with distinction during the Mexican War and upon the breaking out of the Civil War was one of the first to raise and equip a company of artillery in the State of Missouri. During the terrific shelling near Marietta, a shell from the enemies guns exploded near Capt. Bledsoe's battery, killing him and twelve others.

6 ²Thomas Bledsoe, married Miss Wilson. They resided near Lexington, Missouri.

6 ³David, Joseph and two daughters.

Children of Col. Thomas and Sarah (Pruett) Hickman:

6 ¹John Lewis Hickman, born 1804, married Eliza Hutchinson, a cousin, he died near Boonville, Missouri.

6 ²Ann Hickman, born in Jessamine county, Kentucky, in 1805, in 1817, her father moved to Howard county, Missouri; she married in 1819, Robert McGavock, a lawyer, born in Wythe county, Virginia 1794, resident of Clovesport, Kentucky.

6 ³Clara Hickman, born 1807, her first husband was Jones H. Flournoy, a merchant and farmer of Kentucky; she married a second time and was living at Boonville, Missouri, a widow, when last heard from.

6 ⁴James P. Hickman, born in 1814 was at one time a merchant

at Chihuahua, Mexico, married a Spanish lady and lived at San Antonia, Texas. They had five children, James, John, Thomas, David and Sarah Hickman.

6 ⁵Sophia W. Hickman, born 1818, married James O. Toole of St. Joseph, Missouri, her children are John, William, Mary and Sophia Toole.

6 ⁶David W. Hickman, born 1822, a merchant, died in Chihuahua, Mexico.

Children of Lieut. James Hickman and Sophia (Woodson) Hickman:

6 ¹William Hickman, born 1819, died 1832, in Kentucky.

6 ²Mary Elizabeth Hickman, born 1821, married in 1837, James S. Rollins. They resided in Columbia Boone county, Missouri. Maj. Jas. Sidney Rollins was the oldest son of Dr. Anthony Wayne Rollins and Sallie Rodes, born in Madison county, Kentucky, April 19, 1812, died at his home in Columbia, January 9, 1888. He was a graduate of the Indiana University, and in 1832, a law graduate of Transylvania University, Lexington, Kentucky, after which he located in Columbia, in 1838, he was elected to the Missouri Legislature, and introduced the bill under which the State University was located at Columbia by the State Commissioners June 24, 1839. On account of his authorship, and successful advocacy of the bill of 1839 under which the institution was located at Columbia, and his life-long devotion to it, the Board of Curators, on motion of Edward Wyman, of St. Louis, in May, 1872, passed a resolution honoring him with the title of "Father of the University." Col. W. F. Switzler and Dr. John D. Vincil, members of the board, advocated the motion. Major Rollins served with distinction in the United States Congress from 1861 to 1865. His widow now in her eighty-sixth year resides at the old home in Columbia, Missouri.

6 ³Laura Hickman, born 1823, died in St. Louis, Missouri, in 1841.

Children of Capt. David M. and Eliza K .(Johnston) Hickman:

6 ¹William T. Hickman, a farmer of Boone county, Missouri, a deacon in the Baptist church and was once sheriff of the county. He married Fannie Woods; their children are: David M., Martha, who married Mr. Bunton, of Terre Haute, Indiana, and Clara, who now lives at Columbia, Missouri.

6 ²Hon. David H. Hickman, of Columbia, Missouri, married Ann Bryan. He was elected to the Legislature from Boone county as a member of the Committee on Education. He drafted the School Law of Missouri. He held many positions of trust and honor, discharging all the duties imposed upon him, with fidelity and honesty and died June 25, 1869, his wife 1867. He left one daughter, Mary D., who married June 3, 1885, Mr. John E. Price, son of Col. J. B. Price, of Jefferson City, they now live in Seattle, Washington, they have two sons.

6 ³James J. Hickman, resides now in California. He married Sophia Edmonson, their children are: John, Gay, James, Sophia, Sallie, David, and others.

Children of Capt. David M. and Cornelia (Bryan) Hickman:

6 ⁴Thadens B. Hickman, a farmer in early life—later a groceryman, of Columbia, Missouri, married Louise Hickman of the State of Louisiana—both are dead and left no children.

6 ⁵Sarah Ann Hickman married Dr. Achibald Young and resided in Columbia, Missouri. Their children are Dr. David H., who married Addie Foley and have one daughter and live in Fulton, Missouri; Nina Young, who married Henry Walker of Cooper county, Missouri and have one daughter, Nina; Sallie Young, who married James H. Guitar, of Columbia, Missouri, and their children are Helen, Sarah,

375

James and Archie; Archibald Young, the youngest of the children of Sarah Hickman and Dr. Young.

6   ⁶John Lewis Hickman, now living in Kansas City, Missouri, married Ella Walker, their children are: Walker, Cornelia, Mary.

6   ⁷Milton Hickman, died in infancy.

6   ⁸Thomas Harvy Hickman, of Boone county, Missouri, married Amanda Hickman from Louisiana, their children are: Thaddeus, who is now in Iowa and Thomas Hickman, who married Mrs. Austin, of Louisiana.

Children of Mason and Lucy (Hickman) Moss:

6   ¹David M. Moss, married Catharine Coates and resided near Carrollton, Missouri.

6   ²Eliza Margarett Moss married Matthew Jeffries, a farmer, of Boone county, Missouri, they have several children.

6   ³Henry H. Moss married Harriett Egar, started to California in 1849. His wife died when they were in forty miles of Nevada City and their infant child soon after reaching California. He returned with an only son to Missouri and afterwards was deputy marshal at St. Joseph, Missouri.

6   ⁴Benjamin F. Moss, died single in Platte county, Missouri, in 1848, age 25 years.

6   ⁵Charles Mason Moss died single in Calloway county, Missouri, aged twenty-five years.

6   ⁶Clara A. Moss, born 1821, married in 1840, Walter Robinson, he died in Lawrence county, Missouri and his widow resided for many years near Paris, Missouri.

6   ⁷Thomas T. Moss, married first Miss Smith; second, Sarah Brown. He was a farmer near Mexico, Missouri, died in the age of twenty-eight years.

6   ⁸Nancy Buford Moss, died in 1857.

Children of William and Mary (Tureman) Hickman:

6   ¹David Hickman died of cholera.

6   ²Elizabeth Hickman resides in Paris, Kentucky.

6   ³Ann Hickman married John Shackleford, of St. Louis, Missouri, their children Mary now in St. Louis, Martha married Mr. Thomas, of Greenville, Mississippi, they have several children.

6   ⁴Thaddeus Hickman died single several years ago in Boone county, Missouri.

6   ⁵Mary Hickman married Dr. Owens, of Paris, Kentucky.

6   ⁶Martha Hickman married Dr. R. T. Davis, son of Garrett Davis.

6   ⁷Laura Hickman, of Paris, Kentucky.

6   ⁸Clara Hickman married William Hood, of Scott county, Kentucky, now living in Mississippi.

6   ⁹Irene Hickman married William H. Bass, son of Eli Bass, of Boone county, Missouri, their children are Everett, of Greenville, Mississippi, Thaddeus, now of Indian Territory, married Elizabeth Ferris, who died several years ago, he has two daughters, Irene and Elizabeth. James Bass and Robert Bass, of Indian Territory, William Bass married and has several children now living in Indian Territory, Lawrence Bass of Mississippi married and has one son, Everett; Hugh T. Bass, of Greenville, Mississippi and Lollie Bass who lives with her mother and brother Everett at Greenville, Mississippi.

6   ¹⁰Rebecca Hickman, Paris, Kentucky.

4   ³Anna Hickman, daughter of James and Hannah (Lewis) Hickman, born, in Culpepper county Virginia, in 1754, died in Clark county, Kentucky, in 1836, about the year 1783, she married Stephen Holladay, son of Joseph and Betty (Lewis) Holliday; born, September 8, 1760, in Spottsylvania county, Virginia, moved to Clark county, Kentucky, 1795.

Children of Stephen and Anna (Hickman) Holladay:

5   ¹Elliott Holladay, born in Clark county, Kentucky, in 1786, in 1812 he volunteered to fight the Indians. He was a member of Maj. John Martin's Company. After two days

hard fighting on the eighteenth and twenty-second of January, 1813, was taken prisoner at Winchester's defeat at the river Raisin. He suffered much from cold and cruel treatment of the Indians and finally had to give up his gun to save his life. After being exchanged he made his way home, where he arrived in April, 1813. He married in 1814, Rachel Johnson, whose parents were from Maryland. He died in Pike county, Missouri, in 1869.

5 ²Jemima Holladay, born in Clark county, Kentucky, in 1788, married in 1809, Elija Harris, she died in 1812, leaving one daughter, Lucy F. Harris.

5 ³James Holladay died single.

5 ⁴Joseph Holladay, born in 1791, married Sarah Woolfolk, daughter of John Woolfolk and Elizabeth Lewis, granddaughter of Dr. Waller Lewis and Sarah Lewis. He died in Clark county, Kentucky in 1855, their descendants are given in the "Warner Hall" Lewis line.

5 ⁵Lewis Holladay, born 1793, died in Clark county, Kentucky, leaving one daughter.

5 ⁶Elizabeth Holladay, born 1795, married John Huston, died in Fayette county, Kentucky, in 1833.

5 ⁷Waller Holladay, born 1797, married in 1843, Sarah A. Dunahoo, who was the widow of James H. Whittington when he married her. She died 1853, leaving three children: Cordelia Holladay, born 1844, Jemima Jane Holladay, born 1846, and Ann Eliza Holladay, born 1848.

Children of Rev. Henry and Phebe (Eastham) Hickman:

5 ¹Frank Hickman, died young in Virginia.

5 ²Nancy Hickman died in Virginia.

5 ³William Lewis Hickman, born 1776, married in 1801, Sarah F. Thompson, of Kentucky, born in 1782, died in 1848, in Illinois. He moved from Clark county, Kentucky, to De Witt county, Illinois in 1836 and died in 1842.

5 ⁴Lucy Hickman, born 1778, married Belain P. Evans and died in 1838.

5   ⁵Mary Hickman, born 1780, died single.
5   ⁶Richard Hickman, born about 1785, married in 1812, Sarah
    Combs, both died in Saline county, Missouri, in 1854.
5   ⁷William L. Hickman, born 1790, married Sallie Pearson,
    died at Winchester, Kentucky, 1864.
5   ⁸Fanny Lawson, born 1795, died single.

Children of Eleanor Hickman, who married Joseph Hill:
5   ¹Lieut. James H. Hill, born 1779. He was a soldier in war
    of 1812, served under Capt. Combs in a company from
    Clark county, Kentucky, and was in the battle of Thames
    under Col. Richard M. Johnston. He died single in Pick-
    away county, Ohio, in 1830.
5   ²Elizabeth Hill, born 1781, married first, James Haley, who
    died in 1830 in Fayette county, Kentucky, after which she
    married her cousin, John P. Hill, she died in Christian
    county, Illinois, in 1854.
5   ³Nancy Lewis Hill, born in 1783, married John Haley, brother
    to James, who married her sister. He died in Kentucky,
    and she died in Sangamon county, Illinois.
    4   ⁶Gen. Richard Hickman born in Culpepper county 1757,
        was a Revolutionary soldier. He emigrated from Vir-
        ginia to what is now Clark county, Kentucky, was a
        farmer but was called from his plow-handles by the
        citizens of his county and was elected as a member of
        the convention that formed the Constitution of Ken-
        tucky in 1799. He served his country over twenty
        years; a Senator in the Kentucky Legislature. He
        was elected Lieutenant-Governor of Kentucky and
        during his term the war of 1812 occurred. The Leg-
        islature requested Gov. Isaac Shelby to take the field
        in person against the Indians and command the troops
        of the state, which order he obeyed. During the ab-
        sence of Gov. Shelby, Gen. Hickman acted as Gov-
        ernor of the state; Hickman county in Kentucky was
        named for him. In 1787 Gen. Richard Hickman mar-

ried Lydia, the widow of Christopher Irvine, whose maiden name was Lydia Calloway, daughter of Col. Calloway, who was killed by the Indians. Lydia before her marriage was stolen by the Indians, together with her sister Elizabeth and a daughter of Col. Boone, but was recovered by Boone and reached the fort in safety. Gen. Hickman died in Clark county, Kentucky in 1832.

Children of Richard and Lydia Hickman:

5 [1]Capt. Llewellen Hickman, born 1788, was an officer in war of 1812, stationed at Prairie du Chien on the Mississippi river. He married Agnes St. Cyr, a French lady of St. Louis, Missouri, leaving one son named Llewellen, St. Cyr Hickman, who married and lives in St .Charles, Missouri.

5 [2]Elizabeth Hickman, born 1790, married her cousin, John Lewis Hickman, son of David and Clara (McClanahan) Hickman, she died in Bourbon county, Kentucky, in 1833, for their descendants, see page 372 this book.

5 [3]Catharine Hickman, born 1797, married Gen. William C. Prewitt, a farmer of Fayette county, Kentucky, died at the residence of her son R. H. Prewitt, in Clark county, Kentucky, July 11, 1878; her husband died many years before.

5 [4]Matilda Hickman, born 1801, married in 1818, Hon. Samuel Hanson, died in Winchester, Clark county, Kentucky, in 1847, Samuel Hanson was born in Alexandria, District of Columbia, was a very distinguished lawyer and died in Winchester, Kentucky, 1858.

5 [5]Caroline Hickman, born 1803, married David K. Pitman, she died in St. Charles county, Missouri, leaving a son, Richard Hickman.

4 [7]Capt. James L. Hickman, born in 1759, in Culpepper county, Virginia, married Elizabeth Bryan and died in Lincoln county, Kentucky, in 1828. After his

death his widow, with several children moved to Platt county, Missouri. He was a Revolutionary soldier.

Children of Capt. James L. and Elizabeth (Bryan) Hickman:

5 [1] William B. Hickman, born 1795, married Sarah Bronaugh, half sister of Polly, who married James P. Hickman; Wm. B. died in Lincoln county, Kentucky in 1832, and his wife in 1845.

5 [2] Nancy Lewis Hickman, born 1798, died in Cole county, Missouri in 1868. She married James Tinsley, a soldier of 1812, who was at the battle of New Orleans; he died in Greene county, Mo., 1870.

5 [3] Mary Hickman, born February 8, 1800; married Samuel Engleman and died in Lincoln county, Kentucky in 1819, leaving one son, Jacob Engleman, born 1819, who married his cousin Betsy Hickman whose children are found on another page.

5 [4] Henry Terrell Hickman, born 1804; married Elizabeth Logan. He died in Lincoln county, Kentucky in 1835, leaving a son, James, who married Eliza Duncan and resided in Johnson county, Missouri. Their children are: Mary, Laura, William, John, Annie and Luther S. Hickman.

5 [5] Elizabeth Hickman, born 1806; married Simeon Engleman, brother of Samuel; she resided in Boone county, Missouri. Issue Mary, Elizabeth, John, Maria, James W., Barbara, Simeon, Martha Christian & Sarah E. Engleman.

5 [6] Amelia Hickman, born 1808; married John M. Shackleford and resided at Red Bluffs California, names of children unknown.

5 [7] Lucinda Hickman, born 1810; married Joel Hickman, son of Joel and Frances G. (Wilson) Hickman. He died in Platt county, Missouri, in 1847 and his wife afterwards resided in Cameron, Missouri. The names of their seven children are—John W., James, Elizabeth, Louisa, Maria, Mary and Martha Hickman.

5 ³James P. Hickman, born 1812; married Polly Bronaugh and died near Dallas, Texas in 1879. They left seven children —Betsy, Mary Ann, Gleeson, Henry, Louisa, Lydia and Clara, who married a Mr. Terrell and lived in Parker county. Texas.

5 ⁹Louisa Hickman, born 1814; married Thomas J. Thurman and died in Lincoln county, Kentucky in 1866, leaving an only daughter, Bettie Thurman, who married Dr. W. C. Swinney and lived in Greene county, Missouri. Issue, William and Louisa.

4 ⁸Joel Hickman, son of James and Hannah (Lewis), born in Culpepper county, Virginia, August 10, 1761; married, 1786, Frances Garetta Wilson, daughter of Lieut. John Wilson, who was killed at the battle of Eutaw Springs, South Carolina, 1781. He (Joel Hickman) was a soldier of the Revolutionary War and died in Clark county, Kentucky, July 16, 1852.

Children of Joel and Frances G. Hickman:

5 ¹John Wilson Hickman, born 1787; married, first, Betsy Bronaugh; married, second, name unknown. Issue, Adeline Hickman, Boyle county, Kentucky. He died in Boyle county, Kentucky, in 1849.

5 ²James Lewis Hickman, born 1788; married Maria Shackleford. He was for many years a merchant at Lexington, Kentucky, from which he moved to Todd county, Kentucky, where he died in 1855. He was a member of Captain Hart's company from Kentucky in War of 1812. He married in 1818, Maria Shackleford eldest daughter of William S. Shackleford of Fleming county, Kentucky.

5 ³Nancy E. Hickman, born 1790, died 1791.

5 ⁴Polly Terrell Hickman, born 1792; married George Gilmore and died in Christian county, Kentucky in 1828.

5 ⁵Sallie Lawson Hickman, born in 1794; married James Eastham and died in Lexington, Kentucky in 1857.

5 ⁶Thomas Elliott Hickman, born 1796, in Clark county, Ken-

tucky. He died in Winchester, Kentucky, 1838, leaving an only daughter, Mary Ann, who died in 1848.

5 ⁷Sophia Weston Hickman, born 1798; married Thomas Holton, resided in Madison county, Kentucky. Issue, Thomas Holton, died 1855; Adeline Holton married Thomas Jones and lived in Cass county, Missouri.

5 ⁸Adeline D. Hickman, born 1800; she died unmarried in Clark county, Kentucky.

5 ⁹Elisa Byrd Hickman, born in 1802; married John Reed, died in Madison county, Kentucky in 1855, leaving one child, Elisa Byrd Reed, who married Jeremiah Collins. Issue, Edwin H. and John P. Collins.

5 ¹⁰Joel Franklin Hickman, born in 1804; married Lucinda Hickman, a cousin and died in Buchanan county, Missouri in 1847, leaving children.

5 ¹¹Frances Garetta Hickman, born 1807; married Addison T. Elliott and died 1831 in Jefferson county, Kentucky.

5 ¹²Edwin Clinton Hickman, born May 10, 1810; married about 1839, Amanda F. Best, daughter of Dr. Robert Best, born in Cincinnati, Ohio, April 29, 1815, died in Clark county, Kentucky, 1845. He died in Lexington, Kentucky May 5, 1861.

Children of John Wilson and Betsy (Bronaugh) Hickman.

6 ¹William Hickman, resides near Salvisa, Kentucky.

6 ²Lucy Hickman.

4 ⁹Hannah Hickman, daughter of James and Hannah (Lewis) Hickman, born in Culpepper county, Virginia, 1765; married George L. Hill (brother to Joseph, who married her sister Eleanor) of Virginia in 1782. She died aged 89 and her husband 85; both buried near Darbyville, Ohio.

Children of George and Hannah Hill:

5 ¹Susan Hickman Hill, born 1788; married Archibald Shockley and died in Pickanay county, Ohio, 1853.

5 ²John P. Hill, born 1790; married, first, his cousin, Mrs. Nancy Lewis Haley, widow of John Haley and daughter of

Joseph and Eleanor Hill; married, second, Mrs. Bridges, they lived near Chatham, Illinois. He was at the battle of Baltimore in War of 1812, was also in the Black Hawk War, under General Henry. They left no children.

5 [3] Hannah Hill, born 1792; married Rev. George Ambrose, who died in 1850 and was buried near Darbyville, Ohio.

5 [4] James Lewis Hill, born 1794, died single in Norfolk, Virginia in 1814. He was a volunteer in War of 1812.

5 [5] George Hill, born 1797; married Catherine Price and lived near Moundville, Virginia.

5 [6] Silas P. Hill, born 1799; married Paulina Haley, daughter of John and Nancy L. Hill. He died in Christian county, Illinois, leaving no issue.

5 [7] Leroy Lewis Hill, born 1801; married Nancy L. Haley, daughter of James and Elizabeth (Hill) Haley. They lived near Hempland, Mo.

5 [8] Elizabeth Hill, born 1803; married Col. James Mitchell and died in Madison county, Ohio in 1840, leaving two sons (twins) David and James.

5 [9] Nancy L. Hill, born 1805; married Sam Thompson; married second, James Magill and resided near Darbyville, Ohio.

Children of Elliott and Rachel (Johnson) Holliday, grand-children of Stephen and Anna (Hickman) Holladay.

6 [1] Elisa Ann Holladay, born in Clark county, Kentucky, 1815; married in 1836, Samuel Crutcher of Montgomery county, Mo. She died 1847, leaving three sons: Elliott Waller, Obanon and James W. Crutcher.

6 [2] Samuel Wilson Holladay, born 1817. He was a farmer of Pike county, Missouri.

6 [3] Mary Holladay, born 1819; married Ambrose Crutcher, cousin to Samuel. Issue: Elizabeth Ann, Sarah Frances, who married Mr. Wright of Paris, Missouri. Rachel and Samuel W. Crutcher.

6 [4] Sarah Holladay, born 1821; married 1840 Harvey B. Pritch-

ett of Pike county, Missouri. Children, Mary Ann, Edwin, Melissa, Eliza, Samuel W. and Christine.

6. ⁵Nancy Holladay born 1823; married 1843, her cousin Braxton L. Hickman. He was a miller of Ashley, Pike county, Missouri. Their children are: Sarah Ann, Marcellus, Rodney, Laura and David Hickman.

6 ⁶Martha Jane Holladay, born 1824; married 1846 Samuel N. Purse. He owned a foundry at Ashley, Pike county, Missouri. Issue: Irene, Zachary Taylor and Dolly Purse.

6 ⁷Emily Holladay, born 1825; married, first, Wm. Cash in 1844, who died in 1852. She married, second, 1855 Elija J. Strother. Children: Claudius Cash, James E. Cash and Ella Strother.

6 ⁸James Waller Holladay, born 1827, died in Cincinnati, Ohio, 1852. He was a very ingenious mechanic working in metals of all kinds.

6 ⁹Lewis Holladay, born 1829, a farmer of Pike county, Missouri.

6 ¹⁰Owen Holladay, born 1832, was a merchant at Pikes Peak, Iowa.

6 ¹¹Margaret Jemima Holladay, born 1837 in Pike county, Missouri.

Children of Elija and Jemima (Holladay) Harris:

6 ¹Lucy F. Harris, born 1810; married Benjamin R. Waller and resided near Winchester, Kentucky, until they moved to Cooper county, Missouri in 1841. Their children are as follows:

    7 ¹Frances Ann Waller, born 1828; married 1851 David M. Johnson, a lawyer from Ohio. They lived in Troy, Kansas. Issue: John Lee, dead, Benjamin Waller, dead, Waller Sheridan, born 1853, James Y., Eliza J. and Laura Johnson, born 1864.

    7 ²Robert Edward Waller, born 1830; married Ann E. Guthrie in 1862. They lived in Cooper county, Mis-

souri. He was a noted mathematician. Children, John James, etc.

7 ³Jemima E. and ⁴Elizabeth died young.

7 ⁵Mary Jane Waller, born 1834; married Robert J. Parrish, resided near Bell Air, Missouri. They have four children.

7 ⁶John Adams Waller, born 1835; teacher.

7 ⁷Lucy Harris Waller, born 1838; teacher.

7 ⁸Jemima E. Waller, born 1849, died 1860.

7 ⁹Benjamin Franklin Waller, born 1841; a teacher.

7 ¹⁰Elmina L. Waller, born 1844 of Cooper county, Missouri, a poetess.

Children of Lewis Holladay and wife.

6 ¹Martha Ann Holladay; married Samuel A. Woodford of Clark county, Kentucky. Issue:

7 ¹Mildred Woodford, born 1842.

7 ²Elizabeth Woodford, born 1846.

7 ³Mary Woodford, born 1851.

7 ⁴Lewis Woodford, born 1853.

7 ⁵Lucy Woodford, born 1856.

Children of John and Elizabeth (Holladay) Huston:

6 ¹Nancy Huston married James Hall of Bourbon county, Kentucky. Issue: Elizabeth Hall, who married Robert S. Taylor of Clark county, Kentucky. Children: Sallie and Annie Taylor.

Children of Waller and Sarah (Whittington) Holladay:

6 ¹Cordelia Holladay, born 1844.

6 ²Jemima Jane Holladay, born 1846.

6 ³Ann Eliza Holladay, born 1848.

Children of Wm. Lewis, son of Rev. Henry and Phoebe (Eastham) Hickman, who married Sarah H. Thompson:

6 [1]Louisa Verona Hickman, born 1802; married in 1822 George L. Hill, born near Fredericksburg in 1797. She died at Clinton, Illinois, September 25, 1886. He died November 30, 1887 at Clinton Illinois.

6 [2]Laurinda E. Hickman, born 1804; married John Bostick in 1825 and died in 1826.

6 [3]Rosanna B. Hickman, born 1805, died 1827.

6 [4]Emily T. Hickman, born 1806; married Paschal Mills.

6 [4]Mary Byrd Hickman, born 1807; married Thomas J. Rogers, died in Dewitt county, Illinois in 1838.

6 [6]Albert H. Hickman, born 1808; married Harriet Grimes and died 1831, leaving a son Charles Lewis Grimes Hickman.

6 [7]Rodney E. Hickman, born 1809; married Elizabeth Wallace, died in 1842. Issue:

   7 [1]David Wallace Hickman, born 1839.

   7 [2]John Thomas Hickman, born 1841; married Jane McKinney.

   7 [3]Hester Ann, born and died in 1842.

6 [8]Braxton Lewis Hickman, born 1810; married his third cousin Nancy, daughter of Elliott Holladay.

6 [9]John H. Hickman, born 1811; married Rachel E. Giddings in 1853, died 1860, leaving two children, John M. and Sarah L. Hickman.

6 [10]Iantha C. Hickman, born 1813, died 1814.

6 [11]Paschal P. Hickman, born 1814, died 1853 in DeWitt county, Illinois.

6 [12]Llewellen B. Hickman, born 1817; married in 1835 Cynthia Ann Brown. Issue: Wm. Jones, John L., Fannie B. and Warren Hickman.

6 [13]Susan F. Hickman, born 1818; married Samuel Duncan, died 1851, leaving two children, Lewis and Lucretia Duncan.

6 [14]William W. Hickman, born 1820; married, first, Sarah A. Condiff; married, second, Elvira Mintum. He was a Lieut. in the Federal army, 41st Illinois Regiment, during the

Civil War. Children are: Lewis, Henry, Ira, Theodore, Richard T., Sarah V. Nancy and James Hickman, etc.

6 [15]David A. Hickman, born 1821, died 1824.

6 [16]Sarah M. Hickman, born 1822, died young.

6 [17] & [18] Both sons died young.

Children of Belain P. and Lucy (Hickman) Evans.

6 [1]Hickman Evans married Mary Combs

6 [2]Belain P. Evans married Spiers. Issue as follows:

    7 [1]Lucy H. Evans married Albert G. Boggs son of Ex-Governor Boggs of Missouri. Children: Willis Henry, Sam Spiers, Mary Frances.

6 [3]Richard Evans married Mariah Jughs.

6 [4]James L. Evans married Elizabeth Hayden.

6 [5]Peter Evans married Elizabeth Smith.

6 [6]John Evans married Miss ———— Ford.

6 [7]William H. Evans married Miss ———— Smith.

6 [8]Frances L. Evans, born April 10, 1809; married December 18, 1827 James C. Banford of Fayette county, Kentucky.

6 [9]Mary Evans died single.

Children of Richard and Susan (Combs) Hickman.

6 [1]Cuthbert H. Hickman, born 1815; married in 1838 Elizabeth Grimes. He resided near Cambridge, Missouri. Issue, eleven children.

6 [2]Dr. Lawson B. Hickman, born 1816. He was a surgeon in the Confederate army, was taken prisoner at Fort Donelson while waiting on both Northern and Southern soldiers; married Georgianna Baylor, resided with his family at Elkton, Todd county, Kentucky.

6 [3]Sally Combs Hickman, born 1819; married James A. Logan, resided near Dangerfield, Titus county, Texas, where she died in 1856. Their children are: Susan E., Sarah A., Logan married Edward Truitt of Texas; Lydia E., William, a soldier in Civil War, taken prisoner and confined at Little Rock, Arkansas, where he died; Robert and Jay Logan.

6 ⁴Fielding A. Hickman, born 1820; married Agnes Pigg. They have no children.

6 ⁵Dr. Richard William Lewis Hickman, born 1822. He graduated in medicine at Louisville, Kentucky; married, first, Jane Hord; married, second, Miss Kidwell. He has no children and when last heard from was a widower, living near Petra, Saline county, Missouri.

Children of William L. and Sally (Pearson) Hickman.

6 ¹Susan M. Hickman, Winchester, Kentucky.

6 ²Frances L. Hickman married Robert Smith.

6 ³Lucy E. Hickman married John Taliaferro, son of Hay Taliaferro, grandson of William Taliaferro of Caroline county, Virginia.

6 ⁴William Hickman, lived with his father, who was old and afflicted and confined to his bed. He was arrested in 1861 and taken from the bedside of his father to prison in Lexington, Kentucky, because his sympathies were with the South . After his release, joined the Confederate army and after the close of the war resided in St. Louis, Missouri.

6 ⁵Nancy Hickman youngest child.

Children of James and Elizabeth (Hill) Haley.

6 ¹Nancy Lewis Haley married Leroy Lewis Hill, son of George and Hannah Hill of Darbyville, Ohio and resides at Springfield, Illinois.

6 ²Paulina T. Haley married James Bennett.

6 ³Joseph Haley married Nancy Elliott.

6 ⁴Elizabeth Haley married, first Robert McCondie, who died near Springfield, Illinois in 1844. She married, second, William Singer. They resided near Taylorville, Illinois.

6 ⁵Woodson Haley.

Children of John and Nancy Lewis (Hill) Haley.

6 ¹Paulina Haley married Silas P. Hill, son of Hannah and George Hill. She died in Christian county, Illinois, childless.

6 ²Lucinda Haley married Bartlett Haley. Their children are, Angeline, married Joseph Matthews, James, Frank married Miss Harper, William, Mary and Newton Haley.

Children of William and Catherine (Hickman) Prewitt.
6 ¹Richard Hickman Prewitt, born 1833, a graduate of Bethany College, Virginia and the Law class of Louisville, Kentucky. Afterwards practiced law in Lexington, Kentucky.
6 ²David Prewitt, born 1838, was a soldier in the Confederate service under command of Gen. John H. Morgan. He married after the close of the war.

Children of Samuel and Matilda (Hickman) Hanson:
6 ¹Richard H. Hanson is an eminent lawyer, has represented Bourbon county in the Legislature. He married Evaline Talbott and resided in Paris, Kentucky. Issue: Charles G., R. H., Jr., Jennie M. and Samuel Hanson.
6 ²Sarah C. Hanson of Leavenworth, Kansas,
6 ³Matilda R. Hanson married Captain James Stone, who served in the Mexican War as Captain of infantry company, now a farmer living near Leavenworth, Kansas. Their children are, Samuel H., Robert C., James, etc.
6 ⁴Lydia C. Hanson, died single.
6 ⁵ & ⁶Eliza and Caroline died in childhood.
6 ⁷Thomas L. Hanson died single.
6 ⁸Mary K. Hanson married Mr. Gladdings and resides at Leavenworth, Kansas.
6 ⁹Ellen L. Hanson married Major Charles W. Helm. He served in the Confederate army as Major under Gen. Roger W. Hanson. He was born July 16, 1834, died 1888, graduated with honors from the University of Virginia. Mrs. Ellen L. Helm resided in Dallas, Texas. Her children are:
  7 ¹Virgie A. Helm married Mr. Reed; one child, Carl Hanson Reed.
  7 ²Erasmus Helm, resides in Leavenworth, Kansas.

7 [3]Matilda Stone Helm married and resides in Texarkana, Arkansas.

7 [4]James S. Helm.

7 [5]Roger Hanson Helm.

6 [10]Gen. Roger W. Hanson, Lieutenant under Colonel Williams in Mexican War, was a General in the Confederate army, was mortally wounded near Murfreesboro, Tennessee, in January, 1863. In 1853 he married Virginia Peters of Woodford county, Kentucky. Mrs. Hanson served three terms as State Librarian of Kentucky. No issue.

6 [11]Colonel Charles S. Hanson, a Colonel in the Union army, received a wound near Saltville, Virginia, from effect of which he died in Paris, Kentucky. He married Carrie Wheeler of Winchester, Kentucky. Their only daughter married William R. Thomas, Paris, Kentucky.

6 [12]Sam K. Hanson, Jr., died in the Federal service from sickness.

6 [13]Isaac S. Hanson, a soldier in the Confederate service died soon after war.

Children of William B. and Sarah (Bronaugh) Hickman.

6 [1]Thomas B. Hickman, born 1814; married Margarett Culbertson, daughter of David and Sally (Bright) Culbertson, resides near Red Bluff, California where he settled after leaving Kentucky in 1839. Children: Thomas Jefferson, Sarah E., Mary K., Gholson, Eliza T., Elijah H., and Drucilla.

6 [2]Elizabeth B. Hickman, born 1818; married her cousin, Jacob Engleman, she had eight children and died in 1867.

6 [3]Mary Hickman, born 1820; married Isham Gilbert and died in Missouri in 1855, leaving three daughters.

6 [4]Robert L. Hickman, born 1823.

6 [5]Sarah Ann Hickman, born 1825; married John Owens. Issue one daughter.

6 [6]Lucy Hickman, born 1827; married, first, Samuel Shackleford, second, George W. Patterson, and died in 1855, leaving three children.

6 [7]Maria Hickman, born 1829; married William A. Owens: Issue, two children.

6 [8]Catherine Hickman, born 1832; married James Baxter of Missouri and had nine children.

Children of James and Nancy Lewis (Hickman) Tinsley.

6 [1]James H. Tinsley, born 1817; married Mary Dunlap. Issue: Mary E. and others.

6 [2]William Tinsley, born 1818, died in Lincoln county, Kentucky in 1845.

6 [3]Henry H. Tinsley, born 1820, died in Polk county, Missouri in 1869 from injuries received in war of 1861.

6 [4]Betsy Tinsley, born 1821, died 1833.

6 [5]Amelia Tinsley, born 1823; married Dr. B. M. E. Smith and died in Clay county, Missouri in 1852. Issue: Mary L. and Edward L. Smith.

6 [6]Dr. Robert L. Tinsley, born 1825; married, first, Ange Berry, who died in 1859 and he married, second, Amanda A. Paschal in 1866. They have serveral children.

6 [7]John F. Tinsley, born 1827, died 1845.

6 [8]Mary L. Tinsley, born 1829, died 1848.

6 [9]David Anthony Tinsley, born 1833, captain under General Price, was in the battles of Oak Hills, Wilson Creek, Lexington and was killed in 1863.

6 [10]Thomas B. Tinsley, born in 1855, was murdered in Platt county, Missouri in 1865 by Fitzgerald's party.

6 [11]Benjamin S. Tinsley, born in 1840; was in battles of Lexington, Pea Ridge, etc. He married Mary Gilbert in 1869.

Children of James Lewis and Maria (Shackleford) Hickman.

6 [1]Elizabeth F. Hickman, born in Frankfort, Kentucky in 1810, died same year.

6 [2]Mary S. Hickman, born in Fleming county, Kentucky, 1821, died in 1826.

6 [3]William Shackleford Hickman, born in Clark county, Kentucky, in 1823.

6 [4]Dr. Joel T. Hickman, born in Fayette county, Kentucky, 1825; married 1846 Frances Downing Lewis, daughter of Dr. John Terrell Lewis. They were distant cousins.

6 [5]James Lewis Hickman, born in Fayette county, Kentucky, 1828, died same year.

6 [6]Maria Troter Hickman, born in Lexington, Kentucky, 1829; married Charles F. Coppage.

6 [7]Sarah C. Hickman, born Fayette county, Kentucky.

6 [8]Amelia F. Hickman, born in 1834, died 1836.

6 [9]Ellen Douglas Hickman, born 1836.

6 [10]John J. Hickman, born Fayette county, Kentucky, 1839.

6 [11]Edwin Clinton Hickman, born 1842 in Fayette county, Kentucky. Several of James Hickman's children afterwards lived in Todd county, Kentucky.

Children of Dr. Joel and Frances D. (Lewis) Hickman.

7 [1]James Lewis Hickman, born 1847; married 1884 Nancy L. Wright of Audrain county, Missouri.

7 [2]Joel Thomas Hickman, Jr., born 1849; married Cannie Davis of Boone county, Missouri, in 1879.

7 [3]William F. Hickman, born 1852; married 1882 Josie Drumb, died 1887, in Evansville, Indiana.

7 [4]Mary L. Hickman, born 1854.

7 [5]John Breckenridge Hickman, born 1856, died 1860.

7 [6]Charles Douglas Hickman, born 1858, died 1860.

7 [7]Alice Hickman, born 1861, died 1862.

7 [8]Margaret Downing Hickman, born 1863, died 1888.

7 [9]Maria Shackleford Hickman, born 1866.

7 [10]David C. Hickman, born 1869.

7 [11]Martha W. Hickman, born 1871, died March, 1890. Her mother, Frances D. Hickman, died March, 1890.

Children of Charles F. and Maria T. Coppage.

7 [1]Charles Lewis Coppage, born 1848 in Lexington, Kentucky, died young.

7 [2]Mary Meriwether Coppage, born 1850 in Todd county, Kentucky.

7 [3]Sarah Ellen Coppage, born 1851.

7 [4]Maria Penelope Coppage, born 1853, Louisville, Kentucky.

7 [5]Sabina F. Coppage, born 1855 in Christian county, Kentucky.

Children of Charles O. and Sarah C. Faxon.

7 [1]William Henry Faxon, only child born in 1851. The same year his mother died in Clarksville, Tennessee.

Children of George and Polly Terrell (Hickman) Gilmore.

6 [1]James Lewis Gilmore, lives in Illinois.

6 [2]Joel Gilmore.

6 [3]John Wilson Gilmore, resides in Albany Oregon.

6 [4]Alexander Gilmore, New Lancaster, Illinois.

6 [5]Thomas Elliott Gilmore, died in Illinois, leaving a widow and children.

6 [6]Robert Gilmore.

6 [7]Ellen Gilmore married, first, Mr. Salter; married, second, Mr. Little.

6 [8]Mary Gilmore, died unmarried.

Children of Frances G., daughter of Joel Hickman, who married A. T. Elliott.

6 [1]Edwin T. Elliott, lives in Clark county, Kentucky.

6 [2]Priscilla F. Elliott married Ellison A. Daniel, Jr. She died 1854 in Dallas, Texas, leaving one child.

6 [3]Mary Eliza Elliott married William H. Dean, resides in Madison county, Kentucky. Their children are: Addison Dean and Fanny Dean.

Children of Edwin C. and Amanda F (Best) Hickman.

6 [1]Captain Robert B. Hickman, born 1840.

6 [2]Lieutenant Joel Drake Hickman, born 1842.

6 [3]William H. Hickman, born 1845, died 1845.

LEWIS AND KINDRED FAMILIES.

Children of Archibald and Susan H. (Hill) Shockley, grandchildren of George and Hannah Hill.

6 ¹Woodson Shockley married Martha Smith.

7 ¹Mary, George and Nelson Shockley.

6 ²Editha Shockley married Jacob Kiler. Issue: Henrietta Kiler, etc.

6 ³Ewel Shockley married Miss Bowman.

6 ⁴Orilla Shockley married Thomas Bowman.

6 ⁵Celia Shockley married William Gilliland. Issue: John, Mary and Elizabeth Gilliland.

Children of Rev. George and Hannah (Hill) Ambrose.

6 ¹Dr. George Ambrose, born 1824; married his cousin Ellen Frances Hill. They resided in Oregon. Their children are, Utilla, Ann, Lillie, Florence and Willis L. Ambrose.

6 ²Linnie Ann Ambrose married George Ambrose and died in 1855, leaving a daughter, Matilda Ambrose.

6 ³Silas J. Ambrose, born 1828; married Mary Winn and died 1854 without issue.

Children of Leroy L. and Nancy (Haley) Hill.

6 ¹Ellen F. Hill married Dr. George Ambrose, whose descendants are given elsewhere.

6 ²James H. Hill.

6 ³Willis A. Hill.

6 ⁴Leroy W. Hill of Oregon.

6 ⁵Ormizinda Hill married Mr. Twist, of Oregon.

6 ⁶Edward T. Hill.

Children of Samuel and Nancy (Hill) Thompson.

6 ¹Samuel H. Thompson married Theresa Radcliff and resides at Darbyville, Ohio. Their children are, Alice and Emma Radcliff Thompson.

6 ²Paulina Thompson married William A. Miller and resides at

Darbyville, Ohio. Children, James, Virginia, Belle, George and Samuel Miller.

6 ³David T. Thompson is a merchant at Pekin, Illinois. Issue: Cora and others.

6 ⁴William McGill.

6 ⁵Leroy McGill and Susan H. McGill and others.

Children of James K. and Catharine C. (Hickman) Marshall, grandchildren of Hon. John Lewis and Elizabeth Hickman.

7 ¹Bettie Marshall married Henry Buford of Woodford county, Kentucky who died in 1852, in Milwaukee, Wisconsin, leaving a son, Henry Buford.

7 ²John Lewis Marshall married Miss Turner, daughter of Judge Turner of Lexington, Kentucky. J. L. Marshall was living in Milwaukee, Wisconsin in 1857.

7 ³Charles Marshall died single in Milwaukee, Wisconsin.

7 ⁴Alexander Marshall.

7 ⁵James.

7 ⁶Mary.

7 ⁷Kate Marshall, all residents of Milwaukee, Wisconsin.

Children of William H. and Margaret (Hickman) Shackleford, grandchildren of Hon. J. L. and Elizabeth Hickman, great-grandchildren of David and Clara (McClannahan) Hickman, who was a son of James and Hannah (Lewis) Hickman.

7 ¹Bettie H. Shackleford, born 1838.

7 ²Martha Shackleford, born 1840.

7 ³Hickman Shackleford, born 1841, died 1842.

7 ⁴William Shackleford, born 1844.

Children of John Lewis Jr. and Adelia (Edwards) Hickman.

7 ¹Bettie E. Hickman, Margaret S., Caroline D. and Adelia Hickman and others.

Children of William and Caroline P. (Hickman) Duke:

7 ¹John Lewis Duke died young.

7 ²Mary Duke.

7 ³Bessie Duke.

7 ⁴Charlotte Duke.

7 ⁵Caroline Duke.

Children of Robert and Ann (Hickman) McGavock.

7 ¹Randall H. McGavock, born in Howard county, Missouri in 1820; married in 1857 Ann Hite of Jefferson county, Kentucky, afterwards resided near Haynesville, Kentucky. Children are:

    8 ¹Robert McGavock, born in Breckenridge county, Kentucky, 1852.

    8 ²Thomas McGavock, born 1854.

    8 ³Francis McGavock, born 1856.

    8 ⁴William McGavock, born 1858.

    8 ⁵Oscar McGavock, born 1860.

    8 ⁶Maggie McGavock, 1862.

    8 ⁷Lilliam McGavock, born 1864.

7 ²Thomas McGavock, born in Howard county, Missouri, 1823; married 1846 Mary Lightfoot of Breckenridge county, Kentucky. He died in Breckenridge county, Kentucky in 1860 and his wife died the same year in Howard county, Missouri. Children as follows:

    8 ¹Daniel C. McGavock, born 1847, served in Confederate army under General Price and died in Arkansas in 1865.

    8 ²Rosa McGavock, born in Breckenridge county, Kentucky 1850.

    8 ³Annie McGavock, born in Hancock county, Kentucky, 1851.

    8 ⁴Lander McGavock, born in Breckenridge county, Kentucky, 1853.

8 [5]Ada McGavock, born in Breckenridge county, Kentucky, 1855.

8 [6]Emma McGavock, born 1857.

8 [7]Gordon McGavock, born in Howard county, Missouri, 1860.

7 [3]Jacob McGavock, born in Howard county, Missouri, 1824, married 1845, Elizabeth Haynes, of Davis county, Kentucky, issue as follows:

8 [1]Sarah McGavock, born in Breckenridge county, Kentucky, 1845.

8 [2]Mary McGavock, born in Davis county, Kentucky, 1847.

8 [3]James McGavock, born in Davis county, Kentucky, 1849.

8 [4]Ella McGavock, born in Davis county, Kentucky, 1850.

8 [5]Morgan McGavock, born in Tennessee, 1862.

8 [6]Ida McGavock, born in Breckenridge county, Kentucky, 1864.

8 [7]Robert McGavock, born in Athens, Alabama, 1866.

7 [4]Robert McGavock, born in Breckenridge county, Kentucky, 1826 and resided near Franklin, Howard county, Missouri; married, first, 1853, Matilda Bondurant who died in 1854; second, Sally Cruz in 1856. Issue as follows:

8 [1]William McGavock, born in Howard county, Missouri, 1862.

8 [2]James McGavock, born in Howard county, Missouri in 1864.

8 [3]Rosa McGavock, born 1866, and others.

7 [5]James McGavock, born in Breckenridge county, Kentucky, 1828, married 1856, Martha Talbott near Franklin, Howard county, Missouri, where they reside. Issue as follows: Charles and Kate McGavock.

7 [6]Gordon Cloyd McGavock, born in Breckenridge county, Kentucky, 1839, married December 22, 1859, Lucy Mary Lewis, daughter of Rev. Addison Murdock and Sarah Ann (Minor) Lewis. Rev. Addison Lewis was of the

Zachary Lewis line, of Spottsylvania county, Virginia. Issue as follows:

8 [1]John Lewis McGavock, born 1861.

8 [2]Sarah Ann McGavock, born February, 1863.

8 [3]Mary Cloyd McGavock, born 1866.

8 [4]Louisa McGavock, born 1869.

8 [5]Hugh McGavock, born 1871.

8 [6]Robert McGavock, born 1876, in Howard county, Missouri.

7 [7]John McGavock, born in Breckenridge county, Kentucky, 1834, married 1860, Bettie Skillman and resides near Cloverport, Kentucky. Issue: Leon, Marion and Gordon McGavock.

7 [8]Frances McGavock, born 1840, and resides near Cloverport, Kentucky, married 1865, Maggie Cunningham, daughter of Rev. Alexander Cunningham, of Franklin, Tennessee. Issue: Lynn McGavock, born 1867 and others.

Children of Jones H. and Clara (Hickman) Flournoy:

7 [1]Sarah A. Flournoy married Andrew Adams.

7 [2]Eliza M. Flournoy married George W. Cook.

7 [3]Mary L. Flournoy married Robert W. Simpson in 1854 and resides at Boonville, Missouri, their children are: Frank F., Clara A., and Thomas Simpson.

7 [4]Martha M. Flournoy married Robert T. Ross.

7 [5]Napoleon L. Flournoy, died young.

Children of Maj. James S. and Mary Elizabeth (Hickman) Rollins:

7 [1]Sophia Woodson Rollins, born 1839, died 1841.

7 [2]James Hickman Rollins, born 1841, educated at West Point, New York, and graduated in 1862. He married Miss Bowen and died, leaving his wife and three children, H. B., Eulalie and Mrs. J. L. Sehon.

7 [3]Laura H. Rollins, born 1844, married I. O. Hockaday, died in 1904, leaving two sons, Rollins and Irvin, and one

daughter, Eulalie, who married Rev. Sneed, a Presbyterian minister.

7 4Mary Elizabeth Rollins, born 1846, married John H. Overall, a lawyer of distinction, who died 1905; she has three children, John, Florence and Adelle.

7 5Sallie Rodes Rollins, born 1849, died ———.

7 6George Bingham Rollins, born 1852. He graduated from the University of Missouri in 1872, with honors, married January 25, 1882, Margarett B. Clarkson, daughter of John S. Clarkson, they have four children, Clarkson, Frank, James, Sidney and Margarett.

7 7Curtis B. Rollins, born 1853, married Ruth McCune, have two children, C. B., Jr., and Ruth.

7 8Flora Rollins, born 1855, married Rev. Gray, an Episcopal minister, who died; she has two daughters, Mary, who was married April 19, 1906, to Mr. Sidney Stephens, son of Hon. E. W. Stephens of Columbia, Missouri; and Florence Gray.

7 9Frank Rollins, born 1858, died ———.

7 10Woodson Rollins, born 1860, died young.

APPENDIX.

It had been the purpose of the authors to include a genealogy of the Tandy family in this book, but having accumulated considerable data and knowing this could be increased, have decided to publish it in a separate edition hereafter. We are also collecting material for the Beasley and Woolfolk genealogy.

401

INDEX TO LEWIS FAMILY.

[The numbers preceding names indicate the generation.]

INDEX TO LEWIS FAMILIES.

INDEX.

INDEX TO LEWIS KINDRED.

INDEX TO LEWIS KINDRED.

INDEX TO LEWIS KINDRED.

INDEX TO LEWIS KINDRED.

INDEX TO LEWIS KINDRED.

413

INDEX TO LEWIS KINDRED.

INDEX TO LEWIS KINDRED.

INDEX TO LEWIS KINDRED.

CPSIA information can be obtained at www.ICGtesting.com
Printed in the USA
LVOW031916131011

250395LV00014B/75/P